Thinking About YOU
Thinking About ME

Second Edition

www.socialthinking.com

MGW'07

by

Michelle Garcia Winner

Published by

Think Social Publishing, Inc.

Michelle Garcia Winner

3550 Stevens Creek Blvd, Suite 200

San Jose, CA 95117

Tel: (408) 557-8595 ext 303

Fax: (408) 557-8594

Michelle Garcia Winner offers workshops on a variety of social thinking topics.

To order copies of this book, learn more about her workshops or about social thinking in general, visit the author's web site: **www.socialthinking.com**

Book design, layout & typesetting by Dion Desktop Publications • www.diondesktop.com

Also by Michelle Garcia Winner

Think Social! A Social Thinking Curriculum for School Aged Students

Inside Out! What Makes a Person with Social Cognitive Deficits Tick?

Worksheets! for Teaching Social Thinking and Related Skills

Strategies for Organization: Preparing for Homework and the Real World (DVD)

Social Thinking Across the Home and School Day (DVD)

Social Thinking Posters for Home and the Classroom:

- The Boring Moments
- Being Part of a Group
- Social Behaviors Maps

Social Behavior Mapping

Sticker Strategies: Practical Strategies to Encourage Social Thinking and Organization

Acknowledgements

Illuminating the complex world of social thinking for people with social cognitive challenges truly takes the collaborative effort of the educational and parent communities. Writing a book on the topic feels like it takes the collaborative effort of the entire world! This book would not have been possible without the insight, teaching stories, and parenting strategies of people around the nation who have been so generous with their time and efforts. My clients and their families are a constant source of inspiration. They enlighten me to the many wonders of the mind and remind me of the great things we can accomplish when we work together. This collaborative spirit shapes all our lives for the better.

I have hearty respect for my clinical staff: Stephanie, Susan, Deborah, Randi, Jaime, Amy, Cathy, and Shelly who are my close friends, professional collaborators, confidants, and amazing teachers. I applaud them for their professionalism and playfulness and for fostering the development of further social thinking concepts and lessons.

The contingent of "Social Butterflies" (Andrea, Liz, Patty, Lauren, Glenda, Linda, Luanne and Trisha) in Orange County, California, help me remember what it is like to have a social life outside the clinic, and spotlight the "unexpected" in social interactions. These women, together with the Orange County social-thinking mentor team, provide me a wealth of professional food for thought (thanks, Stan!).

I have been fortunate to befriend many folks around the country who are on the cutting edge of clinical treatment services for persons with social cognitive deficits. To Patty, Tamra, and Kathee of Oregon, Gretchen of Washington, Pam of Arizona, and the teams in Illinois, Wisconsin, Minnesota, Montana, Maine, New Hampshire, and states too numerous to list, I applaud your persistent efforts to educate administrations in the importance of teaching social thinking concepts. Social thinking IS part of standards of education. More importantly, it is an integral part of life beyond the public school years! Kathee and Gretchen: special thanks for winging your way here to plant my "friendship garden" at a time when I needed it most.

My deepest and most heartfelt thanks go out to my daughters Heidi and Robyn. You have helped me understand that typical social development and the evolution of perspective-taking is very odd, indeed, especially through the middle school years. Your love and encouragement has kept me going in ways you cannot imagine. As you embark on your own careers exploring the functioning of the mind and body (animal and human), I know you will continue to be my teacher for years to come.

My dad, Max Garcia, a Holocaust survivor, has taught me much about perseverance and humor. You have shown me how to laugh out loud at myself and appreciate that social learning never ends. Even at 82 we need to think about what other people are thinking. We continue to laugh at ourselves when realizing how difficult this concept is to keep in mind, even for us neurotypical folks!

While I have many ideas — sometimes more than I know what to do with — it takes a knack for getting them onto paper in a reader-friendly way. Thanks to my editor, Veronica Zysk, for helping me do just that. Marilyn Dion, my long-time friend and constant source of encouragement, has used her desktop publishing skills to turn text into a presentable format of which I can be proud.

Finally, I want to acknowledge you, the reader, for your willingness to "think outside the box" and explore this sometimes strange yet truly fascinating world of social thinking. In doing so, you forge the pathways that will help our students succeed not just across their school and home day, but for all their days to come.

My heartfelt thanks to you all,
Michelle Garcia Winner

Dedication

In memory of my mother,

Priscilla Alden Thwaits Garcia

1927-2002

She continues to be my anchor and inspiration.

Table of Contents

Bibliography **B-1**

Figures

Handouts

Tables

Introduction

Assessing Social Cognitive Deficits

We began discussing the concept of social intelligence back in the 1920s through the work of Edward Thorndike. Recognized as a major contributor of our overall functioning as members of society, Dr. Mel Levine (2002) highlights social intelligence as a critical aspect of our total intelligence. Dr. Daniel Goleman (2006) defines social intelligence as "being intelligent not just about our relationships, but also in them."

Students with social cognitive deficits face enormous challenges, not only in their day-to-day relationships, but also because few professionals — educational or medical — understand their core difficulties. The social cognitive learning disability is the most abstract of all learning disabilities, making it extremely difficult to assess through standardized measures.

In the field of speech and language pathology, a student is typically assessed for expressive and receptive language. It is commonly assumed that if a child can understand and formulate language, he also has the skills to be successful within the communicative process. However, exploration into social cognitive deficits in persons with autism and Asperger Syndrome reveal that successful interactive communication is dependent not only on a student's technical knowledge of language, but also on the student's ability to use language in a socially meaningful way.

The ability to use language as a means of social communication is referred to as a "social pragmatic skill." In the past decade, formalized tests have been developed that attempt to assess students' social pragmatic skills. They include:

- Test of Pragmatic Language (TOPL) and

- Social Pragmatic Subtest of the Comprehensive Assessment of Spoken Language (CASL)

My clinical experience indicates that results from these assessments, particularly for students with strong IQs, often fail to show the true severity of the social thinking problem. It is not uncommon for a student to score within normal limits on one or more of these assessments, and yet be awkward in the presence of others, have difficulty with elements of class work, and be picked on by peers for not fitting in. (It should also be noted that in most school districts, scoring within the "normal limits" means scoring above the 7th percentile.)

Our attempts to assess social pragmatic skills are frequently limited to assessing superficial social knowledge, rather than the deeper complex knowledge needed to successfully interact with peers. For example, during assessment students may be asked questions such as, "What do you ask when you want to go and play?" or "Amber learns that Erik's grandmother has just died. She sees Erik in the hall at school. What can she say to him?" Our smart students learn the superficial social codes and are able to answer these questions easily, thereby receiving a reasonably high score on the test. However, these scores do not truly reflect their ability, or lack thereof, to successfully, quickly, efficiently, or sensitively interact with others in the real world

I often see written reports about a student with a known medical diagnosis of Asperger Syndrome state that the student "does not have social pragmatic deficits. He scored in the 60th percentile on the TOPL." This same student has no friends, has frequent outbursts in class, and remains intensely focused on his own area of interest at home.

Statements like the one above are not uncommon as educators strive to understand the abstract nature of social cognitive learning disabilities. Indeed, many educators and SLPs assume we can test for this deficit. However, formalized assessments are limited in their practical application and may, in reality, totally fail to identify a student's more abstract deficits.

One significant problem with standardized tests is their need to strip away competing variables to assure each "subtest" assesses in a valid way what it purports to measure. However, social communicative competence is based on social multitasking or executive functioning. If we strip away competing variables we have dismissed the complexity of communication.

The assessment situation is further complicated in that the federal government qualifies students for special education through one of only 13 disability categories. Some of these include:

- Specific learning disability.

- Speech and language impaired.

- Emotionally disturbed.

- Autism.

For students with average to above average IQs, the extent of their social cognitive deficits can be difficult to define. Eligibility criteria provided by the educational system may not qualify them for services, despite the fact that it is obvious to others that these students (1) behave strangely, (2) fail to establish a peer network, and/or (3) cannot do their schoolwork at the predicted levels based on their intelligence and achievement test scores.

Most school districts now use the autism eligibility category to qualify a person with Asperger Syndrome or Pervasive Developmental Disorder-Not Otherwise Specified (PDD-NOS), since many states interpret the federal description of "autism" to include all conditions that fall on the spectrum. Nevertheless, students who present vague but significant symptoms that suggest a social cognitive learning disability fail to qualify for special education services, because they generally have good grades or test scores. IEP teams often report that these students do not have "educational problems" because they equate education with only academic knowledge.

We further assume that academic knowledge is the key to success in adult life. The adults at my clinic have proven the fallacy of this assumption. An education must prepare students for life beyond the 12th grade by helping them become effective communicators, critical thinkers, and problem solvers. Most school mission statements include these characteristics in their overall goals for students, but without social thinking skills students will be ill-equipped to achieve these goals. I encourage educational teams to review their mission statements and address the fact that an education is supposed to render outcomes that are more complex than good grades and test scores.

Differences in Health and Education Diagnostic Systems

Health Diagnoses

It is extremely important for all people working or living with students with disabilities to understand that the medical/mental health community operates independently of the public education system and that diagnosis and eligibility for educational services are two very different things. Health professionals make a medical diagnosis of a disorder; educational professionals decide on eligibility, and a medical diagnosis does not automatically guarantee service eligibility.

Medical doctors, psychologists, psychiatrists, licensed marriage and family therapists, and clinical social workers generally use the Diagnostic and Statistical Manual, Fourth Edition Revised as their primary reference guide when making these diagnoses. The DSM-IV-R (2000) presents the clinical manifestations and diagnostic frameworks for a large variety of disabilities.

Medical diagnoses can be used for a number of purposes, including access to services covered by medical insurance, and providing families with a better understanding of their child's needs and appropriate treatment options.

A medical diagnosis of a disability, however, is not equivalent to eligibility for individual education services. The purpose of an educational eligibility determination is extremely narrow: to assess whether or not a student qualifies for special education services through the public school system.

Education Eligibility Decision

As mentioned earlier, students are only eligible for school services under the 13 eligibility categories established by the federal government. Eligibility categories are not intended to prescribe specific treatment programs — those are decided on a case-by-case basis. Information on the criteria for each of these 13 categories, and the corresponding diagnostic framework for determining eligibility, should be available through the special education office of your local school district. The school psychologist is usually the person most familiar with this information.

It is also important to know that each individual state in the U.S. determines what constitutes eligibility for school services in that state. A student who is eligible for IEP services under the category of autism in one state, for example, may not be eligible in another state. Furthermore, while our understanding of autism has evolved to include the entire autism spectrum, beginning in the 1990s, some states have never modified their original eligibility criteria for autism. As of this printing, the State of California is still using a very old eligibility description that predates the prevailing contemporary understandings of the autism spectrum.

To become eligible for public school special education services, a student must first be assessed by education professionals. These professionals seek to determine whether the student has a disability that affects his or her educational progress during the school day, and whether that disability qualifies a student for services.

Before we can facilitate a deeper understanding of what qualifies as a disability, we must first ask educators in the schools to define what constitutes an "education." I recently asked a panel of professionals who collaborated in the formation of the "No Child Left Behind" education legislation (2001) to provide the definition of an education on which NCLB is based. They responded that there is no definition of education associated with NCLB — they stated it was up to each state to form its own definition.

If students are deemed eligible for special education services, they will receive a "Free and Appropriate Public Education" (FAPE). This does not entitle students to receive every service the school system has available, however, but only those that are appropriate based on each student's specific needs. A team of education and related-services professionals, along with the student's parents, meet to create the student's Individual Education Plan (IEP). The IEP team determines what services the child needs in order to benefit from instruction across the school day.

Understanding the Differences

Understanding the differences between the mental health and educational systems is critical for working within these two systems. Very often the professionals from both groups are unaware that the two systems offer different diagnostic/eligibility frameworks. Mental health professionals are also frequently unaware of the limitations of public school special education services, given that they are only to provide what is "free and appropriate."

As mentioned previously a medical diagnosis in no way mandates eligibility for specific special education services. Educational professionals are required to include the reports written by medical professionals along with their own assessments, but they are not required to agree with the medical diagnosis or to abide by the recommendations in that professional's report. Public school professionals should consider the reports on file from medical professionals, but often the service recommendations made by medical professionals are far more extensive than a school can reasonably provide under FAPE.

Although both the medical and educational communities provide assessment and therapeutic planning services, neither group dominates in its ability to understand students with social cognitive challenges. I have observed both medical and school professionals make inappropriate assessments and treatment recommendations. It should be noted that not one professional field — medical, educational, or within the area of speech/communication — includes the study of social cognition-related treatment as part of its professional training.

Fortunately, more and more professionals in these communities are starting to better understand these students. The best educational team is one that is willing to continue to learn, and many professionals in our school systems are truly interested in figuring out how to meet the needs of students with social thinking challenges. But with regard to understanding how to make a diagnosis and provide appropriate treatment strategies for intelligent students with social cognitive deficits, both the medical and educational fields are still in their infancy.

The Internet makes it possible to find resources quickly. There are also many professionals in our school systems who are truly interested in these students and are trying their best to keep up with the newly developing information about how to serve their needs. The best educational team is one that is willing to continue to learn. But with regard to understanding how to make a diagnosis and provide appropriate treatment strategies for intelligent students with social cognitive deficits, both the mental health and educational fields are in their infancy.

Creating a Framework of Understanding

The lack of formalized assessment tools for social cognitive deficits and the lack of access to services are stumbling blocks faced by families and concerned teachers all over the United States. Slowly, more recognition is being given to these topics as researchers and educators strive to find better solutions, but the progress is slow and often compartmentalized within school districts. Research is also limited in scope and application.

Nonverbal Learning Disorder, Asperger's Syndrome, Pervasive Developmental Disorder-Not Otherwise Specified, and High Functioning Autism all imply the existence of social cognitive learning challenges in the students who carry these labels. As we gain greater understanding of these disabilities we realize the extent to which impairments in social thinking affect students in the classroom, on the job, and in the community. We come to better understand why our students behave the way they do.

Despite the burgeoning knowledge, a student's educational program is never any better than the skills of the teachers and parents themselves! While we wait for research to teach us more about these complex students, we need to conduct grass roots campaigns of our own to teach educators and parents about the very real challenges these students face at home and in our classrooms on a daily basis and work cooperatively to find ways to meet their very real needs.

Evolving from Behavioral to Cognitive Treatment

Up until now, treatment programs for persons with social cognitive deficits have been strictly behavioral based; that is, their emphasis has been on helping students learn to behave like neurotypical folks. As professionals recognize that students with normal to above normal intelligence and language skills can have severe social adaptive and comprehension issues, we have the opportunity to educate these students through a cognitive-behavioral framework rather than a purely behavioral approach.

Rather than teach them superficial rote social codes, actions, and patterns of response, the cognitive-behavioral approach involves teaching students about the thinking process itself (cognition) and how thinking affects behavior. They learn that the behaviors we manifest throughout our day impact our ability to understand and react cognitively to the information around us.

Dobson (2001) explains that all cognitive behavioral therapies share three fundamental propositions:

1. Cognitive activity affects behavior.

2. Cognitive activity may be monitored and altered.

3. Desired behavior change may be effected through cognitive change.

The cognitive-behavioral treatment approach helps students understand the nature of their deficits. It also teaches them to recognize the related behavioral responses neurotypical persons demonstrate throughout their day. *For students with average or above intelligence, and particularly for older students, there is no other way to help them learn to help themselves.* That being said, it is hard work. These students have to learn cognitively what neurotypical persons do intuitively.

However, not all students have the ability to metacognitively analyze their thoughts and environment. Many cannot change their own behavior based on what they are thinking. Therefore, the information in this book focuses on individuals with near-normal intelligence (high 70s to low 80s verbal IQ) who are either verbal or minimally verbal due to apraxia (oral motor planning challenges). Students who function below this level will benefit more from a behavioral social skills approach that relies less on understanding their own and others' minds.

Cognitive Theory that Contributes to Therapeutic Application

Three major theories guide our understanding and exploration of cognitive development in our students. Most professionals who study social cognitive learning disabilities acknowledge that these three concepts help describe the deficits of our students. However, it has yet to be determined whether these theories coexist or if one dominates the others. The concepts are:

1. Central Coherence Theory (Frith, 1989)

2. Executive Dysfunction Theory (McEvoy, Rogers, and Pennington, 1993)

3. Theory of Mind (Baron-Cohen, Leslie, and Frith, 1985)

1. Central Coherence Theory

The Central Coherence Theory states that students on the autism spectrum have difficulty conceptualizing to a larger whole. They tend to think in parts and do not fully relate their pieces of information back to a larger pattern of behavior and thought.

A third-grade boy with high-functioning autism sat in his mainstream class each day, just like the other students, participating in all the same activities. He had a full-time instructional aide to help clarify information he did not understand. When I observed him in class in late fall, the students were asked to take a spelling test. As soon as the teacher said the words "spelling test" all the other students got out a piece of paper, folded it in half, wrote the numbers down the side, wrote their names in the right-hand corner of the paper along with the date, and then titled the paper "spelling test." The boy with high-functioning autism sat there, not doing anything. He did not appear to have learned that "spelling test" meant more than writing down the words the teacher was to recite; it also included the pre-test and post-test sequence of related activities.

It is common for our students to participate well in the rote activities of academics, but struggle with connecting what they know through interpretation and analysis. All of our higher functioning students have access to vast amounts of data stored in their brains, but limited channels through which they can fully integrate or organize the data. Central Coherence Theory reveals that our students have a conceptual learning disability that impacts effective communication, summarizing, recognizing expectations, and written expression.

2. Executive Dysfunction Theory

The term "Executive Functioning" is used more widely in research and in cognitive rehabilitation than in the field of education. In effect, Executive Functioning describes the skills that an executive needs in order to perform in his or her job (or, more realistically, the skills the executive secretary needs for his or her job).

Executive Dysfunction Theory speaks to the fact that people with social cognitive deficits have difficulty solving personal problems, communicating effectively, and creating organizational structures that allow for flexibility and prioritization. These persons crave structure but have difficulty creating their own healthy structures. This affects not only their social relationships, but for students, their ability to succeed throughout the school day. Problems continue as they have difficulty learning the complex skills of managing homework and school projects, solving problems, appreciating the perspective of others — all skills needed for achieving independence.

One high school freshman responded to my query about whether she had homework in her science class by lifting her book toward the light. When I asked what she was doing she showed me she had written her homework assignment on the one-inch strip of scotch tape that she used on the cover of her book. The only way she could read her homework assignment was to lift the book toward the florescent light

to illuminate the pen ink. This behavior was reflective of her ongoing organizational problems, which impacted her ability to account for and complete an array of assignments.

🔲

A student attending graduate school struggled with learning to organize his assignments. He could manage assignments due at the next class meeting, but he had fallen horribly behind with his long-term projects. Some of his difficulties included his inability to:

• Segment his project into smaller parts

• Budget his time to work on the project during the weeks prior to the due date

• Comprehend the information at a high conceptual level, and

• Plan and organize when he could talk to the professor to get help.

When he finally did write his papers, his written work was said to be exquisite. The problem was he rarely completed these projects.

Executive functioning skills, like social skills, are taken for granted by teachers and caregivers. It is assumed that students with normal to above normal intelligence have the ability to prioritize, organize, and solve personal problems.

As mentioned above, the term Executive Functioning is generally used in the mental health community. In schools, students with these types of problems are described as having "weak organizational skills." There are few standard assessments available to explore students' abilities in this realm, and the assessments we do have are shallow. Students with social cognitive deficits generally need direct intervention to address their executive functioning or

organizational weaknesses. Without the skills that allow them to manage complex tasks, it is unlikely they will make it through college, regardless of how intelligent they are.

School districts around the country are beginning to recognize that many students need these skills directly taught to them, whether or not they have a known disability. Special education departments have begun to add Study Skill classes to their course offerings to meet this need. These classes can be helpful as long as teachers teach study skills, rather than allowing students to use the period to do homework and ask questions (assuming the student has the skills to ask for help!).

In addition to homework organization, study skills programs would also do well to incorporate lessons on personal problem solving. Personal problem solving is a complex skill that weaves together social and organizational abilities. It requires us to create an organizational structure to work through the problem and also demands perspective taking, auditory comprehension, abstract thinking, gestalt processing, and initiation of language.

3. Theory of Mind and Perspective Taking

Theory of Mind (or as it is described in this book, perspective taking) is the ability to intuitively track what others know and think during personal interactions. We use this information to understand and then monitor our own responses — verbal and nonverbal — in the presence of others.

For example, if Joe is talking to Frank, who is intermittently checking his watch, Joe might feel compelled to inquire whether Frank is in a hurry or has an appointment, since he appears to be distracted by the time.

Students with social cognitive deficits have different degrees of perspective taking impairment. Just as autism is a spectrum disorder, so too does perspective taking fall along a continuum from less to more. Unfortunately, at present there are no clinically based functional assessments of Perspective Taking skills across the spectrum of functioning levels.

It is my belief that a deficit in perspective taking skills accounts for the most significant challenge faced by students with social cognitive deficits: their inability to relate to others at the pace of a typical human interaction.

To have a perspective taking deficit is to have the most complex, abstract deficit possible. It is nearly impossible to quantify. As you will learn in later chapters, deficits in perspective taking abilities are not directly related to IQ or academic test results. Nevertheless, this deficit affects virtually every form of interpersonal interaction. It also impacts school work, such as comprehension of literature, understanding socially based themes presented in texts or movies, or interpreting directions given by the teacher.

Perspective Taking, Central Coherence and Executive Functioning are synergistic cognitive processes. A weakness in one co-mingles with dysfunction in the others. Based on my clinical observations, there appears to be a strong positive relationship between a person's perspective taking deficit and his or her corresponding level of deficit in central coherence and executive functioning.

An educator was describing a seven-year-old male student, Michael, who was diagnosed with high-functioning autism. Although Michael was nonverbal at three years of age, he developed language and social relatedness methodically through a well-run Applied Behavior Analysis program. The educator felt Michael was now doing so well on tests that he probably no longer qualified as "autistic" according to the school eligibility criteria. She suggested that his eligibility be changed to "speech and language impaired."

The educator requested that I consult on this case to help train the paraprofessional and teachers who would be working with Michael in his second grade mainstream class setting. I met Michael briefly to gain an understanding of his issues. He was an adorable blond-haired, blue-eyed boy who smiled easily and enjoyed making jokes. He required cues to "think with his eyes," he jumped from one topic to the next when talking, and he physically wandered away from direct social interactions to look at objects in the room. I asked Michael to put in sequence a series of pictures that described a birthday party. He attended to the task but then placed the pictures arbitrarily in a row on the table. When asked to explain his sequence, he exhibited difficulty with the social interpretation of the pictures.

One picture was of a boy waving as he and his mom left a birthday party. Michael stated that the picture represented the boy saying "hi" as he arrived at the party. It was necessary for me to present Michael with a series of questions in order for him to understand the meaning of each picture, as well as their logical sequence to conceptualize the story.

His mother explained that Michael had made significant academic gains (although reading comprehension was weak) but that he continued to have difficulty initiating and sustaining relationships with his peers.

Based on the consultation, it was clear that this boy continued to have a number of very significant educational and social issues that stemmed from his core diagnosis of autism. He demonstrated a limited

Theory of Mind both in his spontaneous interpersonal relatedness as well as in his ability to understand the motives and emotions of those pictured in the photos. What his mother wanted most in his current stage of development was for him to learn how to think about other people and what they wanted from him; she wanted him to have lessons to further develop his perspective taking abilities.

In the example above, the educator's desire to change Michael's diagnosis from autism to speech and language impaired was a way to celebrate his progress: Michael had developed to a point that he "looked normal" on the surface. His difficulty processing the world at a deeper, more conceptual level, however, is what keeps him on the autism spectrum.

What are Social Skills?

The term "social skills" is rather nebulous, and is highly subjective from one social group to another, or one culture to another, however we readily identify people as having good or bad social skills. Many people intuitively understand what is meant by social skills, yet operationally defining the concept often stumps us.

When I ask audiences to define social skills, the following terms and concepts are often repeated:

• Turn-taking, reciprocity

• Reading cues

• Maintaining a topic

• Recognizing people's emotions

• Eye contact

• Proximity

All of these descriptions are accurate, but they lack attention to a larger concept: whether or not a person has good social skills is perceived by others, whether or not that person is "talking" to others. Social skills are present (or absent) without direct interaction.

Consider defining social skills this way: "sharing space with others effectively" or "adapting to others effectively across contexts."

If we understand that social skills involve social adaptability and the related social interpretation of others' thoughts and desires, we realize how essential these skills are for not only interactions, but for situations such as quietly sharing space in a classroom or when working at a job.

Pulling It All Together: The I LAUGH Framework Model

In my previous book, *Inside Out: What Makes the Person with Social Cognitive Deficits Tick?* (2000), I detailed a framework by which teachers and caregivers can better define these students' deficits. The framework is referred to as the I LAUGH model. It is briefly reviewed here and forms a reference for the material you will read in the rest of this book.

I LAUGH is an acronym for the different affected areas that contribute to a student's overall social cognitive deficits, deficits that are displayed in academic, life skills, vocational, and social contexts. The model addresses only the social cognitive aspect of functioning. It does not detail other challenges common to individuals on the autism spectrum, such as sensory integration disorder and fine/gross motor skill dysfunctions.

The I LAUGH framework illustrates that persons with social cognitive deficits have a collection of impairments that constitute a syndrome, not just one weak area of development. These students exhibit a predictable set of varied deficits suggested in Table 1. Neurotypical individuals may exhibit some of the weaknesses addressed in the I LAUGH framework; however, their challenges don't constitute the syndrome of severity as with our students.

It is important to note that each student with social cognitive deficits can have an individual pattern of weaknesses even within the I LAUGH framework. Keep in mind that a label is only a red flag as to possible challenges a student faces. Each student must be individually assessed to determine his or her mix of strengths and weaknesses.

Table 1

Summary of the "I LAUGH" Model And Corresponding Treatment Ideas

Type of Deficit	How it affects social interaction	How it affects classroom functioning	What to do...
I = Poor Initiation of Communication or Action	• Does not initiate appropriate social interactions or begin working on a novel activity.	• Does not ask for help. • Sits and does nothing when others are doing something. • In group work, may not participate or only know how to direct the others; weak negotiator.	• Teach a clear initiation response. Reinforce success by helping them gain access to information they do not know or just need to clarify.
L = Listening with Eyes and Brain	• Does not observe others' social cues. • Does not process the meaning of others' messages. • May not "think with eyes" (e.g., poor eye contact).	• Does not easily process the meaning of spoken messages. • Does not predict people's unstated plans. • Poor sustained eye contact diminishes understanding of total communicative message. • Difficulty functioning in large groups; needs more direct instruction.	• Break information into smaller parts to increase attention. • Use visual strategies to help alleviate auditory overload. • Teach how we use our eyes and whole body for listening • Teach how we "read people's plans" (intentions).
A = Abstract and Inferential	• Does not infer meaning from social cues or decipher meaning from words/language.	• Is limited in the ability to infer meaning from books, teacher's lectures, or conversation. • Literal In Interpretation of all modes of communication (verbal, nonverbal, written, etc.).	• Be aware that speech therapists and resource specialists can help! • Be aware that students may provide odd responses when not clearly interpreting abstract information. • Work on students' understanding and interpretation of others' intentional and unintentional communication.

Table 1 (*continued*)

Summary Of "I LAUGH" Model And Corresponding Treatment Ideas

Type of Deficit	How it affects social interaction	How it affects classroom functioning	What to do
U = Understanding Perspective	• Difficulty recognizing and incorporating other person's perspectives to regulate social relationships or just share space effectively.	• Difficulty understanding the perspective of characters in literature. • Difficulty regulating classroom behavior according to the needs of others. • Difficulty working in small and large groups.	• Work with the student to learn cognitively about this concept. Stress thinking about others in the classroom. • Teach that we "think with our eyes." • Understand the reading comprehension challenges associated with inefficient perspective taking.
G = Gestalt Processing; Getting the Big Picture	• Not good at tracking how language fits into the overall concept being discussed. • Tangential. • Off topic remarks.	• Attends to details but misses the underlying concept of assignments. • Writing can be tangential or misses the point. • Difficulty staying with the concept of group work and cooperative learning.	• Use graphic organizers to break information down into visual, concrete parts. • Break information down and then help the student see how it all goes back together. • Teach overtly how to discern the "main idea," etc.
H = Humor and Human Relatedness	• Students usually have a great sense of humor, but may miss the subtleties of humor. • May not understand if they are being laughed at or laughed with. • Above deficits contribute to difficulties relating to others.	• They respond well to a teacher who has a bit more of a relaxed, humorous style, but is still able to follow a fairly structured routine. • The student may produce inappropriate humor in the class in an attempt to engage others.	• Teach that humor has a time, place, and person! • Differentiate friendly teasing from "mean-spirited teasing." • Incorporate anti-teasing programs into your classroom and school! • Be aware: these kids get teased and bullied NON-STOP!

Exploring Social Cognitive Deficits as a Set of Related but Unique Learning Disabilities

The I LAUGH model was developed to create a framework with which we can organize and describe our observations and test results as they relate to social cognition. It incorporates issues related to the Central Coherence theory, Executive Dysfunction, and Theory of Mind/Perspective Taking. It elaborates upon the "triad" of impairments for persons on the autism spectrum: communication, socialization, and imagination (Wing and Gould, 1979).

Students with social cognitive deficits often defy description due to the abstract nature of their deficits, despite their frequently normal to high results on intelligence tests. These students can have a variety of discrete but overlapping learning disabilities:

• Conceptual learning disability

• Inferential learning disability

• Language formulation disability

• Perspective Taking learning disability

• Significant organizational challenges

Addressing students' social cognitive deficits as a series of learning disabilities creates a structure through which we can understand our students' struggles. This sharpens our own observations, assessments, and development of treatment strategies.

A diagnosis of Asperger Syndrome, Nonverbal Learning Disorder, or even the broader diagnosis of social cognitive deficits does relatively little for our students without an appropriate treatment plan. Breaking down the student's challenges using the I LAUGH model helps focus our attention on our students' specific needs.

The following outline spotlights key deficits in the five overlapping disabilities mentioned above.

Deficits related to the **Conceptual Learning Disability** may include:

a. Difficulty with reading comprehension.

> i. *Determining the main idea.*

> ii. *Following the evolving subplots.*

b. Poor personal problem-solving.

c. Poor organization, planning, and prioritization.

d. Weak ability to abstract information from larger concepts.

e. Difficulty with written expression.

> i. *Difficulty with organization, planning, and prioritization of written material.*

> ii. *Difficulty with exploring a main idea not of their own choosing.*

Deficits in **Inferential learning** can account for:

a. Difficulty recognizing nonverbal emotions.

b. Difficulty knowing how to respond to nonverbal expression.

c. Difficulty recognizing implied meanings across all modes of communication (written, oral, and nonverbal communication).

d. Difficulty understanding and using language flexibly (figurative language).

e. Difficulty modifying one's own persona based on the social context within which the person is participating.

A **Language Formulation disability** (in the absence of measured expressive and receptive language deficits) may include:

a. Difficulty formulating and initiating questions to inquire about other people's areas of interest.

b. Difficulty formulating and initiating language to help solve personal problems, even after the student can conceptually explain the problem.

c. Difficulty formulating and initiating language to maintain a conversation even when the topic is conceptually understood.

Students with a **Perspective Taking learning disability** may have:

a. Difficulty determining the needs, intentions, and motives of others.

b. Difficulty gauging how to respond to others' needs.

c. Difficulty recognizing and accounting for other persons' expectations about how that student should participate or behave.

d. Difficulty completing obligatory tasks not of their own choosing.

e. Limited knowledge of what it means to participate in a relationship (formal or informal).

Deficits associated with significant **Organizational challenges** include:

a. Difficulty tracking homework assignments.

b. Difficulty organizing materials in class and transporting materials across environments.

c. Difficulty planning and executing steps toward completing the class work load.

d. Difficulty completing obligatory tasks not of their own choosing.

e. Difficult predicting time to complete a task and prioritize task importance.

Perspective Taking — The Clinical View

In my first book, *Inside Out: What Makes the Person with Social Cognitive Deficits Tick?*, I discussed the variety of challenges faced by students with social cognitive deficits, and how they manifest socially and academically. In this book, the focus is exclusively on the ability to understand the perspective of others (Theory of Mind). While a component of the I LAUGH model, it stands out as the driving force that is interrelated to all others.

Being able to understand the perspective of others, and understand how they perceive you, is critical to establishing successful interpersonal relationships. Each lesson we teach on developing more appropriate social skills is intrinsically linked to students' abilities to "see" the perspective of the people with whom they communicate.

Sharing "Perspective Taking" with Educators and Caregivers

While researchers — thankfully — strive to isolate and describe each of the dysfunctions related to our students, we clinicians are faced with the equally daunting task of helping students acquire knowledge and skills that will help them succeed in social and classroom settings today, tomorrow, and beyond. However, in order to work effectively with our students, we must first increase the knowledge base of the educators and caregivers who interact with them. Bringing these people "on board" is often not as easy as it might seem.

My recent conversation with a director of special education highlights the struggle often experienced when presenting the need for therapy related to perspective taking. This director was genuinely interested in understanding more about Theory of Mind/Perspective Taking. She was concerned that it was one more type of treatment program that would have to be offered as an option to students with autism spectrum disorders and, further, was concerned about whether it had any theoretical or functional treatment history. She questioned whether the concepts of Theory of Mind or Perspective Taking even existed, whether they were plausible to implement, and what the school district's role was in providing therapy geared toward an area of thinking that was so "intangible." This educator wanted explanations, and rightly so, given that parents of her students were now requesting Theory of Mind and Perspective Taking therapy programs for their children.

This book is written to address the questions and concerns expressed by this educator. It is intended to create a path through which readers can better explore perspective taking, consider and develop their own questions, and then try out different ways to implement these lessons when working with their students.

This book is *not* intended as a mandate for how things must be done, as these treatment strategies remain "under construction" for all of us who specialize in this field. Virtually no longitudinal studies have been completed to evaluate the long-term effects of implementing this treatment approach.

However, my staff of therapists and I are truly inspired by the progress made by students who engage in these lessons. We are also inspired by the positive feedback from parents and professionals who find this material helpful and see results when used with their own students. It is my hope that readers of this book expand their own knowledge of "social thinking" and perspective taking techniques,

and then use this knowledge to guide their students toward a greater understanding of social relationships. I truly believe that if our students can cognitively understand the relationships in which they participate, it will be far easier for them to make sense of the related social skills that lead to further interpersonal, academic, and vocational success.

Summary

Social cognition supports our ability to relate to others and successfully engage in social relationships and the school curriculum. The three primary theories reviewed here (Central Coherence Theory, Executive Dysfunction Theory and Theory of Mind) are critical to understanding social cognition. They highlight the underlying constructs of social cognition and overall intelligence.

Having "good social skills" is defined as being able to "share space effectively" or "adapt to others across contexts." By broadening the definition of social teaching, we can more easily recognize the extent to which it impacts the daily functioning of students in all classrooms and how this knowledge also contributes to interpreting core language arts curricular concepts.

Social thinking should be taught to kids with social learning challenges not as an additional school subject, but as a core instructional element that impacts each moment of the school day.

This book focuses on developing a cognitive behavioral treatment approach for students with social cognitive deficits who have language and near-normal to above-normal verbal intelligence. By demystifying what constitutes social thinking and related social skills, I hope that caregivers (parents and professionals) can learn and practice a more explicit approach to social teaching.

Further, the I LAUGH framework included illustrates how we can facilitate the assessment and remediation of students with deficits in social thinking.

A new understanding of the role social knowledge plays in the eventual success of our students is needed if we are to develop appropriate and effective treatment programs for these students. School systems often feel these students don't have "educational problems" since many do well on tests and get good grades. If we are to help these socially challenged students, a new definition of "education" is needed, one that gives equal attention to the social cognitive development of students alongside their academic development.

The more I learn about specific diagnostic categories related to persons with social cognitive deficits (e.g. Autism, Asperger Syndrome, PDD-NOS, ADHD/ADD, Oppositional Defiant Disorder, schizophrenia, Tourettes, etc....), the more I realize the extent to which professionals have compartmentalized these disorders and overlooked how the individual parts relate to the whole functioning of the person. When I feel really confused, I remind myself: God did not create man based on diagnostic manuals! Let us not lose sight of the totality of who we are.

Chapter 1
Perspective Taking: Thinking, Learning and Teaching

The term "perspective taking" describes the ability of one person to consider the point of view and motives of others. While sounding fairly simple, this is an incredibly complex process that is the very foundation of successful interpersonal relationships.

A more formal academic term for perspective taking is "Theory of Mind," described by Dr. Simon Baron-Cohen as "being able to infer the full range of mental states (beliefs, desires, intentions, imagination, emotions, etc.) that cause action (by a person). In brief, to be able to reflect on the contents of one's own and others' minds." Dr. Baron-Cohen is one of a group of researchers who have explored the Theory of Mind of individuals with typical social cognitive development in contrast to those with limited social cognition.

Terminology

Mindblind - Unable to perceive that others have thoughts and feelings.

Perspective Taking - Understanding the point of view of another person; the ability to consider the contents of other people's minds.

Social Cognition - one form of intelligence that creates our overall "smarts," it allows us to interpret and respond to social information through interpersonal communication, written expression, sharing space, or interpreting thoughts and actions of fictional characters.

Theory of Mind - Understanding of your own and other people's thoughts, emotions, physical and language-based motives, intentions, personality, and belief systems.

To describe the significant deficits in Theory of Mind demonstrated by people with autism, the term "Mindblindness" was coined (1995), suggesting that these individuals are not able to see into the minds of others. Persons who are considered to be "Mindblind" lack perspective taking skills.

First-Order Testing

Numerous studies have explored what it means to be Mindblind. Assessment of a person's ability to understand that different people have different thoughts is referred to as "First-Order Testing of Theory of Mind." Developmentally, typical children can pass First Order tests by the age of three to four. A classic research study, commonly referred to as the Sally-Anne Study (Baron-Cohen, Leslie, and Frith, 1985), evaluated the Theory of Mind skills of children with Down syndrome compared to those of children with autism. The following passage describes an autistic child's participation and typical response:

The child with autism (Anne) and a typical peer (Sally) were in a room with a supervisor. A basket and an inverted box were on the table in this room. A marble was placed in the basket with both children observing. The supervisor then had Sally step out of the room while he asked Anne to move the marble under the inverted box. The supervisor then had Sally re-enter the room. Upon Sally's return he asked Anne where she thought Sally thought the marble was. Since Anne (child with autism) could not consider the perspective of Sally (typical peer), she stated that she thought Sally would think the marble was under the box, even though Sally was out of the room when the marble was moved.

In the Sally-Anne study, the autistic child's inability to account for the different experience, and thus knowledge, of her peer demonstrated her very limited perspective taking skills. Anne was therefore referred to as being "mindblind." Interestingly, no child diagnosed with autism has ever been reported to pass First-Order Theory of Mind tests when compared to peers of the same mental age. The students with Down syndrome also did not show a strong Theory of Mind deficit in this study. (Baron-Cohen, 2000).

Second-Order False-Belief Testing

Second-Order False-Belief tests assess a child's ability "to understand one person's mental states about other people's mental states" (Baron-Cohen 2000). This means that a child knows (to some extent) what another person thinks about him or about a third person. For example, Second-Order False-Belief tests evaluate whether a person such as Anne would be able to understand what Sally thought about her sister, Sue.

The ability to pass a Second-Order False-Belief test is acquired by typically developing children by the age of six. While children with significant deficits in Theory of Mind (such as those with autism) continue to struggle with this concept throughout their lifespan, many persons with higher-level autism spectrum disorders, including many with Asperger Syndrome, are able to pass Theory of Mind assessments that explore both First-Order and Second-Order False-Belief tests closer to the developmental age of their typical peers.

Nevertheless, it has been observed repeatedly in my clinic, through others' anecdotal reports, and in research (Baron-Cohen, 1995) that very high functioning students with social cognitive deficits (such as those with Asperger Syndrome) who are able to pass these basic assessments still manifest difficulties in gaining full insight into the mental states of others. Clearly, these students are not fully "mindblind," although they continue to be limited in their ability to recognize the mental states of others. In most cases, they will have challenges while engaging in a spontaneous interaction that requires them to quickly and fluidly monitor an array of features (nonverbal social cues, inferential language, and cues from the surrounding environment) in order to actively comprehend and demonstrate healthy perspective taking skills.

Theory of Mind and Perspective Taking Deficits

Normal Development of Perspective Taking

The development of perspective taking skills appears to begin in the womb. Normally developing babies start making attempts at matching the facial expression of others in the first weeks of life. By the age of nine to 12 months, babies establish "joint attention." This means they look to the eyes of people around them and follow eye gaze to determine what they are looking at. This helps the baby figure out what other people are thinking about. Shortly after joint attention is established, children start to point with their index finger and arm extended to encourage others to share in their thoughts or requests. Alongside these early nonverbal communicative patterns, language also emerges.

As toddlers synthesize language and thought, their ability to see into others' minds springs forth. They begin to understand that they are different from others and have their own desires. (We call this stage "the terrible twos.") Ultimately toddlers realize that people's minds contain different sets of information based on their different experiences. We used to believe this skill evolved by 4.5 years of age; newer research indicates this knowledge may be emerging in the first two years of life.

Subsequently children come to understand that each person's mind is unique, and the information in it can be altered based on personal experiences. During preschool and early school years, children learn how to manipulate others' minds through trickery, cheating, lying, etc.

Throughout our development, from childhood into adulthood, we continue to master our ability to take the perspective of others. We become more sophisticated in the subtle manipulation of other's thoughts, and our awareness of how other people might be trying to manipulate us grows. We become more empathetic and responsive to the needs of others. This ability to anticipate, respond, and encode/decode our own and others' intentions, to "take perspective," is critical for developing the capacity to live independently as an adult.

Persons with social cognitive deficits, such as those on the autism spectrum, all have some degree of weakness in their ability to decode others' intentions: they have a perspective taking deficit. However, the diagnostic labels associated with autism spectrum disorders do not in any way help us predict the level of these deficits in each person.

My clinical experience clearly indicates that perspective taking deficits exist on a spectrum, one that is not directly aligned with the less-functioning to more-abled spectrum of ability in other functioning areas. Perspective taking challenges are not black and white. Once it is determined that a child has a deficit, it is essential to examine the level of deficit and how it impacts the child's overall thinking.

Early Intervention, Learning and Labels

All of us are born with an innate ability or inability to take the perspective of others. The good news is that even those born with limitations can improve to some degree, with consistent intervention. While research in the area of treatment with regard to en-

couraging further development of Theory of Mind towards the goal of enhancing social skill development is in its infancy, Gevers, Cifford, Mager, and Boer (2006) state in their summary of their clinical research that it showed "promising, although preliminary results. School aged PDD children are able to profit from a Theory of Mind based training aimed at improvement of social cognitive skills, provided together with psychoeducation and instruction for the parents."

On the downside, however, it is also clear that students will always struggle to comprehend quickly and efficiently the perspective taking process when compared to their age/developmentally matched peers. However, given the key importance of perspective taking (Theory of Mind) skills towards forming and sustaining healthy relations across our lifetime, any progress is to be appreciated as vital.

Experience indicates that applied behavior analysis (ABA) and programs of relatedness — such as Floortime (DIR) and Relationship Development Intervention (RDI) — can help students tremendously when initiated during the preschool years. Many students who participate in intensive early intervention programs make significant global social and communicative gains compared to their initial functioning levels. However, they continue to have lifelong challenges with complex perspective taking skills. To date, baseline studies on the emergence of perspective taking skills through these treatment programs have not been completed, yet anecdotally anyone who has worked with children in intensive early communication/intervention programs will attest to clear improvement in social motivation and social outreach when compared to the students' own baseline skills.

Regardless of the level of perspective taking, every student — with structured teaching — can learn adaptive skills. All students can learn, but not all students have the capacity to learn all things. The complex and abstract concept of perspective taking is one of the most difficult challenges a person not born with this ability can attempt.

We explore students' capacity to learn perspective taking because it allows us to establish realistic expectations for students. It also helps us determine what services are needed now to develop appropriate social skills required for the students to be successful as adults. Some students with limited perspective taking skills will need their education focused on the development of practical life skills: vocational, leisure, and daily living. Students with a more advanced ability to understand perspective taking concepts need to be prepared for the daunting challenges of college and career life where critical thinking skills are required.

The problem with a label such as "autism" is that it is applied broadly across a huge spectrum of functionality. This renders the label meaningless in determining appropriate treatment — it only acknowledges that the student has some level (undefined by the label) of communication, social, and sensory needs.

Some parents express concern that by acknowledging that their child will not completely resolve his or her social/communication challenges, they are giving up "hope" for their child's future. I believe the opposite. Realistic hope helps us focus proactively on how services can help the child progress beyond his or her current level. In my experience, members of the treatment team who have unrealistic expectations often put unreasonable pressure on the child, parents, and supporting professionals. This creates stress and even animosity related to establishing and carrying out the treatment plan. While the ceiling potential for social cognitive growth may be

based on the student's prenatal brain development, the growth that can be fostered in an appropriate environment and with appropriate teachings is very encouraging.

Spectrum of Perspective Taking Deficits: Proposing Three Levels

By third grade, students with perspective taking deficits function in one of three global ability categories, each associated with prognostic information describing what can be expected of these students once they become adults.

As previously mentioned, perspective taking abilities are on a "spectrum," and there are many students who "blend" across two different levels. Students change rapidly during their preschool and early elementary school years. Thus, it is important to postpone assessing the perspective taking level of a student before third grade.

The three levels of perspective taking are:

1. Severely Impaired Perspective Taker (SIPT)

2. Emerging Perspective Taker (EPT)

3. Impaired Interactive Perspective Taker (IIPT)

Level 1: Severely Impaired Perspective Taker (SIPT)

The student referred to as the Severely Impaired Perspective Taker (SIPT) is a student with autism who also has a dual diagnosis of significant cognitive impairment (mental retardation). These students generally present most of the following symptoms (this is not an exhaustive list):

1. *Inability to take the perspective of others.* SIPTs do not read people's motives, intentions, thoughts, beliefs, and prior knowledge experiences. They likely "read" some level of emotion conveyed through tone of voice and facial expressions,

but they lack the ability to read the nuances of these emotions. It is unclear exactly what they know and don't know since they are not able to communicate beyond stating their basic wants and needs.

2. *Very limited development of spoken language; many are non-verbal.* SIPTs benefit from augmentative communication systems such as PECS (Picture Exchange Communication System) or old-fashioned simple communication boards. (Note: being nonverbal alone does not make one a SIPT. Persons can be very limited in their development of language due to motor speech apraxia. Speech language pathologists and psychologists help make this determination.)

3. *Communicative language, when utilized, is generally used to tell people what is desired (food, clothing, etc.) rather than to share observations about the world.* In other words, SIPTs' communication focuses on functionality. These students may also use echolalia as another functional way to communicate their desires and more abstract thoughts.

4. *No understanding of abstract language.* Language used to help them understand must be short, precise, and literal.

5. *Very limited attention span.*

6. *Very limited understanding of the conceptual world.* SIPTs cannot create their own structures and plans away from finding time to engage in their personal pleasures or routines. Adults have to supervise all aspects of their daily living at home, in the community, and on the job. They need sameness and routine.

7. *At times, limited to almost no acknowledgement of others in their presence.* Very active participation initiated by the caregiver is required to engage SIPTs in reciprocal play or communication.

8. *Significant sensory challenges.* SIPTs may exhibit active and frequent sensory self-stimulation and have very specific habits to keep their senses balanced.

9. *Difficulty with transitions.* Transitions can be extremely challenging. Since these students are not actively aware of the subtle changes in their world, they do not actively anticipate change. Transitions have to be planned carefully.

10. *Limited abstract thinking and problem-solving ability.* Academically, these students can learn some basic skills such as counting, reading, and decoding, even if they cannot speak. However, they are not able to generalize this concrete, rote learning to abstract thinking and problem-solving.

11. *Limited social motivation to engage.* SIPTs can learn routine-oriented play, jobs, and self-help skills when taught in a sequential, positive environment and given lots of practice. They also can learn to navigate the community with close supervision. Their lack of intuitive social and communication skills does not imply they do not like being with people; however, their social motivation to interact is usually limited because of their lack of insight into other people's minds. These students often have personal preferences with regard to who they wish to be with at home, at school, etc. When they relate, they generally do so on their own terms.

SIPT students will do well within an education environment focused on function and teaching them practical, daily life skills. They can and will learn these skills that are critical in preparing them to cohabit with others in a structured environment. Merely teaching them mainstream academics in grade four and beyond is not a good use of their educational time.

Parents and caregivers often share that everything their child knows had to be directly taught to them. Therefore, preparing them for life beyond school will take a lot of planning and teaching of functional life skills. Incorporate trips into the community so that SIPTs learn to interact with persons and in settings outside home and school. Practical and functional communication skills should be emphasized in their educational program.

Prognosis for the SIPT

Learning is not limited to the school years. As these students become adults they will continue to learn and develop new skills. With individualized, structured teaching, many will be able to learn a routine-oriented job and perform it with minimal, but consistent supervision. However, they will in all likelihood always need some level of adult direction.

Effective teaching strategies for the SIPT

A strong focus on behavioral teaching methods (i.e., applied behavioral analysis) will be most effective with this subset of students. Teach social skills concretely, with specific rules, and across various domains. Avoid expecting these students to generalize the information across settings.

Level 2:
Emerging Perspective Taker (EPT)

The students I refer to as Emerging Perspective Takers (EPTs) are often the same students referred to as "mindblind" in the work of Simon Baron-Cohen (1995). These students will often fail First-Order and Second-Order False-Belief testing. However, I do not refer to them as "mindblind" since in my experience, these students can learn to think about the contents of other people's minds if given extra time and explanation.

EPTs have difficulty understanding the abstract qualities of perspective taking, such as figuring out people's motives, or exploring emotions and language in context. In this sense students with EPT struggle to do the "social algebra" involved in determining the hidden meaning within communicative exchanges.

While EPTs cannot process other people's perspectives quickly and efficiently, when encouraged to think long and hard about a social situation, they often come to a reasonable conclusion (with some assistance). Their real deficit is being able to do so within the very short period of time (one or two seconds) of each communicative exchange. If we agree that social thinking impairments fall along a spectrum, it makes sense that some students' impairments are related not only to the quality of their thought, but also the ability to quickly process and respond to multiple thoughts in a very short period of time.

Perspective taking requires us to use our "social executive function skills" (e.g., social multi-tasking) to help us relate efficiently with others. Students with very weak executive function skills are also going to have difficulty with social relations. However, clinical experience has shown that we can help this subgroup of students learn more about other people's thoughts, emotions, motives, and prior knowledge/experiences. This requires direct, intense teaching.

While our intervention will not "cure" the problem, these concrete lessons contribute to EPTs being able to lead a more active and successful social life.

In general, EPTs present most of the following symptoms (this is not an exhaustive list):

1. *Range of intelligence.* They range in their intellectual skills from mildly cognitively impaired to very intelligent.

2. *Inability to efficiently take the perspective of others.* EPTs' ability to intuitively consider the thoughts, emotions, motives, prior knowledge/experiences, belief systems, and personality of those around them is inefficient. They also lack understanding about how they are perceived by others.

3. *Learning disabilities.* EPTs may or may not have mild cognitive impairments or mental retardation. However, all of them have significant learning disabilities that manifest as weaknesses in reading comprehension, written expression, math word problems, and organizational skills.

4. *Language difficulties or disabilities.* The vast majority of EPTs are verbal, although they may have experienced a significant language delay or disorder that continues in some degree throughout their lives. All have some level of language-learning disability, both receptive and expressive. Although they use verbal language, it is mostly focused on their wants and needs. EPTs do not initially share their thoughts about the world spontaneously. They also do not easily initiate language and may become easily frustrated by their inability to get their needs met in different environments.

5. *Lack of abstract language understanding.* All of these students have significant challenges in understanding written or verbal abstract language. This means they may be very literal in both their use and understanding of verbal and written language (stories, etc.).

6. *Lack of cognitive verb understanding.* EPTs may have difficulty with the use of "cognitive verbs," which are words we use to express what we think other people are thinking. Cognitive verbs include "think," "know," "guess," "decide," "forget," or "consider."

For example, a friend's normally developing four-year-old son recently said to his dad, "Dad, remember when you forgot to put the sodas in the refrigerator?" He demonstrated his remarkable ability to use language to code the thoughts (or lack thereof) in other people's minds.

However, a number of four-year-olds with high functioning autism are not yet able to use language to talk about the content of other people's minds. In fact, one of my 16-year-old clients with EPT still struggles to demonstrate his knowledge that the concept of "knowing" is different from the concept of "thinking." We obviously expect most 16-year-olds to be able to say, "I think my mom knows where she is picking me up after school." But many EPTs do not use language to discuss the actions or failures of other people's minds in this way.

7. *Lack of organizational skills.* All EPTs have significant organizational issues. Many will do what is asked of them, but are not able to build their own organizational systems.

8. *Difficulty with reading comprehension.* Most EPTs are good reading decoders but they are not able to comprehend what they read at their level of reading fluency. Reading comprehension requires the reader to understand the perspective of the characters.

9. *Lack of writing skills.* Most EPTs are poor writers, both physically due to problems with fine motor control, and academically in regard to the content of their writing. Written language requires cognitive organization and perspective taking

beyond their abilities. However, some can write stories from their own imagination or based on their own areas of interest that are quite good. But these same students will have difficulty writing a paper based on a teacher-assigned topic.

10. *Lack of problem-solving skills.* All of these students are poor personal problem-solvers. Given that they have difficulties quickly and efficiently reading the intentions or motives of others, they are naïve and can easily be manipulated. EPTs have difficulty identifying, defining, and initiating actions to recognize and solve their problems.

11. *Distractibility.* All EPTs struggle with paying attention to topics not of their personal interest; the larger the group, the more they struggle. These students are not able to regulate their behavior to the needs of the group. They do best in a very small group setting with one-on-one help. In this situation they only have to consider one other person's mind.

12. *Sensory challenges.* Most, if not all, EPTs have serious sensory challenges requiring caregivers to learn how to modify the environment to help them calm or arouse their senses.

13. *Transition challenges.* Most, if not all, EPTs have some level of difficulty with unexpected transitions because they are fairly aloof and not actively attuned to what may be happening in the environment. They do not use prior knowledge to help them predict how a situation might be calmly resolved.

14. *Lack of critical thinking skills.* Academically, EPTs may do well learning the concrete curriculum of the early elementary school years. After that, they may need intensive help in order to fully participate in the mainstream classroom, because they lack critical thinking skills. Many EPTs have paraprofessionals assigned to them or participate in smaller special education classes, which provide them with the direct educational assistance they need.

15. *Behavioral problems.* Depending on their personality, some EPTs develop significant behavior problems when placed in more challenging group educational environments. Some may experience mental health difficulties.

16. *"Quirkyness."* EPTs are often "quirky"; most peers and adults quickly recognize these students as being different.

17. *Behavioral disability labels.* Most of these students are labeled as "high functioning autism" or "PDD-NOS"; others include Asperger Syndrome, Nonverbal Learning Disorder, or ADHD.

18. *Social interaction initiation.* Almost all of these students enjoy being with others and have a very good sense of humor. However these interactions often have to be initiated and maintained by others since these students have difficulty initiating interactions themselves.

Prognosis for the EPT

As these students move into their adult years, they will continue to learn and be able to learn. Some EPTs hold very routine-oriented jobs in the community, take the bus to and from work, and learn to live in their own apartment. However, these same students will always need a caregiver or team of caregivers in the background to assist them during times when critical thinking is demanded (e.g., loss of a job, need to move apartments, changes in the bus schedule, etc.).

Effective teaching strategies for the EPT

EPTs benefit most from a blended teaching program based on behavioral strategies and a cognitive behavioral approach. These methods are explained in later chapters and in *Think Social! A Social Thinking Curriculum for School-Age Students* (Winner, 2005). Other helpful cognitive behavioral teaching strategies include *Social Stories* (Gray, 2002), *Comic Strip Conversations* (Gray, 1994), and *The Incredible 5 Point Scale* (Buron and Curtis, 2004).

Our main goal in working with EPTs is to help the student adopt explicit behavioral guidelines while also teaching him to think about thinking. It is generally noticed that immersing this student in the mainstream classroom environment from elementary through high school is not the best use of his educational day. Rather, these students require a blended curriculum, one that offers some general world knowledge typical of the mainstream classroom while also providing individual instruction in life skills that prepare them for vocational, leisure, and home environments post-high school.

Few EPTs will find success at the community college level, although some go on to earn college degrees. Vocational and community training should be a component of their middle and high school curriculum, continuing on into the adult years. Although EPTs are often very intelligent, these students must be explicitly taught basic skills to prepare them for life in the broader community.

Level 3:
Impaired Interactive Perspective Taker (IIPT)

Persons with Impaired Interactive Perspective Taking (IIPT) have active, quick, and efficient awareness that other people have perspectives different from their own. They can describe the emotions, motives, intentions, belief systems, and prior knowledge/experiences of another person. They understand they can affect other people's emotions and thoughts by what they do and say.

However, they are best at doing this when removed from an interaction with that person. They fall short when it becomes necessary to monitor and modify their own behavior during a spontaneous conversational exchange. Thus their greatest impairment occurs during the actual moments of interaction.

Persons with IIPT often look "normal." Because they can explain other people's thoughts and actions, peers and adults expect them to successfully interact with others in a positive and productive way. In reality, they become overwhelmed by social executive challenges during communication. They default to their own beliefs and thoughts to rule their decision-making when they feel overwhelmed, rather than considering and responding to other people's points of view.

Like all of us, persons with IIPT are self-oriented. But since they do not "filter" what they say or do based on how they think people will perceive them, they are viewed as self-indulgent or self-absorbed. At the same time, they have a very strong sense of how other people should behave and how people should treat them. They may be the first to point out that someone else's behavior is "out of line" or that others are not following the rules, when in fact IIPTs are not able to follow the more "hidden" rules (e.g., hidden curriculum) of participating in the group.

The majority of these students are in the mainstream setting and physically look very much like their peers; this sets them at greater risk for confrontation. IIPTs can describe in great detail how they expect other people to behave. However, they fail to see interactions from other people's points of view while in the classroom, during recreational activities, or at home. As a result, they are often seen as "behavior problems," "emotionally disturbed," or just "spoiled."

✖

Bernadette, a 12-year-old girl in middle school, actively participated in activities to better understand the concept of perspective taking. She was able to verbally describe what others expect from her and what she should do to modify her interaction to keep her peers enjoying their relationship with her.

One day Bernadette and the other girls in her therapy group were provided with visual cues to remind them that their job was to ask questions to find out about other people in the group during their more spontaneous interaction. Bernadette appeared to understand the assignment. I asked who would like to start the interaction; Bernadette raised her hand. She began by saying, "I am auditioning for a school play. I have worked really hard to memorize the lines." She then began to recite all the lines she had memorized. Next she told the group that she also had to sing a song for the audition, and then she launched into singing the song. She stopped only when a girl sitting across from her gave her a strong physical cue to stop singing.

Bernadette never realized during her attempt to interact that she had not done it right. I checked the length of time Bernadette spoke about herself – it was four minutes! The good news was that when she was shown a video of this interaction, and I reviewed with her at length ways she can self-monitor her own behavior when in a group, Bernadette did go on to make considerable progress in this area. By the end of the school year, her principal and classroom teachers were remarking how much more she was acting like her peers at school now that she wasn't making so many inappropriate comments.

In general, IIPTs present most of the following symptoms (this is not an exhaustive list):

1. *Near normal to very high intelligence.*

2. *Fluid verbal language skills, often using an expanded vocabulary.* IIPTs sound impressive verbally, which leads people to think they are highly competent communicators. They may or may not have receptive language challenges.

3. *Have difficulty following the "hidden rules" of the social context (classroom, free time, vocational environment).* IIPTs understand that the rules exist for others but do not necessarily have the insight to see how the rules apply to themselves. For example, these students may blurt out statements when they feel they have something to say in class.

4. *May struggle with complex interpretation of social academics.* IIPTs struggle with reading comprehension of advanced literature and written expression, particularly in writings where many different people's points of view are presented.

5. *Organizational skills are often lacking.* Just as this person has a social executive functioning deficit, they also have challenges with all other executive function tasks, most of which relate to organizational skills.

6. *Weakness in developing friendships and working as part of a group in the classroom.* IIPTs are not able to consider other people's perspectives intuitively when engaged in social exchanges. Most have strong desires to socially relate to others, even if they may appear "caustic" or "uncaring" in the sense that they want to relate on their own terms.

7. *Have difficulty simultaneously reading the social cues of the face, body, voice, spoken language, and environmental context.* IIPTs can be overwhelmed by all these cues, and may depend solely on the person's spoken words to determine the meaning of a message. This often results in misreading the situation.

8. *Mental health challenges.* These may include depression, anxiety, or obsessive compulsive disorder. Mental health problems appear to develop after the student lives through years of not being able to fit into a group of peers in a proactive way. A significant body of research now recognizes the co-morbid mental health challenges of high functioning persons on the autism spectrum.

9. *Excessive competitiveness.* IIPTs can be extremely competitive and insist on winning all games, since they see winning as their victory and may have little sense of how others feel in that situation. At younger ages, some may become very upset when they don't win.

10. *May not be in touch with their own and others' emotions.* They tend to be quite limited in recognizing the existence and power of their own emotions; let a lone make decisions based on interpreting other people's emotional states. However, most IIPTs have empathy and will provide it profusely when they can read the social cues that provoke empathetic responses. As all students age, empathetic reactions are triggered off subtle social cues easily missed by this population.

11. *May not initiate language to problem-solve or seek assistance from others.* IIPTs have weak personal problem-solving and self-advocacy skills. These skills are very important for transitioning into their young adult lives.

12. *Sensory issues.* While sensory problems often exist for IIPTs, they are not so overt in their sensory seeking strategies. These students rarely flap their hands, but may pace or have more extreme reactions to loud sounds, etc.

13. *Disability labels.* Diagnostic labels frequently associated with IIPT include: Asperger Syndrome, Nonverbal Learning Disorder, PDD-NOS, ADHD, Bipolar, and other emotional challenges.

Prognosis for the IIPT

IIPTs have the best chance of leading a "normal" life, and may experience full independence in all domains: leisure, vocational, and home life. However, persons with IIPT have an uphill road to accomplish what most of us learn almost through osmosis. Their maturity is often delayed, they have weak social networks, and they have difficulty establishing the self-advocacy and organizational skills that will help them succeed in their chosen path (college, career, etc.). Parents often need to stay closely involved in the child's life, well into that child's 20s and beyond, to provide that extra emotional foundation and support.

Of course, this only helps as long as the IIPT adult accepts the support. IIPTs often have such poor self-awareness that they blame their problems on others (often the parents) rather than examine and realize how they can help themselves. Ultimately, maturation is the friend of the IIPT, and as adults, they will start to see that they can do more to help themselves.

The good news is that we now have therapeutic lessons for persons with IIPT that have historically not been available to them. Many of today's adult IIPTs did not have lessons to assist them when they were younger and now have to learn so much more as adults. It is our hope that these new supports will result in greater levels of success for students as they grow into adults. On the down side, there are precious few services available to adults in the community, since these persons don't usually qualify for state or federal monies given their "high level" of deficits. We need to try and provide as much help as possible before these students graduate from high school.

Effective teaching strategies for the IIPT

The only teaching approach that appears to be of real help is cognitive behavioral therapy. These lessons teach our students to think through a concept prior to the behavior (skill) being taught. While many of our clients need mental health counseling, cognitive behavioral counseling is a more practical approach than the traditional insight-oriented therapy used by many therapists (Paxton and Estay, 2007). However, some therapists are modifying this technique to make it more beneficial to our clients with social thinking challenges (Jacobson, 2003).

Researchers are now exploring how they can assess Theory of Mind challenges of higher-functioning persons with social cognitive deficits (Baron-Cohen, Jolliffe, Mortimore, and Robertson, 1997). Theory of Mind and Perspective Taking processes are complex. They are rich in interconnected detail and concepts. Breaking down this process to pinpoint the exact nature of the deficit is a daunting process. Even so, astute parents, educators, and researchers immediately sense students deficits in this area when observing them in social interactions and environments.

It should be noted that virtually no professional field — counseling, psychology, psychiatry, neurology, speech language pathology, behaviorism, education, pediatrics, or special education — includes a mandated, intense curriculum to educate professionals about autism spectrum and related disabilities. Recently a few specialized university programs have begun incorporating classes on this subject, but professionals generally seek out this education on their own. Those of us who work in the field are still learning what we need to teach!

Interweaving Developmental Language Concepts and Theory of Mind

Wellman and Lagattuta (2000) in reviewing the normal development of "understanding other minds," cite that typical developing children do not verbally formulate references to thinking and knowing until about three years of age. Tager-Flusberg (2000) demonstrates that lexical development is interwoven with the development of a Theory of Mind. Therefore, children with autism — who have limited ability to understand that other people have thoughts and motives — are unlikely to use cognitive verbs such as "think, know, decide, and guess."

This is a fascinating developmental language marker, and one that may indicate that a person with autism is developing a Theory of Mind. In normally developing children, these verbs of cognition emerge after children are able to pass basic tests of Theory of Mind. However, it also appears that if a child is weak in his development of Theory of Mind but is developing some adequate language skills, it may be possible to teach him a bit more about this fundamental concept through specific language lessons that capitalize on thinking and knowing. This is the case when one works with the Emerging Perspective Taker. In Chapter 4, a therapy strategy will be discussed for teaching these linguistic concepts to EPTs who lack them.

The more sophisticated and language-based concepts related to perspective taking discussed in this book will not be absorbed by all students. But students who function in the middle and higher levels of the perspective taking spectrum — that is, students who are at least beginning to discern between their own thoughts and those of others, and who use language to describe those relationships — are the students for whom this book's strategies are intended.

Some children (those who function more as SIPTs in their late elementary school years) will never be able to grasp these concepts given our current technology and teaching strategies. Still, it is important to emphasize that students who function towards the "mindblindness" end of the spectrum may be able to learn skills that allow them to acquire more independence related to the levels at which they currently function.

Applying Perspective Taking Lessons in the Clinic

Our clinical work at the Center for Social Thinking focuses on persons experiencing IIPT or high-end EPT. At all ages, children, teen, and adult, IIPTs and EPTs have difficulty with relations in all environments: home, work, and school.

For example, a bright 17-year-old boy with Asperger Syndrome, who graduated early from high school, explained that he did not feel he had to do any chores at home because "I do not take anything from my home, so I do not have to give anything back in return." He was unable to consider the perspective of the other household members who "give" to the home by cooking, cleaning, doing laundry, and working at their jobs to pay the household expenses.

At our clinic we work on defining the concept of "perspective" and perspective taking with our older students. When we explore these terms with our younger students (K-Grade 5) we explain it as "thinking about what other people think."

By introducing this concept we provide our students with basic conceptual building blocks that will develop their ability to think about social relationships during the actual moment of social interaction. We continually explore how to take this abstract thought process and break it down into concrete parts. Using these parts, we create a starting point from which we can launch our students' thinking. It is a trial and error process that continues to evolve. Nevertheless, our experiences and results validate that we can work with higher-level students, IIPTs and EPTs, to expand their knowledge in this area and eventually increase their use of appropriate skills.

The first step is to create and implement a core vocabulary to discuss how people think about others. The second step is to use direct experience to show children how the "thinking about others and what they think of you" process plays out in real time. We do this through session activities that build on their knowledge and experiences.

I strongly believe that students at IIPT and EPT levels who are born with some intuitive insight into perspective taking can expand their knowledge in this area. However, we know we do not "cure" this disability. Therefore we must acknowledge that while we help students acquire social skills associated with the concepts, we do not completely "fix" the problem.

Applying Perspective Taking Lessons Outside the Clinic

I counsel families that working within the realm of perspective taking is like learning about a new culture: at first it's only a concept because it's foreign to our current way of understanding and functioning. It is only over time that its meaning is learned, as it is experienced again and again. Perspective taking cannot be taught through behavioral approaches alone. It is not a quick fix — it takes time to learn. Inherent in the process is learning to explore other people's minds as well as one's own, and recognizing the related reactions of others.

As such, all persons who are living or working with these students need to learn the vocabulary of perspective taking. This creates a common basis of communication, one that they can use during teachable moments throughout the day, in all environments.

A 16-year-old, very intelligent boy with Asperger Syndrome, who had a problematic history with regard to social understanding and social relationships, recently told his clinical psychologist, "I now care about what other people think of me!" His psychologist and I have been working with this student on this concept for a couple of years. His statement was fantastic. While he still exhibits some mildly odd social behaviors, improvement in this area is notable as well. Now that he can relate cognitively to perspective taking as "thinking and knowing," we can focus on teaching him to monitor his own social skills and understand how they relate back to the perspective taking of others.

Teaching "Social Thinking" to EPTs and IIPTs to Foster Social Understanding

 As we describe the process of "thinking about others and how they think about you" to students, it is important to keep in mind that this process occurs below the tangible level of human interactions. Perspective taking is constantly in motion, even when spoken language is not at the forefront of an interaction.

For example, one day I entered a large room to give a workshop. I was setting up my laptop computer for the presentation when an audience member arrived early and took her seat. At that point I became keenly aware that this silent observer was monitoring all my actions. I found myself thinking about her while monitoring my own activity much more closely than I did when I was working in the room alone. I began to monitor her activity as well and I finally broke the silence by inquiring, "What brought you here today?"

As I work with students on understanding the use and meaning of specific social skills, I find it impossible to teach these skills without exploring how the skills relate to the mind and motives of the other individuals involved in the interactions. In my clinic we work on these concepts in "social thinking groups." We explain to our students that social thinking is a necessary precursor to the use of social skills.

As educators and parents, it is important to understand that what we are really teaching are the concepts that support the skills we want these students to develop. If we can expand a child's knowledge in the realm of social thinking, we can more quickly help him develop related skills.

Our teaching focus shifts from telling a student what to do in a social interaction (traditional "social skills" program), to helping him learn why he needs to do it and then how he can demonstrate what he knows through his behavior. This, in a nutshell, comprises the "social thinking" program.

With younger children we introduce this using very basic concrete concepts; by middle school, most of our students with high language skills and social cognitive deficits can engage in meta-cognitive discussions about the perspective taking concept itself.

I am often reminded that historically our therapeutic focus for helping students develop better social strategies has been mired in teaching them how to have better conversations. We do this by writing goals about how a child should engage in "three conversations throughout a school day," "maintain a conversation through three to five turns," and "stay on the topic." While these are not bad goals, the fact that these are the only socially oriented goals in an IEP demonstrate our limited insight into the complex process of social interactions. In the past we have assumed that excellent verbal language skills are the key to relating to others. But individuals with social cognitive deficits have proven to us a student can have high language skills yet lack the ability to think about what another person is thinking, resulting in communicative interactions that are weak or confusing.

My books, *Worksheets! for Teaching Social Thinking and Related Skills* (2005) and *Think Social! A Social Thinking Curriculum for School-Age Students* (2005), explore practical ways to teach social thinking concepts at home, in therapy groups, and in the classroom. The information in this book lays the foundation for the use of these other materials.

⧗

Dan was a six-year-old boy with Asperger Syndrome who was fascinated with chemistry. I was working with one of my clinicians to show her that Dan had significant deficits in interactive perspective taking even though he had an exceptionally high IQ and strong language development. I sat down across from Dan and asked him to tell me about chemistry. After I listened for about a minute, I got up from my chair, walked over to the door, walked out of the room and closed the door behind me…while Dan continued to look at my chair and talk about chemistry!

The information below reveals why and how we must first teach students about the communicative process as a whole before we teach specific language techniques to be used when engaged in verbal interactions.

EPT, IIPT, and Overall Intelligence

Intelligence and perspective taking abilities are not directly correlated. A common characteristic of persons with high-level social cognitive deficits (such as those with IIPT) is that their verbal intelligence quotient is significantly higher than their performance intelligence quotient, as measured by assessment tools such as the Wechsler Intelligence Scale for Children, Third Edition (WISC III). Given that advanced or relatively high language skills are strong indicators of potentially good school achievement, one would naturally assume that a child with high verbal intelligence "has it all together."

However, we cannot make this assumption for students with social cognitive deficits. Most people who enter into relationships with these students get the sense that their behavior is qualitatively different, but cannot describe the extent of the impairment, Parents often describe these children as "bright but clueless." Based on clinical observations, there is a lack of correlation between a person's formally measured intelligence and his perspective taking abilities. Some of my "less smart" students appear to have more intuitive perspective taking skills than my "super bright" students. This can be extremely frustrating since we do not have formalized assessments to document the difficulties experienced by persons with social cognitive deficits in their interactions with others. Even for very bright persons, IIPT can often be so disabling that the person has difficulty gaining or succeeding in employment or achieving satisfactory personal relationships, in spite of the fact that he has numerous college degrees and has won awards for academic accomplishments.

It should also be noted that no direct relationship between the "autism spectrum" and the "perspective taking spectrum" exists. Perspective taking skills are not currently considered in diagnoses related to the autism spectrum, and the extent to which they manifest is not tied to functioning level. Thus it is possible for a person labeled "Asperger Syndrome" to function as EPT, and for a person with high-functioning autism to be an IIPT.

⧗

Terry is a 55-year-old man who came to my attention when his 80-year-old mother called me. She had recently become familiar with the medical diagnosis of Asperger Syndrome and was anxious to seek help for her son. She explained that he had been qualitatively different throughout his early childhood and into his youth and adulthood. She had sought the help of professionals when he was a boy, but to no avail.

As Terry became an adult, he continued to search for ways to help himself. When meeting with a psychologist about 20 years ago, the psychologist apparently told him, "There is something wrong with you; we just do not know what it is!" Terry revealed to me that at that point he discontinued his search for answers. He was a good student academically and, upon graduation from college, took a test for the federal government and achieved a high score. That test result gained him employment in a government agency.

Terry maintains that exact same job today, never having received any job promotions in his 31 years of service! He also continues to live alone and describes a life of high anxiety and intermittent depression. Over the years he was frustrated by the lack of progress he made from talk-based therapy. When I met with him to help break down how to comprehend the social world around him, step by step, he felt he was finally gaining some insight.

Recognizing Perspective Taking Deficits

Learning to observe students with social cognitive deficits — and qualitatively describing their place on the perspective taking spectrum — is an important step toward helping educators and parents better understand their unique needs. As mentioned earlier, students who have SIPT and EPT are much more limited in their ability to gain insight into this process than those with some level of IIPT. The more we understand about the spectrum of perspective taking disabilities, the more we can focus our therapy techniques on helping students progress to the best of their abilities.

Later in this book we will discuss ways in which we can gain insight into this complex process through meaningful and relevant assessment techniques. We will also offer a reporting template that better describes social thinking challenges in our professionals' written reports.

While this book focuses on the student with labels such as High Functioning Autism, Asperger Syndrome, Pervasive Development Disorder-Not Otherwise Specified (PDD-NOS) and Nonverbal Learning Disorder (NVLD), I have often considered that IIPT deficits may also affect individuals diagnosed as Emotionally Disturbed (ED). I realize that many of the needs of the emotionally disturbed are different from those with social cognitive deficits; however this population also appears to benefit from the perspective taking lessons described later in this book.

The exploration into these "social thinking" treatment techniques by the scientific community is just beginning. A study demonstrating students not only learned social thinking concepts but could carry them over into a generalized environment has recently been completed (Crooke, Hendrix, and Rachman, in-press 2007). Practitioners are applying these techniques across the U.S. and in Asia with positive results. Social thinking programs have now been implemented in school districts and private practices in California, New Hampshire, Illinois, Washington, Oregon, Maine, Hong Kong, Singapore, and the Philippines, to name a few.

Both parents and teachers comment on how these strategies are user friendly and logical. Hopefully more published research as to the treatment benefits will be forthcoming. Parents from our center (Michelle G. Winner's Center for Social Thinking,

Inc.) responded to a narrative format questionnaire (2006) indicating they found the social thinking vocabulary helpful in how it provides a path to talk about social information with their children. They also indicated that many of the children are generalizing these social thinking strategies into their interactions in their larger communities. One parent wrote, "the simple concepts that can be carried into the home really helped and made total sense to Noah. He is much more aware of his impact on others and uses the vocabulary with us and his 4 year old sister. "

Summary

This chapter explored Theory of Mind more deeply, introducing the concept that perspective taking challenges fall on a spectrum from mild to severe and can be described within three broad categories:

1. Severely Impaired Perspective Takers (SIPT)

2. Emerging Perspective Takers (EPT)

3. Impaired Interactive Perspective Takers (IIPT)

From my clinical experience, a student's level of perspective taking directly correlates to their ability to develop full independence as they achieve adulthood. However, their level of perspective taking ability is not tied to intelligence or their level of functioning on the autism spectrum.

By assessing perspective taking skills, we can design more appropriate treatment programs that will result in positive long-term outcomes.

Students with SIPT need strong behavioral instruction to help them learn basic levels of social interaction.

Students with EPT require a blended approach of behavioral support together with social cognitive teaching strategies. These students need social information broken down into very small parts and the opportunity to practice them extensively over time.

IIPT students will gain the most from a cognitive behavioral program where we introduce social thinking by teaching these students why we demonstrate specific behaviors, how these translate into social behaviors, and how to self-monitor thinking and behavior to stay focused on the appropriate social expectations of the communicative context.

Chapter 2
The Keys to Perspective Taking

Perspective Taking Attributes

As a skill, perspective taking is a marriage of key communicative skills and individual personality attributes working together within the visible and social context of the environment. Perspective taking is an incredibly abstract concept, and those of us working in the field capture the most feedback from our students who are capable of increasingly abstract thought and discussion. Teachers of this concept — and that includes educators, service providers, or parent-teachers — must step outside the box of conventional methodology and develop a firmer grasp of what it means to be an EPT or IIPT. This helps us break down teaching to a level where students can begin to comprehend how to think about thinking. As our knowledge base grows, we can further open the windows to understanding in those students more challenged in this area.

The skills and attributes that contribute to perspective taking are not a finite list and will vary from person to person. In this chapter we introduce you to an ever-expanding list generated through clinical teaching experiences we have had with EPT and IIPT students at our clinic. While we all recognize the benefits of early intervention for students with autism and other developmental disabilities, it is important that within the realm of social cognitive challenges, we do not de-emphasize the importance of late intervention (and all intervention in between). Whether a student is 5, 15, or 25, it is critical that we help students gain foundation skills in social relationships that will help them be successful as they grow and develop. And perspective taking is a key foundation skill. It is equally important that we share this information with parents and family, so strategies are used across the day and within the different life domains. Living with a child who does not have

strongly developed perspective taking skills, even if the child is very bright, can be extremely challenging for a family.

Dr. Steven Gutstein, author of *Autism Asperger: Solving the Relationship Puzzle* (2000), does an excellent job recognizing the basic attributes that serve as precursors for social relationships. While Dr. Gutstein recommends that this social relationship information be used in a 15-20 hour per week treatment program, it is certainly possible to take his well-developed concepts and apply them to activities during a school day or therapy session.

My hope is that the following information encourages parents and educators to think about what drives us to interact with others so that others want to sustain the relationship in return.

Consider this as you read: your friends are the people who make you feel good about yourself!

Thinking About How Others Affect You

1. Recognizing the thoughtful presence of another person.

- This attribute is generally very weak in individuals with autism who are SIPT and EPT. Absence of this attribute results in persons failing to acknowledge others when in direct proximity of them.

  When a child enters the waiting room at the clinic he may physically bump into another person while in pursuit of the toys and never acknowledge any physical contact with that person.

2. Recognizing the individuality of the other person.

- Upon meeting a new person, initial thoughts are quickly formed by people with strong Theory of Mind and perspective taking skills. These thoughts are based on traits of the other person: gender, age, appearance, and apparent intellectual functioning. Individuals with strong perspective taking skills consider these variables and immediately modify their interaction with the person based on what they think they know about them.

- Individuals with deficits in this area may approach another person and begin to talk to him/her without considering the point of view or attributes of the person to whom they are talking.

  Many children at the clinic have tried to explain to me how to play the game of Pokeman without ever accounting for the fact that I am a forty-year-old woman and far from interested in this game.

3. Recognizing that another person has his or her own personal set of emotions.

- A deficit in this area is demonstrated when the student is weak in his recognition and response to each person's unique and changing emotional states.

- It is also common that these students have difficulty understanding and expressing the full range of emotions at a level similar to their age-matched peers.

- Individuals may not recognize that there are many occasions or common experiences where all individuals share similar emotional states.

  When working with a high-school student, I asked him how it felt to return from vacation. He acknowledged it was no fun to return to school. When I asked him how he thought I felt he said, "I have no idea." When I explained that people often share emotional states around specific events he responded by saying, "No one ever told me that before!"

4. Recognizing and responding to the fact that other people have their own desires, motives, and intentions. These are coded through two systems: our physical movements and our language.

Physical movements: When we share space with another person, each of us tries to figure out the intentions of the other person(s) by watching their physical actions. If they are walking down the hall towards us but then quickly go into a room marked "restroom," we figure out they had to use the restroom. We track, almost unconsciously, the physical movements of those around us to figure out why people are near us. We do this for safety as well as to determine who wants to talk to us (e.g., by observing them walk towards us and then look at us).

Language: Language-based exchanges always reflect intention. If a person walks by and says "hi," his/her intention is to be friendly. If a person buying a cup of coffee at a coffee shop turns to the person behind him and asks, "do you have a spare dime?," his/her intention is to find money to help pay for the cup of coffee.

⊙ When a student has difficulty acknowledging and "reading" that a person has intentions, he has a deficit in this area of perception. Our students often fail to read other persons' physical intentionality; if they get bumped into in the hall, they tend to think the person did it on purpose. While this may be true, most likely it was just an accident of sharing space. For example, a nine-year-old client accidentally bumped his head on my clipboard as he walked through the door. He turned and screamed at me, "Hey, you hit me!"

⊙ When engaged with another person, a student challenged in this area has difficulty inferring what the other person wants. He is unable to decipher the nuance of the other person's indirect communication – both verbal and nonverbal. When a student cannot easily discern the motives of another, he may become confused and frustrated or may be tricked by others.

A student I worked with was told by another to pull down his pants on the playground, so he did. As students get older they may continue to be easily manipulated. A thirty-year-old man was asked to marry a woman who was not a citizen of the United States right after he first met her. Luckily, he sensed that something was wrong with this proposal so he spoke to his mother. He personally wanted to marry for the traditional reasons, and it was difficult for him to understand that another person's use of the word "marry" could involve an entirely different motive.

5. Recognizing that another person has his or her own personality (Baron-Cohen, 2000).

⊙ Students with this deficit expect all others to have their exact same values, desires, interests, and so forth. Our students have difficulty understanding the concept of opinions and preferences. They often insist that all others converse about or play games related to their own areas of interest. Many of our high-level students acknowledge that others have opinions, but they have difficulty accepting other's opinions as valid. They tend to become very argumentative regarding another persons' opinion rather than accept this as a natural by-product of human relatedness.

6. Having an intuitive desire, or social curiosity, to learn about others' interests and personal histories.

⊙ A deficit in this area inhibits students' curiosity about others. It is common for our students to know very little information about the interests of peers or even their own family members.

I was recently talking to a twelve-year-old girl with Asperger Syndrome. I asked what her father did for a living; she stated she had no idea. I pursued the topic thinking she just didn't have clear words to describe his job, only to find out that she literally had NO IDEA what he did or where he worked.

7. Developing and using memory of a person to facilitate and sustain interpersonal relationships, as well as create a base of understanding about that person's potential actions.

⊙ This deficit is most often noticed when students fail to recall information about individuals with whom they have an ongoing relationship.

In our social thinking groups, the students regularly reveal information about their areas of interest. Nonetheless, many of the group members do not recall having learned information about another person on a previous day.

8. Formulating language to inquire about another person's interests.

⊙ Students with this deficit tend to be highly verbal when engaged in a topic of their particular interest, but can think of little or nothing to say (question or comment) to another person, even when they can recall that person's interests.

After initial introductions of the participants in a summer community camp program, the students were each given three blocks with which they were to build one common tower together. Each participant could only put a block on the tower by asking a personal question of another person. A boy volunteered to go first, looked directly at another person, took a deep breath, and then exclaimed, "I do not know how to get started!" This deficit involves language formulation based on weak perspective taking.

9. Understanding social conventions surrounding specific environments.

⊙ This deficit shows up when students do not modify their behavior based on the environment or situation. Students need guidance to learn that appropriate communication varies depending on the setting, even though the person may be the same. For example, a student who has a habit of swearing needs to understand which environments tolerate that behavior (socializing with peers at lunchtime) and in which environments that behavior may meet with severe consequences (in the classroom). For school children this may mean teaching that acceptable behavior in the cafeteria differs from that on the playground, even though both of these activities are outside the classroom setting.

10. Understanding social conventions specific to social contexts.

⊙ A deficit in this area is expressed when individuals do not recognize that different contexts in the same environment command different behavioral sets. For example, a student must change how he relates to those around him when he is working during quiet time versus working as part of a small group activity. While the environment stays the same (e.g., the classroom) the context within that environment has changed. This same deficit impacts a child's at-home behaviors, where he is expected to distinguish between appropriate behaviors at the dinner table versus play or getting ready for bed.

⊙ Another skill is detecting the emotional changes in a person and self-adjusting interactive and communicative behavior accordingly. For example, we can act in a jovial manner when another person is very happy. When that same person's emotions change — he becomes somber or angry — the student is expected to recognize this modified social context and use interpersonal communication (verbal and nonverbal) that demonstrates an understanding of the other person's emotional state.

11. Using eye contact to remain aware of the shifting internal states of the communicative partner.

- ⊙ To maintain an interaction with another, we must remain constantly alert to how the other person is perceiving our communicated message and reacting to it. This is often achieved through active eye contact with the other person, to "read" how the other person feels about or comprehends the information offered. Eye contact also helps us gauge whether the communicative partner is staying focused on the discussion or whether he has become distracted or bored by it.

- ⊙ Active eye contact among all participants in a group is also needed to maintain the interaction. In this case eye contact is used not only to ascertain how other participants are reacting to you, but also how they are reacting to each other.

12. Considering the prior knowledge and/or experience of anyone a person may talk to, even if not forming a long term social relationship.

- ⊙ We use narrative language in our daily communication and written expression, and it is generally based on how much we know or don't know about the other person's knowledge base. We consider our prior knowledge of or shared experiences with the person to whom we're talking to choose the best way to verbalize our thoughts. For example, when giving someone directions you consider how much the person knows about the area to determine the appropriate level of detail.

- ⊙ A deficit in this area is demonstrated when students provide either far too many descriptive details or far too few, considering what they know or don't know about their

communicative partner. However, teenagers in general are notorious for providing too little information in their communication and should be factored into our assessments of students in this age group.

Others Thinking About You

We now flip-flop the social thinking concepts, this time applying them to what others think about the student, rather than what the students thinks about others. While this realm of thinking may seem obvious to the person with a solid Theory of Mind, our students have difficulty understanding that the thoughts and expectations they have of others can be the same as what others expect from them.

Many of our students do not take the perspective of the person with whom they are interacting. It is difficult for these students to both interact AND monitor how others perceive them during ongoing interaction. Our students tend to believe that the interaction is taking place for their own personal enjoyment and not for the mutual enjoyment of the group. Moreover, they tend to think they can pick and choose when they send communicative messages to others (verbally and nonverbally). They fail to realize they are always sending some form of communication when they are in close proximity to others.

Social interactions are stressful and anxiety-laden for our students and many become anxious in the presence of others. As a result, they may inadvertently send a nonverbal message that says, "I want

to be left alone!" However, the reality is that the majority of students truly want to have healthy social relationships with others. They yearn to be part of a group or at least have some close, consistent friends. Yet their own neurological wiring keeps them so self-focused and inhibits their perspective taking skills to such a degree that they have a much harder time establishing relationships that are mutual, flexible, and deep.

Unfortunately, I have heard it said many times that the difference between persons with Nonverbal Learning Disorder (NVLD) and Asperger Syndrome is that "persons with NVLD want to have friends and persons with Asperger Syndrome do not." From my clinical experiences I can say that nothing is further from the truth! Persons with Asperger Syndrome want desperately to pursue and succeed in a variety of friendships.

It is fair to say that the more severe the deficits in Theory of Mind, the more difficulty students will have making and keeping friends. The SIPT individual just doesn't have the underlying cognitive base to support an understanding of the needs and perceptions of the communicative partner(s).

As a treatment strategy, I find it helpful to discuss with our students what seems to be a key factor in successful relationships: the ability to "fake" interest in what others are saying. While this may sound deceitful, in reality all good social communicators

become somewhat weary or bored at times when relating to others. Their ability to fake their interest in another person's topic, however, is integral to the overall success of their relationship. When I teach students about this concept, I refer to it as the "social fake." See Chapter 4 for ways to implement this strategy.

The following attributes of perspective taking can help our students better understand how others perceive them. (This information is also summarized in Table 2). Help our students understand that:

1. The other person recognizes you as an individual as long as you are in close proximity to him.

○ Many people with social cognitive deficits feel they only affect other people when they engage in an intentional act of communication with them. The fact is, even without talking, our mere presence is communicative. It is important for students to understand that even though they may not choose to directly communicate with someone, that choice, in itself, sends a communicative message!

A fourteen-year-old student began our session together with his body slumped over the table and his head facing away from me. I told him he was making a strong communicative statement by his lack of alert, directed communication with me. He denied that he was communicating, stating he was just tired. I then videotaped our interaction, with him still turned away from me. We watched the video clip together as I pointed out to him how the interaction looked to me. Directly after watching the video he pulled his chair around, sat up and gave me direct eye contact. Nevertheless, to assert his own control in the situation, he stated the typical threat of a teen: "If you turn that video on again, I won't look at you again!"

2. The other person recognizes your individual traits.

⊙ Others think about you in terms of your gender, age, appearance, and apparent intellectual functioning. Others may form some "impressions" of you based on your physical characteristics. Many of our social thinking-challenged students have no idea that others are thinking of them at all, especially when they are not actively engaged in conversation.

3. The other person recognizes and reacts to your emotional states.

⊙ Communicative partners monitor your facial expression, body posture, and overall reactions. Many of our students, however, can't monitor how their emotional state is being communicated. They also have difficulty communicating effectively with their whole body (words matched with facial expression, matched with other nonverbal communicative features). This often is confusing to the persons who are talking to the student. While people with a stronger Theory of Mind may be able to hide their anxiety when communicating with an unfamiliar person, our students often "wear their emotions on their sleeves." This painful looking expression is often interpreted by others to mean, "This person does not want to be with me!"

4. The other person recognizes that you have a distinct set of desires and motives communicated through physical movements and/or language.

⊙ Others are able to determine quickly and efficiently the student's motive when communicating or sharing space. Once again, this makes it easier for the neurotypical person to gain the upper hand over our students.

5. The other person has an intuitive desire to learn about your personal history and interests.

⊙ Since others often have a natural curiosity about you, they will ask you questions or comment on your areas of interest. The communication breakdown occurs when you do not share the natural curiosity about the other person and ask questions in return. You assume the other person's questions imply he is interested only in talking about you, and the conversation quickly becomes one-sided.

There are also times when the student with impaired social thinking feels that the other person is being overly intrusive by asking personal questions, even when the question is as benign as, "Do you have pets?"

6. The other person formulates language to inquire about someone else and their interests.

⊙ As mentioned above, the deficit manifests itself in the student's inability to effectively develop a set of impromptu questions or comments to reciprocate the inquiry. A later chapter of this book deals exclusively with therapy ideas to expand a student's ability to verbally converse with others.

7. If you have met the other person before, he recalls his memory of his past interactions with you.

⊙ Your past interactions affect your present relationship. The last time you were with someone is often the first memory that person recalls the next time you see him. If your last experience was good, the relationship should be reestablished in a positive voice. However, if your last interaction with the person was interpreted as being negative, reestablishing this relationship could also be a negative experience.

As mentioned above, our students often fail to recall important information about others to use in present conversations. But it can also go deeper. Our students tend to recall negative experiences they've had with others, yet they may not realize that others continue to hold negative memories of them as well. Because many of our students' emotions are either On or Off, they can get very upset, explode, calm down, and then come back to the group and expect everyone to proceed as if nothing happened.

Many parents have described to me horrible outbursts directed toward them when their child was upset, only to have the child go calm down, recover, and then request to be taken out for pizza as planned!

8. They interpret your message based on how your communication relates to the social conventions mandated in specific environments.

- ⊚ Others expect your communication to coincide with the unwritten rules of the specific physical environment in which you are communicating. Our students are generally unaware of these unwritten social rules that dictate what is appropriate or inappropriate language and behavior across different environments (e.g., the library verses the cafeteria). Embarrassment can ensue.

9. They interpret your message based on how your communication relates to the social conventions mandated in specific social contexts.

- ⊚ Others are sensitive to the fact that your communication should coincide with the unwritten rules of the specific social contexts in which you are communicating. Again, our students are blind to the many social contexts within which they interact on a daily basis (e.g.,

classroom participation when working quietly at a student's desk versus circle time activities). Embarrassment can ensue.

10. They tolerate boring moments in the communicative exchange!

- ⊚ All persons occasionally experience the feeling that they are not receiving attention during social exchanges. Most know, however, to conceal these feelings so they don't directly affect the feelings of the communicative partner(s). The deficit appears when our students outwardly reveal their boredom by stating, "I do not want to talk about that," "This is boring!," "That's stupid!," or by physically just walking away from the other person.

Emerging Perspective Taking Versus Impaired Interactive Perspective Taking: How This Appears in the Classroom and at Home

The information above helps to spell out some of the primary attributes of what I clinically identify as Perspective Taking deficits. While we can all understand this conceptually, parents and educators still request a more solid descriptor of what this looks like on a child with a disability.

To address those requests, Table 3 reveals how children with EPT and IIPT appear to function differently depending on their various levels of ability to take perspective of others. The traits summarized tend to co-occur rather than follow in succession.

Like all information in this chapter, if it is not exactly right, it serves its purpose if it facilitates your thoughts in this area.

Table 2

Attributes that Contribute to Forming a Theory of Mind/ Perspective Taking

Overall Concept of Perspective Taking

People engage in interpersonal relationships with an intuitive lens on how their words and personal behaviors affect the feelings of the persons with whom they are communicating. People generally keep the communicative relationship "healthy" through modification of spoken language, clarification, and self-monitoring of nonverbal communication, rather than rigidly adhering to one specific set of behaviors regardless of their impact on others.

Thinking about others using Perspective Taking

1. Recognize the thoughtful presence of another person.

2. Recognize the individuality of the other person.

3. Recognize that another person has his or her own personal set of emotions.

4. Recognize and decipher another person's desires and motives.

5. Recognize that another person has his or her own unique personality.

6. Recognize that another person has an intuitive curiosity to learn about another's personal history and interests.

7. Develop and use memory of others as a resource to facilitate and sustain interpersonal relationships as well as create a base of understanding about the person's potential actions.

8. Formulate language to inquire about another person's interests.

9. Understand social conventions surrounding specific environments.

10. Understand social conventions specific to social contexts.

11. Be aware of the shifting internal states of the communicative partner.

12. Think about others' prior knowledge and experience.

Thinking about how you impact others using Perspective Taking

1. The other person recognizes you as an individual when you are in close proximity to him or her.

2. The other person recognizes your individual traits.

3. The other person recognizes and reacts to your emotional states.

4. The other person recognizes that you have a distinct set of desires and motives.

5. The other person has an intuitive desire to learn about your personal history and interests.

6. The other person formulates language to inquire about you and your interests.

7. If you have met the other person before, he recalls his memory of past interactions with you.

8. The other person interprets your message based on how your communication relates to the social conventions mandated in specific environments.

9. The other person interprets your message based on how your communication relates to the social conventions mandated in specific social contexts.

10. The other person tolerates boring moments in the communicative exchange (and expects you to do so as well).

Table 3

Comparing Levels of Perspective Taking Deficits Between Students who are Emerging Perspective Takers and those who are Impaired Interactive Perspective Takers

Descriptors of a student who tends to function more as an **Emerging Perspective Taker**	*Descriptors of a student who tends to function more as an* **Impaired Interactive Perspective Taker**
⊙ Distractable or disengaged body and/or mind to the point of alienation, making fully engaged group participation extremely difficult.	⊙ Distractable body and/or mind, but redirected with minimum to moderate cues to rejoin the group.
⊙ Needs persistent cues to understand the lesson concept.	⊙ Needs cues when asked to engage in activity perceived as being difficult. Limited task persistence when task is not directly related to the student's area of interest.
⊙ Severe difficulty establishing and maintaining joint attention. May be directed to be part of a group, but has difficulty following the group given that he does not attend well to what others are thinking about.	⊙ Mild to moderate difficulty establishing and maintaining joint attention, but once redirected can understand a group task and relate to it for at least a short period of time.
⊙ Likely presence of overt self-stimulatory behavior.	⊙ Minimal persistence of self-stimulatory behavior, if it exists in the child's repertoire at all.
⊙ Lacks spontaneous insight into the appropriateness or inappropriateness of other persons' social behaviors.	⊙ Is aware when others may be acting inappropriately versus appropriately. Tends to police other children's behavior and ability to abide by the rules, even if he is lacking in the same skills he is tracking.
⊙ Lacks awareness, almost entirely, of how others perceive him or her. When elementary school-aged, not familiar with the concept of embarrassment.	⊙ Understands that others form perceptions of him, but cannot monitor his own behavior to regulate how he appears to others.
⊙ Blurts out completely unrelated comments to the topic at hand, or tangentially related comments often at the wrong time and place.	⊙ Blurts out tangentially related or fully related comments to the topic at hand, but at the wrong time and place.

Table 3 *(continued)*

Comparing Levels of Perspective Taking Deficits Between Students who are Emerging Perspective Takers and those who are Impaired Interactive Perspective Takers

Descriptors of a student who tends to function more as an **Emerging Perspective Taker**	*Descriptors of a student who tends to function more as an* **Impaired Interactive Perspective Taker**
⊙ It is usually immediately obvious to persons unfamiliar with the student that he or she has some sort of disability.	⊙ Appears to look like the neurotypical students. Deficits are subtle and generally more evident to individuals familiar with the student who have seen a pattern of weak interpersonal skills.
⊙ Does not understand the concept of competition and is not competitive.	⊙ Can be extremely competitive and insists on winning all games or mental challenges. Perfectionist traits in many.
⊙ Has a tendency toward large emotional reactions, sometimes with ill-defined behavioral triggers. (At times behavioral outbursts are caused by sensory integration deficits or misunderstanding of information in the environment.)	⊙ Often has a large emotional breakdown to mild triggers that the child can often pinpoint. (A second grader's basketball team loses their game and the child has a tantrum.) Behavioral outbursts are also caused by sensory integration deficits or feeling confused by communicative breakdowns.
⊙ Communication is very functional, serving the student's desires or needs. At times communication will exist to seek brief social attention; however, communication generally lacks a desire for social reciprocity.	⊙ Communication is often socially motivated, with ability to participate in some conversations. However, the conversations tend to be very one-sided around the student's area of interest.
⊙ Does not distinguish between literal and figurative language, even with direct intervention in this area.	⊙ Tends to be very literal, but can qualitatively understand the difference between literal and figurative language, even when the student cannot necessarily interpret it at the moment in conversation.

Table 3 *(continued)*

Comparing Levels of Perspective Taking Deficits Between Students who are Emerging Perspective Takers and those who are Impaired Interactive Perspective Takers

Descriptors of a student who tends to function more as an **Emerging Perspective Taker**	*Descriptors of a student who tends to function more as an* **Impaired Interactive Perspective Taker**
⊙ Initiation of communication to get needs met is lacking. May become very frustrated.	⊙ While these students are highly verbal when engaged in their topics of interest, they can have significant difficulty initiating communication to seek assistance for themselves. However, since they are so verbal in their attempt to relate with others, it is not uncommon for educators to fail to notice that the child does not seek assistance from others. They also are poor self-advocates with personal problem-solving.
⊙ In adolescence and adulthood, often develops some desire for sexual stimulation even if they cannot seek it from others successfully.	⊙ In adolescence and adulthood, develops sexual desires just like their peers; however, can become very depressed or frustrated in their inability to establish an intimate relationship due to weak development of subtle social interactive skills.

Summary

In this chapter, perspective taking is explored in further depth, encouraging the reader to more fully understand the socially algebraic equation associated with perspective taking and its ability to help or hinder us as we navigate through relationships. Numerous points are addressed to analyze how many of our very intelligent students struggle with this more 'intuitive social process. A discussion evolves to explain the subtle but significant differences between how social behavior impacts each of us directly and how others think about us, based on our own reactions.

Comparisons are made between students with EPT and IIPT, while recognizing that a significant number of students are on the spectrum of functioning that hinges the EPT and IIPT together.

Chapter 3
The Four Steps to Communication

Creating a Framework for Understanding Social Thinking Complexity

Teaching social thinking and related skills can feel like a daunting task. When I first started teaching in this often nebulous arena, I didn't always know where to begin or how to organize treatment. I used to arbitrarily work on concepts based on what I thought was interesting to explore each week. Lessons were not necessarily connected, but they were all relevant, if a bit unorganized.

Over time it became apparent that interpersonal (face-to-face) communication unfolds in a fairly organized manner. This was good news for me and my students. The more concrete the structure we provide for students with social thinking challenges, the better chance they have of organizing their own thoughts and recalling our lessons in a systematic way.

Out of these in-the-trenches observations was born the "Four Steps to Communication." These Four Steps help teach not only students, but also educators and caregivers, how communication progresses. The Four Steps also help us analyze communicative breakdowns and take a more systematic approach to teaching social thinking and related skills. The next four chapters of this book are organized around the concepts related to the Four Steps of Communication. Additional information is also offered in my curriculum-based book, *Think Social!* (2005).

Defining the Four Steps to Communication

Each of us approaches the communicative act in a very similar way, whether we realize it or not. It's not something we stop and think about, it just happens naturally for neurotypicals. But for the benefit of your own education and that of your students, observe communication with a Sherlock Holmes spyglass and you will notice that every day you and the people around you engage in these Four Steps.

Step 1. Think about the person with whom you desire or need to communicate.

Step 2. Establish a physical presence to indicate communicative intent.

Step 3. Shift into directed eye contact to seal your intention to communicate with a person or group of people.

Step 4. Use language to communicate with those people, while maintaining and expanding upon the first three steps.

If any of these steps are excluded or misinterpreted, the attempted communication can result in misunderstanding or complete failure. While these four steps seem so obvious to us, they are not obvious to our academically bright students with social thinking challenges. They unknowingly err in these steps, diminishing the success of their communication without understanding why.

⧗

Shelby was a woman in her early forties when she was referred to me by her psychiatrist. She was often angry, feeling abandoned by people "for no good reason." Shelby stated on numerous occasions she felt there was a sign posted on her back instructing people not to communicate with her, even though she was a ready and willing partner.

As our sessions progressed, it became apparent that Shelby rarely focused her attention/thought/perspective taking skills on other people. While she would identify who she wanted to talk to, she mostly thought about her own needs when she started to talk. One of her favorite topics was how hard her life was since people did not seem to like to talk to her.

I learned that Shelby was really upset with fellow students in her adult education class. Prior to class starting the students would socially congregate in a group outside the classroom. Shelby would stand away from the group getting really annoyed, even mad, that the group did not come to her to talk to her. She also avoided eye contact with them. Ultimately, she never got the opportunity (nor did she have the ability at that time) to talk to these peers. She remained on the sidelines and never used language to relate to others.

As our therapy sessions progressed I worked with her explicitly on understanding the Four Steps to Communication. We started by discussing that she has to think about others if she wants to develop a relationship with them. We then established rules: "groups don't move to people, people move to groups." We explored how and why we "think with our eyes" to read other people's cues and that by doing so we show people our interest in them. Finally we worked extensively on ways we code our questions and comments to indicate continued interest, which ultimately results in using language to relate to others.

Shelby calmed down and made progress, albeit slowly, in understanding the depth and complexity of communication and how to meet other people's needs while helping them feel more positive about her. Shelby continues to work with me; she is not "cured" but she is less verbally abusive and feels calmer in social situations. She is now able to hold a job for the first time in years, thanks to not only our

efforts but also the continued support of her psychiatrist and devoted staff from the Department of Vocational Rehabilitation.

A few years into working with Shelby, she asked me to document in writing what she should have learned in a particular session. I pointed out it was actually her job to figure out what she had learned. I encouraged her to sit in my office and write down what she thought she had learned from coming to the clinic. Here is what she wrote:

"What I feel I have learned in the past month: reading empathy in others. Try to imagine how they feel and the impact I have on them. Show an interest in them. Calm down.

Apply what I learn in the sessions outside the sessions. Concentrate on not being so stiff, relaxed face, body, etc. Don't be a talking head.

We've done a lot of role playing. Learning how to approach a group of two or more people and join the conversation. What to do/not to do. Be subtle when I approach a group. Don't just jump in, read the others. Will know it's ok if they turn towards me, their bodies, eye contact, etc.

I realize I want to give them all equal eye contact. If I don't they will think I'm not interested in them. I need to remember that they are thinking about me as well, wondering if I am interested in being part of their group. They won't think I'm interested if I stand 6 feet away from them and don't talk or look at them.

I've been learning about conversation, that we can have conversations about small things like hangnails, freeways, colored construction paper, etc. That there is a world of things to talk about.

That I am not front and center in a group. I am just one of the group. Not to sidetrack what is going on in a session. I really don't mean to!

Another session I learned how to be in a social situation, how to know whether or not somebody is interested in being with me. I need to start small, suggesting to someone that we go out for a cup of coffee, not "would you want to go to Hershey's Park in Pennsylvania with me?" They might get the wrong idea of my motives, particularly if it's a man; he'd be thinking "we'd be going to a distant city together, staying in a hotel," "what would the sleeping arrangements be?," etc. Even if it were a woman, she might think I am gay if I make a suggestion when we don't know each other that well."

The Four Steps to Communication ~ A Detailed Description

1. Thinking about people: anchoring your thoughts on your communicative partner(s).

Establish communicative intention by thinking about the other person and the purpose of your communication with that person or group.

    a. What do you know or remember about them?

    b. What do they think and how do they feel?

    c. What might they want to talk about?

    d. How will they feel about what you want to say?

2. Being aware of your physical presence as well as the physical presence of your communicative partner(s).

Your body's physical presence conveys a desire to communicate, interact, or hang out with a person(s). On the flip side, by not establishing physical presence, you can, by default, unintentionally or intentionally communicate a lack of desire for social interaction.

However, physical presence is more than establishing a physical proximity. It also has to do with how your shoulders and hips are positioned towards the person with whom you want to interact. It also relates to how you use your body language and facial expressions to support the overall message. In addition, it relates to the speed with which you enter and exit the interaction.

Your physical presence "greases" the communication cycle and plants a seed in others' minds that you may wish to communicate with them.

    a. Your body position strongly implies whether or not you want to talk to someone.

    b. Your body movements show what you plan to do next (do you plan to stay or leave?). These movements communicate nonverbal messages to people, even if the messages are unintentional.

    c. Your shoulder and hip positions convey whether you plan to stay and talk or just want to offer a quick message before leaving.

    d. Your body language and facial expression communicates to people how you feel about things or people around you.

    e. An overall relaxation through the head, neck, shoulders, arms and hips conveys a sense of ease and comfort to your communicative partners. At times you need to physically relax your body to comfort your communicative partners.

    f. It is critical to realize that we all actively try to "read" the physical presence cues of people around us to determine their intentions, even if we never plan to communicate with them. For example, you watch a person step off a sidewalk into the street, and you assume the person intends to cross the street. You process this signal and decide if this impacts you. (For example, are you driving and do you need to slow down? Or did you just happen to see the person and can't help but notice his intention?).

3. Using your eyes to think about others and watch what they are thinking about.

In Chapter 6, I will review at length why and how we teach students about the importance of the eyes in establishing and maintaining communication. Briefly, the social skill desired is "eye contact" while the concept we need to teach to our students is "thinking with our eyes."

While physical presence and active eye contact co-exist much of the time, it is pulled out into its own step for this reason: we generally actively look towards our communicative partner only when we actually arrive in close proximity to them.

For example, if I want to talk to Heidi and I see Heidi across the school courtyard, I usually do not fix my eyes on Heidi as I walk across the yard. Instead:

a. I notice where she is.

b. I look all over the place while I walk in that direction to navigate my way toward her.

c. Once I am near her I establish a closer physical presence.

d. Then I look directly at Heidi and the people she may be with to demonstrate my desire to communicate with them.

Once direct eye contact is established with a person, it forms a laser-beam lock-on of communicative intent. We get a very strong message that a person wants to talk to us or is thinking actively about us if he or she keeps looking at us. At times this gives us the creeps, particularly when a person we do not know keeps looking at us without proceeding to communicate verbally.

The direction of our eye gaze and other people's eye gaze provides clear information, much of time, about what each person might be thinking about in their environment. For example, if you are looking at cereal in the grocery store, it is likely because you are considering which cereal to buy.

We also use our eyes to determine how other people feel, whether these other people are interested in the people with whom they are talking, or whether they are interested in what others are doing.

4. Using your language to relate to others.

We assume a person has good overall language skills if he demonstrates measurable strength in length of use, sentence complexity, and word choice. Most language assessments measure these skills, and educators assume students know how to use language well if they exhibit strength in these technical areas.

However, when language is used without the ability to relate to others' feelings, thoughts, emotions, beliefs, and prior experiences, in reality it is not used well at all. When language is used only to convey one person's intellectual ideas, few people want to maintain active social relations with this person. If language is not used to make the listener feel validated or valued, the listener will rarely want to develop a deeper relationship with the speaker.

We must teach our students how language helps other people feel good (or bad, or neutral) about the person with whom they are communicating. We want them to understand that language is qualitative and infused with intent. For example, if you ask me questions about myself, I think you are interested in me. If you continue to tell me what is interesting to you without you appearing interested in me, I think you are self-centered. If you keep telling me how well you do on all your tasks, I think you are trying to show off. We constantly read the intentions behind each person's language — it is an automatic part of our social processing.

As we progress to this fourth step of communication, our goal is to teach students to think more deeply about the impact of their language on others. We want them to understand the "social thinking" behind language, and then learn the related social skills to help them use language effectively. In truth, each one of us can benefit from the information in this lesson, since it is impossible for any of us to use this set of skills perfectly at all times! Some of the ideas to explore:

a. Think about what you know about the person to whom you are talking.

b. Try connecting your ideas to things that are interesting to others.

c. Ask questions to learn more about people; make comments to show interest.

d. Listen with your eyes and ears to determine people's intentions and hidden meanings.

e. Add your own thoughts to connect your experiences to those of others.

f. Make comments that support a person's idea, or add comments that support discussion of the idea without brashly condemning other people's thoughts.

g. Use small units of language (or body language) to support people's ideas, or at least show you are actively listening.

As you review the four steps, you may notice that when we set out to teach students better communication or conversational skills, we often start on the fourth step, skipping the first three. We launch into lessons on how to talk to each other by sitting children down at tables with their bodies frozen in place in their chairs.

However, most children, adolescents, and young adults develop friendships in movement, talking while they walk between classes, hanging out at recess and lunch, or running around a sports field. We need to actively teach all four steps if we are to help our students become effective communicators rather than just "talking heads."

As you review the four steps, they may trigger your own thoughts and opinions on how communication progresses. You may want to add a 5th or 6th step — please do so! The purpose of the information in this chapter and this entire book is to stimulate all educators to think about how we use language to communicate. You may have ideas of your own that further illuminate the communication process; feel free to add that 5th or 6th step! We engage in communication continuously without fully realizing the complexity of the process. Like breathing and swallowing, most of us engage in communication spontaneously and unconsciously, never realizing that — unlike our social thinking impaired students — we use these Four Steps naturally and instinctively.

The Four Steps to Communication are Synergistic

Chapters 4 through 7 offer further teaching ideas that support The Four Steps to Communication. In these chapters you will find detailed suggestions for engaging students in the treatment process.

You will quickly discover that while we can break communication down into these four steps, students cannot master each step before moving onto the next one. These four steps are synergistic. We must also teach about their interdependency.

In our clinic we have explored each of the four steps individually and in different combinations. We have found that more progress is made when we remove the fourth step, (e.g. don't let your students talk) and have them focus solely on the first three steps. This helps our language-proficient students realize the significance of nonverbal communication and physical intentionality.

While we work on these steps in different combinations, we also use them to analyze communicative success or failure. For example, rather than using the word "quirky" as a clinical description of a student's level of functioning, we can now describe the success and error patterns in more detail: "the student does not establish a physical presence before communicating" or "the student does not use his eyes to think about what others are feeling." By carefully analyzing the communicative breakdown, we can better develop relevant goals and related lessons.

Are the Four Steps to Communication an Evidence-Based Practice?

Yes, depending on how you define it. There are many definitions of evidence based practices. The American Speech, Language and Hearing Association (ASHA) has provided a definition of "evidence based practices" that is aligned with other allied health professions. It can be summarized by saying that for clinical services, evidence based practices "recognize the needs, abilities, values, preferences, and interests of individuals and families to whom they provide clinical services, and integrate those factors along with best current research evidence and their clinical expertise in clinical decision making" (2005).

While some of the various concepts in this book have been explored in formal clinical research studies (Miller, 2002; Zweber, 2002; Crooke, Hendrix and Rachman, 2007-in press), much of the information has yet to be explored formally through scientific measures. Nevertheless, the evidence has just walked right by you.

Look around and observe. You will see the evidence supporting these Four Steps everywhere. People cannot communicate with you if you are not physically present for that communication. People will not want to communicate with you if you only talk about your own ideas and fail to seek and consider others' ideas. Teachers cannot teach students in large groups if the students' minds are not thinking about the group topic.

While research is important, with regard to social pragmatics, it is severely lacking. Many of the approaches used for students with ASDs are based on strong behavioral reward systems that lend themselves to concrete quantitative studies. But social thinking is difficult to concretely define and neatly isolate variables that can be studied to the exclusion of others. Social thinking is dependent on the interrelationships among an endless set of variables that can shift at a moment's notice. As such, the social thinking methodology I propose defies easy research in that we will never be able to fully know what someone else is thinking. We cannot research whether or not we made people think more about other people.

However, we can study the overall qualitative outcomes. Do others feel more comfortable in our students' presence? Are our students able to hold a job more successfully? Can they participate as part of a group with greater success?

We absolutely need a series of long-term studies to answer these questions. Helping students shift their thinking requires a process-oriented approach that extends across a long period of time — usually years.

We also must recognize that social deficits often trigger emotional problems. Our students are difficult to study in a Petri dish since their social challenges often impact their emotional and behavioral wellbeing. They also have sensory processing and digestive issues. While we have helped our students widen their social thinking and perspective taking skills, other aspects of their life can also shut them back down — depression, anxiety, etc.

The work we do must be multidisciplinary and interdisciplinary. It is an ever shifting, changing landscape when we work with students with social thinking or social cognitive challenges. The SCERTS model (Prizant, Wetherby, Rubin, Laurent and Rydell, 2006) describes the complexity of using a team approach to address a student's challenges where sensory, communication, and social relatedness are all intertwined. Their model spotlights some of the challenges we all face in working with these students.

But even without definitive social pragmatic research, you will observe the inner workings of the communicative moment. A cascade of highly predictable events converge to trigger successful communication or social coexistence. The evidence is actually right in front of you — by observing your students well you are creating your own evidence-based practice.

While you are at it, as a humorous aside observe how this same set of skills play out with your family dog — we humans are not the only ones who follow the Four Steps to Communication!

Summary

The Four Steps of communication are described as a framework to help parents, professionals and students explore the multilayered nature of social communicative functions. The four steps are listed as a hierarchy for unfolding the social interaction process in face-to-face interactions. This is a synergistic framework with the evidence supporting its use clearly available for all persons to observe; just carefully watch the next person who approaches you.

The four steps of communication can be summarized as:

Step 1. Think about the person with whom you desire or need to communicate.

Step 2. Establish a physical presence to indicate communicative intent.

Step 3. Shift into directed eye contact to seal your intention to communicate with a person or group of people.

Step 4. Use language to communicate with those people, while maintaining and expanding upon the first three steps.

The following four chapters analyze each of these Four Steps in far more clinical detail.

Chapter 4
Communication Step 1:
Enhancing Perspective Taking Knowledge & Skills

In this chapter we focus on concepts and ideas that provide a strong foundation from which interactive perspective taking skills can develop. It has been my experience that these lessons are beneficial to students who function at the EPT/IIPT level. However, they are not appropriate for students with lesser perspective taking abilities, i.e., those who lack a concept of Theory of Mind. Howlin, Baron-Cohen, and Hadwin (1998) produced a workbook for educators that introduces a variety of perspective taking concepts to this more impaired segment of the autism population. While the workbook does a good job in explaining ways to break down these concepts into smaller parts, the exercises are not based on a student's own experiences. It is difficult for the student with autism to understand and apply such abstract social thinking as perspective taking when it does not have a personal connection at the start.

You will find activities in this chapter defined by age groups. Early grade-school children, kindergarten to third grade, are naturally weaker in their ability to conceptualize abstract information than are older students. Situation context also varies as the child ages. "Activities for Younger Children" were developed primarily for early elementary aged students; however, many of these strategies work well with children from Pre-K through Grade 6. "Activities for Older Children and Young Adults" can be introduced to students with, at the minimum, grade-level academic intellectual development, from middle school through adulthood.

Core Beliefs Underlying the Therapeutic Lessons

The I LAUGH model is a framework for more clearly understanding the origin of a student's social thinking deficits. Figure 1 illustrates the interrelationship among the parts of the model and of perspective taking in general. Interactive perspective taking is the foundation upon which a broad variety of therapeutic lessons can be developed.

The lessons in this chapter arose out of sheer necessity while working with students in our therapy sessions. They were then refined, expanded and incorporated into a curriculum that made sense to us and to our students. This will no doubt happen for you, too, as you work with these students. To do this well and with the flexibility that social thinking demands, however, requires a framework of principles or core beliefs that can guide the therapeutic decision-making process. The core beliefs I and my staff clinicians rely upon in developing lessons are reviewed in Table 4.

Figure 1

Interrelationship of ILAUGH Model Variables

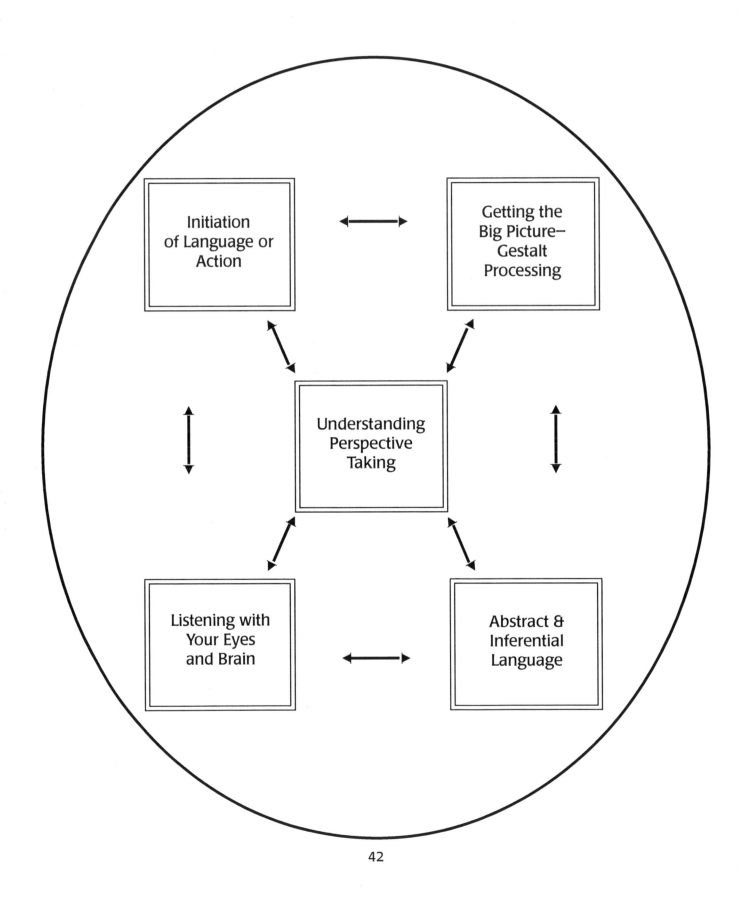

Table 4: Core Beliefs in Developing Clinical Lessons

1. Our job as educators and parents is to teach students information that expands their knowledge about social information prior to teaching them the skills they should use to interact with others.

2. ALL skills related to successful social interaction lead back to understanding the concepts of Theory of Mind and Perspective Taking.

3. For bright students, realize that learning and memorizing schoolwork comes easily, whereas learning about social thinking does not make intuitive sense. Respect how challenging this type of learning is for them.

4. Given that interactive perspective taking generally exists around us with few words to directly talk about it, it is essential that social thinking lessons start by building a vocabulary from which we can describe and discuss thoughts and observations about ourselves as well as others. This is called "Social Thinking Vocabulary."

5. Clinical lessons on social interaction coexist with all other lessons on social interaction. Social interaction is a highly complex process. We need to break down concepts for our students into specific lessons that lead to lower levels of competence. As these levels are mastered, students slowly work towards the ultimate goal of more suitable social interaction. Our greatest challenge is how to help students weave the lessons we provide back together to facilitate their understanding of the ultimate big picture of social interaction: that other people will desire their company if they show interest in these people effectively.

6. All people have socially inappropriate and appropriate moments regardless of whether they are labeled with a disability. The best lessons come from the exploration of our own personal experiences and observations of the world around us. (As much as I would like you to read this book, you might do just as well by observing people at the next meeting or party you go to!)

7. Use the personal interactions (or lack of) that spontaneously emerge (or fail to emerge) in group therapy or classroom lessons as your basic teaching material. For example, if students are working with these concepts as part of the group, create opportunities for the group to observe and communicate. While this may sound obvious, we as teachers often continue to teach students lessons by having them refer to pages in a social skills training book rather than by having them explore the concept directly with the student sitting across from them.

8. When teaching about human emotions, allow students to see and understand your own as well as those of the other students in the group. If lessons are taught only from pictures or role-plays, very little will carry over into real life.

9. Prepare a lesson and understand that there will be chaotic moments in the group. The students are in social thinking groups for a reason: being part of your group is one of the students' more difficult challenges in a day.

10. For older kids, don't ever call your social thinking group a "friendship group." They decide for themselves who their friends are, and not all of these students like each other. When group members appear to dislike each other, create group projects they must work on cooperatively to achieve success. Group projects take the focus off social relatedness.

11. Enjoy your work. Engage in humor with the students and their family members. It opens doors and helps students accept all you are encouraging them to think about!

Lessons for Children that Can Lead to Building a Therapy Curriculum

The following concepts help develop interactive perspective taking in children who benefit most by learning through play. They are listed in the order we use them in our clinic. The activities are accompanied by text that discusses why the concepts are important, and how to explore them with the children.

Much of this work is in its infancy. Be creative and generate activities of your own! Additional curriculum ideas can be found in my book *Think Social! A Social Thinking Curriculum for School-Age Students* (2005).

"Think, Know, and Guess"

As mentioned earlier, a student's ability to competently use the words "think, know, and guess" appears to be directly linked to that student's ability to understand others' thoughts and motives. IIPT students over the age of five should learn and use these concepts easily. However, students with EPT may struggle tremendously.

It is important that students have the basic command of these words BEFORE moving on to other lessons in this chapter. However, it raises the issue of what level of mastery is needed. Does teaching this vocabulary result in expanded perspective taking skills? For some students yes, for others progress may be minimal. We CAN increase a child's understanding of these concepts yet he may not be able to achieve full understanding and fluid use. Some children you work with will have just-emerging perspective taking abilities. We view it as "any progress in learning to understand the minds of others is better than no learning!"

Assessing a student's ability to use "think, know and guess" can easily be accomplished by showing a student a picture or a written social scenario that involves some act of deception and then asking direct questions about what the participants in the scenario are thinking.

A seven-year-old girl named Bernadette who was diagnosed with high functioning autism in preschool was now fully mainstreamed into second grade. The school had done a good job helping her modulate her behavior so she could function without interrupting others in her regular education setting. In fact, Bernadette was doing so well that one educator commented he thought she had "outgrown" her autism. The parents reported that Bernadette continued to have significant attention deficits with large group learning activities and felt she was falling further behind her peers. However, it was difficult for anyone to put their finger on what she did not understand since her academic scores were within normal limits.

I presented Bernadette with a social scenario picture. It showed a breakfast scene: a younger sister sitting at the table pouring milk into her cereal while a boy stood behind her chair outside the girl's field of vision. He was clearly looking at the girl with a mischievous grin on his face while he poured salt into the sugar bowl. I asked Bernadette what he was pouring into the sugar bowl and she correctly replied it was salt, also making a facial expression indicating it tasted bad. When I asked how the boy felt she said he looked "evil". When I asked what the boy was planning to do, she reported he was going to give the sugar bowl to the girl who would end up putting salt on her cereal. When I asked what the boy "knew," she said he knew there was salt in the sugar bowl. When I asked what the girl "knew" she said the girl also knew there was salt in the sugar bowl. When I asked what the boy was thinking, she was unable to report that he was planning to trick his sister, even though she repeatedly noticed his face looked "evil," and Bernadette knew the boy was looking directly at the girl.

Despite many different attempts to encourage Bernadette to rethink what the girl knew, Bernadette was unable to perceive that the girl had a different knowledge set than her brother. Her apparent gaps in taking the perspective of all persons in the situation, even though she was able to notice appropriate related details, was important in helping Bernadette's parents understand that she had significant difficulty with perspective taking.

Using Videotapes to Teach "Think, Know, and Guess"

Use of "Wallace and Gromit" videotapes

Wallace and Gromit stories (Dreamworks, 2005) were created by the makers of the movie *Chicken Run* and are great for teaching the concepts of think, know, and guess. They are each about 30 minutes long and the story is mostly told through action and body language. Each of the three videotapes involves some mystery that Gromit (a smart dog) ultimately solves. They offer many wonderful opportunities to discuss with students what one character thinks verses what another one knows. The students can then guess what a character might do based on what others know and/or think.

For example, in the film *The Wrong Trousers,* Wallace is the technically smart but socially weak adult, Gromit is the socially smart dog, and a penguin turns out to be the villain. The penguin treats Wallace very nicely, so Wallace THINKS the penguin is a good bird. However, Gromit KNOWS the penguin is evil because he sees the penguin doing sneaky things behind Wallace's back.

When watching with students, the therapist can lead a discussion regarding what the students KNOW about each of the characters verses what each character THINKS about the others. There are many opportunities to observe how one character can trick by misleading another character, as well as observe how the thoughts and emotions of each character are conveyed through body language and facial expression. Analyzing this information helps students build knowledge about what the other characters think, know, and guess. The twists and turns in these movies facilitate discussion of these complicated concepts while keeping things light and fun. This type of movie can be used with students of all ages.

The rate at which a student learns and can discuss these concepts is further information about his ability to easily and readily shift perspective. For many students with high-functioning autism, this vocabulary is just emerging and they make frequent errors. Some of our students work hard to figure out what Wallace thinks about the penguin in specific situations, but it is almost impossible for these same students to perceive what Gromit thinks the penguin is thinking, even when Gromit is not near the penguin. Observing where students' perspective taking breaks down is extremely helpful in further understanding their confusions about the world around them. We can then create better educational lessons that impact their social thinking across the day, both in personal and academic areas.

The "Thinking About You" Game

"Thinking about other people and how they think about you" are words commonly uttered by therapists and students in our clinic. These words are key in developing an awareness of interactive perspective taking. Explaining this concept to young children is a mindful task, as well as a mouthful!

Younger children learn through whole body experiences. We, therefore, introduce this lesson in the clinic using part of a story from a very old book that was originally my mother's when she was a child, entitled Fair Play (Leaf 1939). It starts out with the author asking children to imagine they are each alone in the world, just the child and all the wild animals. Leaf explains that being the only person in the world would not only be scary, it would also mean you would not have any shoes to wear, beds to sleep in, stores to buy food in, or schools to go to, since the people responsible for making that happen would not be around.

Leaf (thankfully!) explains that children live as part of a group of people who assist him in gaining his worldly necessities and is why the world has rules, which become laws, that help create our government. The author then describes a group of children playing together where one child does not want to follow the rules and ideas of the group members. That child is referred to as "JustMe." JustMe always insists on doing things his way. Interestingly, while illustrations show the group of children always looking happy, JustMe always looks sad.

During this first section in the book, the therapist guides various student activities:

a. The teacher or therapist asks children to explore the idea of having no possessions. Shoes, socks, glasses, books, tables, and chairs are taken or pushed away to show that none of these objects are available when you live as the only person on the planet. Be prepared for your students suggesting they take off their clothes too! Remind them this is not a good idea to do in the public setting of a clinic!

b. The teacher or therapist has the children explore the experience of being alone in a room with no toys.

c. The teacher or therapist has the children explore the concept of each of them being "alone" while other kids pretend to be wild (within reason) animals.

d. After the children have worked through the above activities and concepts, they are taught how to play the game "Thinking About You." This game involves all children but one receiving "thinking of you" cards. This card means they play in a group where their job is to remember to think about other people while playing a cooperative game. One person in the group is arbitrarily chosen to be "JustMe". The appointed JustMe does not get to play with the group; he gets to choose anything he wants to play with except he is not allowed to communicate or play with any of the Thinking of You kids. Every child gets a chance to be JustMe. The game helps children contrast what it is like to be a JustMe verses a Thinking of You player. See Table 5 for printed instructions for this game.

The Thinking About You game is a wonderful way to introduce the vocabulary and thinking that are part of interactive perspective taking. It is remarkable to watch children acquire the vocabulary and then use it to begin to describe the behavior they see in others and then eventually describe their own thoughts and actions..

⧗

The Thinking About You game was introduced to a group of three boys, ages eight and nine years old. On the first day one of the boys was initially excited to receive the JustMe card, but within moments of playing alone and not being allowed to join the play of the group, he verbally bemoaned, "I do not want to be a JustMe, I want to play with the group. Being a JustMe is boring!" Nevertheless, when he reentered the group he insisted that he get to go first and have the longest turn. We used the same vocabulary of a JustMe even though he now was supposed to be a "thinking of you" person. I asked, "How do you think the other boys are thinking about your behavior?" We then talked about ways to negotiate the situation so all students could enjoy it together.

Another boy, Sam, with less Theory of Mind ability, had the most difficulty of all the boys in intuitively thinking about how the others were thinking. He had difficulty understanding the concept of the game and continued to try and play by himself even when he got the "thinking about you" card. This child was prone to throwing himself on the floor and crying when he did not get his way. He had a wonderful, no-nonsense mom who listened to me explain our lessons so she could work on them at home. At the next session she told me when she had asked her son what he was playing in the therapy group he recalled, "a game called JustMe and thinking about ME!"

During this next session the kids once again got the opportunity to play the Thinking About You game. The vocabulary was reviewed and then the kids chose their cards. Sam once again received the Thinking About You card. What was remarkable during this session was that Sam now stayed in the group and continually reported how others in the group were doing. He appropriately stated when one of the others was acting like a JustMe and he distinguished when they were demonstrating Thinking About You behaviors. Sam appeared to be developing more awareness of this concept, a critical building block toward self-monitoring and self-control. The moral of the story: our kids learn more than we sometimes realize!

The Thinking About You game also gives educators a chance to assess children's group play skills. Sustaining group interaction is hard work. Some skills to observe include the ability to:

a. Maintain a group interaction around another person's area of interest

b. Take turns

c. Use their eyes to monitor the social exchanges of others as well as regulate their own interactions with others

d. Initiate interactions toward others

e. Sustain interactions

f. Maintain a physical presence with others

g. Negotiate with others

h. Play flexibly by shifting focus as the group adjusts play schemes

Table 5
Rules for Playing the "Thinking About You" Game

1. Children are presented with a set of cards: one card for each child in the group. All but one of the cards has the phrase and instruction, "Thinking About You. Play as part of the group." written on it. One card in the set has "JustMe! Play by yourself."

2. The children take turns selecting a card. All of the children who receive the Thinking About You cards play together in a cooperative group activity arranged by the teacher. In our clinic this often involves taking turns crawling through a fabric tunnel or bouncing a ball to the members in the group (who are standing in a circle). The ball is to be passed to members of the group who are looking towards the person in possession of the ball and have their bodies ready to receive the ball.

3. The child who received the JustMe card gets to pick anything else in the therapy room to play with as long as he does not play or look towards the other children.

4. After a few minutes of play, the whole group is brought back together and the set of cards is shuffled and dealt again, with the group leader (parent, educator, or therapist) supervising so a different child receives the JustMe card each time.

5. Eventually all children experience the distinction of playing as a member of the group verses playing alone in close proximity to the group.

6. The group leader facilitates comments or discussion about the different thoughts of the children while they engaged in these two different types of play.

Example of playing cards:

Thinking About You!

Play as part of the group

JustMe!

Play by yourself

Whole Body Listening

One of the concepts that emerges from the idea "I think about you and you think about me" is that the individual can observe others and make judgments about them. When children participate in a group, they are frequently told to "listen." Interestingly, when I asked a group of children with social cognitive deficits to listen, many of them turned their faces away from me so they could turn their ears toward me.

In doing this, they lose their ability to fully interpret the interaction, since they have removed their eyes from the group. All children interpret the world in a fairly concrete way, but children with social cognitive deficits tend to be far more literal in their thinking when compared to their same-aged peers, even when the children with social cognitive deficits score much higher on tests of language comprehension and expression.

Listening is a concept that is crucial to social relationships in early developmental play as well as structured learning activities. Many children intuitively know that when someone says "listen," he actually is alluding to the gestalt concept of "pay attention," which means: sit up straight, look at me, keep quiet, do not fidget (if possible), think about what I am thinking!

"Listening with your body" refers to teaching children to focus on a message by paying attention through their whole body. The book *Can You Listen with Your Eyes?* (Everly 2005) is targeted for preschool and early elementary-school aged-children. It illustrated in pictures the concepts related to listening with our whole bodies.

We can break down the concept of active listening as follows:

⊙ You listen with your shoulders, hips and feet by turning toward the person who is talking.

⊙ You listen with your chest by keeping it up and pointed toward the person who is talking.

⊙ You listen with your hands by not distracting other people or yourself.

⊙ You listen with your ears by hearing what other people are saying.

⊙ You listen with your brain by thinking about what other people are saying.

⊙ You listen with your eyes by looking at people's faces and eyes when they are talking to you, to think about how they are feeling.

⊙ You listen with your mouth by making comments or asking questions only about what the person is discussing.

For young kids, "listening with your body" is another way to introduce the concept of thinking about what other people are saying, doing, and thinking. Young children enjoy exploring each of the above points and contrasting the position of various parts of their bodies when they are listening actively versus when they are not (e.g., super-distracting hands and feet compared with hands and feet that may move but do not distract others or themselves from paying attention to the speaker).

Once the various listening positions/body parts are described you can then reinforce children's specific behaviors by telling them they are doing a nice job listening with their eyes, listening with their hands, or listening with their brain, and so forth.

Pantomime

Pantomime or charades is useful in teaching children that you can "read" body movement to understand what others are communicating nonverbally. There are games on the market — "Charades" and "Guesstures" — that help children develop more awareness of how their bodies communicate.

Many of our students don't understand that they may need to use many gestures to communicate a single concept. For example, when a boy was trying to show me with gestures that he was "rolling dice," he used the same hand movements over and over again, even when I told him I did not understand what he was trying to show me. I encouraged him to use different types of gestures to give me more information (e.g., such as what he might do when he was picking up the dice, how his arm moves to get ready to shake the dice, etc.) but he could not understand that his single hand movement was insufficient for me to figure out his intended meaning. He could only look at the gestures from his point of view.

This was a perfect opportunity to explain that even when a person is engaged in a nonverbal action such as gestural communication, he still has to think about his partner's interpretation of his message. Teachers need to guide students in learning to modify all parts of their communicative expression to help others comprehend their intended meanings.

Videotaping the Group

Videotape can be introduced to help children observe the behavior of the group, individual people in the group, and even themselves. Showing a video of children as they work and play together helps develop insight into the real world of interaction. Videotape the children in two distinct settings:

a. As they sit together in a group being taught a lesson

b. When they are attempting to play together as a group

Show the video to the children and have them each look for an example of people who are listening with their hands, eyes, and mouth. Then have them look for contrasting examples of obvious breakdowns in specific components of listening. Children really enjoy being "detectives" as they analyze their own videotape. They generally tolerate comments that illuminate appropriate and inappropriate demonstrations of the concepts being worked on in the clinic or classroom that day, as long as the teacher makes a point to balance examples of a child's inappropriate behavior with more examples of when that same child was doing it just right.

We refer to times when children comment on their own and others' behavior as watching a "video moment." Video moment analysis promotes self-awareness and self-monitoring skills related to specific sets of behaviors. By learning to identify their actions, we hope they gradually learn to control them also. Behavioral self-awareness and self-monitoring are crucial steps in the development of self-control. In the curriculum, *Think Social!* (Winner, 2005), a video moment worksheet is included in the back of most chapters to help guide students towards exploring on the video clips the specific social thinking vocabulary concepts in this book.

Digital video cameras that record directly onto DVDs are ideal since they show a perfect picture when the video is paused, and it is easy to jump from one clip to the next to show students their progress across or between sessions. School personnel with small budgets might consider asking their school's parent group to help purchase the video camera. It is a must-have tool for working with this higher-level population. Our students generally have very weak observation and self-monitoring skills. The video lessons are ideal because students can review them over and over, pausing at any point to discuss or review something they don't understand.

A good set of video social scenarios of appropriate and inappropriate social behaviors can be found at www.socialskillbuilders.com

Summary of the Whole Body Listening Strategy

⊙ Introduce the concepts related to listening with your whole body.

⊙ Have the children role-play activities where they contrast appropriate and inappropriate use of these concepts.

⊙ Use pantomime or charades. Have children learn that they can understand what people are communicating even when language is not used.

⊙ Encourage parents and educators working with the children to use the vocabulary of "listening with your whole body" throughout the day and evening, during teachable moments.

⊙ Create a videotape of the children during structured and unstructured activities. Have the children be "detectives" and monitor these concepts as they see them in other children and themselves.

⊙ Teach children ways in which listening with your whole body contributes to learning what other people are thinking. (Also see section in Chapter 6 on eye contact/thinking with your eyes.)

Using Literature to Teach Social Awareness

Classic tests to assess Theory of Mind use fairy tales such as "Snow White" and "Little Red Riding Hood." These familiar stories (and others like them in today's marketplace) encourage children to probe the minds of characters and laugh at how easily a character was duped when he wasn't thinking about the motives or intentions of other characters in the story.

We can use these books within therapy settings to expand Theory of Mind in our students, too. For instance, in the story "Little Red Riding Hood," Red Riding Hood ("Red") is duped into believing the wolf is actually her grandma when the wolf dresses in her grandma's clothing. After reading the story to students, explore what clues Red should have seen to avoid the catastrophe that unfolds in this story. Other lesson options include:

a. Have the students role-play the traditional story, particularly the scene where the wolf tricks Little Red Riding Hood into believing he is Grandma.

b. Have the students "listen with their eyes" and explore all the visual clues Red should have noticed to more accurately distinguish the wolf from her grandma.

c. Have the students figure out the wolf's intent. Why did he want to dress up like Grandma? Who was he trying to fool? What did he have to know about Red in order to trick her like this? How many people did the wolf have to trick to make his plan (intent) succeed?

d. Have fun encouraging them to summarize what Red did wrong!

In this story the wolf clearly has a much stronger Theory of Mind than does Red. The wolf knew that Red loved her grandma and was too trusting of everyone. The wolf guessed that if he pretended to be Grandma, Red would allow the wolf (dressed as Grandma) to get close to her (which he did successfully). Ultimately his plan was to eat both Grandma and Red. The wolf's intent was to trick Red and Grandma to get what he wanted. The whole trick was dependent on the idea that Red would not guess what the wolf was thinking and her associated inability to pick up the physical cues and clues.

e. Have students problem solve. At this point in the lesson students should be much smarter than was Red: they not only understand Red's weak Theory of Mind but they also understand the wolf's strong intent to be a rotten scoundrel! Work with the children to come up with a better solution for Red.

f. Create a new solution and have the children guess how it would change the ending of the book.

g. Role-play the new version of the story and discuss how much smarter Red is now!

h. Explore the students' life experiences: have they encountered other mean-spirited people? Discuss that bullies can look like regular kids but can really have intentions more like the wolf.

"Little Red Riding Hood" is just one of many books and stories that can be used to expand students' understanding of Theory of Mind. Virtually all stories by Disney have a character who starts out sweet but ultimately acts very badly towards others.

A note about using fairy tales: The very talented therapists who work with me voiced strong concerns about the use of "Little Red Riding Hood" in our social thinking curriculum. It does, after all, have quite a disgusting middle and ending (depending on the version you read). The prevailing opinion (but not without long debate) was that by using the story, we could help children create Red as a powerful heroine rather than the bland, useless character presented in the book. We ultimately felt that we could empower children by helping them understand that changing how a person or character thinks can modify specific outcomes. That lesson, we all agreed, was more important than the disgusting details of the story. We also reminded ourselves we were all raised on the story and we prevailed!

Making Smart Guesses

Social success (reacting to others, knowing and choosing when to apply specific social skills, and choosing what words to say) depends on our own ability to "read a situation" and infer what actions to take, based on that information. Inferencing is the ability to take what you know and make a guess. Inferencing tends to be a process most of us engage in cognitively but often not consciously. People with good social cognitive development receive and respond to social cues intuitively and fluently. They also interpret the actions of others' and regulate their own social behavior based on the inferred expectations in that communicative environment.

For example, if I am in a group discussion, I consider the environmental context, watch how people are responding, consider the words being said, and formulate the message I feel contributes to the ongoing conversation. Moreover, during this process I have to monitor the discussion to make sure it has not moved away from what I want to say. Then I have to track others' speech to find the smallest pause that will allow for me to jump in with my words without making it appear I am interrupting anyone else's ideas!

Social inferencing is a continuous process in all communicative interactions, but it happens at many different levels. At any moment it involves interpreting:

a. The meaning of spoken words.

b. How a person's body language contributes to the overall meaning.

c. How a person's facial expression contributes to the overall meaning.

d. How a person's eye contact contributes to the overall meaning.

e. The person's overall intent or motive.

f. How the social context and social environment helps us better interpret all of the above.

The point of social inferencing is to be able to simultaneously think about yourself and others, what you and everyone else is thinking about the topic, before you further contribute to another's voiced comment or opinion.

Inferencing as a social thinking skill is also required in academic work. Elementary school curriculum shifts significantly in the second half of third grade. By then, children are expected to have mastered basic academic skills and now are required to apply their knowledge to gain new insight in the learning process. The curriculum moves from procedural to conceptual.

In our math curricula, word problems become more abstract, asking students to take previously learned facts and apply them in new and interesting ways. In reading, students are encouraged to comprehend a deeper meaning from the text. Written expression assignments expect students to express more abstract thought. In academia we refer to this ability to infer (use past learned skills to formulate more creative thought) as "critical thinking." Critical thinking is a highly prized construct. While it is not directly taught, it is highly encouraged and viewed as part of school success.

For individuals with social cognitive deficits, critical thinking is far easier when it involves making inferences about information that is grounded in factual knowledge, such as science, history, and math facts. Many, but not all, our students who have high intelligence can be extraordinarily creative in these

realms. Math is a possible exception. Some of our students cannot intuitively grasp fundamental math concepts or conceptually organize math word problems.

Critical thinking is also required to interpret information that is not grounded in concrete fact, but involves social interpretation. This is much more difficult for our students to master. This type of socially grounded critical thinking is required for a deeper analysis of literature, social studies, group projects in the classroom, and interpreting a teacher's class assignments.

Helping children acquire these pivotal skills — interpretation and inferencing — is another "must do" part of the therapeutic process. We begin by teaching children that inferencing is "taking what you know and making a guess." This is a fairly concrete explanation of this abstract process. Making an "educated guess" is synonymous with inferencing. Do keep in mind that all of these words (interpretation, inferencing, educated guess) are a bit complicated for young children in early elementary school. We therefore describe this process as learning to make a "smart guess."

In teaching children about smart guesses, we encourage them to realize that even though they know a lot of factual information, their biggest job is to learn to hook it together to form a new thought or idea — a smart guess. This can be harder to accomplish than it appears, as we found out after leading a group of kindergarten through second graders through a summer club we called "Make A Guess." Even after offering multiple examples this concept was still difficult for many students, especially those who had more limited Theory of Mind abilities.

⌛

In one summer club experience, the six children were getting to know each other by making guesses about each other and about the adults leading the group. Charlie was an eight-year-old boy with high-functioning autism and normal intellectual functioning, who appeared to have significant trouble with perspective taking. He was asked to guess if another boy, who was two grades higher than he in school, was older or younger than himself. Even though we repeatedly explained to Charlie that the other boy was two grades higher, Charlie could not draw upon what he already knew (that kids who are in higher grades are usually older) to formulate his answer. He whimpered, "This is too hard," and was not able to make the smart guess.

With young children it is more fun to tackle this concept indirectly by forming a "detective agency" in the classroom or therapy setting and then teaching children about what detectives do: first they must find the clues (facts) and then make a smart guess to try to solve the problem.

Activities enjoyed in the detective agency include:

1. Pretending to be a detective by dressing in make-believe detective hats and parents' suit jackets.

2. Finding different types of clues, concrete and abstract.

   a. Concrete clues:

      i. Hide a series of written clues, each clue providing information on locating the next clue so they can ultimately find a hidden object. For example, in our program we always hid the students' snacks. The young students loved finding the clues and discovering where the snacks were hidden. Each clue should have an inferential quality to the message so children can practice using information to make small guesses.

      ii. Children create their own clues. After the children have practiced finding concrete clues, have them write their own set of clues that guide another person to a hidden object. Each clue must imply where the next clue is hidden. This gives students practice formulating and writing inferential information. The teacher or therapist will need to work with students to make sure they are thinking about how the other person will read and interpret each clue. Some students wrote clues that were too difficult because they did not consider the perspective of the other person, and thereby did not provide enough information to interpret the clues to make the guess. Others wrote clues that were too obvious, and then the student who wrote the clue became frustrated when another student found the object too easily.

   b. Abstract clues: Usborne Books publishes *A Spy's Guide Book* (Sims and King, 2002) and *The Detective's Handbook* (Civardi, Hindley, and Wilkes, 1979). Information in many of the chapters can be used to teach children how detectives and spies evaluate other people. Chapters cover topics such as wearing disguises, changing your walk, and hidden messages, all of which provide opportunities to teach children about body language, facial expression, tone of voice, and staying alert to what is going on around you.

3. Using DVDs. Use movies, TV shows, or commercials to make "smart guesses" about what will happen next. Some of clues are encoded in the environmental context or body language of a character. Pause the video in places and encourage students to make guesses about what will happen based on the information already provided; discuss how the information helped them make the guess. Most of our students are successful at this task. This allows the therapist to reward students for a job well done and inspire them to search out this same type of information in their day-to-day interactions.

4. Code messages in different ways; use secret codes to reframe information. This develops mental flexibility and again teaches that all information is not presented exactly as it is to be understood. The book *Secret Codes* (O'Brien and Riddell, 1997) was helpful in developing these lessons.

As with all of the above lessons, the real value is in establishing a vocabulary and environment that actively promotes the concepts of inferencing and smart guessing as an important component of the educational and social day. Help students see the connection between the fun of "playing detective" and actually using these detective skills in everyday activities: relating to others, reading a book, guessing what he or she is to do in class, and so on.

As mentioned above, children with more limited perspective taking skills (those students with lower EPT than IIPT) have great difficulty with these tasks. These students need individual speech and language therapy to help them focus on the idea of inferential thinking and how it relates to their daily life, if they can comprehend the notion at all. With EPT students I usually start with teaching them to visually sequence pictures of daily living skills and then explore sequences of short social scenarios.

I Can Change How You Feel

Interactive perspective taking includes the ability to understand that your behaviors affect how other people relate to you. Our students appear to understand that other people's behavior affects how they feel, but they often lack the insight to recognize that their own behaviors affect others! It is extremely common for our students to "patrol" the behavior of peers at school, telling adults when they have identified misconduct or when they feel they have been personally violated. However, these same students fail to be self-aware of their own behaviors and how they affect others. (This statement is not indicative

of the fact that our students are often teased or bullied by others, nor does it lessen the need for educators to create an environment of acceptance, as well as enforce a zero tolerance policy on bullying.)

To help our students better understand how they affect others, I use students' behaviors in the educational setting to teach them how they affect other people in the group, including me. As I develop a safe environment where the students are comfortable sharing their strengths as well as their challenges, I then widen the circle of the lesson to include the impact of a student's behavior on others. This lesson goes beyond showing students traditional pictures of emotions and having them label them. It encourages students to explore another person's reaction to their behaviors and how this reaction contributes to how other people feel about them and ultimately treat them.

Using an Emotions Poster

When I first start working on this concept with younger children I hang an "emotions" poster in the educational room. An emotions poster pictures a variety of facial expressions and is often found hanging in many classrooms or the office of a speech language pathologist. These posters can be purchased at local teachers' supply stores or in specialty catalogs familiar to most teachers or speech and language pathologists.

Students' behaviors are monitored in their educational environments and the teacher identifies certain behaviors that contribute to the emotional climate in the room. For example, if a child is being really cooperative, his cooperative behavior is clearly identified by the teacher and then the teacher can show the child that "you helped to change how I feel!" As she again describes the child's behavior she points to how she feels on the emotions poster. She can also ask the child how that makes him feel, knowing he has made someone else feel good.

On the flip side, when a child demonstrates uncooperative behavior, the teacher can clearly define what behavior she is seeing and then show the child how "you changed how I feel!" This is accomplished by showing the child how you were feeling before (e.g., happy, proud) and that your emotion has now changed to an emotion such as worried, frustrated, or sad, based on the child's behavior. A short discussion usually clarifies what behavior on the child's part "changed" how the teacher felt. The teacher should also encourage the student to discuss his emotions and how they changed during the same time period. The entire purpose of this lesson is to illustrate to students that they can have a good and/or less than stellar impact on others, and that our feelings often shift based on the behavior of others around us.

Scotty was an eight-year-old boy with high-functioning autism who worked with me in individual language sessions. One day he came to the session in a particularly difficult mood. I walked in the room and happily said, "Good morning, Scotty!" but he was under the therapy table refusing to come out. I got him out from the table by asking him to look at the picture chart with me.

When he came over to me I asked him how I felt when I first walked in the room, and then I reiterated for him the cheerfulness in my voice when I said good morning to him. Scotty showed me that I felt happy. I then explained that "he changed my feelings," now demonstrating for him the more serious tone in my voice as I asked him to come out from under the table and look at the poster.

Scotty now looked at the emotions poster with me as I showed him how my mood changed from happy to sad, now pointing to the picture of sad. Scotty and I then went back to the therapy table and worked together successfully. I then asked him to go back with me to the emotions poster and I exclaimed, "You changed my feelings again!" This time I reminded Scotty that I had felt sad when he refused to do what I asked, but now that I noticed how cooperative he was, I felt happy and he could show me that emotion on the poster chart. Scotty was able to show me, as well as verbally state that he felt happy now too.

This lesson is important but it must be used with extreme caution. It should never be used as a form of discipline or to embarrass the child to force him to do better. It is a visual tool that can educate students about the effect their actions have on others, but teachers should use it to show how students' behaviors affect the teacher positively with much more frequency than the negative effects of their undesirable behaviors.

There is a strong sense of political incorrectness in this lesson. Simplistically stated, positive behaviorism was built on the idea that children needed to know what they should do and be rewarded for doing it, rather than focus on what they should not do and be punished for their negative behaviors. Behavioral lessons that focused on negative behaviors were strongly discouraged. Nevertheless, purely positive behaviorism assumes the child either understands how he impacts the world, or he does not have a strong enough cognitive capacity to understand.

We cannot assume that high-functioning children with social cognitive deficits understand how they affect others. For those with good language skills, I believe it is important they learn more about their own behavior and how it affects others. The educator or parent exploring this type of lesson must therefore monitor her/his own feedback to the student to make sure they provide both perspectives: the positive and the negative.

The value in these lessons lies in the opportunity to show a student that he can make you feel better about being with him, compared with other moments when he can make you feel frustrated or angry. As with all lessons that help to expand a student's ability to consider the needs or feelings of others, caution must be used to make sure you are accounting for the student's perspective as well as your own.

Using Personal Memories of Others to Make Educated Guesses About Them

 Interactions exist in the moment, but relationships exist over time. The development and growth of a relationship is strongly dependent on the memory we have of the people or individuals who are part of that relationship.

As an undergraduate in a speech and language program, I had the good fortune to have been a student of Dr. Carol Prutting, an early pioneer in understanding the social pragmatic deficits of students on the autism spectrum. I recall one class lecture where she introduced the idea, "the last time you saw a person is the first memory you have of them the next time you see them." I really enjoyed her lecture, but at that time I could not understand how this related to language development. Now I see it so clearly. We use social memory as a tool to decide with whom we interact and how we choose to interact with them. Memory not only encodes the behavioral impressions we have of others, but also plays a key role in what activities we may choose to do with them, what we may choose to talk about, or even how we choose to behave.

In my clinical experience, students often appear to have a weak ability to encode social memories about other people's areas of interest and personal life history. Part of the clinical experience must include helping children learn to use memory as a primary tool for making and keeping friends, in addition to its impact on forming accurate judgments about what to say to whom.

For example, if you are a devout member of a religion, you may enjoy discussing your ideas about your religion with others. Nevertheless, for social success it is imperative that you carefully choose your audience for this discussion. If you were in a public forum you would have to first remember which of the people present share your interest in your religion, and those would be the people you would engage in discussion. Engaging in a discussion with a person who does not share your interest puts you at a strong risk of offending this person. People who are offended hold that memory and may well avoid you during their next opportunity to relate.

Students with social cognitive deficits have difficulty initiating conversations with others. While part of this deficit has its origins in how to formulate language to relate to others, it also appears that another aspect relates to not having encoded important information about the person or not retrieving that information when needed.

⧗

At our summer camp for middle-school students, each morning the students gathered at the clinic before going out to an event in the community. As the week progressed the students engaged in discussions to learn more and more about their camp peers. Remarkably, at the start of each day, the campers sat together around a therapy table in complete silence. No connection was made between what they did or learned about a person the day before and how to use that information the next time they saw each other!

Teaching students about the concept of social memory and its importance in developing relationships appears to be a crucial and ongoing task. The lessons on the following pages can be introduced to both younger children and older children alike.

Using Body Drawings to Teach Children about Memory

The concept of storing memories can be introduced to younger children using a body drawing of the child, either life-sized or a miniature version. A line is drawn through the middle of the body from head to toe to divide the body in half. One half of the body represents the child, the other half represents other people.

Half of the body is all about me:

The teacher works with the child to identify things the child likes to think about or do. She can identify members of her family, her pets, her friends, and so on. These words or concepts are either written or pictured directly on the half of the body that she has identified as being "all about me." The teacher should validate to the child that she knows about herself and takes pride in her personal attributes.

Half of the body is all about other people:

When students are ready to explore what to do with the empty half of their body, the teacher explains that the brain makes "files" to store information about people or things. As we get to know people our brain makes a file about them that will be opened the next time we see them. By opening this file we remember important things about them.

Each child is then encouraged to share three important pieces of personal information with others in the group. All students are encouraged to listen so they can make a picture or write in the information on the other half of their body, especially in the brain area. Generally students draw small boxes that represent files in the pictured brain. (See Figure 2.)

From each of those files the students draw a line that extends outside the head to another box, or to a set of three lines. In the box/on these lines they write the three pieces of information they learned about each person. This demonstrates to students in a visual, concrete manner that to become friends with another person you have to store information about that person inside your brain. The body drawing and related facts create a graphic organizer of sorts, helping students conceptualize this social idea.

Students can also create a "visual web" of facts they remember about another person after completing an interaction together. The visual web also helps students think about the different types of questions to ask people to gain more information about them. (See Figure 3.) All of this information is useful when talking to students about storing memories of others. The visual representations make these abstract social concepts more meaningful, and students have a tool they can use with or without their teacher.

Therapy sessions focus on encouraging students to open their brain's files and think about what the other person might want to discuss. This process does not come intuitively to our students, and they need lots of practice to learn to use it in their daily lives. It is important that parents and educators encourage interaction based on the information learned, repeatedly and intermittently across many lessons in various settings. Remind our students about the concept of "memory of others" in teachable moments throughout the day.

Table 6 summarizes lessons for younger students that were reviewed above, along with previews of concepts to be discussed in other chapters in the book.

Figure 2

Body Drawing to Teach Children about Memory and Storing Information About Others and Themselves

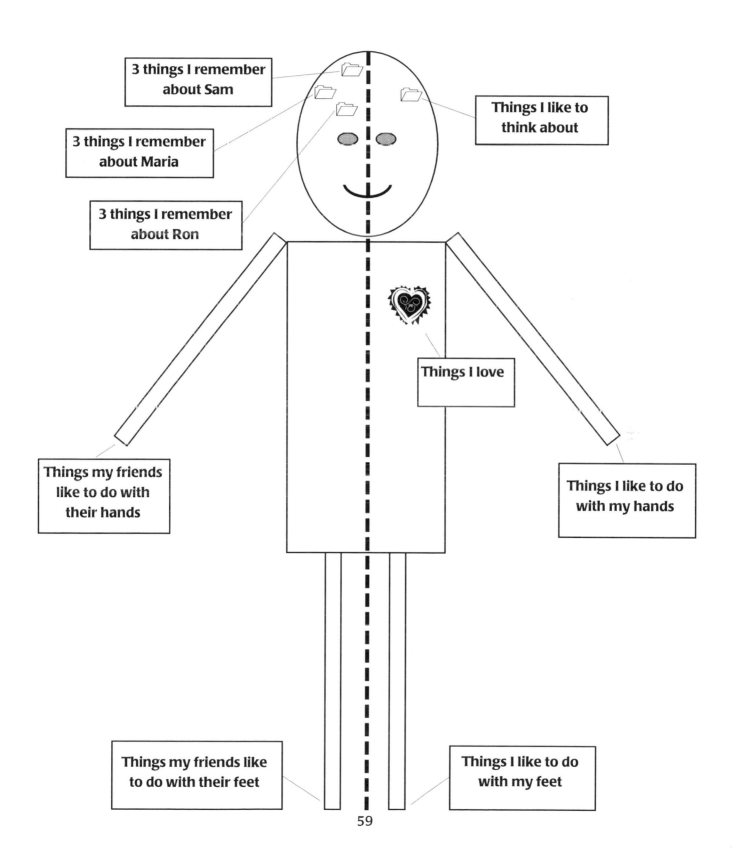

3 things I remember about Sam

3 things I remember about Maria

3 things I remember about Ron

Things I like to think about

Things I love

Things my friends like to do with their hands

Things I like to do with my hands

Things my friends like to do with their feet

Things I like to do with my feet

Figure 3

Visual Web — What You Remember about Others

Name _____ Date _____

Things he likes to do:	Information about his family:

Name of a person you are getting to know:

_____

Information about his school or job:	Types of foods or restaurants he likes:

Table 6

Concepts Related to the Development of Perspective Taking

Think, Know, and Guess

~~~~~~

Thinking About You Game

~~~~~~

Listening with Your Whole Body

~~~~~~

Use of Children's Literature to Build Awareness

~~~~~~

Lessons in Physical Presence (Chapter 5)

~~~~~~

Lessons in Eye Contact:
What You See in Others Means Things About Them (Chapter 6)

~~~~~~

Making Guesses as Part of Being in a Detective Agency

~~~~~~

Using Memory of Others to Talk to Them and Play with Them
(applicable with young and older students)

~~~~~~

I Can Change How You Feel, and You Can Change How I Feel!

~~~~~~

Using Social Behavior Mapping with Pictures (Chapter 8)

Building a Curriculum For Older Children and Adults

"Older children" are those in their late elementary school years and above who can comprehend more abstract information (higher level EPT and IIPT). Among typically developing children, the concepts discussed in this chapter are meaningful by the third or fourth grade. However, children with social cognitive deficits are usually immature for their age, unable to handle as much abstract social information as their peers.

These students' maturation level is often one-third behind that of their peers. This means a twelve-year-old boy with a social cognitive deficit might function socially at about the level of an eight-year-old. I have also worked with thirty-year-old adults operating developmentally as if they were twenty years old, just beginning to get a firm footing in the area of independence.

Girls with social cognitive deficits do not appear to follow this general rule as neatly; some are very immature while many others act years beyond their age. A friend's daughter is twelve years old but the girl believes she is functioning more closely to an eighteen-year-old; she identifies with adults more than children. Some girls have a hard time relating to or understanding the silly or flirtatious traits of their peers as they socialize in cliques, especially when students move into middle and high school. These girls may believe since they are not so silly, they must be more mature. An erroneous assumption since they usually remain weak in other social thinking areas, as well as developing independence, job skills, and college success.

The Four Steps of Perspective Taking

In my earlier book *Inside Out: What Makes The Person With Social Cognitive Deficits Tick?* (2000), a number of concepts were introduced to guide both students and educators in understanding abstract lessons related to interactive perspective taking. A three-step process was presented to help explain the ongoing act of perspective taking; this has since been modified to a four-step framework. These four steps of perspective taking are listed as a synergistic hierarchy — they also occur whenever people are just sharing space, most commonly when people are not sharing intentional communicative interactions (for example, when standing next to a stranger in an elevator or walking around a person you encounter in a grocery store aisle).

Four Steps of Perspective Taking:

1. I think about you.

2. I think about why you are near me. What do you want from me? What is your intent?

3. I think about what you are thinking about me.

4. I regulate my behavior to keep you thinking about me the way I want you to think about me.

Handout 1 details these four steps in a chart that can be posted on a classroom or therapy office wall, bedroom, or refrigerator. These four steps may seem simplistic, but they provide a basic overview of the dynamic process that should happen when we are in the presence of others.

Many of my students tell me they do step 1, but not 2, 3, or 4. They tend to view these four steps as a process that happens only when you first meet someone; it creates the "first impression." I usually need to explain that interactive perspective taking is actually an ongoing process; it doesn't stop from the time you establish contact with another person until the time you leave the person's presence. In fact, the process can extend even beyond that moment: people replay interactions in their minds and review their words and actions to ascertain whether or not they have made a bad impression by not regulating their own behavior in relation to the other person. This can lead to further conversation to clarify the misunderstanding or apologize for one's carelessness.

The act of taking perspective is perpetual; it continues well beyond the time one is physically involved with others as, for better or worse, thoughts are carried about others in our minds. *Inside Out* offers more information on the topic of making impressions. One lesson contained in the book comes from *Book A: Social Skill Strategies* (Gajewski and Mayo, 1998). It helps students understand that specific aspects of a person's behavior contribute to the overall perspective others form of them. Making impressions and taking perspective is a dynamic, synergistic process.

Table 7 summarizes for the reader the interrelationship between the act of interactive perspective and the ways we form perspectives and impressions about others. It breaks down this complex process into the core steps we use to perceive and react to each other. Students can use this information as a framework to evaluate their own functioning and better assess the minds and motives of others.

The inability on the part of our students to fully engage in these four steps of perspective taking affects their daily social, academic, and work environments. These lessons help students develop a common vocabulary and conceptual framework in order to better understand perspective taking and practice the skill in their daily lives. It is critical that all people working and living with these students help them learn and internalize these steps, at school, at home, and in community settings. Therapists can share this information with all caretakers so they think about and discuss this process in concrete terms with students. Parents and educators with strong social cognitive development need to consider what they do and how they intuitively negotiate social interactions with others so they can better explain the process to students who need to learn it cognitively. Most neurotypical adults have never thought about interactive perspective taking as a cognitive process that can be dissected, explored, and taught. This is unfamiliar ground for many and may be difficult at first. However, it is also interesting and rewarding.

I constantly remind parents and educators that if our goal is to be effective teachers, we have to be able to articulate what the child needs to learn. Not only that, we must then be able to explain how we are going to teach it! This is not always easy within the realm of social thinking and perspective taking skills. Even well-seasoned professionals flounder, because the process is so intuitive to us.

Table 7 reviews the basic concepts presented in Chapter 2. For more specific therapeutic information and worksheets please refer to my other books:

- *Inside Out* (Winner, 2000)

- *Think Social! A Social Thinking Curriculum for School-Age Children* (Winner, 2005)

- *Worksheets! for Teaching Social Thinking and Related Skills* (Winner, 2005)

- *Social Behavior Mapping* (Winner, 2007)

- DVD: "Social Thinking Across the Home and School Day" (Winner, 2002). In this four-hour presentation, Michelle reviews the I LAUGH Model and critical aspects of social cognition that impact social and academic skills (two hours). Observe Michelle in a clinical setting, engaged in related lessons with students (two hours). (DVD or Video format)

Consider This:

The majority of time we are engaged in perspective taking we are not talking and we may not even know the people around us. Consider how you take perspective in the following environments:

1. A public bathroom

2. The supermarket

3. Driving

4. Walking in a park

Handout 1

The Ongoing Process:

The Four Steps of Perspective Taking

1a. I think about you.

1b. You think about me.

2a. I think about your intentions. Why are you near me? What do you want from me?

2b. You think about my intentions. Why am I near you? What do I want from you?

3a. I realize you are having thoughts about me. I think about what you might be thinking about me.

3b. You realize I am having thoughts about you. You think about what I might be thinking about you.

4a. I regulate my behavior to keep you thinking about me the way I want you to think about me!

4b. You regulate your behavior to keep me thinking about you the way you want me to think about you!

Table 7:

Infusing the Perspective Taking Process into the Therapy Setting

Four Steps When Taking Perspective Of Others Even When NOT talking

1a. I think about you.
1b. You think about me.

2a. I think about your intention. Why are you near me? What do you want from me?
2b. You think about my intention. Why am I near you? What do I want from you?

3a. I realize you are having thoughts about me. I think about what you might be thinking about me.
3b. You realize that I am having thoughts about you. You think about what I might be thinking about you.

4a. I regulate my behavior to keep you thinking about me the way I want you to think about me!
4b. You regulate your behavior to keep me thinking about you the way you want me to think about you!

Making Impressions: Variables by Which People Interpret Another's Behavior

1. How they look (affects others whether they are relating with them or not).

   a. Clothes they wear   d. Tattoos
   b. Hygiene   e. Make-up
   c. Hair style   f. Other appearance traits

2. What they say (when they are with others). Just the words (not how the words are interpreted through body language). Exploring the meaning of language, including friendly and unfriendly words.

   a. Truth
   b. Sarcasm
   c. Humor
   d. Emotions: anger, fear, kindness, sadness, etc.
   e. Literal versus figurative language

3. What they do (when they are with others).

   a. Body language   f. Tone of voice
   b. Eye contact   g. Volume of voice
   c. Facial expression   h. Posture (relaxed? rigid?)
   d. Proximity   i. Other physical expression or communication
   e. Speed/Pace of language

All People Have Thoughts About Others

Whether alone or in a group, we all have thoughts about the other people with whom we interact. And many times our thoughts are based on first (and last) impressions. Students with social thinking deficits may readily acknowledge that they think about the behaviors of others, but may not realize that others, in turn, think about them.

Robbie is a thirty-year-old man with high-functioning autism. He lives in an apartment and has a job in the community that he travels to by riding the public bus. I work with Robbie on an individual basis. His mother sits in on every session so she can extend our therapeutic discussions into social thinking moments across his day. Robbie has a limited Theory of Mind; he functions as an EPT.

My first clinical lesson with Robbie was to teach him that other people think about him and form opinions about him, even when he is not actively seeking their attention. This amazed Robbie, who loudly protested, "No, they do not!" Nevertheless, Robbie had shared with me that he hated "bums" and would never sit next to someone on the bus he thought looked like a bum. I used this information to explain to Robbie that he has clear opinions about others and that his impression of a bum is made mostly by "how a person looks." When put in terms related to his own understanding of the world, he was able to comprehend this idea. Robbie grasped that people look at him and make decisions about whether they

would want to sit next to him, based on "how he looks" as well. This lesson helped Robbie understand that perspective taking can be a very small moment-in-time act and is not restricted to face-to-face conversation.

We make impressions in various ways but they all pretty much fall into three general categories:

1. How you look

2. What you say

3. What you do

I often introduce this concept to my students by sitting or standing on top of the therapy table. I get up on the table and explain what we are going to do that day, then continue the lesson well past the time students are laughing at me or commenting about my strange behavior. Staying on the table adds to the humor of the experience, but also gives them ample time to realize they are noticing and reacting to what other people are doing. This lesson is simple, yet practical. It makes students aware of the fact that they have strong expectations about others and that they form their impressions the same way everyone else does. Be creative in helping your students understand the concept of social impressions. Have fun with it!

One teenager spent the first thirty minutes of a summer program talking with a strong European accent that he refused to shake, even when other students made comments about his odd use of the accent. At that point, I climbed up on the table and continued to teach, but this time speaking with an accent myself. Interestingly, it was the student who was using an accent who became the most upset, absolutely insisting that I get down and "talk normally!" When I did, he also discontinued his accent, never to use it again during our summer camp experience.

Be sure to incorporate conversation about the impressions we create often in your social thinking therapy sessions. How we look, what we say and do when with others is an integral part of our social experiences. They are at the core of how we perceive each other. At times I give "impression-making awards" at the end of a clinical session. It often involves a lot of humor as the group votes on who made the best or worst impression that day, based on these three factors. It's important to have students think back about the less-than-desirable behaviors alongside the desirable. This reminds students that other people see their behaviors — good and bad — and remember them. However, do balance criticism with equal attention to what students are doing well, and repeatedly point out that we all make mistakes, we all make social blunders, and that's OK.

Teamwork versus Friendship

Desperate moments in the clinic often result in creative new ideas! A small group of teenaged boys in one of our therapy groups disliked each other. That was acceptable to us, because with this age group, the focus of social thinking sessions should never be solely on creating friendships. Teens are old enough to pick and choose their friends. Our goal was to increase their social thinking skills and give them the tools they needed to succeed in their social environments. These boys didn't need to become friends, but it was critically important that they learn to tolerate others even though they may not choose to be friends with them. The focus of this group was more about learning to prevent students from strongly disliking you, rather than encouraging group members to enjoy each other's company. But how could we teach this valuable lesson with boys who didn't particularly like each other? We needed a project that would focus on teamwork rather than friendship.

We decided to write and create a video during the therapy sessions, one that would demonstrate each of the three types of impressions defined above. The project required group participation and cooperation to demonstrate the concept of making impressions. At the same time it required group members to be responsible for their interactions with each other if the project was to be a success.

Students were encouraged to monitor their own impressions while they constructed the video, and there were ample opportunities for each to do so. This type of project involves a heavy emphasis on organization — from content exploration to creating a timeline for shooting the video, to the actual shoot itself. It is an excellent teaching tool on many levels. Participants are required to:

a. Organize their ideas into clear video segments, creating enough segments so that each group member gets a chance to lead the production of one of them.

b. Choose the leader of each segment.

c. Brainstorm ideas for each segment, while being tolerant of different ideas among the members.

d. Write a brief, basic script.

e. Allow each student a turn directing the others' actions for the production of each segment.

f. Cooperate and pay attention throughout the filming.

g. Watch the videotape without criticizing the actions of other participants.

Handouts 2 and 3 are used to direct the students through the video planning process. Our students crave structure but have a very difficult time creating structure. Handouts such as these break down tasks that may seem overwhelming into smaller, more manageable tasks. This promotes an attitude of success within the group.

Making a video is a great team-oriented experience for any social concept being explored. The end product, of course, will vary greatly, based on the conceptual level and teamwork abilities of the group itself. It is important not to lose sight of the fact that our students have to work extra hard at a project like this. In addition to learning the concepts being taught, they are also honing their planning and organizing skills. The vast majority of students enjoy this process, and the videotape can be used effectively to expand students' own self-awareness of how they look to others, even if the final product is not as impressive as all the effort that went into creating it.

The idea to create a video as a team project was born out of in-the-trenches desperation. The teens in the social thinking groups at our clinic had sharply contrasting personalities, and the group dynamics were less than functional. Individuals with social thinking disabilities who do not get along with each other are a particularly troublesome combination. It was decided that in order to keep these groups learning together we had to encourage participants to come together in teamwork, if not in affection for each other. These video projects have turned out to be remarkably successful adventures; we use the idea in other groups, even where the personal dynamics of the group is not problematic. As often refer to the old axiom: "When life gives you lemons, make lemonade!"

During one of our team video projects a high-school student, Phil, came into the group with an attitude. Although he appeared to enjoy the group at some level, his participation was not always, or even often, cooperative. I went to extra measures to make sure he understood how important his cooperation would be toward making the video project successful for everyone. Phil did marginally well when being directed by others, though he tended to make off-the-cuff remarks and needed plenty of cues to follow their directions. However, it was a pleasure to watch Phil when it was his turn to direct his segment: he communicated clearly what he needed the other students to do, and they did exactly as he asked. He received high praise for his success in taking the leadership role so effectively.

Toward the end of Phil's stint as the leader, he stepped out of the room for a moment. While he was gone I instructed the other students to briefly become very disruptive and not obediently follow Phil's instructions. When Phil came back into the room, I videotaped as he began to give a final set of instructions. This time, however, the students did not attend to his message. Phil repeated his message several times to no avail. Finally he turned to me and stated, "I can't direct them if they won't listen to me!" I let Phil know we had set him up, and he took this well. We replayed the videotape showing Phil how he felt when others were uncooperative during his segment. I then made the comparison to his own disruptive behavior when others were directing their segment, and how that affected others' impressions of him. First-hand experience is always a powerful teaching tool.

The value of having students work on social concepts together in a group cannot be overstated. It is real life in action! This type of interaction also helps students consider these concepts in other environments.

Handout 2
Brainstorming the Team Video Project

Name _____ Date _____

Making this video requires planning

We will make some video segments to show concepts we have been working on in our group. Each segment will have a director. That person will help organize the segment and then film it. The rest of the students will then become the actors. Your teacher can be an actor too, but it is up to the students.

Now that you have the basics, you have to figure out how to organize it among all the group members so that it goes smoothly. Project planning and organizing means you have to break the project down into smaller steps. Brainstorm. What plan should we put in place so that we use our therapy meeting time efficiently and everyone gets a chance to be the director?

Brainstormed ideas

1.

2.

3.

4.

Rules of group behavior

To do this project we will be working together as a team. Teams require cooperation and negotiation to create a successful product. What are some of the most important rules to follow to help a group of people work as a team?

Handout 3
Breaking the Team Video Project Down into Basic Elements
Define the overall theme: _____

Brainstorm 3 or 4 different video segments for the project

1.

2.

3.

4.

Order Of Production Clips for Video Making

1. Video Clip Segment Title: _____

Director _____

Story idea for the filming of the concept: _____

_____

_____

2. Video Clip Segment Title: _____

Director _____

Story idea for the filming of the concept: _____

_____

_____

3. Video Clip Segment Title: _____

Director _____

Story idea for the filming of the concept: _____

_____

_____

Reading Other People's Reactions

Face to face communication never starts with words. It always starts by looking at the other person or considering what that person may be thinking, based on the context of the situation. This helps us make educated guesses about what that other person may want to talk about. THEN we say something.

The discussion of how we make impressions on others is a springboard to deeper thinking. Appropriate responses to social interaction require that we not only recall what we know about the other person(s) but we also consider the impression we may be making upon them. For example, if the person is looking really bored by yawning and looking away while we are talking, make the guess that we need to change the topic and talk about something more interesting to our conversation partner. This gets confusing for our students. On one hand we teach them they should never yawn or look away when people are talking because these behaviors are considered rude. But the reality is that many people exhibit these behaviors, though slightly more subtly, to indicate they are getting tired or are in a hurry to wrap up the current discussion.

As much as we try and create concrete lessons to deal with abstract concepts, we can never completely overcome the amazing complexities of social interaction. *Comic Strip Conversations* (Gray 1994) or similar methods help visually demonstrate what people are thinking and then encourage the student to make educated guesses about their role in the interaction. Our students generally do much better when we support our verbal lessons with visual tools that illustrate these concepts. The educator need not be an artist; any type of line drawings will do well, especially if the educator tells the students what they are drawing!

Comic Strip Conversations are often used in our clinic to demonstrate the process of thinking about others and how they think about you. (See Figure 4.)

Figure 4

Example of an Illustrated Visual Conversation*

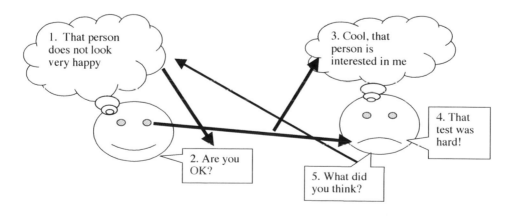

*When drawn in the midst of a clinical lesson they do not look this neat!

71

Using the Rubber Chicken to Keep Students Thinking

Humor is one of the most important elements of social thinking sessions. Students with social cognitive deficits quickly tire of the complexity of the social world around them. Breaking it down into finer elements and having deep lessons about it can be downright boring if not handled with humor! Rubber chickens are used in our clinic as a goofy way to express ourselves through humor. Interestingly, virtually all people enjoy the presence of the rubber chickens, young children to adults. In addition to the rubber chickens serving as "fidgets" to soothe the hyperactivity or sensory needs of many of our students, the chickens also serve as a funny way to approach the concepts being explored.

The writings in this book acknowledge the complexities of communication. No one avoids making social communication errors on a regular basis. The rubber chicken humorously acknowledges the many ways in which communication can fall apart. When a person errs, we call it a "rubber chicken moment."

Rubber chickens are used to touch, prod, or tap the older students who are able to understand and discuss the social concepts in a lesson, but are not yet demonstrating these concepts through their behavior. The rubber chicken "tap" is generally not used with younger children; many find it funny, and it can easily become an action-response model for naughty behavior. Older children (upper elementary, adolescents, and adults) are better able to control their actions and appreciate the humor, remaining relaxed when errors occur.

On a cautionary note, rubber chickens, while fun, can also be physically dangerous if someone holds the chicken by its feet and swings the chicken hard at another person. Therefore, I have established the rubber chicken holding rule: the chicken must be held between its wings, not by its feet.

Blake is a fourteen-year-old boy with Asperger Syndrome. He is very bright intellectually, but has significant impairments in his ability to engage with others reciprocally through his words, facial expression, and body language. Peers do not often have the patience to sustain a relationship with him. As I worked with him on the meaning of eye contact, he was able to share with me how others perceive his behavior, as well as verbalize what he can learn from using eye contact. Yet all the while we had this discussion his head was turned fully away from me as he rested it on the table. At this point, the rubber chicken beak nibbled his ear, and lightly tapped his head. The boy started to laugh, sat up, and looked at me. The next week his mother shared with me that she was trying to get him to understand something and he just was not engaging with her. She became really frustrated and realized she did not have much of a sense of humor at the moment, so she picked up a stuffed fish (the closest thing she could find to a rubber chicken) and she lightly "bonked" her son on the shoulder. He started to smile, and then assured her that he was only smiling because it was so silly. At the same time he engaged with his mother and they moved forward with their discussion in a more positive way.

⧖

I was working with a group of high-school students on the concept of organizing their free time so they could complete some chores at home. One of the boys in the group inferred where I was going with the topic and responded by saying, "Michelle, don't you be messing with my free time!" When I asked him what his mother did in her free time he replied, "Chores!" I picked up the rubber chicken and gently poked him on the shoulder. The rubber chicken prompt helped him realize the irony in his thoughts without my having to give him a serious explanation about his statements.

Before you start thinking we're "crazed rubber chicken whackers," know this: students respond to the chicken. So much of their lives are "serious," even a small break like this in the routine can bring renewed motivation for them to do the hard work that social thinking requires. Plus, how often can they participate in humor in a way that makes sense to them? My general rule is whatever I do with a rubber chicken, the students can do right back to me. Some days I have a hard time keeping track of the names of all the different children I see and I'll call a child by the wrong name — that's when I often deserve the "rubber chicken bonk." At times the rubber chicken never even comes out within a session, but I can say, "I think we are having a rubber chicken moment!" After I explain the use of the rubber chicken, workshop participants often come up to me later mentioning they are going to get a rubber chicken to use with their spouses at home. I think we all need a little more levity throughout our day!

Teaching Older Kids About Files in Your Brain

While the full body diagram is appealing to younger students, older kids need a more "mature" handout to understand the concept of memory and mentally storing information about their social partners. Handout 4 helps guide the older student through this concept and reinforces the importance of memory in forming relationships with others.

With both age groups, however, you will want to actively discuss this concept, over and over again. You'll find it is a natural part of social relationships and is easily incorporated into most discussions. It appears to be a crucial component of successful conversations and friendships. The ability for neurotypical people to engage in the making and keeping of friends appears as effortless as breathing, but as this process is stripped down to its core, we find it is based on incredibly abstract information. Storing information in our brains about other people is just one example of how complex this process truly is.

Because of the intricate nature of social communication and social relationships, it important to support lessons with worksheets as much as possible. As students add information to personalize the worksheet, it reinforces their understanding of the concepts being discussed. The worksheets in this book offer examples and ideas, but they are just a starting place. You can create your own materials using basic word processing programs, as you develop your own ideas with your students. Additional materials are also available in my book of worksheets, aptly titled *Worksheets! for Teaching Social Thinking and Related Skills* (2005).

Handout 4
Creating Files in Your Brain to Remember About Others

Your brain holds all the information you think and know. Getting to know someone else means you have to store information about that person in a file in your brain. You will need to work at remembering to put the information into your brain. Then the next time you see that person, you can brainstorm, which means when you think about that person you will be able to open your file about them!

Below, brainstorm what you remember about the different people you have met in this group.

I remember 3 things about

_____

1. _____

2. _____

3. _____

I remember 3 things about

_____

1. _____

2. _____

3. _____

I remember 3 things about

_____

1. _____

2. _____

3. _____

Empathy

Empathy is the ability to understand and relate to emotions another person feels. Individuals who lack empathy are often seen as cold and uncaring. Many people assume that persons on the Autism Spectrum lack empathy, but I have not seen this in our higher-functioning students. Tests of empathy have traditionally shown cognitive empathy as being weak in persons with Asperger Syndrome; however, they do well in measures of affective empathy (Rogers, Dziobek, Hassenstab, Wolf, and Convit, 2007).

What do I find? If the students are able to understand the emotions of another person, they react appropriately. For example, many of our students become sad when they see someone is hurt. Nevertheless, they cannot read the emotions of the other person or understand how they should react; many do not realize they share emotional states with others. If a student doesn't understand that others experience the same set of emotions as he does, it is more difficult for him to appear empathetic.

For example, eight-year-old Marc was so upset when he lost a game that he cried. However, he became confused when another child lost a similar game and cried. Marc told the other child he was "acting like a baby." Marc was unaware the other person shared the same reactions or emotions as he did; his response appeared to lack empathy. However, when Marc saw another child fall down and hurt himself, he recognized that as painful and rushed to the side of the hurt child to help him. This lack of consistent emotional recognition and response can be confus-

ing. It is surprising how many parents describe their high-level child as empathetic and then go on to describe all the behavioral challenges this child displays when confronted with a situation that requires empathy.

⌛

Damon, a twenty-year-old young man who has great difficulty with perspective taking (high-level EPT), describes that many, if not all, people tend to treat him with "disrespect" from time to time. Damon is keenly aware of other people's facial expressions, meaning implied by their tone of voice, body language, and so on, even though his interpretation of these factors is weak. He feels people act in a less than kind manner toward him, and this is what he defines as "showing him disrespect."

Damon's fairly accurate identification of others' negative feelings toward him is an ongoing point of contention in many of his relationships. Nevertheless, Damon does not recognize that other people also have emotions, and not all of the emotions Damon sees in others are directly related to him. For example, his mother was having a bad day for a variety of reasons, all of which Damon knew about. When Damon was late getting to the car to come to our therapy appointment, Damon's mother used an angry or impatient tone of voice when talking to him. Once again, this caused Damon to become upset by her "disrespecting" him. When we evaluated his mother's emotions he was surprised to realize that her being upset about other things could carry over to how she conveyed her message to Damon – no disrespect was intended! We then discussed that Damon also projects his negative emotions onto others with whom he is not upset. Damon is often unhappy due to his unemployed status and he routinely carries over his frustration to his relationship with his parents.

Daily life, with all the interactions, thoughts, and reactions experienced by our students, is a veritable sea of opportunity for detailed analysis in the clinical setting of communicative emotions and intent. While these are not traditional lessons on emotion and language expected in sessions led by speech language pathologists, they are at the core of teaching how language and communication work to sustain relationships with others.

Social Expectations: Differences in Age Affect How People Treat You

Early intervention provides excellent initial treatment strategies that step our students onto the path to social functioning, yet it is really only the beginning of their social education. Many students who go through good early intervention programs and show improvement may well appear to get a bit worse rather than better with age. The reality is that we as a community are much more accepting of social awkwardness in younger children than in adolescents and adults. For children with social cognitive deficits, their disability becomes more obvious as they age, in large part because social behaviors shift to nuance and sophistication.

To help students make more sense of the information they are learning, they also need to realize how social expectations change with age. Children grow gradually, without realizing social rules evolve as well. They often think what they learned at six still applies to them when they are ten; this is not usually the case. For example, it is socially appropriate for six-year-olds to be in close physical contact when they are talking to others, to change the topic abruptly, and to be very distractible in their play. None of these skills are socially acceptable for a ten-year-old. Social expectations evolve, from childhood into adulthood, with each acquired skill building on the next.

Tom is a twenty-year-old man with a mild presentation of Asperger Syndrome. Unlike our stereotypes of individuals with Asperger Syndrome, Tom is a "cool" person who has tattoos and who experienced gang life earlier in his adolescence. Tom is also a determined person; he has clear career goals even though his lack of organizational skills and ability to see the big picture prevent him from taking the path of least resistance. Tom continues to live with his mother while working part-time and attending a junior college. He also has an active social life although his friends have "used" him on many occasions because of his social naiveté.

Tom arrived at one therapy session furious at his mother for setting a curfew for him. As I discussed the situation with Tom and his mother, it turned out that Tom was staying out until three in the morning on his mother's work days, making it difficult for her to sleep well and then be fresh for work in the morning. (Tom started his job later in the day.) Tom felt it was incredibly unfair of his mother to have a curfew for him since many of his younger friends had no curfew at all.

We worked with Tom to understand that the curfew originated not only from his mother's worries about him (he had managed to get arrested on previous occasions) but also her own need to be well rested for the next workday. While Tom could cognitively understand his mother's needs and concerns, he still was upset that he had a curfew when some of his younger peers did not. At this point I began to talk to Tom about how changes in our age also change the behavior that is expected from us. I explained that he was right; he basically should not have a curfew at twenty years of age because it is expected that a twenty-year-old can start to make decisions based on how his own behavior affects others. I encouraged both Tom and his mother to toss out the use of the word "curfew" from their vocabularies and exchange it for Tom setting "reasonable restrictions" on his own behavior. The reasonable restrictions were to be based on thinking about the needs of others as well as his own.

Tom liked the idea that he could take control of setting his own limits. We then discussed what time Tom thought he could be home to keep his mother comfortable with their living situation. Surprisingly, when Tom set his own restrictions, they were not too far off from his mother's curfew time.

Strategy: Work with students to compare and contrast the differences in socially accepted behaviors of various age groups: preschoolers, early elementary school students, late elementary school students, middle school students, high school students and adults. Have students observe others during recess, classroom breaks, or when watching videotapes about their peers, and discuss their different social behaviors. During the observations define the social behaviors they see as being appropriate and inappropriate across the changing years. Help students be aware of their own peer group and learn what is socially appropriate behavior within that group. Break behaviors into sets and help students learn each behavior in the set. This process encourages independence, so they can further help themselves step by step with other behavior sets.

Although we often have the goal of helping children approximate normal development, do not lose sight of the fact that each student is an individual first, on his own learning curve. Most students with social cognitive deficits are not able to approach functioning at the social level of their peers; they are the most difficult group of people to understand. Most of our students prefer to spend their time with people who are either significantly older or younger than themselves. To help students understand their own peer group, teach them to understand that different aged children are expected to have different sets of social behaviors, and then define for the student the behaviors belonging to his peer group. While it would be convenient to have this all written in a book, the reality is that peer groups share not only a developmental norm but also a cultural norm. The best way to gain access to information about a student's peer group is to go observe that group yourself.

Explore the concept of emotional maturity with middle and high school students. Most of our students perceived as immature are using the social code of young children. Those perceived as "more mature" use the social code of an older set of children. Those who are "emotionally mature" communicate their emotions more through words, and with greater

nuance, than they demonstrate the larger more elementary ones (anger, etc.)

Chores and Gift Buying As Treatment Strategies at Home

Raising and living with a child with social cognitive deficits can be hard on the family. The child with the social thinking deficits tends to be "ME focused" and has difficulty considering the needs or wants of other members of the family.

Individuals with social cognitive deficits often create distinct boundaries between their behavior and willingness to cooperate with the program at school and at home. While many of our children "pull it together" as best they can in the school environment, these same students can cause havoc at home. Our students consider completing homework assignments or chores as "beasts of burden" and they react strongly to their burdens. Families tend to cope by spending their energy on getting the child through the homework assignment and minimizing the child's participation in other less desirable activities, such as chores, that he or she is likely to complain about.

I have full respect for the hard work it takes to raise a child with social cognitive deficits, and I am careful not to assign a lot of extra work to a family that is already overwhelmed by the demands of parenting special-needs and typical-needs kids.

All that being said, it is important that all children, special-needs or typically developing, have at least

 one chore per day they must do around the house. This can be as simple as setting the table before dinner or sweeping the floor after dinner. By assigning chores and having children consistently engage

in them, we are encouraging them to partake in activities that make them think about the needs of others. We do a disservice to our students and families if we send the message to a child that the only thing important is behavior and skills related to success at school. Developing independence goes far beyond managing behavior at school; it also means knowing how to manage a home, negotiate with others, and tolerate participation in activities not of one's choosing.

If a child complains or becomes angry about the chore assignment, his reward should be for managing his behavior while doing the chore, rather than completion of the chore itself. If a family feels that adding a chore into the family's routine would "break the camel's back," I encourage them to adjust the child's homework load by talking to the teacher. When a student is frequently in need of a modified homework schedule, I encourage the accommodations or modifications be written directly into the Individual Education Plan (IEP) or 504 plan.

By the same token, it is also important that our students engage in the act of selecting gifts for friends and loved ones on appropriate occasions, rather than having the parents shop. Gift buying is another opportunity for students to think about what they know about another person, their likes and preferences, and then receive the natural reward of thanks for the presentation of the gift to the recipient.

The Social Fake: "Truth" and How It Plays into Social Expectations

A fascinating segment of social relatedness is exploring how genuinely interested each of us feels as we engage in social dialogue with others. Most of us are genuinely interested in getting to know another person even though we may not be fascinated by everything the other person has to say. In reality, we tolerate other people's conversational topics in order to pursue the highly prized social relationship, and

in doing so we often employ the "social fake." This is the intuitive ability of persons with good social cognitive skills to appear they are interested in their conversation partner's words, when actually they are not that intrigued. While this sounds horrible, it is, in fact, what good social communicators do on a regular basis. It's part of what we as a society consider "being polite."

At times students are taught that if they maintain a conversation and take turns with others they will enjoy the conversation. Many of our students learn to participate in some aspects of conversations at a fairly scripted level, but do not enjoy the process. Teaching children about the social fake clues them in on one of those 'hidden' social rules that govern our behaviors: that many people engage in conversations without enjoying all the messages shared, knowing that the real enjoyment is the emotional connection of the moment. The concept of the social fake also helps students learn the importance of nonverbal communication and how it either supports or negates what we are saying with words.

Many of our students believe the sole purpose of conversation is to learn more interesting information; their thinking is devoid of the notion that they are actually building a relationship through the reciprocal communication. As I work with older students we enjoy exploring the concept of the social fake. For students who consider themselves smart, I teach them the social fake is a way to "out-clever" other people by making others think you are interested, even if you are not!

In the clinic, when a student's mind starts to wander during a conversation with others (which happens often with this population), my response is: "You are not faking it well enough!" We then explore what they need to do with their bodies, faces, or words to help convince the conversational partner they are still interested in what this person has to say. This is one more way to teach the lesson that others form opinions about you even when you do not think they are thinking about you! When instructing a child to "fake it better," it should be said in a humorous tone, rather than punitive.

Not everything goes the way I plan. I was with a group of very bright high school students preparing to introduce the concept of how long a person can talk about themselves before everyone else tires of the topic. As the students settled in for the start of their therapy session, I began to talk about myself. With each student's attempt to broaden the topic, I brought it right back to talking only about me. The students continued to listen to me going on and on, nodding their heads, showing apparent interest in what I was saying, even asking questions to get me to talk more. Finally I stopped my monologue to ask if they were getting tired of my talking only about myself. They said they thought I was testing them to see how good they were at doing the social fake! Clearly, they had improved their skills in this area.

As I explain the social fake to people with good social cognitive skills, some look appalled and others laugh. On occasion parents react with concern that they want their child to truly enjoy the social experience, not fake it. The reality is that all good communicators are adept at faking their participation or interest in others at least some of the time, which is in part what makes them such good communicators. As we work with our students, it is important that we honestly dissect what we do socially and teach even the grimmest of realities, all with a dose of humor.

The Boring Moment

Another one of the "honest" social concepts is the boring moment. Students with social cognitive deficits tend to focus on their own wants and desires. Because of this they are less able to see themselves functioning as part of the group. In addition, all children live in an increasingly fast-paced world, where information presented through the media is delivered quickly through sound bytes, and even meals are presented as "fast food." All children, and especially our students, are increasingly unfamiliar with the idea that while boredom may not be fun, coping with it is expected in daily living!

As I observe mainstream classrooms, it consistently amazes me how well typically developing young children (first and second graders) have adapted to the concept of the boring moment throughout the school day. (This is not to say that school is always boring, but it is filled with plenty of boring moments during which children are expected to cooperate as part of one large classroom group, even though the students learn information at different rates and interest levels.) These little children will sit straight and continue to attend to the teacher, even when they fully understand what she is about to say next or have already completed their lesson.

Children with social cognitive deficits have much more difficulty tolerating boredom, and it shows through their class behavior. A classic example is not maintaining attention to the topic. These children also tend to blurt out, "This is boring!" expecting their comment will force educators to change the activities immediately. While it is always easiest to teach a child when he is fully engaged in a lesson, this is not part of what being in a mainstream public school classroom is about. To help children function in the mainstream and in society, we need to help them understand that the world does get boring, and they need to learn how to put up with it, without distracting others or themselves. Coping with boring moments is key to successfully holding a job later in life.

⧗

I was working with a group of second and third graders and introducing a concept for us to explore prior to playing a game that required the use of that concept. As I spoke about the concept a child blurted out, "This is boring!" I looked at the written schedule on the board and responded, "I am sorry, I forgot to write on the schedule that we would have a boring moment today!" I went on to explain that every day we would have to talk a little bit before we got to play our games. I would try not to make the discussion boring but if they thought it was boring, their job would be to try and listen and not distract others until the discussion was finished.

In another example, a ten-year-old boy was being very disruptive to the social thinking group in which he was participating. I was not his therapist for the group, but I did meet with him to discuss his behavior. I asked him why he was having a hard time being part of the social group when he reportedly did an excellent job being part of his group in his classroom. He protested, "It is so boring here until we start to play games!"

My response was, once again, to apologize for the fact that no one had told him there would be a boring moment, which was the time when the therapist leads a discussion about the targeted social concepts for the week. I then went on to explain that while I didn't think the therapist was trying to make it boring, if he thought it was boring we could call it the boring moment. The boring moment usually lasts for about ten minutes during each session. He then got to help make the schedule for the session, and I asked him, "Do you want the boring moment during the first ten minutes of the session or would you like to come play a bit before you have your boring moment?" He responded by saying he would like

to have the boring moment during the first 10 minutes! The child demonstrated much more tolerance in the group after our discussion.

Another example: having learned the above lessons from my students, I set up the schedule for my middle school community campers to include a boring moment the first fifteen minutes of each session. One day we had to leave early for the community and we skipped the boring moment, at which point a student commented on its absence from our schedule. I assured him we would do it when we got back to the clinic toward the end of the day. Later that day when we had time for the boring moment, we also worked on who was doing the social fake to get through it.

If you are not comfortable with the vocabulary created to describe these social realities, come up with your own that explores the concept from your point of view. Once you create the vocabulary, teach others to use it consistently across the day. The most important idea is that we do not try to teach our students that all interaction is fun and exciting. It isn't. When we act as though it is we lose their trust, and the students rightfully feel disappointed when they deal with the daily reality of social interactions.

Exploring Motive Through Hidden Agendas

Whether it is a bold-faced lie or subtle manipulation, people with stronger social thinking abilities use these tools well. Individuals whose Theory of Mind abilities tend more toward EPT often do not understand the concept of lying: they do not tell lies or understand those produced by others. For some students the ability to actually tell a lie is proof of the child's social cognitive developmental progress. Exploring the many shades of truth is an important lesson for older students.

⧗

Rick is a thirty-year-old, very able man, with high-functioning autism. He had a credit card in his name that his parents had shown him how to use. After using his card successfully on a limited basis, Rick became more confident and began to use it more often, finally amassing a debt of $3,000, which was difficult to pay off with his low-salaried job. Both his mother and I attempted to work with Rick to help him problem solve the situation, but it became very apparent how abstract the concept of credit cards is to a very literal mind.

Some of the many gaps in Rick's knowledge related to his belief in the advertisements credit card companies use. For example, after we visually mapped out and explained to Rick how credit card companies charge interest on the money they lend the customer, he summarized the lesson by saying, "Oh well, I will get rid of this one and get this other one because this other one says it gives free interest in its advertisements!" When we tried to explain to Rick that the credit card company was only offering free interest for up to six months as a promotion to try to get people interested in using the card, he was indignant stating, "Then they are lying!" because the company did not blatantly state the limited time for the free interest in their advertising campaign.

To help Rick we started a series of lessons on understanding the "hidden agenda." We defined hidden agenda to mean a secret plan, and the job of the student was to reveal the plan (motive). We also explained that having a hidden agenda is not always to encode untruthful information, but simply an indirect way to communicate basic facts. For example, when a man wants to ask a woman out on a date he may start by asking her about her job and hobbies.

At times, though, hidden agendas are used to encode less-than-admirable intents on the part of the communicator. All students with social cognitive deficits need lessons to help them understand that all people — the student included — have hidden motives or intent. The job of the communicator is to determine the hidden agenda of others, whether their underlying message is good or bad. A hidden agenda exists at any level of communication:

1. Human interactions

    a. Social relationships with friends and family

    b. Formal relationships (i.e., teacher and student)

    c. Relationships with strangers

        i. Verbal

        ii. Nonverbal

        iii. E-mail messages

2. Advertisements

    a. Print advertisements

    b. Television advertisements

    c. Telephone or door-to-door solicitors

    d. Product endorsements embedded in television shows and movies

Our children who end up being the target of teasers or bullies are generally those who have a great deal of trouble reading the hidden agendas. A common occurrence, unfortunately, is the socially savvy bully who targets the socially naïve child by saying he wants to play with him. The bully then asks that child to pull down his pants, which our student does without ever recognizing the hidden agenda of the bully until the child is publicly humiliated. Even then, he has a difficult time understanding the bully's less than humane intent.

The vocabulary of hidden agendas or secret plans can be infused into lessons, especially those that center on making inferences from communicative tools such as body language, facial expression, and words. This vocabulary has been discussed earlier in this book and in my other books. With younger children we call this, "reading people's plans."

Discussions about hidden agendas inevitably lead to discussions about the concept of truth. All children, at one time or another, are told not to lie. Nevertheless, when it comes to social interactions, completely truthful thoughts about the other person are not always greeted with enthusiasm by the recipient of the news! For example, a student I had not seen in a long time greeted me by saying, "Wow, your hair has really turned gray!" When I spoke to him about it, he replied by saying "I was just telling the truth!"

When students are honestly confused by when/when not to tell the truth, we need to explain that truth exists on a spectrum. On one end of the spectrum is "truth", in the middle are "white lies," and at the other end are "bold-faced lies"; this idea is illustrated in Handout 5. The concrete information presented in the worksheet provides examples of rules that are meant to be broken.

It is also important to help students understand that the communicative world is not the "black and white" place that our therapy lessons often make it appear to be. For example, we often tell students to be happy when other people win games, and we then tell the loser to tell the other student, "Good job!" However, the reality is that the student really doesn't feel happy to lose, and when we tell him to say "good job" he is really doing a bit of a white lie.

Helping older children understand this concept also helps them be more socially savvy about the world around them. While we certainly do not want to convey the message that it is expected they lie all the time, they do need to learn that in social circumstances their factual, truthful thoughts can be as painful to people as bold-faced lies. Learning how to present information to people so they still feel good in your presence is a skill worth exploring.

Handout 5

Truth is Not Always the Ultimate Goal!

Name _____ Date _____

Truth is what we are taught to share with all people at all times. Yet, if we always told the truth it would be difficult to find anyone who would want to be with us. Remember the time that you thought that someone had really bad breath, looked really bad in their clothing, or said something you thought made them sound dumb? What happens when you tell people exactly what your thoughts are about them? How does that make them feel about you? All people have their fair share of negative, as well as positive thoughts about each other. To be a person other people want to be around, you must learn how to express only the thoughts that make people feel safe or good when they are with you.

Bold-faced lies are to be avoided at all times. Some people are purposefully hurtful and will say mean things to you to get you upset or in trouble and to avoid getting themselves in trouble. Bold-faced liars are usually only thinking about themselves while intentionally hurting other people.

Below is one way to explore the very gray area between ultimate truth and bold-faced-lies.

$$\longleftarrow \hspace{8cm} \longrightarrow$$

TRUTH   WHITE LIES   BOLD-FACED LIES

Truth

Can be defined as describing what you believe to be the facts, exactly as you know them.

When would be an important time to tell the truth?

_____

White Lies

Can be defined as stating information that you feel is not the ultimate truth, but you do so to protect how other people would feel as long as the white lie does not cause harm to anyone in the long run.

When would be appropriate to tell a white lie?

_____

Bold-faced Lies

Can be defined as stating information you know to be false in order to protect yourself from people becoming angry or disappointed with you. Sometimes bold-faced lies unintentionally get other, innocent people, in trouble.

Why are bold-faced-lies never considered good options?

_____

Exploring Motives Through Truth in Advertising

Lessons should also be developed that explore ways in which advertisers market products; these are critical lessons for individuals working toward independence. The most readily accessible tools to teach these lessons are within the print media delivered to our homes: newspapers, magazines, and junk mail. Magazine advertisements are my tool of choice because of their high quality.

Like real communication, some advertisements are literal in nature and some are abstract. Those that are literal are selling exactly what is on the page. For example, in one advertisement there is a picture of a stomach being coated by pink medicine. This is a literal advertisement selling a product to soothe the stomach lining. Many of today's ads also market products abstractly by not directly telling you what they are selling. For example, one advertisement shows a family floating together on a raft in a pool even though the product being advertised was a family-style car. The abstract ads allow us to not only look for the hidden agenda, but to also point out all the clues that lead us to infer what they are selling.

I provide the students with a framework called LOOK, THINK, DO to decode the hidden agenda in advertising. This same framework can also be extremely helpful in decoding the meaning hidden in social interactions. This framework is presented in Handout 6, followed by Table 8, which summarizes the strategies for older students presented up until now in this chapter.

.

⧗

When working with a group of teenagers, we explored the meaning of a series of cigarette ads. While we could immediately see (LOOK) they were trying to sell cigarettes because everyone in the ads was smoking, we then had to THINK about what else they were trying to sell us by seeing all the skinny, young, and seemingly healthy people who were smoking in the ads. The students then summarized that the cigarette companies wanted us to buy their product with the secret meaning that they were trying to sell you on the idea that smoking would keep you skinny, healthy, and young. Therefore, if we believed the advertisements, what the cigarette companies want us to DO is buy cigarettes. We then discussed the idea of "truth in advertising," recognizing that just because something is printed in a magazine or newspaper, that does not mean it is true.

Thinking Through Hidden Agendas

LOOK

with your eyes to try to get clues from what you see.

THINK

about what you see to connect it to what else you already know.

DO

Do I believe this information to be true?

What should I DO with the information?

Table 8
Teaching Concepts for Facilitating Development of Perspective Taking
Ideas for older children and adults

- Thinking About You Thinking About Me: The Four Steps of Taking Another Person's Perspective

- All people have Thoughts About Others! The three ways people make impressions:

    1. By how they look

    2. By what they say

    3. By what they do

- Making a Video

- Making an Educated Guess

- Using the Rubber Chicken to Keep Students Thinking

- Establishing and Using Memories of Others in Our Social Relationships

- Making Educated Guesses Through Reading Other People's Reactions

- Using Our Experiences to Predict the Emotions and Knowledge of Others

- Exploring Social Expectations:
  How Differences Such As Your Gender and Age Affect How People Treat You

- Using Language to Develop and Sustain Relationships (chapter 7)

- Establishing Chores and Gift Buying As Necessary Treatment Strategies in the Home

- Exploring Truth and The Social Fake

- Lessons in Reality: The Boring Moment!

- Exploring Motive Through "Hidden Agendas" in our Social Relationships and in our Media

Ideas on Writing Goals and Objectives for this area of Treatment

Teaching Think, Know, and Guess:

Marilyn will demonstrate comprehension and use of the words "think, know, and guess" with 80% accuracy during activities that explore other people's thoughts.

a. Marilyn will demonstrate comprehension of the words "think, know and guess" by pointing correctly to pictures that demonstrate these concepts, with 80% accuracy. (For example, the student should point to a picture of the person who is looking at an ice cream cone and licking his lips, as opposed to another person in the picture who is not looking at the ice cream cone, when asked "Who is thinking that it would be nice to have an ice cream cone right now"?)

b. Marilyn will use the words "think, know, and guess" to describe the thoughts of other people pictured with 80% accuracy.

Teaching the JustMe and Thinking About You concept:

Benjamin will define the difference between being a "JustMe" verses a "Thinking of You person" with 90% accuracy.

a. Benjamin will monitor and describe the other student's "JustMe" versus "Thinking of You" behavior when in a group with 85% accuracy.

b. Benjamin will monitor and describe his own behavior as being "JustMe" or "Thinking of You" when in a group, with 80% accuracy upon request.

c. Benjamin will demonstrate "Thinking of You" behaviors related to cooperation in a group such as: calm turn taking, complimenting others' success, listening to others even though it is a

bit boring, keeping in close physical proximity, keeping his eyes thinking about what is going on in the group; with 75% accuracy and initial cues.

Teaching Whole Body Listening:

Shelby will demonstrate and describe how she pays attention and listens using her whole body 75% of the time with initial cues.

a. Shelby will describe, with 75% accuracy, how each part of her body (ears, eyes, brain, hands, feet, bottom) help her to listen to others.

b. Shelby will demonstrate how she listens with her whole body with initial cues, 75 % of the time.

Teaching Making Guesses:

Randi will make "smart" or "educated" guesses when directly questioned about information presented both visually and/or verbally, with 70% accuracy with initial cues.

a. Randi will describe the difference between a "smart guess" and an "I don't have a clue guess" with 70% accuracy.

b. Randi will be able to make smart guesses with 70% accuracy using visual cues such as graphic organizers.

c. Randi will make smart guesses 70% of the time with an initial cue.

Teaching about emotions and how they change:

Robyn will describe how people's emotions change based on what is going on around them (other people's behaviors or things that happen in the environment) with 75% accuracy.

a. Robyn will describe or demonstrate (either through physical demonstration or by using an emotion picture chart) how other people feel, based on different ways in which others are treating them, with 75% accuracy.

b. Robyn will describe how her own emotions change based on how others treat her, with 75% accuracy.

c. Robyn will increase her emotional vocabulary to include words such as "confused, embarrassed, frustrated, annoyed, excited," demonstrating knowledge and use of these words with 80% appropriateness.

Teaching Impression Making:

Alex will define the concept of "perspective taking" and how he makes impressions on others during free time and during class time.

a. Alex will increase his awareness of how his behavior affects others by explaining how he thinks others feel about him intermittently across the session, with 60% general accuracy.

b. Alex will define the three ways in which a person makes an impression on another (by what you say, how you look, and what you do).

c. Alex will define how others make an impression on him using these three same parameters, with 75% accuracy.

d. Alex will define how a specific behavior of his makes an impression on others with 65% accuracy and why that is important.

e. Alex will define how a specific behavior of another makes an impression on him, with 65% accuracy and discuss why that is important.

f. Alex will explore how he feels when he knows others have positive or negative thoughts about him.

Teaching the use of memory to sustain interactions:

Reesa will describe the importance of recalling key information about others, with 75 % accuracy.

Reesa will utilize information she has recalled about others to ask them questions about their areas of interest, with 75% accuracy.

Teaching about intent or hidden agendas:

Tania will describe the intent of a person's communicative interaction with 75% accuracy, when shown a variety of video clips both from movies or videotaped interactions in the clinic.

a. Tania will describe the key indicators in a person's tone of voice, body language, facial expression or chosen words that helped determine a person's intent, with 75% accuracy.

b. Tania will describe the intent of a character in a book, describing the key indicators that helped form that opinion, with 75% accuracy and initial cues.

c. Using a graphic organizer, Tania will complete the various sections to explore key indicators that help form a concept about a character's intent, with 75% accuracy and initial cues.

d. Tania will describe the difference between friendly teasing and mean-spirited teasing, describe the variety of ways these concepts can be demonstrated by their peers and role-play these concepts, with 75% accuracy.

Teaching about the different levels of truth and opinions when interacting with others:

a. Caleb will describe the difference between appropriate and inappropriate use of truth-telling, with 80% accuracy. Caleb will demonstrate the appropriate use of this skill 70% of the time.

b. Caleb will describe the difference between "white lies" that protect the feelings of others and "bold-faced lies" that only protect yourself, with 80% accuracy.

c. Max will verbally describe the difference between a fact and an opinion, with 80% accuracy.

d. Max will monitor the body language, tone of voice, facial expression, and words that others communicate, as well as his own personal talking time to determine when it is appropriate to share his opinion with 75% accuracy, and when it is appropriate to stop sharing his opinion with 50% accuracy.

General self-awareness goals:

Nick will journal his own thoughts and related experiences one time per week, with regard to the specific social relatedness areas he is working on to improve as noted in his other IEP goals. Increase Nick's ability to state what aspects of social communication he needs to work on in the group and at school to increase his own personal awareness of his treatment plan.

a. Given one specific social-communicative behavior, Erika will describe it and then monitor her own performance related to that behavior (self-monitor), with 80% accuracy without the use of videotape.

Summary

This chapter reviews a number of useful therapeutic approaches to introduce and facilitate the active use of perspective taking skills across a variety of situations. The goal of the lessons provided in this chapter is to make the implicit explicit by teaching parents and professionals how to think socially about the more intuitive social tasks we engage in on a daily basis and then break down and teach the task in a user friendly way to our students.

The beginning of the chapter provides information for working with younger elementary school-aged students; the later half of the chapter defines strategies for the older student. Relevant goals and objectives pertaining to these abstract concepts are offered.

Chapter 5
Communication Step 2: Establishing Physical Presence

All of our students are weak in the art of social interaction, which is usually equated to poor conversational skills. Traditionally, social skill therapy programs have focused on helping students develop awareness and use of their language during conversational exchanges.

During this teaching process students are often prompted to "stay on topic" across multiple turns. While verbal skills are vital to conversations, language alone does not create or destroy conversations.

Successful social interactions have as much to do with our bodies as our words. Table 9 offers a hierarchy of skills a person needs to establish and maintain a social experience.

It is essential that we help our students develop an awareness of communication skills in two areas: "physical proximity" (described in this chapter), and "thinking with your eyes" (more complex than "eye contact" and described in Chapter 6). These skills are vital to achieving success in all social interactions.

Physical Presence: The Basis of Social Interaction

While language is the exchange of ideas, physical presence is the gateway to forming an interactive relationship with another person in which ideas can be exchanged. It is fascinating to work with our students and observe their difficulties in physically sustaining interaction with another.

In this chapter we will define the concept of "physical presence" to include not only maintaining an appropriate physical distance (proximity) but also having one's body (shoulders, chest, feet, and head) facing in the direction of the partner. In a recent summer program for high-level middle-school students, our main goal was to keep the students functioning as a group by maintaining physical presence. Language used in that group was secondary to maintaining a physical partnership, whether we were in the clinic or the community.

Sally was a middle school girl with higher-functioning autism. She loved to swim, and on this day we had taken her group of summer club participants to the local community pool. Sally was pleased to demonstrate to the therapists her ability to swim using many different types of strokes, while the other students played together in the pool. Upon completion of her swimming demonstration she came and sat with the therapists exclaiming that she was tired. The therapists informed her that her job was to stay in close proximity to the other summer club participants. When she again repeated that she was tired, she was told she could go sit at the side of the pool and simply face in the direction of her friends. She sighed and then went and sat on the pool's edge, looking toward her friends who were playing together.

Within a single minute, her friends spontaneously noticed her sitting and watching. The whole group of five moved their game over in her direction. They then began throwing her the ball as she reentered the group interaction. Language did not establish this interaction; physical proximity was the key!

Establishing physical presence is the source from which interaction and conversation develop. The direction in which a person orients his body is an essential precursor to interaction. Fine-tuning this

Table 9

Hierarchy of Knowledge and Skills Needed to Foster a Social Relationship with Other Persons

Thinking about the other person:

a. If I have met this person before, what do I remember about this person?

    i. What are her interests?

    ii. Who is in her family?

    iii. Who are her other friends?

b. If I have not met this person before, I have to make some guesses about her:

    i. How old is the person?

    ii. What gender?

    iii. How is he or she feeling?

    iv. From what this person has said or how he or she looks, what might he or she be interested in?

    v. Does the person seem interested in me? (Is he or she looking at me?)

c. Establish a physical presence with the other person.

    i. Turn your shoulders, chest, feet, and head in the direction of the other person(s).

    ii. If entering into a group where two other persons are already talking, observe their bodies to see if they shift their physical presence to welcome you into the group.

    iii. Keep your body relaxed from your legs up through the top of your head.

Table 9 *(continued)*

Hierarchy of Knowledge and Skills Needed to Foster a
Social Relationship with Other Persons

d. Establish and maintain intermittent eye contact: think with your eyes.

  i. If you want to engage with another person, look toward that person's face to establish communicative intent.

  ii. Look at that person's face (cheeks, eyes, mouth, eyebrows) to try and discern emotional reactions.

  iii. If you are part of a group of more than two people, move your head and shift your eye gaze to track the speakers. This shows active interest.

  iv. Monitor the eye contact of the communicative partners. Are they distracted or focused on the people in the group? Do they show a preference for one person with their eye gaze?

e. Maintain interest in another person's topic/comments.

  i. Make comments or ask questions related to what the other person is talking about to acknowledge you are attending to what they are saying. (Chapter 7)

  ii. Create a bridge between what they are interested in talking about and what you are interested in talking about. Add your thoughts to connect to their thoughts.

  iii. Monitor your own talking time — avoid monopolizing a conversation.

concept begins with teaching students about the direction of their head, shoulders, torso, and feet as they start to relate with others.

⧗

Corey was a very bright student in high school but had difficulty relating to his peers. He desperately wanted to be part of a group at lunchtime. However, he was overwhelmed by the thought of interacting with up to eight people at one time. As part of his homework assignment he was asked to simply stand in the school courtyard at lunch and observe students in social groups. Through our discussions of his observations we noted that for students to succeed in a large social group it was necessary that they do the following:

1. Face their head and shoulders in the direction of the individual with whom they wish to communicate.

2. To join a pre-existing group, it was important to approach the group, slowly entering the group with one's body facing others. We noted that the group of people automatically "opened" their shoulders with a subtle turn of the body to allow the person who approached the group to enter.

3. Persist in keeping one's body turned toward others with one's face shifting between the speakers. Actively listen to their topic without immediately interjecting comments. Laugh when appropriate (usually when others are laughing.). Group members will acknowledge the presence of this other person by looking towards him. At this point, interject comments into the conversation if appropriate.

4. Another key observation was that large groups of people socializing together rarely communicated as one large group. For the most part, success in a large group meant that a person was successful communicating with one to two other people. Generally one large group naturally breaks into subsets of smaller groups that consist of two or three people.

5. Notice that people can actively be part of a group by sustaining physical presence and eye contact in a group. The reverse is NOT true; one does not sustain appropriate communication in a group if the physical presence and eye contact are not maintained.

A simple but effective activity to introduce this concept is to have the students stand together in a group; then the therapist introduces a topic for the students to discuss. When teaching social thinking we often work with students seated in chairs around a table, yet peer interactions in school often consist of standing or moving together in an open space. If you are working with younger children, many of them interact while running in play or sitting in an open space on the floor. Create natural settings with these younger children accordingly.

Whether they are standing or sitting on the floor, monitor the physical presence students establish (or fail to establish) with each other as they attempt to interact. Allow students to describe the body positioning of others and how it affects their own feelings/emotions and desire to communicate with the person. Begin with the position of feet, hips, shoulders, and head. Eventually you will want to explore the position of the face and, ultimately, the position of the eyes themselves. (See the section on "Thinking With Your Eyes" in Chapter 6.)

The importance of establishing a physical presence through proximity and subtle turns of the body cannot be over emphasized! It is essential that this concept be explored with students of all ages, preschool through adult. Even older students with high-level language skills need to understand and experience the importance of physical presence as a key to interactive social success.

Interestingly, our students often have a clear understanding and expectation of how **you** should physically approach and sustain a physical presence with them, but they often do not fully understand that others have the same set of expectations for **them**. The following ideas are useful in introducing this concept in clinical sessions:

Whole Body Listening

The concept of "whole body listening" helps children learn that you attend to information by using your whole body and not just your ears. With younger children we often work while they are sitting in a circle on the floor. Carpet squares are used to give the children a sense of physical boundaries. We discuss and demonstrate concepts such as: how you listen with your hands, by only using them to keep your mind focused but not distracted (meaning it is okay to fidget, but not to the point of distraction); your feet, by keeping them by your side and away from others; and your bottom, by sitting on it and not letting it roll up into the air. These easy exercises reinforce that we listen with far more than just our ears! A sweet book that explores this concept for preschool and early elementary school students is called *Can You Listen With Your Eyes?* (Everly, 2005).

This lesson can also be taught to the older child, but through discussion and analysis of videotape, either of their own social thinking group participants or of TV or movie clips that illustrate how other people "listen" to others with their entire body.

Children DO Understand!

It is important to proactively help students realize that they themselves have clear expectations about how other people use physical presence with them. A fun way to work on this is to upset what students expect to naturally occur. With young children who are seated in a circle, the teacher can come to the group and sit turned away from the group as she starts teaching her lesson. Very quickly the children will start to giggle and tell the teacher she is doing it wrong. The teacher can then ask the students to describe what appears to be wrong and how to fix it.

When I did this with a group of children, they immediately told me my head was facing the wrong way and I was supposed to look at the people in the group. I then kept my body turned away from the group, but I awkwardly turned my head so that I could see the students. I said, "Okay, now I am looking at you; let's keep going…" but the young students kept giggling, saying, "No, your body also has to face the group." I then turned myself around so I was completely in the group, and we observed each of the other students in the group to see if they were listening and speaking with their whole bodies.

One child in the group was not; she was rolled up in a ball with her bottom up in the air. We discussed how this child did not really feel like she was part of our group since she did not appear to be listening with her whole body. We could only see her bottom and that part of her body did not have ears or eyes!

When working with older students, I encourage them to think about their expectations of others, with regard to physical presence, when they enter a group. I do this by sitting or standing on the table in the classroom at the start of the lesson. I explain what we are going to do that day, but they cannot concentrate because they are so surprised to see me trying to teach them while standing on top of a table or desk. I continue for a couple of minutes and then stop after enough students ask me questions about what I think I am doing. I then lead a discussion about the expectations they have for other people when communicating. After that, I ask them to consider and monitor the expectations that others have for them as they communicate in the social thinking group.

My position on top of the table instills humor into the lesson and is not readily forgotten by the students. A girl I have worked with all year just recounted to her parents that she will never forget the first time she met me because I was standing on a table talking to them, acting like everything was normal.

Open and Closed Shoulders

Older students (third grade and above) need to learn how to enter and exit a group using their own body positioning and also "reading" the body language of others. We teach this by exploring how a person enters into a pre-existing discussion between two or more people. In the classroom, I have at least two persons stand and engage in a conversation while a student walks up to the group. We then observe what happens to the body positioning of the people who are already talking. We take note of the fact that a very subtle shift of position to open their shoulders, chest, and ultimately a turning of their feet occurs to show they welcome others into the group.

It is equally important to teach students that sometimes when you approach people who are talking, they don't shift their body, and their shoulders stay "closed" to the person who approaches. This indicates they don't want you to break into their conversation and you should walk away unless what you have to say is extremely important. In that case you say, "Excuse me, I just need to give you a quick message."

Students need to practice both parts of this conversational process: being the person who is entering into the group, as well as being the person being approached by another. This may seem so obvious to those of us without social challenges, but it is an extremely important concept to teach!

Discovering One's Zone of Comfort

The distance speakers stand from each other varies from culture to culture; in the U.S. it is about an arm's length away. Our students have difficulty determining this space intuitively. They often move in way too close, or stand too far away. Each person has his or her own internal "comfort zone" relating to how close or far away people should stand from them. Some activities to explore this concept include:

a. Have a child stand on a carpet square and have another person approach him. The student on the mat is then to indicate when he feels the other person has entered into his "private space." Measure the distance and see how close it is to the "one-arm rule." Have each student in the group stand on the mat and then compare the similarities or differences in their tolerance level for physical proximity. Encourage them to practice getting a sense of what it means to stand "one arm's length" away, without having the child extend his or her arm each time to measure.

b. Use hula-hoops to help children get a sense of walking around but maintaining a distance from another person. In this case each child holds a hula-hoop at his waist and then practices talking to others but maintaining the distance of the hula-hoop between them.

c. Encourage others to invade the personal space of each student and then encourage the student to talk about how it feels when others invaded his "private zone."

It is also important to remember (and teach!) that different environmental contexts or types of relationships may require a different understanding of personal space. For example, if you are in a crowded room or on a crowded bus, people will have to stand closer simply because we don't have the privilege of maintaining the rules of personal space in that context.

Different types of personal relationships also reflect different understandings related to personal space. An intimate relationship allows for people to become physically close, but only when both people agree to that degree of intimacy. Parent-child relationships often allow for more physical touch and hugging. Of course, the student must learn the difference between socially appropriate family hugs and touching versus inappropriate sexual touching. When working with our students, these "fine lines" need to be much more carefully considered and more clearly defined.

Furthermore, as children become teens, they need to learn to adjust the personal space they share with their parents, especially in public settings. Teens do not normally readily hug and kiss their parents in public.

Sitting As Part Of A Group

While I have emphasized that we need to practice standing and defining space in our interactions, we must also ensure that students understand the impact of their sitting postures when interacting with others.

Sally, a twelve-year-old girl, persistently felt "outside" the group. Other members of the group had developed a strong social relationship and increased their social chatter when sitting together. Sally always had her chair pulled about a foot away from the table, and she would sit with a slumped posture looking at her lap while the others girls talked.

At my insistence, I had Sally pull herself up to the table, letting her know that it was okay to slump as long as she slumped on the table (like the rest of the teenagers). Interestingly, when her body was pulled up to the table, the other girls naturally engaged with her more in the discussion, and Sally appeared to feel more open to participation. At the end of the session, each girl was to speak about something good they noticed in another. One of the girls looked at Sally and stated, "You were really part of the group today!"

Frank, a married man in his 40s with Asperger Syndrome, wanted to discuss why "no one ever listens to me" when he is in meetings at work. I asked him to create with blocks a model of how he and others were positioned during meetings. He set a block down to represent a table and placed corresponding blocks to represent two other people who sat at either end of the table, talking. He then put himself sitting along the side of the table, but he pulled his block further back from the table than the other two participants at the meeting.

When I asked him why he had pulled himself back, he stated he did not feel comfortable sitting directly in their line of vision. He also noted that his eyes usually were looking down into his lap, indicating that while his body was not pushed up to the table he also was not following the discussion with directed eye-gaze. When I asked if a fourth person ever came to the meeting he said "yes" and added another block to represent that person sitting across from him at the table. He then took his block and pulled it off to the side a bit. When I asked him why he did that, he indicated he was not comfortable with that person having direct visual gaze to him.

We then discussed how other members of the meeting might interpret his removed physical presence – they probably think he is not interested in the people in the meeting. Consequently, they may not be alerted to the fact that he wishes to speak, or they may feel that his comments would not be relevant. Furthermore, his lack of physical presence could be offensive to others, making them feel uncomfortable

In both of these examples, the first instinct would normally be to figure out what the clients are "saying" that is keeping them from successfully participating as part of the group. Before teachers or clinicians concern themselves with the spoken language they need to first consider how a person brings his or her body into the group!

Physical Presence : On the Move and Standing Still

While many of us work with students in our offices, sitting around tables, a reality is that many friendships are established and maintained on the move. A middle school student once asked me how other students seem to "magically" pop into groups when the bell rings at school. His question reminded me the importance of teaching students to be more actively aware of their physical presence, not just when directly engaged in conversa-

tion, but also when quietly hanging out as part of a group. Just as we can practice how to enter and exit physically from a group, we can practice how we just stand in a group.

Try standing very rigidly and communicating to another person with stiff legs, hips, arms, neck, and face. Very quickly you will notice that few people feel comfortable communicating with you.

Evaluate each of your students' physical presence when not talking. Do they respond with facial expression? Do they move their heads to look at the different communicative partners? Do they shift their weight back and forth from leg to leg? Identify people's different physical movement, then discuss and practice these subtle body movements with your students. Show movie clips of people to look at physical movement of actors. Make videotapes of your students' movement.

Students whose bodies are rigid or appear "locked" in position convey they are uptight. This may make others feel uncomfortable. Learning to relax our bodies as we communicate, and using our bodies to communicate emotional messages, is where drama and theater skills come into play.

Alongside these lessons, teach students that when standing and talking, communicative partners' bodies often shift in their positioning. Work with clients to learn to shift their stance or position when other people shift. For example, while standing and working with a group of teenaged boys, I shifted my position in the group to stand (deliberately) in front of another very bright boy in the group, blocking his body from all the other group members. Unfortunately, this boy did not move – he allowed me to stand right in front of him, without shifting his position to remain visible to the group.

We then discussed that when in a group, a social expectation exists that each of us adjust our physical positions to keep our bodies actively in the group, rather than allowing ourselves to be blocked out. We physically practiced adjusting our own body presence in a group, when other people's bodies shifted near us. At times, I teach our more shy students they have to "fight" to keep themselves in the group. They need to learn to be subtly assertive.

Try one or all of the above suggestions, or create some of your own. Just avoid lessons that teach students to become "talking heads," which means they learn to talk to people while always seated at a table. Our students need to learn to "talk and walk." Lessons on physical presence can be integrated into sessions across time. At first, just help them practice being more comfortable with their bodies. Eventually you can teach them to think about what their physical presence conveys to others while they are also engaged in talk. Like all lessons, these can be fun. But realize this type of social learning takes a significant amount of time. We are changing not just thinking, but accompanying physical actions.

⧗

Eileen was part of a middle school girls group that usually met by sitting around the therapy table. One day Eileen came to the group and asked, "How do the other kids magically pop into groups when the bell rings at school?" I told her she had a very good question, and explained that from here on out we would push the therapy table to the side and practice our social thinking and related skills while standing, sitting on the floor, or moving.

We began that day with my asking two of the four girls in the group to start to talk to each other about shopping at the mall. In the meantime, I had asked Eileen and Marilyn to stand off in the corners, and wait for further instruction. Once the first two girls began to converse, I pointed to Eileen and asked her to walk over and join the group. Eileen had a history of challenges with establishing eye contact and appropriate physical presence — on this day Eileen walked into the group with her face pointed to the ceiling, her arms rigidly glued to her sides, her chest pointed in the direction of the other girls and stiffly standing with legs together. She stood in the group staring at the ceiling.

At that moment I said, "Pause girls, we need a rule: 'Boobs do not enter first!'" The girls laughed and then we talked seriously for a moment, discussing that we enter conversation first with our body; this demonstrates to others we are thinking about them. Eileen then relaxed a bit, used more eye contact, and began to engage with the other girls.

Next I asked Marilyn to join the group. She left her post in the corner and began to talk loudly to the group about her favorite stores to shop in at the mall, talking to them before she even got to the group. As she did this I once again paused the group and said, "We need another rule; you have to enter as a nobody to become a somebody." We then explored the idea that we enter groups silently but observantly to be able to figure out the topic and how we can connect our thoughts to those already being discussed in the group. Then we wait to talk until an appropriate moment.

More on Teaching Physical Presence

It is one thing to approach familiar persons for social contact; it is a whole different experience for our students to approach unfamiliar people: for instance, those with whom we interact in community settings like the grocery store, the library, or a doctor's office. Once your students have had plenty of practice approaching familiar persons and are successful in their interactions, practice these same lessons with unfamiliar persons. Have a student go up to an unfamiliar person to ask him a question of importance to the student. The student is to learn to observe how quickly a person acknowledges and moves towards him once the student demonstrates a physical intent to communicate.

Joe, a 21-year-old master's student, reported great hesitation when having to go to a person with whom he is not familiar to ask questions. I took him to a large bookstore and had him approach the counter on numerous occasions with various questions such as "Where is the bathroom?" or "Where is the science fiction section?" We observed that within two seconds of Joe approaching the counter, turning his body towards the clerk and establishing a steady eye-gaze, the store clerk moved towards him asking how he could be of assistance. This communication appeared to be effortless for both Joe and the clerk.

When I discussed with Joe that I was wrong to assume that this was going to be difficult for him he responded, "I would like to tell you that I do this all the time, but the truth is I hardly ever do it and it is nice to know that I can!"

Being Part of a Group: There Goes My Body, There Goes His Brain!

Even when students grasp the importance of monitoring physical presence when they are with one or two other students, they still may not understand the importance of this social action when they are in a larger group. Our students tend to get lost in large groups. They feel that if no one is specifically paying attention to them, they do not have to pay attention either.

This becomes a problem in the school setting, where children are required to learn and socialize in the context of a group. Some of my students tell me they are "invisible" when they are in their classrooms — they believe that neither their peers nor their teachers notice them. I asked a boy who frequently tantrums in class, "Who notices you during your tantrums?" He replied, "Only my teacher."

Teaching students with social cognitive deficits requires us to consider the complexities involved in what we neurotypicals consider to be "simple situations." Our responsibility is then to teach our students the hidden information embedded in these seemingly simple, but truly complex situations.

One summer I led a "Social Thinking Day Camp" for a group of five children with social cognitive deficits. They ranged in age from eight to ten years old. Our mission was to teach them the hidden skills involved in establishing and maintaining social relationships. While the ultimate goal was for the children to verbally interact successfully with others, it was not the primary goal of this camp. Instead, our focus was on developing the knowledge that underlies social interaction: taking perspective of another and participating as part of a group. We began by exploring what it means to physically and cognitively be part of a group.

Most students with social cognitive challenges experience the mixed blessing of having their minds wander to thoughts of great interest to them. While this can lead to a highly motivating inner world, it diminishes social connectedness. As we conducted our day camp lessons, we watched as children impulsively and intermittently got up from the table and walked over to an object of interest in the room. Each time this happened it destroyed the group interaction. It was very frustrating to those of us trying to teach new teachers as we introduced a new concept to the campers.

Keeping in mind that we educators must take abstract concepts and make them concrete, I grabbed a big ball of play-dough and created from it five small balls, one to represent each of the campers. I then made two taller rectangular play-dough figures to represent the teachers in the room. I arranged the play-dough figures in a small circle on the center of the table and gave instructions that only the adults were allowed to touch them. I explained to the campers that each of the play-dough figures represented one of us, and that for all of us in camp to be part of the group, we needed to stay physically close, just like the play-dough figures.

Each time a student impulsively got up from the table to explore the room, I made his ball of play-dough roll off the table and followed with a comment that we were no longer a complete group. The student who had moved away from the table quickly returned to the group and also wanted to make sure his play-dough ball was re-established in the group formation on the table.

The lesson was that it was not good enough to say you were listening. (Some kids who wandered away from the table would say, "I can still hear you.") We explained if your body was not part of the group, you were not perceived by others as

being connected to that group. Furthermore, when your body is not in the group, even if you hear everything said, you are not following the plans (intent) of the group.

Interestingly, introducing the play-dough motivated the students to stay in their places and keep the whole group in close physical proximity. The students quickly adopted the vocabulary represented by the play-dough people. When a student left the group to go to the bathroom, the other group members wanted the play-dough figure to also leave the group until the child returned. We would describe this by saying, "His body is out of the group."

Students developed self-awareness that they were actually operating as a group, and it was a concept they sorely needed to learn! *It is fascinating to realize that we readily assume children know what it means to function as part of a group, yet many of our students with social cognitive deficits do not intuitively understand their role in that context.*

Our second challenge arose when I noticed that while the children were now maintaining "group physical presence," one boy had great difficulty keeping his attention on the group lesson. While we were playing at the table or talking about a certain topic, he would be looking away and talking to himself about dinosaurs.

I took the play-dough ball that represented this boy and divided it into one larger piece and one very small piece (the size of a grain of rice). I left the rice-sized piece in the collective circle of play-dough figures while I rolled the larger piece of play-dough out of the circle. I then explained that while it was great that everyone's body was still in the group, it was unfortunate that this boy's brain had "rolled away." While making that comment, I simultaneously rolled away the larger portion of his play-dough figure.

We discussed how other participants feel when someone's brain is not part of the group. The student whose brain wandered away immediately returned his attention to the group discussion. Furthermore, he clearly stated, "I want my brain to be part of the group!" I explained to him that group members can often see when someone's thoughts have "rolled out of the group."

(Figure 5 demonstrates how to introduce the play-dough lesson to the group.)

It was fascinating to watch the speed with which this concept was learned. The children began to actively observe where their own and others' bodies and brains were focusing in relation to the group. Campers would make comments such as, "Oops, I almost took my brain out of the group." Very quickly we were able to move from the visual representation to communicating this concept verbally: "Uh-oh, who is about to roll his brain out of the group?" After the initial play-dough lesson the campers were able to sustain this concept and discuss it without using the play-dough balls. This lesson not only worked on the importance of physical proximity but also joint attention.

After seeing the success of using play-dough to teach the concept of physical presence and maintaining attention while in a group, we became increasingly more creative. One boy in the group had a particularly difficult time maintaining eye contact. For that boy, we took his play-dough and created big eyeballs on it, to cue him to concentrate on using appropriate eye contact. (See Chapter 6 for more information on making eye contact and "Thinking with Your Eyes.")

A couple of boys continually wanted special attention. They repeatedly asked to be first to participate in group activities. When we made it clear that no one can always go first, each boy then made a big deal about wanting to be the

last. For these boys, we took their play-dough and stretched it out of the ball shape into a much larger, awkward shape. I then explained that by always seeking to be different from the rest in the group, they actually were trying to make themselves look "bigger" or "different" from the others. I then convey that when working together in a group, it is important that all group participants "stay the same size."

Using play-dough to concretely demonstrate abstract social concepts requires only a good imagination and a solid conceptual framework. I have since gone on to use play-dough people with students of all ages (even teenage boys!). Experience has shown that using this concrete visual strategy to teach basic group relationship skills is quite powerful.

For older children, an alternative to play-dough is Barbie dolls. One Barbie doll represents each child in the group, and if a child's brain rolls away, you can pull the head off the Barbie! However, to do this you should use imitation Barbie dolls, since it is almost impossible to pull the head off an original Barbie!

(Any effective therapy lesson requires that you keep students interested and laughing as you teach them about these abstract concepts. Have fun; be playful!)

Figure 5

The Use of Play-Dough to Illustrate
Physical and Cognitive Presence to the Group

The Set-up: Create play-dough balls to represent each student, a play-dough tower to represent each adult in the group.

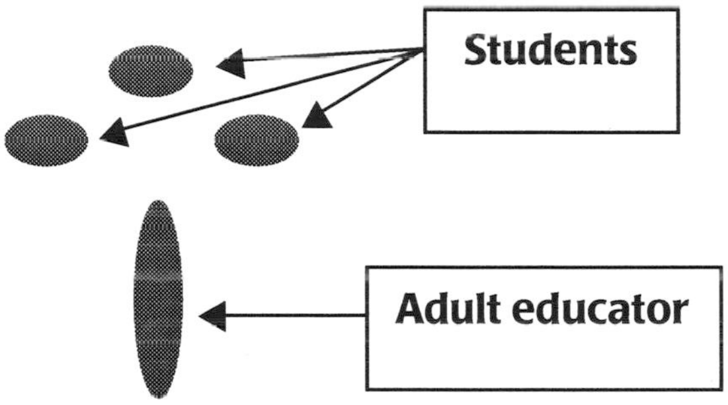

Students

Adult educator

Option 1:

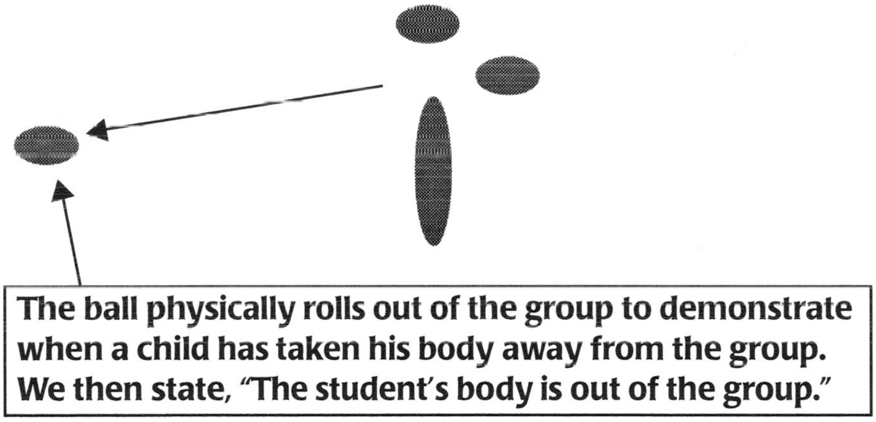

The ball physically rolls out of the group to demonstrate when a child has taken his body away from the group. We then state, "The student's body is out of the group."

Option 2:

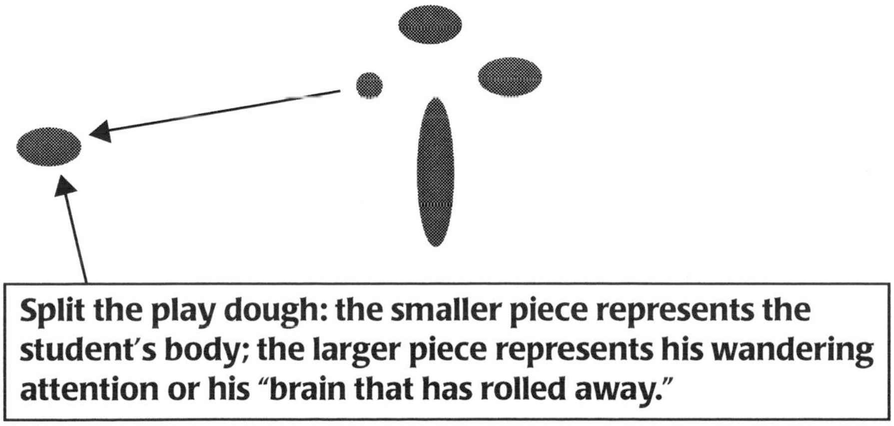

Split the play dough: the smaller piece represents the student's body; the larger piece represents his wandering attention or his "brain that has rolled away."

Goal Ideas for Physical Presence

1. Sam will describe what is meant by observing physical presence and facial expression of others to help understand the meaning of other's messages, with 85% accuracy.

2. Sam will establish an appropriate physical presence when participating as part of the group, 80% of the time.

3. When observing social scenes videotaped interactions or a movie with the sound turned off, Sam will accurately describe the implied meaning of the body language and facial expression of the people, with 80% accuracy.

4. Dirk will maintain the appropriate physical proximity when participating as part of the group, 80% of the time.

5. Given one specific social-communicative behavior related to physical presence, Erika will describe it and then monitor her own performance related to that behavior (self-monitor), with 80% accuracy with the use of a videotape.

6. Nick will increase his awareness of reading non-verbal cues of others by identifying which cues he will observe and then will accurately define these physical behaviors and their implied communicative intentions with 75% accuracy when watching a movie with the sound turned off.

7. Nick will self-monitor his own production of a specifically defined non-verbal communicative behavior (e.g. shoulder turn, shifting posture, etc.) with 75% accuracy when watching himself on video and 60% accuracy when having to monitor himself in the actual moment.

8. Joe will observe and be able to identify when other group members physically are part of the group with their eyes and thoughts as opposed to when they are not, with 90% accuracy as measured by directly asking the student to report.

Summary

Teaching the underlying physical concepts that support verbal interactions shows great promise in helping students interpret and participate more successfully in social interactions. The key to teaching these abstract concepts is to break them down and demonstrate them in visual and concrete ways. From my experience, the best lessons are those that also involve a bit of humor.

It also appears to be far more effective to teach why we are expected to use physical presence rather than constantly verbally reminding our students to employ each skill with cues such as "Join the group!" or "Pay attention!" This type of cueing only tells students what is expected of them in the moment, rather than fostering self-awareness of how their behavior affects their overall participation with others. It is important to remind ourselves that self-awareness is the first step in modifying behavioral and cognitive changes.

In this chapter we have also discussed specific education goals that can be written into a child's IEP in relation to teaching these abstract concepts. Some of them follow.

Chapter 6
Communication Step 3: Thinking with Your Eyes

Thinking With Your Eyes: Conveying Social Knowledge and Social Skill

Our higher functioning students lack social skills, not because they lack a desire to interact with others, but because they lack social cognitive knowledge. Exploring the skill we routinely call "eye contact" helps us better understand this point.

Establishing and maintaining eye contact in our daily relationships is a natural part of communication for those of us considered neurotypicals. Indeed, it is nearly impossible to avoid looking at the person to whom you are talking. Just as social interaction is forged through physical presence (see Chapter 5), it is maintained through eye contact or "directed eye-gaze." I prefer to use the term "directed eye-gaze"; it more accurately describes what we do. We don't look at people's eyes just to show them we are paying attention, we use eye-gaze to also decipher subtle but important information about how the interaction is progressing.

For the typical social communicator, the information gained through directed eye-gaze is critical to social communicative success. Eyes feed the brain information about the possible thoughts and/or reactions of others. Through the use of directed eye-gaze we are able to:

a. Monitor the emotional state of our interactive partner(s).

b. Consider whether the interactive partner is highly interested in the interaction or internally or externally distracted.

c. Monitor our interactive partner's interest in the topic being discussed.

d. Demonstrate our interest to our partner.

e. Distinguish the facial features of the person that help us recognize him or her in future meetings.

f. Demonstrate our attention to our partner (even if we are secretly thinking about other things!)

g. Explore the communicative context to determine the intent of a message: Does it carry true meaning or should we be alert to something else?

h. Synthesize all the above information to develop an appropriate response.

From the above list, it is apparent that directed eye-gaze helps a person "think with the eyes." Research substantiates that "seeing leads to knowing," even with chimpanzees (Emery, 2000). Emery explored a variety of ways in which the use of eyes establishes the lead in acquiring knowledge about others, including: mutual versus averted gaze, gaze following, joint attention, shared attention, and Theory of Mind.

Baron-Cohen, in his book *Mindblindness* (1995), discusses Eye Direction Detection (EDD) as one of the four steps toward mind reading, or what I call "perspective taking." EDD describes the fact that humans, as well as animals, detect when people look at them — that action establishes a physical arousal. We humans also consider the intent of eye-gaze directed at us and begin to form questions in our mind about the other person. EDD supports our ability to understand what others think and know. Students who are unable to detect others' eye movements and gazes lack the ability to develop more comprehensive perspective taking.

The previous chapter explored ways to teach the concepts related to thinking about what other persons are thinking. In this chapter, we explore lessons that link thinking with the eyes. It is virtually impossible to separate these synergistic concepts.

Development of Eye Contact and Abstract Communication in the Early Years

A critical milestone in the first year of life is the formation of a skill called "joint attention." Joint attention is the ability to follow someone's eyes to see what they are looking at, which then allows us to determine what they are thinking about. This skill typically develops by the age of nine to 12 months, after the infant has spent his first year learning to monitor the face, body, and emotions of his caregiver. Ninety percent of children who do not develop joint attention by age one are autistic (Jones and Carr, 2004).

While we traditionally celebrate more obvious developmental milestones in infancy — rolling over, crawling, walking, and speaking — we as a society do not celebrate the recognition of other people's thoughts and intentions, characterized by the development of joint attention. Once this skill is established, a cascade of other symbolic social communicative acts begin to emerge. For example, infants who are establishing joint attention begin to use an index finger to point (interrogative) to symbolically show others what they are thinking about. They begin to understand their caregivers' increasingly symbolic gestures (facial expressions, tone of voice, pointing). Further, they begin to "read other people's plans" and recognize their intentions. For example, a baby may get excited when she sees someone open a refrigerator, anticipating being fed a favorite food.

As if by magic, when a baby moves to this level she begins to use language to communicate her own intentions. At first she may say "dada" or "mama" to more efficiently gain her caregiver's attention. Then she begins to request desired objects and even comment about what is interesting to them. Intuitively she uses language in association with eye contact, understanding pre-linguistically that our eyes show people what we are thinking about.

Symbolic language slowly but surely moves toward more abstract and symbolic play in neurotypical kids. The developing abstract mind facilitates cognitive flexibility; children in their first couple of years are already considering what other people know and don't know. At this point language development blossoms beyond the confines of a child's own mind and shared imagination with others emerges. Children move from parallel play to interactive pretend play.

By age four, another critical milestone occurs: group imaginary and cooperative pretend play. Often overlooked, this enormous milestone is a precursor to successful classroom participation. It is also indicative of the ability to infer what other people mean by what they say, not only in face-to-face communication, but also in storybooks read during the early school years.

All of these developmental steps are rooted in joint attention — the ability to "think with our eyes" about what another person is thinking. Remarkably, we have no tests that probe this and other social cognitive developments in infants, pre-schoolers, school-age children, or adults. Yet we assume these skills are emerging or fully developed when children enter preschool, elementary school, secondary school, and when they enter the workforce as adults.

How to Teach Eye Contact or "Thinking With Your Eyes"

Students who avoid eye contact are traditionally encouraged to look at the person with whom they are speaking, as if this cue alone will teach them that seeing leads to knowing. The physical act of eye contact can be taught by reinforcing close approximations of looking at another person. When a child has poor eye contact, we generally teach him to get better at this skill by saying, "Look at me"; we then praise close attempts.

The question I pose to therapists and teachers is this: When the child does look at his communicative partner with "good eye contact," who feels better, the child or the partner? From my experience, it's the partner. Once the student does look, the partner internally feels the connection he or she needs to maintain the ongoing interaction.

Unfortunately, the student who required the cue in the first place usually still lacks the ability to make sense of what he sees or why he even needs to look at you!

It appears the origin of poor eye contact is not simply the lack of a skill, but the lack of associated social knowledge. If a student does not gain insight into another person through eye contact, then what is the motivation to maintain it?

Kyle was a ten-year-old boy with high-functioning autism and normal intelligence. He had very poor use of eye contact. His mother sat across the table from Kyle and me in all our therapy sessions. One day I was explaining to Kyle how to play a game where his mother would see things differently from how we saw them, because her game board showed the same information but in a different order. Neither team was allowed to look at each other's game board. Kyle and I were going to play against his mother. To help Kyle get used to the idea that his mother would see a different board from ours, I asked him to describe what his mother saw in the room, because she was sitting on the opposite side of the table. To my surprise, Kyle described not what his mother saw, but only what he saw!

This example illustrates how eye contact contributes to perspective taking. If a student does not have the insight that other people's eyes provide that person with a unique perspective on the world, then why bother to look at other people's eyes at all? What would be the purpose of eye contact if a student felt that all people saw exactly what the student saw? How limited are some of our students in their ability to understand that the eye movements of others indicate a shift in visual and cognitive perspective? How sensitive are these students to the visual movements of others' eyes?

Noting that Kyle was not able to understand that his mother saw the world differently based on her physical position, I then explored his deficits further. I asked him to stare at his mother's eyes and tell me where she was looking. I had his mother arbitrarily pick out points of reference in the therapy room and stare at them. Again, I was fascinated to see that Kyle did not understand that another person's physical eye movement indicated the person was looking in a different place. For example, when Kyle's mother was looking to the right, I asked him to tell me what she was looking at, or to point to what his mother was seeing. The result? Kyle made a series of completely random guesses about where his mother was looking in the room. Furthermore, Kyle had no understanding that knowing what other people see helps to figure out what other people are thinking about.

⧗

A six-year-old girl with high intelligence and a mild to moderate presentation of social pragmatic deficits visited my office. The parents described her most worrisome social behavior as producing tangential comments when interacting with peers.

During my initial interviews they never made mention of her weak eye contact. When I first met the girl she gave me a lovely social smile and looked directly at me. Her parents observed the rest of our interaction, during which time she demonstrated difficulty establishing any type of consistent directed eye-gaze toward me.

I told her I was going to play a game with her, and I wanted her to watch my eyes and tell me what I was looking at. I started by looking at the clock on the wall. She said I was looking at the ceiling. I then looked at a poster on the wall, and she thought I was looking out a window. The only time she accurately determined where I was looking was when I looked directly at her.

As we continued the assessment, we also found that she was extremely weak in her ability to formulate thoughts or questions about other people. Her parents were fascinated. Because the girl was better at giving them eye contact, they had not noticed how weak this skill was when she interacted with less familiar people. They also immediately saw how her lack of eye-thought association contributed to her larger social pragmatic problems.

Intrigued by these revelations, I began to explore the eye-thought association ability of many of the students who were coming to me for assessment. The assessment process was simple; I asked students to do two things:

1. Follow my eyes and point to or tell me where I was looking.

2. Make a guess and tell me what they thought I was thinking about.

In my clinic, almost all of my clients have high intellectual abilities but notable social cognitive deficits. As I continue to assess students I find that about 50% are weak in their ability to accurately respond to the above eye-thinking probes. Most of my students have the ability to understand that other people see the world differently from their perspective (unlike Kyle), yet it is astounding to learn how many struggle with the precision of direct eye-gaze.

⧗

Doug, an adult with Asperger Syndrome who is married and holds a research job in the community, meets with me on a monthly basis. He has spoken to me on many occasions about his difficulty recalling the faces of others and using eye contact consistently in his interpersonal relationships. On a whim, I asked him to follow my eyes and tell me what I was looking at. While I looked at a picture on the wall, Doug reported he thought I was looking at the hinge of the door two feet away from the picture!

Doug's difficulty in localizing eye movements of others, and subsequent difficulty in gaining knowledge about what others might be thinking, is a common deficit even for people with Asperger Syndrome who are considered intelligent. At dinner one night, I asked my two teenage daughters to tell me what I was seeing when I looked at a range of small objects in a cabinet by our dinner table. The precision they demonstrated was amazing. They were able to define what I was seeing within one to two inches of where I was looking.

Yet at the clinic, many of my clients were having difficulty locating an object within one to two feet of where I was looking! Clearly, a person's difficulties in gaining access to what other people are seeing affects his ability to understand others' thoughts. If we teach eye contact before the student has acquired the knowledge to support the skill, are we teaching the most efficient way?

This discussion illuminates the complexity of establishing meaningful eye contact. To help students learn to use this skill effectively we must better assess their deficits in this area, then define a more specific treatment program, one that teaches them knowledge about the "why" of eye contact, that eyes help us learn not only what others see, but also what others might be thinking.

Thinking With Your Eyes: Ideas for Therapeutic Intervention

The following concepts can help students learn more about meaningful eye contact or directed eye-gaze. As with any cognitive learning process, this is not a quick fix! Nevertheless, in my clinical work, teaching students the knowledge that is embedded in social thinking is proving to have long-term gains. Erin, a thirteen-year-old girl who has a strong desire to interact with peers, had very weak eye contact. At the end of her year in our social thinking group I asked her what she learned. She stated, "I learned what eyes mean. All my life people have told me to use good eye contact but I never knew what that meant before."

1. Eyes Are Like Arrows: Teaching students to localize what others are seeing.

a. If the student has very limited ability to locate where others are looking, the first step is to teach the concept, "Eyes are like arrows"; they point toward what people are looking at.

b. Teach about the eye itself by having the student look at a picture of eyeballs. Discuss how the white of the eye and the iris of the eye work together to show us in what direction the eyes are looking. Draw some eyes on paper, showing different gaze directions. Have the student then draw arrows to indicate the direction to which the eyes are pointing. (See Figure 6.)

c. Have the student practice making observations of what another person is looking at. If

possible, use another reliable student who can stare at one place for an extended period of time. Help the student notice the movement of the eye in the eye socket and then relate that to the direction in which the person is looking with the iris. In my experience, most children, even those with very poor eye contact who say they don't like to look at people's eyes, can stare into someone else's eyes when they are doing it for a defined purpose.

2. Teach that what a person is looking at is often what they are thinking about.

a. When a student reliably starts to tell you where another is looking, add the idea that where one looks is often associated with what one is thinking about. For example, when I look at the clock I am thinking about time; when I look at you I am thinking about you!

Charlie, an eight-year-old boy with probable Asperger Syndrome, was fascinated by carnivorous plants. He had few friends and was not able to converse about anyone else's ideas unless they related to his area of interest. In a therapy session I had encouraged him to talk about one of my hobbies, playing tennis. All my attempts to get him to discuss tennis resulted in him cleverly weaving his way back to carnivorous plants. I then asked him to tell me where I was looking. As I began to look at objects in the room, he was able to guess objects within two feet of where I was looking. His guesses were fairly random, but they were in the general vicinity. I then added the next step: I told him where I was looking and then I asked him what he thought I was thinking about based on where I was looking. When I told him I was looking at a picture on the wall, he replied, "You are thinking about tennis!" When I looked at a toy on the shelf, he said, "You are thinking about tennis," and when I looked at his school psychologist, he said, "You are thinking about tennis!" Clearly we needed to back up our lessons and break this concept down further!

b. Teach the student that you can often see his thoughts based on where he is looking.

I keep this very simple. At first I just want him to learn that I can see where he is looking. "I see you are looking at the candy." "I see you are looking at your mom."

It is fun to play with this idea. Let the student be the one to look at different objects and you make a guess where he is looking. You can then expand this concept to confirm continually that you probably know what he is thinking about. "Since I see you looking at the ball, I know you are probably thinking about the ball."

c. Bridge the concept of looking at objects to looking at the teacher. In lieu of saying, "Look at me," when I want a student to look toward me, I explain to the student:

"I see you are looking at the toys; that means you are thinking about the toys. What do I expect you to think about right now?" This generally is sufficient information for the student to quickly refocus her eyes on me. By doing this you are helping the child think more deeply about the meaning of the eyes.

3. Putting it together: I can see what you think!

a. Use photographs where you can see the eye-gaze direction of the people in the pictures. Have the student predict what the person in the photo is looking at based on where his eyes are looking. For example, a mom is looking at the girl; the mom is thinking about the girl.

b. Design activities where the student has to make a guess about what you are thinking at that moment. Constantly reiterate that what he sees about you (including your eye-gaze location) will enable him to make a good guess about what you are thinking.

c. In Chapter 7 we will discuss forming language based on what you know about another person, with many of your thoughts coming from what you observe in another.

4. The speaker versus the listener: Define the difference in the use of meaningful eye contact.

Much of the information upon which lessons in this book are based I learned from observing people engage socially in the community. At a Christmas party I realized that the use of eye contact varies depending on whether you are the speaker or the listener. Providing this real-life information to students is one more key to further awareness and knowledge about this concept and related skill.

a. The typical listener in a one-on-one situation needs to use his eyes as if they are laser beams. The listener focuses intently on the face of the speaker, especially in social communication. The slightest eye movements away from the speaker's face can indicate a distraction or lack of attention on the part of the listener.

b. The speaker can let her eyes wander while she is formulating and speaking the message, particularly if the speaker is saying something that requires deeper thought or language organization. It is accepted by listeners that speakers can have wandering eyes, indicating they are thinking intently about what they want to say. This is generally not taken as a sign that the speaker is distracted, unless she has a prolonged gaze in one particular direction or her gaze follows a moving object.

Establishing Norms by Observing All Children in a Specific Social Context

Demystifying the experience of social interaction is helpful. Breaking it down, step by step, creates a context in which this complex interaction can be understood. Nevertheless, each school or environment often has its own social culture and conventions. The best way to help students learn the non-verbal rules of the environment is to observe the interactions in that specific environment. They need to learn to be aware of the "hidden curriculum" or "hidden social rules" (Myles, Trautman, and Schelren, 2004).

I am often asked for the research that demonstrates the social pragmatic norms for a given grade level. While I think research is an invaluable tool to help us learn, I also believe that the norms for a child's peer group are established in the social settings in which the child participates. For example, if I am consulting on a third-grade child with Asperger Syndrome, I will often go observe him and all of his classmates in his classroom setting and during recess. It is only by observing the entire group that I will understand the therapeutic needs of the student with Asperger Syndrome. Social rules are context-based and cultural, not usually factual to carry over in all situations.

It is important for us all to remember, somewhat humorously, ALL CHILDREN NEED TO LEARN SOCIAL LESSONS. It is vitally important we understand a child's current stage of development and his environment, and anticipate issues that correspond to specific developmental phases.

For example, after raising two typical children who are now in high school and college, it is quite apparent to me that "normal" development means that all children in the middle school age bracket lose some of their ability to take perspective of others. They

become more egocentric and less tolerant of others. Then with continued maturation they slowly reacquire this skill with a more mature understanding of the needs of others as they grow into their young adult years.

Therefore, one cannot consider that being selfish or egocentric is necessarily unusual for middle school age students. We decide if it is a clinical problem based on the extent to which this lack of skill is demonstrated when compared to other typically developing peers.

The book *Can You Listen With Your Eyes* (Everly 2005) uses a bear to teach younger children this most important concept: we listen with far more than just our ears!

This lesson can also be taught to older children through discussion and analysis of videotape, either of their own social thinking group participants or TV or movie clips that help them observe how other people "listen" to others with their entire selves.

Figure 6

Teaching Students About Eye Movement

Use this diagram to show students how the eye movements of others are related to what the other person sees. The student should draw the arrows that are pictured below. (When I do this in my clinic, I hand draw the eyes on paper to start.)

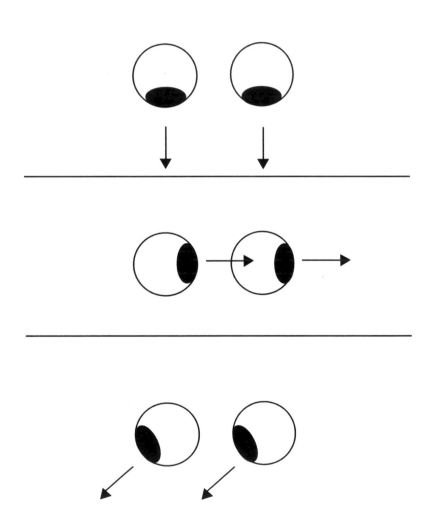

Goal Ideas for Thinking With Your Eyes

The following goals are useful in teaching these abstract concepts.

1. Brandon will orally define the concept of "thinking with your eyes" and demonstrate what it means when given a direct cue, 85% of the time.

2. Based on where a person is looking, Demetri will describe what he thinks the other person is thinking, with 80% accuracy (when looking at photographs, movie clips, and then other people with whom he is communicating).

3. When observing social scenes, Brandon will be able to tell the therapist the plan (intent) of the other person(s) based on where they are looking, with 80% accuracy.

4. Using his eyes to think about what other people are thinking, Tad will notice changes in other people's behavior and modify his own behavior to match the change, with 75% accuracy and initial discussion.

Summary

Communication never starts with words. It begins with taking the perspective of those with whom you desire to communicate. Then our bodies and eyes assume a communicative posture to facilitate the total communicative experience, considering "physical presence" and "thinking with your eyes."

It is crucial that the concepts covered in this chapter, no matter how simple they sound to the reader, be reviewed with the student's caregivers, both parents and educators. Students need considerable time and practice to process and apply this information. Even though this information sounds very basic it requires continual exploration and repetition across a variety of contexts for students of all ages and intellectual levels.

The ability to "think with your eyes" to determine the thoughts, feelings, and plans (motives/intents) of others is a core skill in human relatedness. The concept of teaching students to understand eye-gaze direction and the associated thoughts of others provides far more information than simply requiring them to "use eye contact."

This social cognitive skill plays an active role in all levels of personal face-to-face interaction. It functions synergistically alongside the other three steps of communication: thinking about others, physical presence, and use of language to relate to others.

Chapter 7
Communication Step 4:
Using Language to Develop and Sustain Relationships

What is Conversation?

Conversation is the foundation of social relationships. Many believe the ability to converse is nearly as easy as breathing – that it is a process that occurs spontaneously and intuitively. For most people, this is true.

Individuals with social cognitive deficits, however, teach us that this basic process we call "conversation" actually consists of an incredibly complicated array of skills woven together with subtle precision. A conversation requires skills similar to those possessed by a musician in an orchestra: the conversationalist has to read, interpret, and respond to another person, just as a musician reads, interprets, and responds to the music, his fellow musicians, and the conductor. While we understand that musicians spend years learning to play their instrument – and then learn how to play it in sync with a group – we often expect that the ability to converse should be a rapidly acquired skill, even for those who show obvious deficits in this area. In this chapter we discuss educational strategies that provide the much-needed conceptual conversational tools that allow our students to do more than just produce the conversational music.

Conversational success, or for that matter, all verbal communication, is based on social cognitive knowledge. It is not just the performance of certain skills. As students learn more about communicative interaction, or any type of human interaction, they must learn more about the cognitive processing through which the skills develop. Previous chapters helped define the nonverbal knowledge that feeds into our communicative success. This chapter explores how language is added to this nonverbal base of understanding to create more successful interactions.

Creating a Realistic Set of Treatment Goals and Objectives

Working on successful conversations is **never** a starting point in our therapy sessions, nor is conversational success the ultimate goal of our sessions during the early years of therapy. Rather, our goals for these students are related to helping them become better social thinkers, as well as teaching them to learn an array of related verbal and nonverbal skills. All that being said, the focus of many students' IEPs relate specifically to the student's ability to succeed at conversations.

Unfortunately, when we push a child to demonstrate conversational success we are pushing the child to perform skills he does not have the knowledge or understanding to support. When children demonstrate skills in the therapy room such as "eye contact," but lack the related underlying knowledge, generalization of the skill into different settings outside the therapy room is virtually impossible.

IEP meetings occur at least annually to review the special education program established for a child. When IEP team members write goals that cannot be met within a year or possibly a lifetime I refer to them as "Wish and Prayer" goals. Wish and Prayer goals sound good when they are being written, but they are a source of frustration for the student, teacher, and parent when the subsequent year's IEP approaches and the child is not able to meet – or even come close to meeting – the goals and objectives presented previously.

The following example describes some of these "Wish and Prayer" goals written into a child's IEP. No relevant strategies were provided to help the child learn skills that might enable him to reach any of these goals within the school year.

⧗

Charles is going into third grade. He is generally a cheerful boy with high-functioning autism. He has the typical intellectual discrepancy expected of a student with his diagnosis. On the Wechsler Intelligence Scales he has a full scale of 84, his performance scale is 99, and his verbal scale is 73. These scores indicate he has borderline average cognitive development. He has a full time 1:1 aide in a fully included classroom setting. He demonstrates high anxiety during times of transition, which include having to talk to people unfamiliar to him. At these times his speech becomes highly repetitive. He has a significant deficit in his ability to understand what other people think or how they view the world; he is close to functioning as SIPT with regard to perspective taking. The following IEP goals were written for his social development through his speech and language program.

Goal 1: The student will develop age appropriate social language skills.

   Benchmark 1: The student will demonstrate appropriate eye contact during greetings and farewells in eight out of ten observations.

   Benchmark 2: The student will increase eye contact during conversation. Prompting will decrease to one prompt during four to six continuous reciprocal interactions.

   Benchmark 3: The student will demonstrate turn taking during conversations in five out of eight observations.

   Benchmark 4: The student will demonstrate "good communication body language" (face the speaker, head nods, listening noises, facial expressions) during a five-minute conversation in five out of eight observations.

   Benchmark 5: The student will express feelings using words (i.e., angry, frustrated, happy, glad, etc.) in situations that would ordinarily be upsetting in four out of eight observations.

   Benchmark 6: The student will begin to verbally provide solutions to situations that are upsetting in four out of eight observations.

While these goals address the areas of concern, they are not realistic given Charles' level of functioning. Areas of concern need to be explored to determine accurately what is preventing the child from performing the skill. In Charles's case, the educators should explore:

• How well he understands the meaning of other's eyes,

• How well he is able to use information he sees to make accurate assessments about others,

• How well he is able to shift his thinking to focus on the thoughts or interests of another person,

• The physical presence of his body to initiate and maintain communication, and

• What type of language he uses when he is communicating.

When writing goals, we need to establish smaller steps for teaching this information to Charles so he can learn to think about the underlying concepts while practicing very specific skills.

⧗

Joe is a five-year-old boy enrolled in kindergarten. He had received excellent early intervention and preschool services, but the family recently moved to a new community where they found it difficult for one of the administrators to understand Joe's need for any services, even though the teacher and principal were very supportive of Joe's needs. Joe has a diagnosis of very high-functioning autism; he appears to have normal intelligence.

The parents worked hard to convince the school district of their child's needs, including an expensive reevaluation by a trusted psychologist in their new community. When the school administrator finally acknowledged

Joe's need for services, his teacher described Joe as "having a very hard time socially in his kindergarten class." He often hits, kicks, or bites his classmates. He often rolls on the floor or under his chair. His speech and language therapist wrote, "Joe's language disorder interferes with understanding of oral directions and/or questions, peer interactions, and giving appropriate responses in the classroom environment." He also qualified for services from an occupational therapist to address fine and visual motor skills.

The IEP goals written by the special education teacher for increasing social relatedness in the classroom included:

Goal 1: Joe will improve social behaviors.

Benchmark 1: When faced with a transition that he knows about ahead of time, Joe will redirect himself with not more than one prompt and with no arguments on seven out of ten occasions by 1/02.

Benchmark 2: During a quiet activity time, Joe will sit appropriately at his desk and attend to the task with no more than two prompts by 1/02.

Benchmark 3: Joe will express frustrations and communication in an appropriate way on seven out of ten occasions by 1/02.

The IEP goals written for increasing social relatedness by the speech therapist included:

Goal 2: Joe will improve his pragmatic skills in the classroom and in small group settings.

Benchmark 1: Joe will make eye contact when someone is approaching or speaking to him and will address others using their name with 90% accuracy as judged by SLP or other school personnel.

Benchmark 2: Joe will practice the rules of conversation in structured, small group situations. He will exchange appropriate information, maintain a

topic, take turns, and enter and exit a conversation with increased accuracy as judged by the SLP and appropriate school personnel.

The examples above demonstrate a Wish and Prayer approach to helping students with significant deficits in social cognition overcome their obstacles. While no one can dispute that these goals and benchmarks encapsulate what we truly want for these children, they are not goals and benchmarks that speak to the specific underlying gaps in knowledge and skill that each of these children present.

How will the student develop the appropriate behaviors discussed in the above goals? It is easy enough to say in an IEP meeting that we want the student to behave appropriately, but what does that mean for the student? The team should define what part of appropriateness they want him to accomplish. Should it be that he just stays seated in his chair rather than under the desk? If that is what is meant, that is what should be written into the IEP. IEP goals that encourage social relatedness should be explicit. They serve as an "alternative educational strategy" to assist the team in focusing on core social thinking concepts. These concepts should be applied broadly across all environments.

Students such as Joe and Charles, with IEP goals such as those above can be found on every school campus. While the intent of educators to help these children is clearly visible, the need to address social thinking information at a more fundamental level and through a step-by-step teaching process is critical through all stages of functioning and development for these students.

Our therapeutic and educational programs are gradually moving in the direction of incorporating the verbal and nonverbal skills needed for social relationships. Helping our students achieve independence in this area however, requires us to do more than use Wish and Prayer thinking. We must approach the realm of social knowledge as a conductor, analyzing each individual piece that makes up whatever we want the ultimate outcome to be and then teaching and guiding the student every step of the way.

Conversations that explore the interests of all participants are products of social knowledge. Our therapeutic time is valuable and expensive; it is best spent exploring social thinking concepts that are the foundation of conversation.

The Mechanics of Conversations: Questions and Comments

Comments and questions create the social rhythm of language. The ability to produce related comments and questions to form ongoing communication is not necessarily related to a person's overall command of language. For example, many of our students with social cognitive deficits score extremely well on expressive and receptive tests of language, but they cannot generate language to sustain a conversation or even produce effective basic interpersonal communication such as asking for help.

For these students, we should teach them about these language structures (types of comments and questions) to help them learn the *function* of their communication.

Figure 7 outlines these categories and the importance of perspective taking.

Questions: Creating Conversational Knowledge

We use questions to seek information about and from others. Many conversations begin with "small talk," a process of making quick inquiries about a range of topics as conversationalists explore areas they can potentially talk further upon. Asking and responding to a range of questions is the nature of small talk. Individuals with social cognitive deficits often have a strong disdain for this conversational phenomenon.

Beyond small talk, asking questions allows us to gain access to new information, or probe deeper into the topic being discussed. Questions allow the listener to control the content of the information the speaker is delivering. Questions are fundamental to learning about others and our world.

Our students learn the use of questions as a way to use language to relate to others. Students start by learning to ask other people questions about their areas of interest. This guides students toward thinking about others when using language. All students with social cognitive deficits need to review these lessons, regardless of how old they are or how well they do on standardized assessments.

The Special Case of the "Why" Question

For students with language delays it is appropriate to assess their comprehension of the different forms of questions. For students with autism, many have difficulty understanding and using interrogatives or inquiry words, especially when requesting more than their immediate wants or desires.

Most of our students with stronger language skills understand the meaning of questions as well as their purpose in gaining information about their particular areas of interest — with the possible exception of "why" questions. Answering "why" questions requires a gestalt-oriented comprehension of the topic in order to provide a complete response.

Figure 7

Language Forms Used in Conversation

Comments:

1. Supportive comments
   - a. Verbal
   - b. Nonverbal
2. Add-on comments
3. Add a thought

Questions:
Exploring the wh--- words

1. Classic social greeting questions
2. Questions about the other person to initiate an interaction
3. Follow up questions
4. Baiting questions

Keeping Perspective:

In conversations or less formal dialogues, the types of comments and questions utilized stem from thinking about other people and how they are thinking about you!

⧗

When working with an eleven-year-old student with high-functioning autism who attended a mainstream classroom and tested within normal limits on his reading achievement scales, we explored how to respond to questions beginning with the word "why." One day I asked him to respond to "Why are some rooms dark during the day even though they have windows to the outside?" His initial response was, "I don't know." I then demonstrated this idea by turning out the lights in our therapy room, which then became nearly dark even though there was a window in the room. He was still unable to explain why the room became dark.

To help the student respond, we explored what information he knew about windows and wrote the information on a graphic organizer. He was able to state that windows open and close, allow light into rooms, and often have window coverings like curtains to keep the light out. He clearly conveyed he had knowledge of windows even though he required verbal cues to organize his knowledge. But even when the graphic organizer laid out the information he knew, he continued to have difficulty answering the "why" question. His general response was to repeat the facts as he knew them, and then when I repeated the question while showing him the graphic organizer, he would respond, "I don't know."

With moderate cues he was finally able to answer the question. With repeated practice using a number of exemplars, his ability to respond to "why" questions improved significantly as he began to recognize how to connect what he knew to more largely organized concepts (gestalts.)

The use of graphic organizers or concept maps is critical for teaching students how to think conceptually, such as when answering why questions. Figure 8 demonstrates the type of concept map we used in the above scenario.

Formulating Questions

While our students are familiar with the "wh" words (who, what, where, etc.), many are inexperienced in how to use these words to connect socially with another person. Help students by reminding them of the words, using index cards with the words printed on them to provide visual cues. You can either write each word on a separate index card or list all the words on one card. Practice choosing a topic and then exploring all the interrogatives the student can think of to gain further information about the topic. This is not yet done in the setting of a conversation; it is done purely to introduce the student to using these question words to probe for information on a variety of topics.

As we study how these specific question words are used to create conversation, it is important that students realize there are different purposes for questions, and that we use these questions to figure out what people think. Students can learn that not all questions carry the same value in social interaction. Questions used while interacting socially involve seeking information about another person while simultaneously monitoring how that person is reacting and responding to what you have said (a perspective taking task.) The information below summarizes some of the primary forms of questions we use in day-to-day conversation. This is also reviewed in Table 10.

Classic Social Greeting Questions

Classic social greetings involve the rapid exchange of questions about the other person, including "Hi, how are you?" "Fine, how are you?" Many of our younger students need to be taught this purely routine exchange of words and why we do it: to acknowledge another person. Social greetings are a language-based form of acknowledging, "I am thinking about you and you should be thinking about me."

Figure 8
Mapping Out "Why" Questions

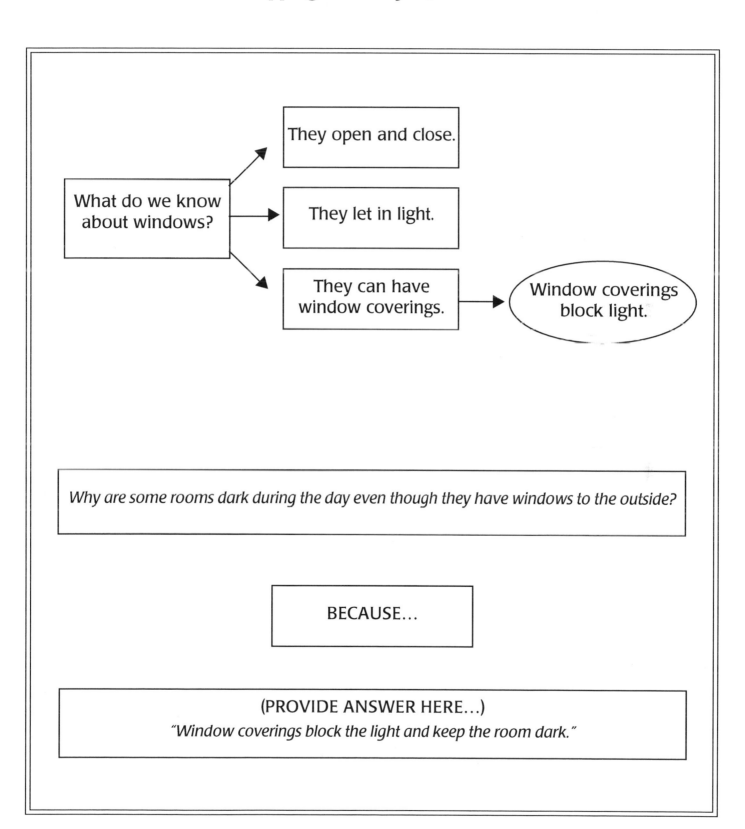

If a person passes one of our students and asks him how he is doing and our student does not respond, this indicates to the initiator that the student has little interest in him (even though this may not be a correct assumption if the student is lacking in his development of perspective taking.) Our primary lesson with this question form is that while it is important to respond to someone else's greeting by returning the greeting, it is not important to give an actual, truthful response! The response simply verbally encodes an act of perspective taking. For example, it is expected that when an acquaintance asks, "How are you?" you should generally respond with "fine" or "okay" even when you feel worse than that. It is only with your close friends that you would tell them how horribly you really feel.

A young man I was recently talking to explained that for years he stumbled over the greeting "What's up?" He said each time a person said that to him he became confused and wanted to reply with a very literal response describing what he has been up to. He has now learned that he should just say, "Nothing, what's up with you?", but he continues to struggle to make sense of it.

Questions to Initiate an Interaction

Scripting is an approach where we give students very clear, concrete information telling them exactly what they should say in response to specific information. Questions to initiate a social interaction are the most easily scripted. For example, whenever a student meets someone for the first time he or she can inquire, "What do you like to do?" after the initial social greeting. If the scripting approach is being used, scripts need to be updated from time to time since they become stale or overused. Nevertheless, they can be a good way for the student to develop confidence in initiating social language when talking to a less familiar person.

When teaching students to ask questions to engage another person, a primary rule is that their initial questions should seek information about the other person. For example, the student can ask, "What did you do last night?" In reality, all people do not start conversations this way, but because we are infusing the idea of thinking about someone else into our lessons, we teach this strategy first in our therapeutic sessions.

Questions to Probe for Deeper Information and Sustain a Topic: "Follow-Up Questions"

Students with social cognitive deficits have difficulty questioning a person about a topic not of their own interest. Our students may ask another person one question about his or her interests but then fail to follow up with other questions to learn more about the topic or the person.

Many of our students have limited ability to engage in social wondering. They accept information at face value and don't realize how little they know about another's experience. Inquiring about another's experience implies you are interested in that person. We work with students on learning that conversation relates to "sharing an imagination" by imagining another person's experience, thoughts, and emotions, and then asking questions to clarify what we still don't know.

A sidebar lesson to the above is teaching students that *we are not supposed to know this information.* We can never really know what another person thinks, but by asking questions we show an interest in the other person and his thoughts and ideas. This helps us learn about other people's experiences and points of view.

Table 10

Questions Used to Engage Others in Social Interaction

The classic social greeting:

⊙ "Hi, how are you?" or "What's up?"

To initiate an interaction:

⊙ "What have you been up to lately?"

To probe for deeper information and sustain a topic:

⊙ "What did you do when you went to Lake Tahoe?"

To take control of the topic (baiting or bridging question):

⊙ A conversation partner is talking about New York, and your student inquires, "Have you ever been to Hawaii?"

Questions that actually form a comment:

⊙ "Wow, did you really do that?"

Note: Appropriate questions are not just scripted responses, but language-formulated when thinking about the thoughts or experiences of others.

⧗

During a recent summer program, the middle-school students were sitting together quietly at the start of a new day's session. I encouraged them to ask some questions of each other to find out what each person did during the days we had not been together. Cathy looked at Mary and said, "What did you do this weekend?" When Mary responded, "I went to a concert," Cathy said, "Oh" and became quiet. I directly cued Cathy by saying, "Hmmm, that makes me think of a question!" Cathy then looked at Mary and said, "Oh yeah. What concert did you go to?" When Mary replied, "The Beach Boys," another person in the group became excited and they started to talk about The Beach Boys' music. Cathy continued to sit silently while all of the other students in the group continued to talk about music groups. I finally asked Cathy whether she knew what type of music The Beach Boys played, and she shook her head "no". I asked her how she could put that thought into a question. She then looked at the group and asked, "What type of music do they play?" at which point a couple of people started to sing one of their songs while Cathy smiled, having finally connected with the group.

The lack of follow through in our students' language implies a lack of interest in others, even though this may not be the case. It also prevents them from gaining access to deeper information they could use to learn more about another person. Teaching our students to wonder about another's experience and to think in questions is critical to helping them expand their discussions with and about others. Use the Conversation Tree (see Figure 10) to further teach the concept. Once students refine their ability to talk to others by inquiring about others, a strategy called Paper Clips and Thumbtacks can be employed. Both the Conversation Tree and Paper Clips and Thumbtacks lessons are reviewed toward the end of this chapter.

"Baiting" or "Bridging" Questions

The stage had been set for the middle-school students to get to know each other by asking questions. I gave each student in the group two colored blocks and told them to collectively build a "question tower" by asking a question of another person about that person. Each time a person asked a question of another person, he or she placed his block on the tower. When each person had used his two blocks he could no longer ask questions, but each person had to use his blocks before we could go on to the next activity.

Roger volunteered to start. He then said to me, "I don't know how to start!" After I reviewed with him what constitutes a social thinking question, he then looked at the group and asked, "Has anyone ever thought about freezing gophers cryogenically?" The other students looked at him blankly not knowing how to answer the question, with few knowing what cryogenics is. They all realized that Roger wasn't thinking about them!

Roger's attempt to ask another group member a question about him or herself was not successful given his continued focus on his own area of interest. (We all learned a lot about cryogenics that summer!) What he needed to do was ask an initiating question to encourage the others in the group to introduce topics they could relate to. However, Roger continued to use questions to encourage people to talk about his own area of interest. Roger was using a "baiting" or "bridging" question to maintain his control over the topic.

Bridging questions attempt to "bait" others into talking about what the speaker wants to talk about. The questions follow the intent and thoughts of the speaker, rather than the speaker following the intents and thoughts of the others in the group. Baiting or bridging questions are not "illegal conversational maneuvers," but students need to self-monitor and balance these with socially relevant initiating and follow-up questions. Those who only ask baiting or bridging questions are quickly perceived as self-centered and not interested in what others think or experience.

Lessons on baiting and bridging questions are some of the last lessons taught when dissecting the language of conversation. After working with students to show them that language carries the hidden intent of showing interest in others, I then delight them with the idea that language can also be used to talk about what interests *them*, in moderation. The section below on bridging comments provides more detail.

Comments:
Creating the Conversational Glue

Like questions, comments can also be dissected to teach students these more meaningful and deliberate forms of language. When we write goals such as, "a child will maintain the topic through four conversational turns" we assume children can simply make relevant comments during a conversation. However, making related comments to sustain a topic actually requires the speaker and listener to maintain a shared point of reference and appreciation of each other's perspective. As we are discovering, what appears simple on the surface is actually quite complicated. Why would anyone maintain a topic if he didn't think about the interests or needs of his communicative partner?

Start by teaching students how and why to use questions as an initial tool in interacting with others. Nevertheless, after the initial lessons on initiating questions, it is important to contrast questions with comments. Teaching about the different forms of comments becomes intertwined with lessons on asking questions.

Supportive Comments

Supportive comments are communicative signals made by the listener to show the speaker she is following or appreciating what he is saying. Supportive comments can be nonverbal as well as verbal in nature, and they are not always happy looking in appearance. When a speaker is discussing a sad topic or a personal problem, it is important that the listener's comments demonstrate support for the content of the topic, rather than having the listener looking happy for the opportunity to be interacting with another person.

For example, as the listener follows the speaker he can nod his head in agreement, smile at the funny parts of the speaker's message, frown during a sad message, or verbalize little comments to connect with the speaker's message: "Wow," "Cool," "Oh no!" or "Uh huh." Students need to appreciate the power of small signals to the speaker that demonstrate the listener is engaged in the topic.

Most supportive comments originate from a minimally verbal — or nonverbal — mode of communication. This is an opportunity to review the variables that contribute to how a communicative message is interpreted, as shown in Table 11.

Videotaping students as they engage in communication is extremely helpful when practicing these question and comment forms, or when advancing to practicing at the conversational level. The videotape provides an excellent opportunity for students to get direct feedback on how they objectively look to others.

Michael, thirty-year-old adult, had completed a worksheet on how to formulate language to talk to his mother about topics that were of interest to her. After his initial difficulty thinking of things that she liked to talk about, he was

able to formulate a list of questions to ask his mom. I then videotaped Michael talking to his mother with one rule: the conversation could only be about her.

Michael did a stellar job with his verbal comments and questions to maintain topics based on his mother's interests. His mother even remarked at the completion of the conversation that it was the first time Michael had ever had a conversation with her that was about her.

Nevertheless, the videotape showed his body and face communicating messages of boredom throughout the conversational process. Michael watched the videotape with us and commented on how his body and face did not look interested. We then brainstormed on how he could communicate with his body to show interest in his mother's topics even if he was doing a bit of the "social fake." Some of these techniques included sitting at the table with his hands casually folded in front of him; maintaining a fairly alert posture while leaning the trunk of his body toward his mother; thinking with his eyes about mom; nodding his head slightly; and having a pleased look on his face. The next videotape we took revealed Michael's ability to follow through on the techniques discussed once he had practiced them in a structured environment.

Michael did not leave the clinic that day cured. He continued to exhibit socially awkward verbal and nonverbal communicative messages, but in the sessions at the clinic, he was developing an awareness of how these smaller aspects of communication feel, sound, and look. Months later his parents were pleased to tell me he had increased his conversational interactions with others when he came for dinner at their house.

In the description of the Conversation Tree later in this chapter, pay special attention to the techniques used to visually demonstrate to students when they are succeeding with effective supporting comments versus when they are communicating messages that indicate they are not interested in what is being discussed.

Add-On Comments

Comments that maintain the current topic are called add-ons, meaning they add information to what is already under discussion. If a speaker is talking about her vacation in Hawaii, a listener's add-on comment could be something like: "I went there," "I've never been there," "I hear they surf a lot there." These comments share the student's knowledge of the topic but do not shift the topic. Add-on comments also encourage students to share their own experiences related to the topic, making the topic more interesting to them, and allow others to learn their knowledge of the topic, while still respecting another's experience or ideas.

Add-a-Thought and Whopping Topic Changes

Like baiting and bridging questions, "Add-a-Thought" comments serve the distinct purpose of moving the conversation toward a particular topic or idea that a person wants to discuss — a topic that is related to the topic previously discussed, but not directly about the current topic. Add-a-Thought comments allow participants to demonstrate they are partaking in the speaker's topic, yet enable them to spin the topic in a direction they choose.

If Mary is talking about her trip to Hawaii, Add-a-Thought comments made by Sue may include:

- "I would love to go to Hawaii, but I had a great time in summer camp!" (transitioning the topic to her summer camp experience).

- "I have been to Hawaii and I loved scuba diving," (transitioning the topic to scuba or similar activities).

- "I didn't go anywhere for vacation; I had to go to summer school," (transitioning the topic to summer school).

- "Have you ever been to Europe?" (transitioning the topic to other travel destinations).

Table 11

Variables Affecting Interpretation of the Communicative Message

VERBAL STRATEGIES TO FACILITATE COMMUNICATION	NONVERBAL STRATEGIES TO FACILITATE COMMUNICATION

1. Asking Questions
 	
  a. Initiating about others
 	
  b. Follow-up
 	
  c. Baiting questions
	1. Nonverbal Strategies
	
	  a. Facial Expression
	
	  b. Gestures
	
	  c. Eye Contact (think with your eyes)
	
	  d. Body Language (physical presence)
	
	  e. Proximity

2. Making Comments
 	
  a. Supportive comments
 	
  b. Add-a-thought comments
 	
  c. Add-on comments
	2. Non-language based Verbal Strategies
	
	  a. Tone of voice
	
	  b. Volume of voice
	
	  c. Pitch of voice

3. Verbally Mediated Strategies
 	
  a. Topic maintenance
 	
  b. Turn taking
 	
  c. Shifting topic while maintaining continuity of the conversation
 	
  d. Acknowledging change of topics or return to previously discussed topics	

From my observation of neurotypical adults engaged in conversation, Add-a-Thought comments are frequently used. They allow all the participants to stay personally connected to the information by subtly turning conversations in more desired directions (from the perspective of the person making the Add-a-Thought comment).

It is important to note, when trying to understand the language used to create social interaction, that each of us is very egocentric. While we easily identify our students as egocentric given their social challenges, we are lax in identifying our own egocentricity, largely because we are better at "faking it." Many "normal adults" almost exclusively use their own Add-a-Thought comments to sustain conversations, commenting about their own lives but connecting these comments to the experiences or thoughts of others. We all then feel justified in our own egocentric comments and all participants feel they experienced a good conversation, even though everyone really just talked about themselves!

Add-a-Thought comments must show some relationship to the topic being discussed, but they can stray far from the actual topic as long as there is a clear connection.

When the student adds a thought that is not logically connected to the current topic under discussion, we refer to it as a "Whopping Topic Change." Our students may understand in their own minds the connection between the two topics, but if no one else can make the connection then it is inappropriate. Again, this requires a student to think about how someone else may be thinking to determine if his or her message is connected to the current topic in the minds of others. Usually Whopping Topic Changes occur when a student's mental thinking path has moved three or four thoughts away from the original topic. When he finally makes his comment, it seems far removed from what others are discussing.

As with most skills, some of our students have complete command over Add-a-Thought comments, while other students almost never use this language form. Observing how your students use language before discussing any of these ideas. The student who is exceptionally good at Add-a-Thought comments generally needs to practice other comment and question forms described here. This type of student usually dominates conversations, pursuing discussions related to his or her own singular interests without regard for other people's interests.

The goal for students who almost never use Add-a-Thought comments is to increase their level of awareness of this language form and practice connecting ideas from the current discussion to their own ideas or experiences.

The following example illustrates a conversation sustained by Add-a-Thought comments. Note that each person is only talking about his own experiences, which is often perfectly acceptable as long as it is not a long-winded account, monopolizing the conversation.

Marilyn: I had a great time on vacation in Mexico!

Bobbi: I wish I had time for vacation, but I have enjoyed some family trips to Colorado to visit my daughter at college there.

Cindy: I love going to Hawaii; I can't go there enough.

Michelle: I travel too much; I can't wait to stay home for awhile!

The Add-a-Thought Game

It is fairly easy to visually and concretely introduce the idea of Add-a-Thought comments. Prepare five index cards for each student in the group by writing "Add-a-Thought" at the top of each one. Give the cards to the students. The students will use their cards to "add a thought" to the conversation (see Figure 9).

One student starts the process by introducing a topic. The next student practices adding a thought to the first person's topic by making a comment that relates to the original topic. When he successfully makes the comment, he places one of his index cards in the middle of the table. The next student responds to the second person's comment by making her own Add-a-Thought comment, then places her card on top of the one already on the table. Continue by going around the entire group until all participants have used up their index.

Placing each index card on top of the prior one demonstrates that all the comments connect to each other. It is fun to subsequently track where the conversation started and how it evolved across the different Add-a-Thought comments..

⧖

Heidi, Robyn, and Wendy were part of a group. Heidi introduced a topic by saying "I went to see the movie Legally Blonde *last night." Robyn then commented by saying, "Last week I saw this cool TV show on Animal Planet," and placed her index card on the table. Wendy then said, "My dog is really sick; she keeps eating plastic toys!" and she put her index card on top of Robyn's. Heidi then put her card on the pile after she made an Add-a-Thought comment about the last time she felt really sick.*

In the above paragraph, the comments open the door to a range of topics. For example, with Heidi's comment "Last night I went to see the movie *Legally Blonde*," conversational participants can appropriately connect with any comment about:

1. What they did last night

2. Things they saw

3. Any form of media

4. Specific comments about the movie *Legally Blonde.*

Once a person makes their Add-a-Thought comment, it opens the door to a whole new set of potential topics. Thus with Robyn's response other participants can now add comments about:

1. What they did last week

2. What they saw on TV

3. Animals

4. Anything in the media.

The key is to recognize that in relating to others, we *don't strongly* maintain topics in conversation — rather, we maintain conversational threads that link our thinking around related topics.

There are times to "maintain a topic," but this occurs in more structured contexts, such as during a classroom discussion, job interview, or business meeting. This context difference is another important concept to teach our students.

The Add-a-Thought game can be repeated as often as needed to help students make connections between others' thoughts and their own more automatically. This same procedure can be used for lessons on bridging questions as well.

Figure 9

Template of Index Cards for Add-a-Thought Comments

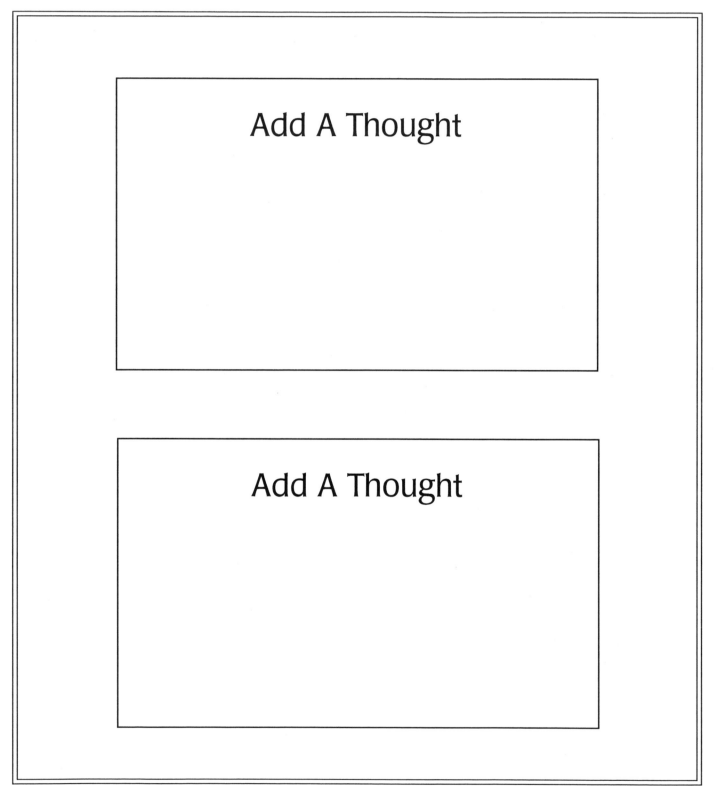

The Conversation Tree

The communication-based strategies above need to be practiced first within therapy sessions. Even when they appear obvious to educators, they need to be specifically reviewed and taught to students. Mastering these strategies increases students' familiarity with the smaller forms of language and the related social thinking skills that form a successful conversation.

The Conversation Tree is a concrete treatment strategy developed to help students visualize these abstract concepts while participating successfully in a conversation. The goal of this exercise is to physically grow the Conversation Tree form across a table. This helps students visualize concepts such as turn taking and maintaining threads to link topics, while applying the different language forms described above. Components used in building the tree also encourage students to monitor less desirable conversational behaviors, such as interrupting, abruptly changing topics, or failing to participate with appropriate nonverbal skills during the communicative exchange.

While the use of the tree itself is very straightforward, the deeper social understanding behind it is important for caregivers to grasp as they work with their students.

The tree consists of four basic parts:

a. The base

b. The top

c. The multi-colored trunk, which gradually grows from the appropriate and targeted use of the language forms

d. Branches that can sprout from the trunk of the tree to document less desirable behaviors, as needed.

The base and top of the tree

The base and top of the tree are permanent components that are always on the table as the tree grows. Philosophically the base of the tree represents the perspective of all the conversation participants. The top of the tree represents the growth of a relationship. Figure 10 pictures these components.

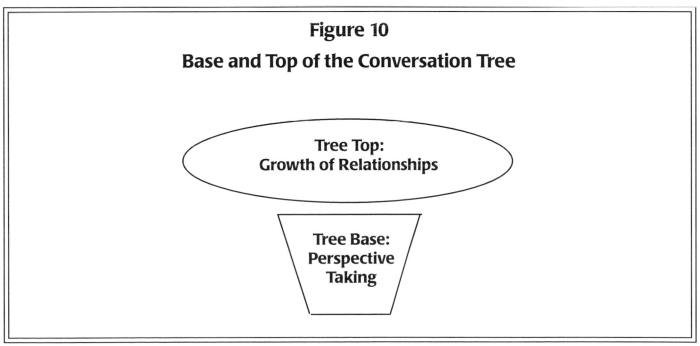

Figure 10

Base and Top of the Conversation Tree

Tree Top:
Growth of Relationships

Tree Base:
Perspective
Taking

The tree trunk

The tree trunk gradually grows from through student participation. Each student is assigned a colored set of trunk pieces; each colored set should consist of up to eight trunk pieces. Participants are identified by the color of their trunk pieces. As many students can participate in growing the tree as you have colored pieces available. Three to five students is ideal.

Every time a student participates in an interaction using the language structure requested by the teacher, he places his trunk piece on the tree. As all students participate, the trunk will extend in length, marking the participation — or lack thereof — of each student. Figure 11 illustrates this process.

We often use the Conversation Tree after we have worked with students on asking supportive questions to other people. Students are then allowed to place their trunk piece on the tree trunk when they have successfully asked a question to another student. The other student can then answer, but she is not permitted to place her piece on the tree until she has also asked a question back to that student or another student in the group.

If a student responds to a question with a long-winded answer, but does not turn the information around to ask a question to someone else, the educator can point out that while the student is saying some interesting comments the tree is not growing.

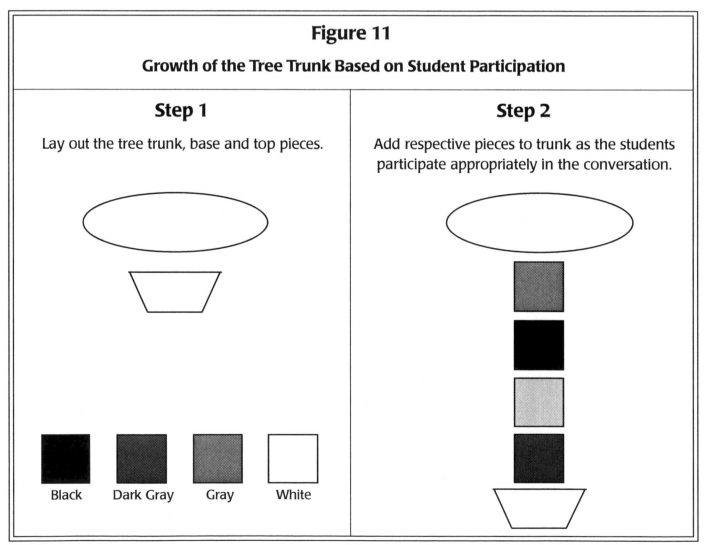

Figure 11

Growth of the Tree Trunk Based on Student Participation

Step 1	**Step 2**
Lay out the tree trunk, base and top pieces.	Add respective pieces to trunk as the students participate appropriately in the conversation.

Black Dark Gray Gray White

Tracking responses based on the appearance of the tree

By observing the appearance of the trunk (as illustrated in Step 2 of Figure 11), participants can visually see the conversation dynamics of the group. For instance, Figure 11 indicates that the student represented by the white squares has not yet participated in the interaction. The teacher can then encourage her to become part of the process by developing specific verbal (question or comment) strategies to place her trunk pieces on the tree. The teacher should prompt the student's thinking without telling the student exactly what to say.

It is also important to note when one student dominates the discussion, indicated by that student's color dominating the tree. The educator can work with this student to demonstrate nonverbal interest in what others are saying while practicing NOT saying anything himself! This is a difficult lesson for many of our hyperactive students.

The growth of the tree trunk is a positive way to commend students for their attempts at productive socially interactive behaviors, as well as monitor active, over-active or minimal communicative participation.

Tree Branches: An approach to encourage self-monitoring

Tree branches provide an opportunity for students to monitor their appropriate participation as part of the interactive group. A branch is placed next to the tree trunk when a student's inappropriate behavior has temporarily halted the tree's upward growth, causing the tree to "branch" outward. The branch signifies a student's verbal or nonverbal communicative blunder that distracts from the healthy growth of the conversation.

⧗

Judd was fourteen years old and worked hard trying to say the right thing during the group meetings. But he had difficulty monitoring his body language, facial expression, and eye contact to look like he was part of the group. As we built the conversation tree with his group, Judd started to stare off into space. A branch was placed next to the last tree trunk piece placed on the tree to indicate to Judd that his staring off into space was not contributing to the group interaction.

Figure 12 demonstrates how branches are placed on the tree. From the intermittent use of branches, Judd became keenly aware of how his whole body supports a successful interaction. He did not want the branch to stay on the tree, so it was agreed it would be taken off as soon as he was able to describe why he received it. Judd quickly understood the meaning of the branch. He then commented on his own or other students' less desirable traits when interacting by making comments such as "Oops, I just branched."

Over time Judd became increasingly able to self-monitor his communicative behavior during conversational exchanges, which, his mother reported, eventually carried over to some extent into the community.

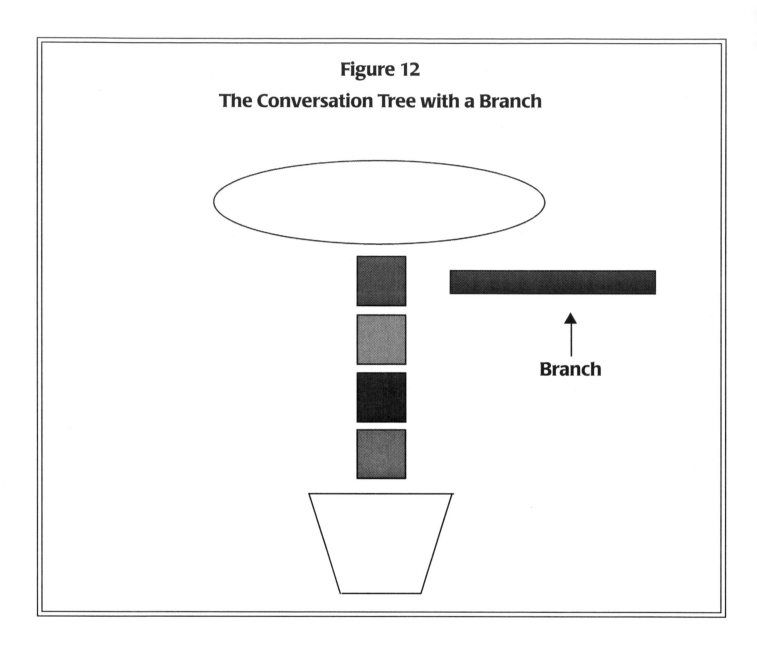

Figure 12
The Conversation Tree with a Branch

Branch

A note about branches: It is best if a set of branches is made for each student that corresponds with the color of his/her trunk pieces. Students want to clearly identify who "branches," making sure they only get one when they deserve it. Making the branches the same color as each student's trunk pieces clearly identifies who owns the branch. While branches have a negative connotation, they are generally placed on the tree to help the stu-

dent understand the factors (verbal and nonverbal) to be monitored to create interactive success. The students I have worked with have accepted the occurrence of an occasional branch when a rational explanation accompanied it. Almost always the branches are removed as soon as the student reviews what social interactive behavior was expected in place of the branch. Table 12 reviews communicative behaviors that may merit a branch.

The Three Strikes Principle

Using the branches with students who demonstrate uncooperative group behavior

On occasion I have worked with a student who is uncooperative in the group and blames other students for his difficulties. This student is often defiant and attempts to modify any activity so that he gets all the attention. I tend to leave this student's branches on the tree to give him an idea of how his behavior affects other people over time. When this type of student gets three branches while building a tree, it generally means the student is not able to cooperate in the group-thinking activity. He is asked to leave the room for two minutes to let him think about what it means to be part of the group.

When the student leaves the room, or goes to sit in a part of the room away from the group, he sits in the "think chair." Posted on the wall near the think chair are the group participation rules. The three-strikes policy is applied only to students who are choosing not to cooperate in the group, not those who have momentary lapses in acting on all the social cognitive information being reviewed.

Ultimately, the educator has to determine which children need a behavioral lesson in group cooperation, and which need an occasional branch applied to them to help them learn to self-monitor. The occurrence of unspecified social interactive behaviors may be ignored by the educator in some instances, given that the student can only focus on learning to control just one or two behaviors at a time.

As with any lesson, we do not expect perfection from students when using the Conversation Tree. We do expect to help a student learn, piece by piece, to build toward a more successful conversational interaction. For a child with significant social cognitive deficits, the educator would carefully choose interactive behaviors (verbal or nonverbal) on which she is going to focus, then help him gain more awareness of that specific behavior.

A Practical Note About Branching

Students with significant social cognitive disabilities tend to be very precise with their knowledge. Many students have questioned the concept of branching based on the very logical premise that trees do have branches, thus branches should not be construed as a bad thing. Most students are readily appeased when you explain that this is a tree cared for by a gardener, and he trims the ugly branches that grow straight out of the trunk to allow for more growth in the top of the tree!

Table 12

Verbal and Nonverbal Behaviors that May Merit Receiving a Branch While Growing a Conversation Tree

POTENTIAL INAPPROPRIATE VERBAL BEHAVIORS	POTENTIAL INAPPROPRIATE NONVERBAL BEHAVIORS
Interrupting and blurting out	Looking away from the group
Off-topic remarks	Constantly physically distracted
Offensive comments that demonstrate a lack of perspective taking (e.g., "That's a stupid hobby!")	Lacking a nonverbal response to comments being stated
Swearing (unless determined to be appropriate in the social context!)	Facial expressions that look offensive to the other participants (e.g., rolling of the eyes)
An inadequate verbal response that the listener cannot understand because the speaker did not give enough information to the listener	Body language or facial expressions that show a lack of interest in what others are saying
A whopping topic change: Making a comment that is so tangential it is hard to understand how it fully relates to what others are saying	Physically walking away from the group as others are talking
Perseveres with one topic of conversation even after cues are given to minimize discussion of the topic	

Using the Conversation Tree with the Overly Verbal Student and the Minimally Verbal Student

As mentioned above, the pattern in the tree trunk can help identify the student having difficulty initiating comments. To establish a stronger expectation for a student to participate, modify the number of trunk pieces each participant receives. The next time you build a tree, give more pieces to students who participate minimally than to verbal participants. For example, if two students in a group barely participate provide them with six tree trunk pieces and give all the other participants only three pieces. The less verbal student is then encouraged to participate twice as much.

The educator may need to initially provide close support of this student to guide him on how to use language and connected thought to jump into the Interaction. This approach works nicely to help older students monitor their level of contribution to verbal interactions. It not only sets the expectation that the quieter participants will initiate more often, it also encourages the more verbose students to give other students chances to talk. If one or two students are dominating the interaction, focus their instruction on learning to be better listeners rather than interjectors.

With students who are highly verbal and have little ability to control their blurting, I emphasize the importance of less verbal participation in the group, while still remaining an active thoughtful member. I begin by setting a predetermined block of time (two to five minutes) when the student needs to use appropriate body language while listening to the group discussion.

During that time the student is not allowed to verbally participate. This helps the student work on nonverbal skills required for interactive success.

A product called the "Time-Timer" (see Figure 13) is extremely useful for helping students visually monitor the passage of time by the minute. It displays the minutes within an hour visually and concretely, showing literally how time passes. Digital and traditional clocks do not provide a mechanism for the student to monitor the passage of time as they regulate their behaviors. The Time-Timer is used in our clinic for all-aged students to help set limits or goals related to monitoring behavior across the passage of time. It works well for most students.

Figure 13
Picture of a Time-Timer

A visual timer that helps students monitor the passage of time within a pre-established activity, whether work related or fun.

Available from: www.timetimer.com

The Many Uses of the Conversation Tree

The Conversation Tree provides a strategic framework for motivating students to participate in a variety of lessons. The educator chooses the specific lesson the students explore with each use of the tree during the therapy session. Table 13 reviews the variety of ways the Conversation Tree can be used during the many stages of teaching social interaction with language.

Topic Cards

To help students initiate conversations on a variety of topics, I use visual "topic cards" as a prompt. A single topic is written on an index card. The stack of index cards is then kept next to the Conversation Tree, or remains available to students any time they are working on topic-directed language skills. The topic cards help students learn to engage in conversations about topics that are not of their own choosing or liking. To become a proficient conversationalist, students must practice speaking about topics that are randomly introduced and possibly not of interest. After a recent experience where a student complained that she was not talking because the topic was so "boring," we discussed that in conversations topics often can be boring. However, by using Add-a-Thought comments we can learn to shift the discussion to a topic more of our choosing.

It is critical to also teach that the developing relationship is more important than the actual language being exchanged. For this girl we then created "boring topic cards" and practiced talking about topics all people would find boring (e.g., moss on trees, my office, etc.)

Some examples of topic cards include:

1. A good teacher
2. Disgusting food your parents make you eat
3. Restaurants
4. Computers
5. Games
6. Weekend activities
7. Thanksgiving
8. Sports
9. The thing you hate to do the most
10. Your family

Some examples of boring or wacky topics include:

1. Airplane seats
2. Fingernail paint color
3. Railroad tracks
4. Annoying drivers
5. Things parents like to do
6. Color of socks
7. Hygiene schedules
8. Dog hair
9. Food sold at school
10. Things on people's t-shirts

Table 13

Lessons That Can Be Used
When Growing a Conversation Tree

Possible Tree-Growing Lessons	Descriptions of the Lessons
Asking questions to others, about these other people.	Instruct the students they can only place their tree trunk piece when they have asked a question of another participant. If a student talks and talks, but does not ask a question point out to him that the tree is not growing!
Keeping a conversation going with Add-a-Thought comments.	Instruct the students they can only place their trunk piece when they make a comment from their own experience or thought that relates to the topic.
Maintaining a topic using supporting comments and add-on comments.	Instruct the students they can only place their trunk piece when they make reaction and add-on comments. Other types of comments and questions may exist, but the only way to add the trunk pieces is by making a specific reaction or add-on comment.
Using appropriate body language during conversational speech.	Instruct the students that while they can converse on any topic, the educator will be in charge of placing tree trunk pieces when she observes students using appropriate nonverbal conversational strategies. (She will have defined what "appropriate" means for the specific students with whom she is working.)
Having a regular conversation (advanced lesson).	Students can place their tree trunk piece on the tree for any verbal exchange that succeeds in the context of the conversation.
Encouraging group participants to increase or decrease verbal interaction during the conversation.	Students who are overly talkative are given fewer tree trunk pieces to use during any of the above tasks, when compared to students who are minimally verbal. This encourages more participation from the less active, and less participation from the more verbally active.

Derivatives of the Conversation Tree Concept

The Conversation Tree provides a visual template for teaching students about many different aspects of interactive communication. The tree is but one idea. A talented speech language pathologist in my clinic, Stephanie Madrigal, was faced with having a thoughtful nine-year-old boy, Eric, politely refuse to use the Conversation Tree because he liked branches for climbing and did not want to have to grow a tree without branches! Stephanie then worked with him on what they could use to create a similar lesson and "Conversation Street" was born. For the Conversation Street, the street vocabulary was defined to discuss all the concepts that go into helping create conversational knowledge and skills. A street is constructed using the colored blocks like in the conversation tree. This concept then became more and more elaborate as different students (Sasha, Erika, Anna, and Kristen) provided further input. Eric was so interested in the Conversation Street that he went home and cut up the pieces for it, and began to create some of the rules.

Table 14 lists street-related vocabulary that has references to social cognitive knowledge and related communicative skills. Perhaps the best lesson is that after introducing the Conversation Tree or Street, the students were encouraged to develop their own visual metaphor to conversation functions. Regardless of how much knowledge we educators have, our ability to teach is dependent on our ability to motivate the students to participate in their own education, especially with concepts as abstract as communication!

Table 14
Conversation Street Vocabulary
Developed by Stephanie Madrigal

1. Tunnel Vision:
Talking without "thinking with your eyes." Talking without looking.

2. Overload Road:
Talking without thinking about how the listener is taking in the message. Tendency to provide too much detailed or scattered information.

3. Interruption Junction:
You interrupt someone's thoughts with your own thought or with an inappropriate body movement.

4. Dead End Bend:
You respond to someone else's question by not giving any solid information for someone else to think about and respond to. For example, someone asks you, "What did you do today?" and you answer "nothing."

5. Missed the Turn:
The conversation changed slightly onto another topic and you did not realize it changed, and you kept talking about the same old topic.

6. Detour:
A person changes the topic (which is not always appropriate!).

7. Cop Stop:
Clearly inappropriate comments or actions, such as walking away from the group.

8. Crash Mash:
Body language and tone of voice does not match what the words mean.
(Yelling at someone when you simply meant to share a new idea.)

9. Speeding Ticket: Talking too fast.

10. Running a Stop Sign:
Making a lot of negative comments in a conversation so that people just wish you would stop.

11. Broken Engine:
Shut down from conversing (body and words).

12. One Way Street: Only talking about your interests.

13. Carpool Lane:
Sharing the conversational topic/asking questions about others.

14. Good Driving Award: Doing everything just right!

Beyond the Conversation Tree: Improvisational Games

A seventeen-year-old boy in one of my high-school groups participated in his school's improvisational comedy club. He shared with us ideas about improvisation, and we began to discuss how conversations are the ultimate act of a real-life improvisational scenario. They require you to follow topic transitions and immediately provide related information. From that discussion we created some conversation games to practice the use of comments and questions around randomly introduced topics.

What's My Thinking?

The first game is called "What's My Thinking?" This game requires students to refine their questioning and commenting skills. The game uses the topic cards described above. At least two students and one educator must play this game. The teacher is in charge of secretly showing a topic card to one of the students. That student then needs to ask questions to try to get the other student to talk about the topic (commenting) without directly revealing it.

For example, if the first student were shown the "Thanksgiving" topic card, he could ask the other student "What do you like to eat for Thanksgiving?" The student who starts with the first topic card has it the easiest. The educator now shows a randomly chosen topic card such as "What do you hate to do most?" to the second student, who is answering questions about Thanksgiving. At this point the first student no longer needs to ask any more questions. He now prepares to respond to the second student's impending questions. The second student must finish up comments on the Thanksgiving topic, then offer bridging questions about the newly introduced topic, which in this case was "what he hated to do most."

The job of the second student is to figure out how to bridge to the new topic subtly by providing comments that are relevant to the old topic, but also bridge to appropriate questions to get the first student talking about this new and unknown topic. For example, the first student asks the second student, "Who comes over to your house for Thanksgiving?" The second student now sees the topic card the educator is secretly showing her so she knows she is now responsible for making the transition to the "What do you hate to do the most?" topic. The second speaker then could respond to the first with something like: "My aunt and uncle come over for Thanksgiving. They are really cool, but they always make me play the piano in front of them! I hate to play in front of people. What do you hate to do when you have guests over?"

The activity of working with students to make the transition from one topic to the next when given two completely unrelated topics often results in some funny comments, questions, and facial expressions. The students enjoy the process, all the while working toward a very valuable skill. Intermittently the educator may ask the students to stop and guess the new topic introduced.

Keep It Connected

The second improvisation is called "Keep It Connected," and is played with a video camera after we have reviewed therapy concepts in a lesson format. The purpose of this exercise is to tell the educator — who is using the video camera — about a concept and its related skills that have been taught to the group. For example, the educator may say something like, "Explain to me why perspective taking is important." Here is the hitch: the students cannot convey the information in a typical conversational format. In this game the educator starts by pointing the camera lens at a student and asks him to start the discussion. As long as the video camera is pointed at a student it remains his or her turn to talk; however as soon as the educator shifts the lens of the camera on another student, that student must continue the message where the first student left off.

The actual topic discussion may subtly shift many times among participants as the camera moves back and forth among the participants. The stream of information, however, is supposed to stay nearly steady. This can result in hilarious outcomes as students work hard to integrate what they have heard another person say into what they want to add without making any obvious topic changes, without knowing when their turn will end.

This game works not only on maintaining a topic while thinking about the message other people are trying to convey, but it also helps increase auditory as well as visual attention as students participate in a group. Aside from being fun to play, the game also creates videotape that can be replayed for further analysis, lessons, and laughter.

I am sure there are many more related games that await creation. I heartily believe that as educators become intrinsically aware of the concepts they are teaching, they will branch out in the diversity and creativity of their lessons.

Paper Clips and Thumbtacks: Teaching Toward Generalization

As students acquire the concepts and related skills discussed throughout this book, we, as educators, need to be mindful that generalization of these skills is not a strong suit for most of these students. Therefore, we must plan for and teach our students to continue being social thinkers outside the walls of the educational environment. Arranging therapy sessions away from the clinic or classroom is a first step, yet to truly promote independence and encourage social self-evaluation, we need more; we need a concrete framework within which students can apply the lessons whenever and wherever they are needed and know how they are doing.

Start by having students work on their social pragmatic concepts in different environments with same-aged peers. This helps promote generalization, especially when the interaction is sheltered enough to allow direct adult observation and some level of participation. We found that students needed some form of tangible, visual "gauge" of their social functioning — similar to the concept of a token system used in behavior modification. Thus was born Paper Clips and Thumbtacks as a teaching tool with our students. These simple, yet effective elements help remind students of the importance of monitoring and adjusting their own social behavior when in a less structured environment.

Paper Clips

The educator brings paper clips and thumbtacks into the less structured environment, and gives students paper clips when they are "caught in the act" of making a good social communicative connection with another person. In advance of this activity the educator defines for each student the specific skill(s) they are to self-monitor and regulate to earn a paper clip.

For example, if a student has difficulty with appropriate physical proximity during interactions with others, he is given paper clips just for keeping appropriate proximity. (Of course, what is "appropriate" would have already been worked on in the more structured setting of a classroom or clinic.) Another student may be working on using more supportive comments or add-on comments, and fewer whopping topic changes in conversation with others. In that case, a paper clip would be given for each identified positive comment.

Students can accumulate a number of paper clips during a session. At the end, students enjoy making paper-clip chains. The idea of using paper clips originated when I needed a handful of small, inexpensive objects to use as token rewards in community outings. One of our terrific therapists, Linda Draa, became somewhat philosophical about the paper clips as she saw the students making the paper-clip chains. To her they represented "the connection we make with others through our communication." Thus, simple paper clips now have a deeper communicative meaning!

Thumbtacks

A single thumbtack is used by the educator as a visual reminder when a student acts or makes a verbal statement that is harmful to the health of the communicative interaction. Thumbtacks are used to help students develop awareness of their less desirable behaviors and how they affect others. Thumbtacks are generally used sparingly and never handed out to a student. The educator simply holds a thumbtack up for the student to see while carefully explaining his or her offensive behavior.

⧖

Evan was an intellectually gifted fourteen-year-old student with Asperger Syndrome who had been home schooled for the past two years. He had difficulty relating to his peers. He was highly verbal, spoke predominantly about his areas of interest, dominated conversations, and impulsively stated unintended offensive comments when he did not approve of someone else's topic or behavior. Aside from his social pragmatic deficits and overbearing nature, Evan was a delightful young man with a good sense of humor. He very much wanted to be like his peers. His parents celebrated his strengths and were perplexed by how to handle his weaknesses. They worked hard to understand how to help him.

Evan participated in our community summer day-camp program for high school students. On the first day, he dominated the group and attempted to make all decisions. At the start of each camp day we explored social

pragmatic concepts, and then the students took the bus into the community to partake in activities together while continuing to work on monitoring and regulating their own specific social pragmatic skills. The paper clip and thumbtack strategy was developed with Evan's group, in part to help him learn to monitor his verbosity and how it affected others.

Paper clips were given throughout day to all students. Evan "received" a couple of thumbtacks for bluntly changing the topic to discuss his areas of interest and for dismissing other people's ideas. Another boy was given a thumbtack for not standing with the group at the bus stop. The students began to work hard to earn more paper clips and minimize the presentation of the thumbtack.

At the end of the first day of camp, Evan bet the others he had the most paper clips. They each created their paper-clip chains and then the members of the group held them up for comparison. Evan had the shortest chain. I reminded Evan about the specific strategies he could think about and use to make positive connections with others. Each day his chain grew a bit longer and the thumbtack appeared less often. Evan's presence in the group mellowed, he was no longer the supreme leader, and he was now "one of the guys." He still made social pragmatic blunders but they were not nearly as obvious or intrusive as those made earlier in the program.

All through the summer Evan spoke about his desire to go to a regular high school. When he enrolled in the high school, I met with his staff to help them understand his unique disability. He had many people helping him learn to help himself. Much to his parent's delight he made a successful transition back into public school with relatively few glitches, compared with his past school experiences. As a school project, he had to write about himself and his hopes. The final paragraph of that paper reflects how much social thinking growth Evan had attained. He wrote:

"To accomplish all this I must stay in school, work reasonably hard, and demonstrate that I can learn and succeed not only for myself but also for others. To have a chance at doing this I must learn to be happy and remain focused regardless of the difficulties presented by others. I must also learn to change my behavior so that more people are willing to help me in these goals."

Table 15
Review of Language-Based Social Interaction Therapy Strategies

Questions: Introducing Question Words or Interrogatives

1. Social greeting questions

2. Questions to initiate an interaction

3. Follow-Up questions

4. Baiting or Bridging questions

Comments:

1. Supportive comments: verbal and nonverbal

2. Add-On comments

3. Add-a-Thought comments

Exploring Students' Abilities to Answer "Why" Questions

The Conversation Tree:

1. Growing the tree

2. Behavioral lessons using the tree, including the use of the Time-Timer

3. Monitoring students participation while growing the tree

4. A variety of language lessons to use while growing the tree

5. The use of topic cards

Improvisational Games:

1. What's My Thinking?

2. Keep It Connected

Promoting Generalization of Lessons Outside the Therapy Room:

Paper Clips and Thumbtacks

Language Skills for Communicative Success: Suggested Goals

The suggested goals that follow have a two-fold purpose: 1) to present examples of goals that can be added to a student's IEP, and 2) to act as a catalyst for your own discussions with parents and other staff about helping students develop verbal communication skills that allow them to be more successful in social settings. These goals remind us of the many components of conversation that need to be worked on and written into a student's IEP, aside from the obvious goal that the student will easily and readily "converse" with others by the end of the IEP year.

1. The student will define and demonstrate the difference between a comment and a question with 90% accuracy.

2. The student will define and demonstrate the differences in various types of questions (social greeting questions, bridging questions, follow-up questions) with 90% accuracy.

3. The student will define and use words that inquire about others (Who, what, where, etc.) with 90% accuracy.

4. The student will answer the fact-based "wh-" questions with 95% accuracy (who, what, when, where).

5. The student will answer how and why questions, using a visual organizer to visually map out the information to be considered, with 75% accuracy and initial cues.

6. The student will define and demonstrate the differences in various types of comments (supportive, add-on, and add-a-thought comments) with 90% accuracy.

7. The student will describe how the use of different comment and question types can affect the perspective of the interactive partner, with 90% accuracy.

8. The student will initiate questions and comments around a pre-selected topic, along with nonverbal means to demonstrate interest in what other people are saying, at 80% accuracy with initial cues.

9. The student will use questions to discover other people's hobbies or interests, at 80% accuracy with initial cues.

10. In settings away from the classroom environment, the student will ask related questions and make comments regarding someone else's topic of the moment with minimal cues, 70% of the time.

11. The student will use questions or comments to bridge an existing topic to one he is interested in, at 80% accuracy with initial cues.

12. The student will monitor changes in topic during a conversation and make appropriate related comments and contributions as topics shifts, with 80% accuracy.

13. The student will tolerate being in a group that contains people he doesn't like by offering supportive comments to the speaker, rather than sighing or uttering other unsupportive comments or gestures, 80% of the time.

(Note: we don't write goals for conversation maintenance or turn-taking; both will naturally occur when these other skills are worked on. Ultimately our job is not about the quantity of communication the students produce, but about the quality.)

Summary

Successful communication involves the application of multiple skills and different levels of social knowledge. It is next to impossible to teach our students to improve their verbal language skills by just having them practice conversations with peers while we, as educators, point out what they are doing right or wrong. To success in social conversation, students need to learn specific strategies that are part of a healthy verbal exchange between communicative partners. A variety of classroom strategies and visual teaching tools are introduced in this chapter that assist students in understanding the dynamics of conversational language. At the end of the chapter, a set of goals are presented that can be considered when developing an educational path for teaching these critical social language skills.

Chapter 8
Social Behavior Mapping:
Behavior is Linked to Perspective Taking

 The term "behavior problem" is often applied to children who use aggressive or very assertive behavior that causes another person to feel unsafe. It is also frequently used to describe a person — especially children — who can't or won't act in accordance with socially recognized behavior "norms" for the situation. In the educational and home setting, however, behavior problems should be seen as any behavior that interferes with the process of learning or participating.

Almost all individuals with social cognitive deficits have some form of behavior problem. At home, these children may have a difficult time completing chores or homework tasks without constant cueing from a parent. At school, a child may sit and do nothing while the class is working through an assignment, or act in socially inappropriate ways that disturb the teacher and other students. Behaviors that arise from our students' social cognitive deficits exist on a continuum, from mild to severe. But they exist, and therefore need attention and amelioration.

Virtually all of an individual's attempts to coexist with others are coded through a set of behaviors. When our behaviors fail to gain what we (or others) perceive as success, we have a problem — a behavior problem.

A Brief Summary of Behavioral Interventions

Behavioral treatment strategies are a core component of education for any child, but especially for children with social cognitive deficits. When parents and educators are dealing with problematic behavior, they often use a traditional behavior approach:

A. Determine the origins of the behavior (antecedents);

B. Clearly define the behavior; and

C. Develop alternative strategies (consequences) for dealing with the behavior — strategies that encourage the emergence of different, more appropriate behaviors.

This can be thought of as the A-B-C approach (antecedent-behavior-consequence) to help modify behaviors.

Behavioral treatment strategies can also be used to help people learn a variety of new skills: academic, social, and daily living. These strategies deliver clear and direct rewards contingent on the performance of specified target behavior(s).

For children on the autism spectrum, early intervention in the form of intense behaviorally oriented teachings is becoming more common. These programs are rooted in Applied Behavior Analysis (ABA) methodology and generally employ discrete trials training (DTT). They rely on carefully detailed behavioral teachings, with tasks broken down into small steps. Students are rewarded for progress within each step, with the idea that they build their knowledge towards larger concepts.

An ABA approach successfully helps children with autism learn concrete, specific skills; however, it is best applied when the tasks can be kept simple and clear. This makes it doubly difficult to use such an approach to teach abstract concepts to students about their own behavior.

Recent research reveals that when behavioral lessons are tailored to a child's natural environment and understanding of the world, the child is more likely to learn and retain the concepts (Durand and Merges 2001). Keep in mind that behaviorally based treatment programs are those that "happen" to the child. Activities are created to encourage the child to practice specific skills, and then tangible rewards are given to the child for a job well done.

While the child's unique skills and challenges are the focus of the program's development, the child is rarely informed about the process of changing his or her own behavior during these programs. Their behavior changes in response to their pleasure in earning rewards; they seek the rewards by engaging in the task or behavior the educator has directed them to accomplish. While these traditional programs for helping students learn to modify their behavior have been effective for many students, I find they quickly lose their power among many of our brighter students with social cognitive deficits.

For students with high-level language skills, it is also appropriate to provide them with a cognitive behavioral approach. This means the child is taught to think about the behavior and consider when it is appropriate versus when it becomes problematic, rather than simply being directed to demonstrate an appropriate behavior based on a contingent reward.

Since the 1960s psychologists have been exploring the connection between cognition and a person's emotional or behavioral response to their environment. Cognitive Behavioral Therapy (CBT) helps students gain a higher level of cognitive understanding, which in turn helps to alter behavior (Dobson and Dozois 2001). It has proven essential in helping students who have good academic cognition (normal or above verbal IQ scores) and highly developed language skills yet lack equivalent development in social cognition (Sofronoff, Attwood, and Hinton, 2005; Attwood, 2007; Paxton and Estay, 2007). These students can grasp the more sophisticated descriptions of how the mind thinks, and relate that to human behavior.

However, CBT does not appear to be as effective for students with low verbal IQ scores (below 65). These students cannot easily process the cognitive explanation of the lessons.

Students with learning challenges such as Asperger Syndrome often find A-B-C type behavioral programs demeaning or ineffective — these bright students quickly find their behavior plans tedious. It is also a struggle to find a meaningful external reward for students who get their greatest pleasure from their internal thoughts and ideas. Bright kids often find holes in their behavior plans, often reflecting their very literal interpretation of the behavior command. For example, if you ask them not to sing in class, they will start to hum, insisting they are not singing. (They're right, they are not! They miss the intent of the teacher's message — to keep quiet.)

Social Cognitive Gaps

As typical children age they think more abstractly about the world. School-aged children with social cognitive deficits, particularly those with at least normal intellectual functioning and those who are in their pre-teen and teen years, have gaps in their understanding of social relationships, and they require more sophisticated behavioral treatment strategies. We cannot assume that by rewarding a student for exhibiting the correct behavior we are teaching the child why that behavior is important in the first place. As their teachers, we need to not only provide functional lessons, but also teach them about the abstract: how their own behavior affects others and themselves.

Children with social cognitive deficits do not easily recognize the many ways their own behaviors affect others. These students must often be taught cognitively what others understand intuitively, including the following concepts:

- Perspective Taking: Our students have little insight into another person's perspective, which causes them to behave without recognition of how another person may be interpreting their actions.

⧗

Lisa, a seven-year-old with Asperger Syndrome, consistently cries when she loses a game or is not selected to go first. Others, including her peers, remind her it is fair to share turns and victories, but this does little to calm her because she does not know to consider the perspective or desires of other students or adults.

- That consequences link back to their own behaviors: Our students have difficulty seeing the "big picture," which often makes it hard for them to understand that the consequences they receive are linked specifically to a set of behaviors they produced earlier.

⧗

Mark, a twenty-year-old man with Asperger Syndrome, had a habit of solving his personal problems by lying about the facts. He used this problem-solving strategy repeatedly with the same outcome: his parents would become furious when they ultimately learned the truth. I asked Mark to bring in his bank statement to one of our therapy sessions because we were working on budgeting his employment earnings. When he realized he did not know where the bank statement was, he decided not to come to the therapy session. He did not cancel the appointment and told his mother that he had attended.

Within a day his parents knew the truth – that he had lied about coming to see me. His mother, desperate to try to teach him that his lying could negatively affect his independence, took his car away as a consequence. He now needed to be driven around the community by his mother so she could supervise his actions, demonstrating to him that his lying cost him his independence. The next time I worked with Mark, I asked him why his car was taken away. He was able to tell me that it had to do with

telling the lie but he had NO IDEA how this consequence related directly to his act of lying!

It is very common for our students to feel that people around them treat them unfairly when, in fact, their behaviors toward others are sometimes less than kind. They perceive themselves as being the victims of other people who impose arbitrary and harsh consequences on them for no clear purpose. They are not able to create the mental link between the facts: students' behaviors trigger a reaction in other people that results in the delivery of specific undesired consequences back to the students.

- Appropriate social behavior: Individuals with social cognitive deficits have difficulty determining what set of social behaviors are appropriate (expected) or inappropriate (unexpected) in specific settings in which they often are insensitive to changes in context. They miss interpreting the "hidden rules."

  ◉ Frequently, people with social cognitive deficits fail to modulate the volume level of their voices to the environmental context in which they are communicating.

  ◉ Some of our students are overly formal, never shifting into different personas to meet the contextual needs of the setting.

⧗

A nine-year-old boy with Asperger Syndrome gave very formal greetings when acknowledging others, regardless of how familiar he was with a person. This boy would attempt to shake hands with classmates when he wanted to recognize that someone else had done a good job. His inability to alter his greetings or compliments according to whom he was speaking was recognized by his peers as odd behavior.

- Gaining access to a vocabulary of emotions: People with social cognitive deficits are often deficient in their awareness and use of words related to their own and others' emotions.

- Many of our students in upper elementary school and middle school tend to use very general emotional terms (e.g., happy, sad) in an attempt to convey complex emotions. Other students completely avoid discussing their world in terms of an emotional framework.

Social Behavior Mapping

As I work with educators, parents, and students I am constantly struck by the fact that we assume our students understand the underlying concepts of the social-behavioral world around them. So many of our students are gifted intellectually and use excellent language skills that people assume they have naturally acquired a sophisticated level of understanding human relatedness. The reality is that these students are often lacking in this knowledge and the accompanying words to explain their abstract emotions.

I developed Social Behavior Mapping (SBM) as a tool to teach individuals about specific relationships between their behaviors, others' perspectives, others' actions (consequences), and the student's own emotions about how people treat him or her. The SBM is a visual tool that displays these abstract concepts through a flow chart, or a graphic organizer of social behavior.

The Core Principles of Social Behavior Mapping

1. Different environmental contexts command different behavioral expectations. In other words, people are not expected to act exactly the same way across the day. There are different expectations during teacher talk time versus small group work time.

2. Context-specific behaviors are defined as expected (socially appropriate) or unexpected (socially inappropriate) through the eyes of the person who is interacting with the student.

3. Behaviors, whether they are expected or unexpected, affect the emotional state of those who are in close proximity.

4. Consequences occur not because of the behaviors themselves, but from the impact of these behaviors on others' emotional states.

5. The emotional state of the student is affected by the consequences he or she experiences.

Given these five core principles, it is easy to note that behaviors cause a chain reaction as demonstrated in Figure 14.

Figure 14
Chain of Behavioral Reactions

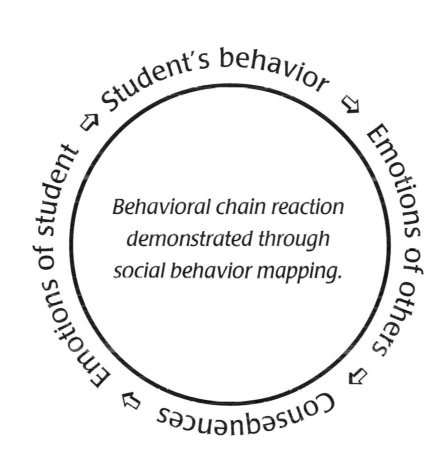

Student's behavior → Emotions of others → Consequences → Emotions of student → (Student's behavior)

Behavioral chain reaction demonstrated through social behavior mapping.

The Social Behavior Map (SBM) Template

SBM templates are shown in Handout 7. Each Social Behavior Map consists of two pages that are photocopied, back-to-back, on one sheet of paper. The philosophy of the SBM is discussed in more detail in the next section of this chapter.

Handout 7

Social Behavior Map Template-1: Behaviors that are **EXPECTED**

Context _____

Behaviors, feelings, and consequences are listed in categories in arbitrary order. There is not a one-to-one correlation between the information listed in each column. For example, whatever behavior is listed first does not have to match the first emotional reaction or the first consequence, and so on.

Expected Behaviors	How They Make Others Feel	Consequences You Experience	How You Feel About Yourself
1.	1.	1.	1.
2.	2.	2.	2.
3.	3.	3.	3.
4.	4.	4.	4.
5.	5.	5.	5.
6.		6.	
7.		7.	

→ → →

Handout 7

Social Behavior Map Template-2: Behaviors that are **UNEXPECTED**

Context _____

Behaviors, feelings, and consequences are listed in categories in arbitrary order. There is not a one-to-one correlation between the information listed in each column. For example, whatever behavior is listed first does not have to match the first emotional reaction or the first consequence, and so on.

Unexpected Behaviors	How They Make Others Feel	Consequences You Experience	How You Feel About Yourself
1.	1.	1.	1.
2.	2.	2.	2.
3.	3.	3.	3.
4.	4.	4.	4.
5.	5.	5.	5.
6.		6.	
7.		7.	

→   →   →

Completing the Social Behavior Map

Defining the Context

Different sets of behaviors are expected — or un-expected — in different contexts. The behaviors required of a child to sit in class and participate are different from the set of behaviors required of a child on the playground. While there may be some overlap of specific behavior across environments, there are also unique behaviors expected that help define that setting. These expected behaviors are generally "hidden knowledge." Most children gain this information intuitively. When we teach our students this information, we describe the information as the "hidden rules."

From a practical point of view, persons expect specific sets of behaviors from others. For example, when sitting in a classroom, there is a whole set of hidden rules that characterize a cooperative student. Understanding that behaviors occur in these "sets" helps us teach our students "gestalt" of a situation — the bigger picture of how to function. If we micro-focus on each behavior, isolating and treating one behavior at a time, the child may have difficulty realizing that behaviors work together toward a larger good.

For example, if a child is kicking the legs of the table in front of him, the teacher may respond to his behavior by saying, "Stop kicking the table." While this may cease his kicking behavior, he may then start tapping his pencil on the shoulder of the person in front of him. Behaviorally, change did occur, but the result was a new behavior replacing the old one because there was no appreciation of the effect his behavior had on others. In this context his behavior remained the same: he distracted others.

To follow is the complete set of goals and benchmarks taken from the IEP of David, a nine-year-old boy with Asperger Syndrome. David is fairly disruptive in his current placement: a mainstream environment in which he has an instructional aide. Notice how the goals only focus on what he is doing wrong, with no explanation of why they are wrong. We simply assume that students know how to think about the social impact of their behavior.

Goal 1: David will reduce incidents of verbal inappropriateness (insults, rude comments, etc.) made to both adults and peers from two times a day to one time a day for eight to ten days.

- Benchmark 1: Reduce to one time per day for three out of ten days.

- Benchmark 2: Reduce to one time per day for five out of ten days.

- Benchmark 3: Reduce to one time per day for eight out of ten days.

Goal 2: David will reduce inappropriate behavior toward peers (grabbing, poking, kissing, etc.) from two times a day to one time a day for eight out of ten days.

- Benchmark 1: Reduce to one time per day for three out of ten days.

- Benchmark 2: Reduce to one time per day for five out of ten days.

- Benchmark 3: Reduce to one time per day for eight out of ten days.

David's behavioral goals do not indicate at any point what David should do in place of the negative behaviors he currently exhibits. Teaching the student explicitly about how and why students regulate their bodies is a worthy concept, which would encourage him to monitor others' behaviors as well as his own. (This child would also likely benefit from occupational therapy strategies in the classroom.)

Goals must provide tools with which we can help the child learn about himself and ways to relate to others. David's IEP behavioral goals fall short. They don't focus on what David needs to learn to help himself and others. They just describe what he should not do.

Teaching children about behavior by helping them understand how the behaviors are interpreted by others, in each environment, is important. Working with educational staff and parents to explore the sets of behaviors that facilitate success in that environment is useful for all students. Observation of peers within this context is crucial.

Classroom students who have difficulty staying on task and learning as part of a group need to be actively taught the behaviors that will allow them to be successful. Depending on the student, the classroom, or the school expectations, this set of behaviors might include:

a. Stay in your chair.

b. Keep your body, shoulders and head turned forward.

c. Keep your feet on the floor.

d. Look at the teacher when she is talking.

e. Keep your voice quiet except to speak when the teacher has called on you.

f. Raise your hand when you need help.

g. Do the class work when the other students are working.

I encourage parents to also explore the sets of behaviors that are expected or tolerated in the home. Parents can create social behavior maps for behaviors expected at dinner time, while in the car, getting ready for school, when doing chores, getting ready for bed, etc.

Social behavior maps can be created to explore any social context. For instance, at school this might include:

a. Learning in the classroom

b. Participation at an assembly

c. Eating in the cafeteria

d. Playground behaviors

e. Rainy day behaviors

f. Working as part of a group

g. Being in the library

Clearly there is a variety of behavioral settings we can help define and describe for a child, but we cannot do it all at once. Decide which contexts are the most difficult for the child and begin there. No more than two to three settings should be explored at any one time.

Defining Expected and Unexpected Behaviors

Behaviors can be defined as expected (socially appropriate) or unexpected (socially inappropriate) through the eyes of the persons interacting with the student (first column of the SBM, Handout 7).

To further break down the notion of "sets of behaviors" anticipated in specific settings, explore with a student what behaviors are expected (socially appropriate) versus unexpected (socially inappropriate). The terms "expected" versus "unexpected" arose during a therapy session where two boys were together and one of them screamed loudly for no apparent reason. The other boy looked at me and said, "Mrs. Winner, that kid is weird!" Always determined to teach students how they affect others in their environment, I went to the whiteboard and wrote down "weird" and "normal." I then paired the word "weird" with the word "unexpected" and explained that screaming for no apparent reason was unexpected and when people do things that are unexpected, others often consider that "weird." I countered this by explaining that behaviors considered "normal" are the ones that people "expect" in specific settings.

I have found that use of the words "expected" and "unexpected" are easily taught and understood by even young children in elementary school. It is generally accepted that expected behaviors help a child learn and be seen in a positive light by peers and educators. It is unexpected behaviors that cause a child to be perceived as "weird" or "odd" by peers and may frustrate those trying to support him.

A set of expected behaviors for learning was reviewed in the last section. Below is a list of possible unexpected behaviors within a learning environment:

a. Falling out of your chair

b. Wandering around the class

c. Making noises or talking to classmates

d. Saying things unrelated to the teacher's discussion topic

e. Looking in a direction other than where the teacher wants

f. Yelling out answers in class or never raising your hand to give answers

Remember: context drives behaviors and this qualifier needs to be frequently pointed out to students as you discuss their behaviors. Once context has been established, start by defining the unexpected behaviors the student is currently exhibiting. Generally parents and educators can easily verbalize what the child is not doing to conform to the group. Once the unexpected behaviors are outlined, it is then fairly easy to describe the opposite of each behavior to create the list of what is appropriate within that context.

I cannot emphasize strongly enough that determining what is expected or "normal" versus unexpected or "weird" in a particular setting is best accomplished through an observation of typical peers in that setting. For example, while I might believe that swearing is never expected at a middle school since we have rules against it, when I observe typical peers in their cliques at lunchtime or even in some classrooms, I observe a lot of swearing.

As you define what is expected or unexpected, always keep in mind what behavior the student observes in his typical peers and then help him make sense of it. Using my example above, it is important to explain to our students that while we adults prefer they do not swear, we know that some kids swear in social groups. The socially savvy students, however, are usually careful to pick the right time and place to "break the rule."

For example, we cannot tell middle school or high school students that swearing is never allowed on campus, since they observe so much of it going on around them. The key is knowing when to use certain behaviors and when not to use them. Swearing at a teacher is never tolerated; however, it is sometimes okay to swear about an assignment (outside of the classroom).

While we try to be extremely positive when working out behavioral teaching plans, our socially challenged students have a difficult time knowing when they have exhibited an unexpected behavior. When adults only attend to their positive behaviors we may not be giving students all the information they need to see the bigger picture of how and why their behavior affects their environment. For this reason we list both the expected and the unexpected behaviors.

The last rule for listing expected behaviors is that the behavior added to the map must be one the student can attain. If a student flaps his hands and the team has not found a suitable replacement behavior strategy, don't list "calm hands" as an expectation. The student will fail at it.

Defining How People Feel Based on Behaviors

Behaviors, be they expected or unexpected, affect the emotional state of those who are in close proximity. In column 2 of the Social Behavior Map we chart ways in which one's behavior affects the emotions and/or perspectives of another person. (See Handout 7.)

Our students have difficulty taking perspective of others. Once we have determined what behaviors are expected or unexpected in specific contexts, we then need to explain how these behaviors affect other people's feelings and emotions. Our students often fail to fully account for the emotional context

that surrounds them. First, they fail to realize that a behavior is inappropriate, then they don't understand how it affects others' feelings about them.

For example, when a student is sitting up at his desk and watching the teacher, the teacher feels proud of him, happy he is learning, and other students may also notice that he is doing a good job. But when a student falls out of his chair or makes "monkey" sounds, the teacher may feel frustrated and worried that he is not learning, and other students may notice the distraction and become frustrated with the student.

Some educators may not feel comfortable talking to a student about the more negative emotions they experience in response to a student's behavior. However, if we don't talk to the student about this, we are assuming he understands how his behavior has affected the environment. With these students we cannot make that assumption. While typical students have learned since early childhood that their behavior affects others' emotions, and they can read social cues that provide this information, our students have not. Our students struggle to make this connection and do not readily recognize others' social and emotional cues.

All that being said, there are times when one of our students behaves maliciously, and is fully aware of his effect on other people. I have observed a student purposely misbehaving and then also observed that same student exhibiting an unexpected behavior with no awareness of how it was affecting others in the environment.

In the second column of the SBM there is space to write a range of emotional words to describe common reactions to expected and unexpected behaviors.

On page 1 of the SBM (expected behaviors), words to express how a person feels can include:

- *Happy*
- *Proud*
- *Pleased you are working as part of the group*
- *Thrilled*
- *Calm*

On page 2 of the SBM (unexpected behaviors), expressing one's emotions takes on a more serious tone:

- *Sad*
- *Angry*
- *Frustrated*
- *Worried you are not learning as part of the group*
- *Confused*
- *Stressed*

Have the student work with you as you fill out the SBM. Discuss these concepts as the student helps you complete the map. By doing this you will get a sense of how much he or she understands about behavior and how it affects others.

It is enlightening to see that most children can provide a relevant list of emotional words for both pages on the SBM. Other children need to be taught there are more emotions than just happy and sad. Older students (middle and high school) can be taught to create their own SBMs; this gives them an opportunity to think through their own impact on their environment, which is a critical skill for them to learn as they move toward adulthood.

As children have the opportunity to see the behavioral expectations and emotional responses mapped out for them, we are also teaching them that behaviors provide a fairly predictable loop of reactions. Our students like concrete information,

and while emotions are abstract concepts, linking them to concrete behaviors and reactions helps children understand that behaviors and emotions are part of the bigger picture of getting along with others.

How People Treat You is Based on How They Feel

Consequences occur not because of the behaviors themselves, but from the impact of these behaviors on others' emotional states (third column of the SBM, Handout 7). In this column, we begin connecting others' behavioral expectations and the resulting emotions to the related natural consequences, good or bad.

Begin by defining for students the meaning of the word "consequence." A consequence is simply what happens next, based on a preceding event or emotion. Consequences can be either positive or negative, good or bad.

Students who are weak in determining how their behavior affects others' emotions tend to think that it is the behavior itself that is the cause for consequences. In fact, the behavioral systems we impose on students often teach them that their behaviors directly cause them to receive certain consequences: "First do your work, then earn a star."

In social contexts, such as the classroom, playground, or dinner time, people actually receive consequences based on how another person feels about their behavior! This is an important step of the process not to be overlooked!

If a student is doing what is expected, people feel good, and the student is far more likely to get some type of acknowledgement, including verbal praise, playmates who desire his company, and participation in an environment free of criticism. If the student exhibits unexpected behaviors, others in the environment may notice and react to the behavior by giving the student less desirable consequences.

For example, if a student is being highly distractible to himself and others, the teacher may speak to him in a stern voice, the aide may "nag him to work," the other students may move away from him, and he may get three opportunities to pull it together before he is removed from the classroom to calm down so other children may continue to learn. Depending on the behavioral system in place, there may also be a less direct consequence, such as removing points from a behavior chart.

When writing the list of consequences in the third column of the SBM it is extremely important to list not only the rewards a student may earn as part of a behavior plan, but also list the naturally occurring negative consequences to which he may not spontaneously be attending (i.e., criticisms rather than compliments).

Our students with significant behavioral problems often have behavioral systems that allow them to amass a lot of external rewards. For showing more positive behaviors they are rewarded with material goods such as stickers, tokens, money, food, or toys. The negative side to this is that relatively young children become the kings or queens of their homes or schools as they develop their personalized token economies! They come to expect rewards for doing any expected behavior.

A nine-year-old boy with Asperger Syndrome frequently had behavioral meltdowns for being asked to do his homework, a chore in the house, or because his mother was spending time with his sister. A variety of reward systems had been established for him over the years. At this point in his life he wanted to specify or negotiate for all possible rewards before participating in any activity presented. His desires became fancier and larger over time to the point that he required fairly expensive rewards to have him participate in basic activities of daily life.

While external token rewards continue to have value when working with our children, we also need to help children appreciate the rewards that naturally occur around them. As they move toward adulthood, all persons who function independently are expected to self-regulate their behaviors based on the natural consequences that in and of themselves are the reward for doing so.

A sixteen-year-old boy with Asperger Syndrome was fidgeting with a rubber chicken in my therapy room. I explained to him that it was fine to fidget with it during our discussion, but if his play with the chicken escalated to the point that it became a "distracter," he would have to move the chicken away from himself. When the rubber chicken was literally swinging around the top of his head while we spoke, I asked him to either put the chicken in his lap or next to me where he did not have access to it. His reply was, "What will you give me if I do that?" I responded that his reward would be the knowledge that he could do it. I explained that at the age of sixteen I would think he would want to know he was able to do that! I then asked him to put the chicken in his lap and I timed how long he was able to talk to me without being distracted by the chicken. After three and a half minutes he began to touch the chicken again. I told him I thought it was fantastic that he was able to go three and a half minutes without touching the chicken!

We then continued our discussion and he noticed that the chicken once again distracted him, but this time he took the chicken, without my cues, and placed it next to me where he could no longer touch it! Within a short period of time he had progressed from wanting to be externally rewarded for his actions to being able to personally problem-solve, make a good choice, and follow through on an action to develop an appropriate behavior. In response to his actions I verbally acknowledged that he was doing a great job.

Consequences given by others based on how they feel in response to a student's expected behaviors might include:

a. People use happy words (compliments).

b. People use happy faces.

c. People use a happy or calm tone of voice.

d. Friends want to play with you.

e. Your teacher pats you on the back. (Don't list this one unless you are sure the child is not averse to touch.)

f. A token reward (earn a point or a star that builds up to some larger known reward.)

An example of consequences given by others based on how they feel as a result of the student's unexpected behavior, might include:

a. People "nag" you (use words to tell you what you need to do).

b. People may show unhappy faces.*

c. People may use an unhappy tone in their voice.*

d. Other children may not want to work with you.*

e. You are asked to leave the room.

f. You do not earn your reward, or a point or star may be taken away.

* While it may be considered inappropriate (politically incorrect) to tell a student that people are using unfriendly communication styles with him based on what the student is doing, this is in fact what is really happening to the student! If we are going to teach our students about emotions and offer lessons on facial expression and so on, the best place to teach him the value of emotions is in the natural setting.

The list of consequences for expected or unexpected behaviors is just a list from which the caregiver can choose when deciding what reaction should take place. Not every consequence needs to be implemented each day the SBM is used. The list provides a set of choices to allow the caregiver to apply the most appropriate one to a specific behavior.

How You Feel About Yourself Based on How People Treat You

A student's emotional state is affected by the consequences he or she experiences (fourth column of the SBM, Handout 7).

So far in the process, sets of behaviors have been explored as having an expected or unexpected value. Students have learned that these behaviors affect another's emotional state and that these events lead to specific consequences. The last part of the SBM helps students observe how this chain of events ultimately affects their own emotional state, either positively or negatively. Use the fourth column of the map to record emotion words related to the students' feelings in response to the behavior chain of events.

It has fascinated me to work with some teenagers and adults who have led tough lives given their challenges (e.g., are in prison, etc.) who readily acknowledge that when others feel good about them and provide them with positive consequences, they feel good themselves! The reverse is also true; they will also state that when others react to them badly, they end up feeling worse about themselves.

You will find that your students can often supply the words for this column that describe how they feel about the reaction from others. Typically, the words are fairly simple and often include (when doing what's expected):

a. *Good*

b. *Happy*

c. *Calm*

And, when doing what's unexpected:

a. *Sad*

b. *Mad*

c. *Stressed*

Once again, it is important to point out that these words express emotions experienced by the student. By listing them in the SBM you are not forcing these feelings. Instead, you are recognizing that this is the way human relationships work.

The SBM is a great tool to teach children how they affect their own social success. By using this visual tool, we are able to document and demonstrate that when a student behaves appropriately in a specific social context he receives a good emotional response from another person, a positive consequence follows, and the student then acknowledges

that he feels good about himself. The reverse is also true. We can teach students how they affect their own and others' negative feelings by using the SBM.

Figure 15 is an SBM used to help a fourteen-year-old boy learn about his mother and her needs during the summer months when he was home all day. After we completed this, his mother commented that the mapping process helped put words to the feelings and reactions to the student's behaviors she had been experiencing for many years.

Figure 15-1
Social Behavior Mapping
Behaviors That Are EXPECTED: Being with Mom All Summer

Behaviors, feelings, and consequences are listed in categories in arbitrary order. There is not a one-to-one correlation between the information listed in each column. For example, whatever behavior is listed first does not have to match the first emotional reaction or the first consequence, and so on.

Expected Behaviors	How They Make Others Feel	Consequences You Experience	How You Feel About Yourself

• Nice:
  - Use friendly words.
  - Show interest in her.
  - Say "please" and "thank you."
  - Give her a compliment.
	• Good	• She compliments you.	• Good!

	• Happy	• She does something nice for you.	•
	• Proud		•
• Smile at her.	• Thrilled!	• She returns nice words, a nice tone of voice, a smile, back to you!	•
• Look at her when talking to her.			•
• Have your body be alert; do not slump over at the table when you are with her.			•
• Follow directions.			
• Anticipate what she wants you to do before she asks you!	→	→	→

☺

166

Figure 15 - 2
Social Behavior Mapping
Behaviors That Are UNEXPECTED: Being with Mom All Summer

Behaviors, feelings, and consequences are listed in categories in arbitrary order. There is not a one-to-one correlation between the information listed in each column. For example, whatever behavior is listed first does not have to match the first emotional reaction or the first consequence, and so on.

Unexpected Behaviors	How They Make Others Feel	Consequences You Experience	How You Feel About Yourself
• Not Nice: - Unfriendly words. - Don't show interest in her. - Doesn't say "please" or "thank you." - Rude remarks.	• Bad • Frustrated • Angry	• She "nags" you to use more skills. • She yells! • She leaves the house.	• Bad • Angry •
• Flat facial expression (not smiling).	• Worried you won't ever get along with others		•
• Not looking at her.		• No special treats.	•
• Body always slumping.			•
• Not following directions.			
• Doesn't anticipate what she wants me to do. $\rightarrow$	$\rightarrow$	$\rightarrow$	

The Behavioral Tornado

After using the social behavior mapping process with students, they begin to see some patterns. It is very likely the better they feel about how people react to them and the related consequences, the more likely they are to continue to produce expected behaviors; the worse they feel about it, the more likely they are to produce more unexpected behaviors.

A seventeen-year-old student summed this up well when he explained that the behaviors on the expected side of the page resulted in a "tornado of daisies" but the behaviors/feelings on the unexpected side of the page resulted in a "tornado of *#@^!." He reiterated that when he exhibits behaviors his mom expects, she feels good, and treats him well; he then feels good about himself, which helps him produce more expected behaviors. He then stated that when he does unexpected behaviors, his mom feels upset and treats him poorly, which makes him angry, and that makes him act even worse!

Social behavior maps can help students see that behaviors can lead to a "Catch 22" or continuous spiral. Behavioral events have a fairly predictable outcome. That is not to say that none of us should ever engage in negative or unexpected behaviors (since we all do), but this is a lesson in outcome. Students learn that the behavioral responses they gain from their actions are generally predictable right down to how they affect their very own emotions.

How to Use Social Behavior Maps

Once a behavioral setting has been described and information has been placed into each of the four columns on both pages of the SBM, it is ready to use. Make sure to mention to the student that information placed in each column does not directly correlate with the word to its immediate right or left side.

The goal is to catch the student in the act of doing what's expected. Circle the expected or unexpected behavior (column 1) that you (the caregiver) noted, then circle an emotion the caregiver feels is appropriate in column 2, then circle an appropriate consequence (column 3), and finally circle the student's emotion (column 4.) Connect the four circles with lines to create the "map" to help the student see the gestalt as it relates to interpersonal behavior.

Because the map provides visually detailed information, verbal interaction while using the SBM can be kept to a minimum. SBMs can be used on timed intervals or intermittently. The SBM itself can serve as a data sheet. I use one SBM for each hour the child is in that behavioral setting. Once the initial information is put into the columns, you will circle repeatedly on the same page, even if circles and lines collide. At the end of the hour, there is a good visual representation of how the student behaved in that setting.

The goal is to have many more circles/lines on the expected, rather than the unexpected side of the sheet. If we catch the student doing well, we socially reinforce positive behavior!

Focus On The Expected

The real power of using the SBM is to CATCH THE STUDENT IN THE ACT OF DOING WHAT IS EXPECTED! While we educators and parents spend much of our time lamenting the more dysfunctional behaviors presented by our students, the reality is that most students do what is expected the majority of the time!

I was consulting about Sam, a boy with Asperger Syndrome who attends a middle school. His behavior was erratic with him frequently calling out irrelevant information or questions in class. The boy was requiring frequent behavioral intervention with little obvious effect. A SBM was designed and implemented for him. After a few weeks, his parent sent a group e-mail to Sam's educational team indicating that he thought the use of the SBM could be effective, but it was currently only being used when the boy had unexpected behavior. The parent was concerned that not only was the child never being acknowledged when he did things well, but he was actually getting a lot of attention for presenting the wrong set of behaviors.

By coincidence I was in the boy's classroom the next day to observe a different child during a classroom social skills lesson. To my surprise, Sam was as good as Sam could possibly be during a lesson, yet his expected and positive set of behaviors was never acknowledged in the thirty minutes that I observed! When his behavior began to deteriorate, however, he was immediately admonished and "nagged" to do what was expected.

It is crucial to catch the student in the "act of doing what is expected" if there is to be any power in turning the sheet over to the unexpected side. In my experience, students grumble far less about having to complete the unexpected side when they have received a lot of positive strokes for their expected behaviors. When mapping an unexpected behavior, don't make a huge deal about it. Simply explain the behavior happened and it needs to be acknowledged on the map.

Using SBMs in Retrospect

Social behavior mapping can also be used quite effectively in retrospect. The SBM was actually developed while I consulted with a group of educators in a middle school. Their concern was that a student was using inappropriate sexual humor, and it was becoming quite serious. True to many middle school students with Asperger Syndrome, when the educators attempted to discuss the inappropriate humor with the boy, he would argue with them about his actions. A SBM about expected versus unexpected humor was designed for the school psychologist to use with him. On a day when he had once again used inappropriate sexual humor, the map was presented to him after the fact, revealing how others reacted and why he was getting a specific consequence. His reaction was to say, "Well, I can't argue with that!" When we get a teenager with Asperger Syndrome diverted from an argument, we've done something right!

169

Summarizing the Concept of Social Behavioral Maps

Social behavior maps were developed to educate students about the chain reaction of interpersonal behavior, emotions, and consequences. They were not designed to replace reward-based behavioral systems, but instead to embellish upon them. The strength of the SBMs is in the "social thinking" vocabulary established between educators, parents, and students. The power of the SBM is that in using them we can acknowledge when students are doing what is expected and contrasting that with the unexpected behaviors. Social behavior maps also allow us to use our emotional experiences as part of the daily lesson.

The visual and concrete nature of the SBMs helps facilitate a student's understanding of the abstract concepts being discussed. It also serves to clarify the different sets of behaviors called for in different environments or social contexts. This technique is being applied In public and private school classrooms across the USA, with mainstream teachers reporting that they like the explicit way the map lays out the social information. For further reference, a book called Social Behavior Mapping (Winner, 2007) provides over 40 generic examples of SBMs that can be used at home and at school.

Handout 8 illustrates how circles and lines create the "mapping" component of the social behavior map. Circles and lines connect behavioral reactions, helping the student see and understand the bigger picture: how she affects her environment and how the environment affects her in return.

Handout 8
Social Behavior Map Sample

Context: Behaviors that Are Expected While in Speech Therapy

Behaviors, feelings, and consequences are listed in categories in arbitrary order. There is not a one-to-one correlation between the information listed in each column. For example, whatever behavior is listed first does not have to match the first emotional reaction or the first consequence, and so on.

Expected Behaviors	How They Make Others Feel	Consequences You Experience	How You Feel About Yourself
• Doing the activity. • Look at things we are working on together. **Stay in your seat!** • Have your body be alert; do not slump over at the table when you are with her. • Follow directions. • Anticipate what she wants you to do before she asks you!	**Hopeful!** • Happy • Relaxed	• Get a star: 4 stars equal a treat **Michelle says "good job!"** • Michelle pats you on the back! • Michelle smiles. • Michelle has a "happy voice."	**Great!** • Happy • Successful • Proud

→   →   →

☺

Summary of Instructions for Creating and Using the Social Behavior Map

Creating the SBM

1. Write a brief description of the behavioral setting on the top of Page 1 and Page 2.

2. In the first column on Page 1 list the expected behaviors associated with the behavioral setting. List the unexpected behaviors in the first column on Page 2.

   It is actually often easier to start by describing the unexpected behaviors, and then listing the opposite on the expected behavior list.

3. In the second column on Pages 1 and 2, list words that describe the emotional reaction of others to the student's behaviors.

4. In the third column on Pages 1 and 2, list the consequences others might administer based on their emotional reaction to the student's behaviors. Remember to acknowledge the naturally occurring consequences in these environments!

5. In the fourth column on Pages 1 and 2, list the emotions the student may feel in response to others' emotional reactions and consequences directed toward him with regard to his behavior.

Using the SBM

1. Create a set of circles, at least one in each column to reflect the chain of events triggered by a student's behavior.

2. Draw a line to connect the circles across the page. This set of connected circles creates the visual map of the behavior. You can draw many circles and lines on one data sheet. Even when the lines and circles overlap, the student usually understands each mapping entry.

3. Show the students how behaviors become cyclical: your unexpected behavior leads to negative consequences, which make you feel bad, and that often leads you to have MORE unexpected behavior!

4. The SBMs are a type of data sheet. Generally, a SBM data sheet is used each hour the student is in the defined behavioral setting.

5. A graph can be made from the data collected each hour.

6. Focus on "catching the student in the act of doing what is expected" as the primary goal of the SBM; this will motivate the student to attend to both sides of the SBM.

7. Use the vocabulary established by the SBM even when the hard copy data sheets are not readily available.

8. REMEMBER!! The SBMs are used to teach students about their own behavior and how others react to them. They are not to be used as a "quick fix," nor do they replace traditional behavioral analysis and associated reward systems.

9. Share the completed SBMs with the entire team of parents and educators working with the student so all members of the team have a consistent core vocabulary and behavioral concept.

Supplements to Social Behavior Mapping: Teaching Students How Behavior Change Develops

Our students need explicit information about the expectations we set for them. Helping students change some aspect of behavior is central to working with most students with social cognitive deficits. Nevertheless, behavior change is hard work, especially as the child ages. We only have to look as far as our own personal experiences to realize how difficult it is to modify our behaviors once we get set in our ways.

To appreciate the challenges expectations of behavioral change present, it is fair — and important — to teach students AND caregivers the steps we all must go through to modify our behaviors. Adults must modify the way they react to a student if they are going to help the student change his own behavior! For example, when using SBMs it is critical that the adult begin to pay more attention to when the student is "doing it right," rather than focus primarily on when the student is "doing it wrong."

Four Steps To Changing One's Own Behavior

There are four steps involved in changing one's own behavior. Each step is defined and described below.

1. Self-Awareness

The person must have an awareness of the personal behavior he or she needs to change. It is helpful to carefully define the behavior and assign it a name so it can easily be discussed. For example, with a student who is constantly interjecting comments while the teacher is talking, we can call that behavior "blurting" or "interrupting."

Traditionally, to teach students self-awareness of a defined behavior, educators often give children stars or checks on a piece of paper when they are doing a good job producing the specified desired behavior. In reality, we also point out when they are not producing the desired set of behaviors. In step 1 the student is externally monitored to teach him to develop awareness about this behavior.

Doing this with tricky teenagers:

Some students in middle school and high school who are trying hard to be "cool" and fit in may not respond well to anything overtly positive, such as a check on a paper, when they are doing things well. For these students I write their desired behavior on an index card. If the student fails to produce the expected behavior I make a slight tear in the edge of the index card. This is effective for most of the students. On occasion, some of our more defiant students indicate they are pleased to get a "tear." When this happens I counter them and draw happy faces on their cards whenever I see them doing it right. They sigh in pain and laugh, but at least they are paying attention to the behavior, which is the primary goal! Basically, anything (that is not abusive!!) that draws their attention to the behavior while appreciating their own developmental phases is a good idea! Working with these older students on behavioral awareness can be tricky. These students require a lot of energy and constant creativity to inspire them to keep learning and help them learn common sense approaches they can handle.

2. Monitoring/Observing Others

Once a behavior is identified and labeled, the student is encouraged to watch this defined behavior in other people. It is far easier to be unbiased in our observations of other people's behaviors. Encourage the student to observe the specified behavior in other students and how people around that student respond to the behavior. A student who has had a lot of behavior problems may also enjoy and benefit from keeping his own data sheet in which he can surreptitiously administer stars or checks regarding the behavior of students he is observing.

Some students have great difficulty understanding how to observe others. We discuss with them the difference between "seeing" and "observing." Giving them very specific details to observe is helpful. At times students need to practice observing before they can be expected to do so successfully in a less structured environment.

For example, I asked a group of eight-year-olds to observe ("think with your eyes") my secretary and tell me what she was doing. When they returned two children told me she was working on the computer and the other two told me "she's there." These latter two students needed more information on what details to think about *(e.g., What are her hands doing? What are her eyes looking at? Is she talking and if so, to whom? What do you think she is thinking about?)*

As you are comparing and contrasting "seeing" versus "observing," continue to play with the idea that Little Red Riding Hood saw people or wolves, but did not observe them carefully, which ultimately caused her to be eaten!

3. Self-Monitoring

Once the student is familiar with how the specified behavior appears in others, he can begin to monitor that behavior in himself. He can give himself stars or checks, with the supervision of an adult to document he is doing it correctly. This phase in behavior change is the ultimate phase as the student begins to internalize his own behavior.

4. Self-Control

Self-control is the product of consistent self-monitoring. In step 4 the student has internalized the appropriate behavior and can produce it without frequent intervention from adults. It is vital that caregivers acknowledge the positive and appropriate dem-onstration of the behavior. Do not take behavior change for granted. The student needs to know that his behaviors affect how others feel in a positive way, producing more desirable consequences for the student!

A group of high school students was struggling with the differences among being "self-aware," "self-monitoring," and "self-control." They reasoned that when you are aware of the behavior you will stop doing the negative aspects of it.

To demonstrate the difference to them, I picked up a bowl of candy that was in my office. As I complained to them about my weight, I kept on eating candy, showing them that I was aware of my weight problem, yet I kept eating the candy anyway. I then showed them I was moving into the phase of self-monitoring by eating candy and saying, "I really have to do something about my weight."

At that moment I looked at the piece of candy I was about to pop in my mouth and I threw it away, but a few minutes later I picked up another piece of candy and ate it. Finally, I demonstrated self-control by picking up the bowl of candy, talking about my desire to lose weight, and putting the bowl back down on the table without taking any.

I find it helpful for students, particularly in middle school and beyond, to identify specific behaviors they would like to adopt in place of ones that trigger more negative outcomes. I then have the students complete the Four Steps of Behavior Change handout (Handout 9) to help them identify which step they are currently working on.

A Behavioral Plan is Different from Behavioral Action!

A group of older students had worked with me extensively on studying their personal behavior as well as that of others in the group. As our sessions were ending for summer, I had the students write out a sequence of smaller behavioral goals to help them accomplish a larger goal.

For example, the student who wanted to enroll in college listed all of the mini-goals ("action plans") he needed to accomplish to actually enroll: get an application, call about enrollment dates, and choose his classes. I then asked the students to sequence each action in order to achieve their goal.

To my surprise, they initially could not distinguish between a goal and an action. The more I spoke about the difference between a goal and an action, the more the students balked. Rubber chickens were flying! They argued that the goals implied an action and that it was ridiculous to list what action needed to be taken.

I pointed out to them that their lack of behavioral follow-through, demonstrated in their school programs, at home, and at work, was not related to the fact that they could not make goals; indeed, many had noble post-high-school goals. Their problems stemmed from the fact that they rarely followed through with appropriate actions!

They filled out their worksheets (Handout 10) where they had to meticulously define not only their goals, but also the related actions to be taken to accomplish the goal. The actions then needed to be mapped onto a timeline to which they were to be accountable during the summer.

Students teach us that no aspect of behavior should ever be taken for granted!

Handout 9: Four Steps of Behavior Change

Name _____ Date _____

Behavior change happens gradually! The older you get the more deliberate behavior change becomes. You can teach yourself how to change your own behaviors.

What behavior are you trying to change? _____

Read the four steps below.

Which step are you on

in helping yourself

to become more

aware of your

behavior?

Step 4: **WOW!**

Catch yourself, and change your behavior to what you want it to

Step 3:

Observe yourself caught doing the behavior you want to eliminate.

Step 2:

Observe other people doing the behavior that you desire or the one that you want to eliminate. Talk or think about your observations.

Step 1:

Label the behavior you want to try to change.

Handout 10: Defining the Difference Between a Goal and an Action

Name _____ **Date** _____

Setting goals for ourselves is a really important part of learning how to become more independent.

Goals help guide us in the choices we make. However, setting a goal is only wishful thinking until a plan is put in place to make the goal a reality. Plans are also only useful when we accompany them with actions to carry out our plans.

Goals and plans are things we *think* about.
Actions are the *things we do* to make our goals happen!

Most goals are accomplished in the future and can be broken down into a group of smaller plans to help you eventually meet the goal.

Fill out the template below to help you map out your specific plans to meet the goals and the associated actions you need to do for each plan.

Remember, plans are things you think about. Actions are things you do!

Write out your goal:

1. Write the first plan to meet the goal:	1. Write the action to make the plan happen!
2. Write the second plan to meet the goal:	2. Write the action to make the plan happen!
3. Write the third plan to meet the goal:	3. Write the action to make the plan happen!

"The Incredible 5 Point Scale"

Another cognitive behavioral strategy that can be used across environments is the "Incredible 5 Point Scale" developed by Buron and Curtis (2004). Using this strategy, students learn how they manifest behaviors at different intensity levels in an environment. When a student is demonstrating level "1" behavior, meaning the student is relaxed and feeling good in the environment, his behavior is generally flexible and appropriate; the student feels good about what he or she is doing. A level "3" behavior is when a student is starting to feel less "in control" but is still sustaining marginally in an environment. In contrast, a level "5" behavior is when the student is completely out of control.

Buron and Curtis encourage us to teach students to recognize the level of behavior they are manifesting in different environments and then to learn associated strategies to help them maintain a level of behavior that allows them to functionally adapt. Generally this means they are functioning at the level "2" range (e.g., good behavior for school/group functioning).

The Incredible 5 Point Scale dovetails well with the cognitive behavioral concepts of Social Behavior Mapping. Where SBMs encourage students to consider their impact on people in a group environment and how this in turn affects how they feel about themselves, The Incredible 5 Point Scale encourages students to consider their personal feelings and internal stressors. This helps them learn strategies to calm themselves, preparing them to self-regulate in groups. Specific examples of "5 point scales" can be found in their book, *The Incredible 5 Point Scale* (Dunn and Curtis 2004).

IEP Goals Related to Social Behavior Maps

Using SBMs as part of the student's special education curriculum ensures that students will learn about their own behavior and the effect it has within social situations. SBMs are an effective tool and their use can be specified in a student's IEP. Nonetheless, related goals involving the use of SBMs are difficult to write because they deal more with exposing a student to a concept than actually bringing about an immediate behavioral change. The goals and related benchmarks that follow suggest some ideas of how to do this. As you will see, these goals also encourage the development of skills related to monitoring their behaviors.

If use of an SBM or any other specific worksheet is to be written into the IEP, it is important to attach a copy of the template to the IEP itself. That way people reading the IEP now or at any point in the future can understand the tool that is to be used to work on a goal.

Goals & Benchmarks for an IEP

Plan: A social behavior map (SBM) should be constructed for Max regarding working independently during classroom time; another can be made regarding his playground time.

1. Max will demonstrate comprehension and use of the social behavior map by verbally reviewing the map with 85% accuracy.

   a. Max will explain the four columns of the social behavior map, especially how the columns relate to each other, with 85% accuracy.

   b. Max will complete his own SBM, filling out all four columns, with initial cues, with 75% accuracy.

   c. Max will review the direction of behaviors described on both sides of the SBM, demonstrating comprehension 85% of the time.

2. Alex will describe the three parts of behavior change: self-awareness, self-monitoring and self-control, with 90% accuracy across three sessions.

   a. Alex will label one specific behavior to become more self-aware of and monitor this behavior in others with 80% accuracy while working with me in the clinic.

   b. Alex will self-monitor his one targeted behavior by making a physical mark on a paper or with a token each time he produces the behavior he desires to change.

   c. Alex will demonstrate increasing self-control of the behavior, reducing it 50% over its baseline levels in the clinical setting.

   d. Alex will explain to his mother how he can use this same system at home or in the community when with his family.

Summary

Traditional approaches to behavioral intervention assume that students understand how their behavior affects others. Students with social cognitive deficits need solid conceptual information to help them understand this process. Social Behavior Mapping is a bridge between traditional behavioral programs and our students' need for cognitive insight into the behavioral process. SBMs demonstrate to students how their behaviors affect the perspectives of those around them and lead to consequences based on how others feel about their behaviors. Social Behavior Mapping is not a replacement for traditional behavioral programs but a supplement to increase cognitive understanding. IEP goals and benchmarks are presented for the reader to illustrate how to incorporate SBMs into the student's formal educational plan.

Chapter 9
The Me Binder: Teaching Students about their Individual Education Plans

 Individualized Education Program (IEP) meetings focus on identifying the strengths and weaknesses of a student and determining the need for and extent of future special education services. It is not unusual for these meetings to run two or more hours in length.

Discussions that occur during these meetings can be enlightening and encouraging. As required by federal law, educators and parents discuss a student's current functioning levels in any/all areas in which a student struggles, and the team devises a plan to promote further specialized education in the coming year. At the conclusion of the meeting, ideally, the team has refocused and is ready to help the student move forward into his or her next phase of learning.

The special education frontier offers a range of services, including:

- Resource specialists

- Special day teachers

- Occupational therapists

- Speech and language therapists

- Adaptive physical education

- Vision therapists

- One-to-one paraprofessional instruction

- Counselors

- Psychological assessments

A myriad of services and modifications may be built into the IEP to facilitate the student's success in the school setting.

Children with special needs, especially children on the autism spectrum, often receive a lot of special education and/or supplemental services, both in school and after school. It is not uncommon for these children to receive at least three or four services from the list above incorporated into their school schedule.

It is ironic that typically developing children, who are the most adaptable, have the least number of transitions during their school day. They stay within their assigned classes, leaving only when the clock indicates a transitional point in the general schedule.

The student with special needs, however, is the one with the unusual schedule. Each school day is a bit different depending on the time his specialized service providers are available to him. While this is not a perfect system, these are necessary interruptions during the student's educational day and week, as they help him achieve the goals and benchmarks in his IEP.

Problems arise, however, when the student does not understand why his schedule and services are different from his typical peers. Many students refuse to leave the mainstream classroom for services, even though it is difficult to provide for the students' needs in that setting. Thus, the problem is not whether to provide the services, but how to help the student understand their purpose.

Our students have difficulty understanding their unique learning disabilities and what educators are doing to help them. Their brains tend to focus on the parts of the day rather than grasping the "gestalt" of their schedule as it relates to the bigger picture of helping them learn specific skills. When students are asked why they go see their speech therapist or why they have a paraprofessional working with them, they generally answer, "I don't know."

Each special education service provider (speech therapist, resource specialist, occupational therapist) optimistically hopes students will take what they learn from their sessions and apply that knowledge and skill to their daily thinking routines. However, unless these students are actively taught why this information is important and how to connect it into their daily thinking routines, the benefit of these specialized services will not be fully realized. When a student does not understand the need for a service or transition, he may end up questioning the service or refusing to use it at all. It is rather ironic that in our best efforts to help students learn, we may also be unknowingly facilitating their defiance!

Another factor contributing to a student's inability to apply a learned skill or learn social thinking strategy from one person to another is that different educators and caregivers often do not know what others are working on with the student. I am always impressed by the level of devotion that educators bring to their work with students. Yet I am also struck by the lack of communication and planning time available for them to work as a team. Paraprofessionals or one-to-one instructional assistants who help students throughout the day — and who likely spend the greatest amount of time with a student during the day — often have never seen a copy of their students' IEPs, or do not know how to interpret the IEPs, so they are unfamiliar with the specific goals and objectives written for their students.

As an aside, at times administrators say they cannot give a copy of the IEP to the paraprofessional or classroom teacher because it breaches confidentiality. This is craziness! All types of educators need access to the educational plans of special needs students. How else can educators know and understand the purpose and value of the goals that are to be implemented? If administrators feel that sharing an educational document breaches confidentiality, they can easily correct this problem by having the

parent sign a note indicating that the information in the IEP is to be shared with all persons who are directly working or consulting with the student. If the parent refuses to sign, then the treatment team cannot function as stated in the IEP.

Another problem arises when a specialist within the district or from an outside agency assesses the student and writes a report which details specific services for a student, and then it is shared with relatively few people or sits unused in the student's file.

Given these lapses in communication, two questions should — and must — be considered:

1. . *How can we educate students directly about their own IEP services so they can more fully integrate what they are learning into their day?*

2. *How can we educate and communicate to team members the student's needs, the responsibility of the other team members, and the progress being made with the student?*

Using the "Me Binder" to Teach Students About Their IEPs

As much as I like to include older students in their IEP meetings, I still see that students have a lot of difficulty following the proceedings of the meeting and understanding it in a meaningful way. When we want to teach students with social cognitive deficits, we know that the lesson must be:

Visual:
Information needs to be presented for visual processing as well as auditory processing; and

Concrete:
Tightly defined and broken down into small steps.

Teams who embrace the idea of teaching students about their IEP services can systematically describe the treatment plan to them using language they can comprehend by using the "Me Binder."

The Me Binder provides the student with an outline of his own individualized educational program in a concrete, visual product. Like its name suggests, the information is assembled in a portable binder the student can use. Since it is difficult for a team to constantly communicate, the binder also provides information for fellow team members about why the student receives each specific service and the progress being made.

Furthermore, the Me Binder defines the roles and responsibilities of the educational team members in a way that is meaningful to the student. This sharing of information contributes to a more cohesive educational program for the student. The paraprofessional or mainstream teacher can read about goals or objectives being worked on during speech-language sessions or his time with the resource specialist. The student can read about the difference between the paraprofessional, resource specialist, and the mainstream teacher. All people working with the student will also have access to his behavior plan.

At home, the student's parents can read about the social stories or services that have been implemented in school and use the same vocabulary to reinforce similar concepts, as well as be able to expand upon the child's unique educational program.

The Six Sections of the Me Binder

The Me Binder has six sections that organize the educational program for the student:

1. Define learning strengths and challenges of the student as well as map out his schedule of services for the week or month.

2. Describe the jobs of the people who work with the student, why they work with him and how he is expected to use the skills gained across different settings.

3. Define his key goals and benchmarks, in language he can understand.

4. Provide a description of his behavior care plan, if one is needed. (See Chapter 8: Social Behavior Mapping.)

5. Include all social stories or other specific information designed to help him.

6. Use the last section to note homework assignments and maintain an academic planner.

The Me Binder Paragraphs

The following pages provide further information about each of these six sections, as well as templates that can be photocopied and modified by the educational team to develop their own Me Binder templates. The time spent on this will be invaluable. Educators will have a product that can be used on a regular basis to help demystify a student's educational experience.

Many parts of the Me Binder will be applicable to more than one student. For example, the speech language pathologist can write a paragraph about a lesson during one of her sessions with the student that will likely suffice for all students who share that same therapy group. The mainstream teacher would need to write only one paragraph, describing her role, that could be used for any student in her class. The ten minutes it takes to complete the paragraph or template is time well spent.

One of the most critical aspects to consider when writing material for the binder is that it be written at the student's level of reading comprehension. Our goal is to present information the child can easily interpret! The benefit is obvious. If the student can understand it, then all people working with the student can easily understand. No one will need to wade through a lot of special education jargon!

Overall, the Me Binder is written in a bottom-up approach: by making the information clear to the students for whom IEPs are created, all individuals working with these students, regardless of their familiarity with the formal IEP proceedings, can understand and define every facet of their students' programs. This approach is the opposite of the formal IEP proceedings, which are written from a top-down perspective. The formal proceedings produce an IEP document that can only be interpreted by those who specialize in the IEP process. The Me Binder is easy enough that it can be used every day!

One person on the student's educational team should be responsible for coordinating the different sections needed to complete the binder. Throughout the year it will need occasional maintenance and updating.

Two books can be helpful in developing the Me Binder: *What Does It Mean To Me?* (2000) by Catherine Faherty, and *I Am Special* (2000) by Peter Vermeulen. Both of these workbooks encourage the development of self-awareness and life lessons for students with high-functioning autism or Asperger Syndrome. Catherine Faherty's book takes the form of a Me Binder itself, and contains helpful templates and suggestions.

How to Use the Me Binder with the Student

Many pages in the Me Binder will be written with the cooperation of the student. Once the binder is completed, each member of the educational team should have the student read the specific description of how that adult contributes to the student's learning, until the student can describe it without the visual cues of the paragraph in the Me Binder.

The educator should also, on occasion, read another educator's description with the student, and encourage him to talk about how he can work on the other educator's targeted areas during his school day, including when he is with you! For instance, the resource room teacher might discuss ways the student can work on a social language lesson while in her classroom. The speech language therapist might explore ways the student can practice following directions during their time together.

The more familiar a student is with the behaviors expected of him, the easier it is for him to meet these expectations and achieve his IEP goals and objectives successfully!

Creating the Me Binder

The following pages describe the six sections of the Me Binder in more detail. Templates are provided in some sections to complete the Binder more quickly.

Section 1: The Student's Schedule

Many students with social cognitive deficits have difficulty predicting all but the most routine changes in their day. Our young students benefit from having a schedule to help them anticipate and prepare for transitions in their day or week. For preliterate children this can include an icon-based schedule. The computer program "Boardmaker" by Mayer Johnson has an excellent set of materials to help produce icon-based schedules or communication boards.

The amount and depth of information presented in the schedule depends on the unique needs of the student. Some of our students need very detailed schedules constantly reiterated to them; others manage with having just the weekly schedule laid out for them with special attention paid to atypical transitions they will be experiencing.

It is important that students in upper elementary school, middle school, and high school learn to be accountable for their own homework assignments and for tracking long-term class assignments such as state reports, book reports, and so on. Because these students have notoriously poor organizational skills, keep all assignment information in the same location, and use the same format to record the information. Remember we need to teach students how to organize and manage their responsibilities.

When assignments or schedules are placed and carried in a routine location, all educators and parents can then easily locate that information and be aware of upcoming expectations. It is also critical that teachers always post their homework assignments in the same area of the room each day to help the student locate the information he is to record in this planner. It is never enough to just orally state the assignment.

As mentioned earlier, the first page in the Me Binder should provide the daily and/or weekly schedule for the student. Handouts 11 and 12 suggest ways to present this information. However, always make sure the schedule sheet design is meaningful to the student and is based on his unique needs and level of cognition.

Handout 11: The Daily Schedule

The daily schedule for _____

Today is _____

Things to do this morning and changes to get ready for:

_____

_____

_____

_____

Behaviors for me to work on today:

_____

_____

_____

Choices at recess and lunch:

_____

_____

_____

_____

How does the teacher think I am doing on my behaviors?

_____

_____

_____

Things to do this afternoon and changes to get ready for:

_____

_____

_____

_____

My feelings keep changing throughout the day.

How do I feel right now?

☺   ☹

_____

Why? _____

Handout 12: The Weekly Schedule

The weekly schedule for _____

During the week of: _____

Time	Monday	Tuesday	Wednesday	Thursday	Friday

THINGS TO REMEMBER THIS WEEK!

_____

_____

Section 2: Strengths and Weaknesses

Handout 13 outlines a student's personal strengths and weaknesses. Helping students learn that each person has both strengths and weaknesses is essential. As I explore their strengths and weaknesses with students, I often map mine out as well to help them learn that part of the human condition is to be less than perfect! This is a worthy lesson because many of our students have significant issues with perfectionism that can cause them great anxiety. A good book on this topic when working with pre-teens and young adults is *Perfectionism: What's bad about being too good?* (Adderholdt and Goldberg 1999). Also review with students the meaning of the saying, "I'm just being human," meaning to be human is to make mistakes.

Most importantly, this worksheet can be a vehicle to introduce students to their IEP services and to the IEP team members who work directly with them to attain their goals. Fill this page out with the student. It is often helpful to have some outside information from the parents about the student's strengths if the student is not able to convey the information himself.

Strengths

The "My Strengths" column has three sections to complete with the student.

a. *What does the student really enjoy doing or thinking about? List these subjects or activities.*

b. *Who helps the student learn more about these activities? We usually have someone who helps us learn more about a subject — even those we're good at. List the people who help the student in these areas.*

c. *What does the student want to do better or learn more about related to this area of interest? List some examples or state a goal. Teach that we all should have goals to improve ourselves even in areas where we already excel.*

Weaknesses

The "My Weakness" column also has three sections. Generally you will need to guide the student through completing this section.

a. *What is hard for the student? List a few areas that the student struggles with at school or at home, academically or socially.*

b. *Who helps the student get better at what is hard for him? List his IEP team members who help him at school, and list his parents as well!*

c. *What is the student doing to get better? List a few IEP goals, written at the student's language level so they are easily understood!*

The person who is taking the lead role in coordinating the Me Binder should be the professional who helps the student fill out this page on strengths and weaknesses. If the student has a one-to-one aide, he or she would be the ideal person to update the scheduling page(s) as needed, once they are developed.

Parents and teachers of older students have shared with me that the concepts of the Me Binder can be modified as students age. By the time students are in high school, they should be writing their own sections in the Me Binder. This helps them develop self-advocacy skills they will need in their post-high school years.

Handout 13: Strengths and Weaknesses

My Strengths!	**My Weaknesses**
I am good at:	I need a bit more help with:
_____	_____
_____	_____
People who help me keep learning about what I am good at are:	People who help me learn how to improve include:
_____	_____
_____	_____
_____	_____
I plan to improve myself even more! My goal is to:	To make improvements, I need to have a plan. My goals are to:
_____	_____
_____	_____
_____	_____

Section 3: Learning About the Adults Who Work with the Student

In this section each direct service provider writes a few short paragraphs about his work and the scope of services provided to the student. Use the following guidelines on how and what to write.

1. Provide your job title and your name. Describe your job in general terms.

    a. Establish your purpose as it relates to the student. If you are a general education teacher your job is to work with twenty or thirty children while teaching them all one big curriculum lesson. If you are a special education teacher, speech therapist, and so on, your job is to help teach this student a more specialized lesson that focuses on his or her specific learning needs for the classroom, playground, etc.

    b. Make sure the student knows that you work with other students, not just him or her.

    c. Inform the student that you have many responsibilities during the day, only one of which is teaching him or her.

2. If you are a consultant, list the days you are at the school to see this student.

3. Label the location where you generally work with the student.

4. If you are a special educator, including a paraprofessional, describe what lessons/concepts you are working on with the student — and why — to assist his learning.

5. If you are a paraprofessional, mention the teacher's name with whom you work to develop curriculum adaptations for the student.

6. Describe where and when you want the student to continue to work on these lessons even when you, the educator, are not present.

7. Describe how you collaborate with the student's parents and other teachers so they all know what skills the student is working on. (This lets the student know that everyone is working as a team.)

Handouts 14 to 20 are a series of templates describing various personnel with whom the child might work. You can use these templates in place of creating paragraphs from scratch.

1. Go through the handouts and select the descriptions of the personnel with whom your student works. The first template is more general, the rest are job specific.

2. Once you select the template that most closely matches your job with the student, review the description and modify it to match what you specifically do with the student or elaborate on the current paragraph. You certainly are encouraged to write your own paragraph, at the student's level of understanding, following the guidelines above.

3. The professional in charge of assembling the binder should establish a date by which each educator submits his or her paragraphs.

4. Alert the various educational personnel and family members that these paragraphs are in the binder; encourage each staff person to review the related information with the student until the student is familiar with the description and can repeat it effectively back to the adult.

5. As the school year advances, contact team members to update their paragraphs as needed.

6. Remember, there is relevance in using a Me Binder with the older student (high school, upper middle school). A parent used this concept to help her son develop a stronger role as his own advocate. He had to write paragraphs about his different educators, what he needed them for, and how to access more information from them.

Handout 14-1
A General Description of Some School Employees

PEOPLE WHO HELP ME LEARN: A GENERAL DESCRIPTION OF SOME PEOPLE AT SCHOOL

Many adults help me learn. Some of them I see every day and others I may only see once a week or once in a while. Each one helps my teachers or me in a special way.

All schools have:

1. THE PRINCIPAL

Principals are people who are in charge of making sure all the people in the school are doing what they are supposed to be doing. Principals are in charge of the teachers and the other adults who work at the school. Principals also work with parents to make sure families and schools work together. Sometimes principals even help students who need special attention, good or bad. Principals are very busy people.

2. CLASSROOM TEACHERS

Classroom teachers teach lessons to their classes of students. Teachers MUST teach very specific lessons. These lessons are called "curricula." For example, there are different curricula for math, science, English, social studies, and so on. The textbook used in the classroom usually contains a lot of curricula for the class. The principal works with the teachers to make sure they are following the curriculum. In elementary school one teacher can teach one group of students all day. In middle school that changes, and a student often has many different classroom teachers, with each one teaching a different curriculum. The main job of the classroom teacher is to teach a large group of students at one time.

Every student has some type of learning he or she does really well and some type of learning that is harder for him or her. The classroom teacher has to monitor each child to see how he or she is doing with each part of the curriculum. In order to teach a large group of students, the teacher has to have every child work hard at thinking about what she or he is trying to learn. Because classroom teachers have so many students to teach, they need everyone to work together. When a child has a hard time learning a certain lesson or doing what the teacher asks, then special education teachers might be called on to help make learning easier for that child.

3. PARENTS

Parents are really important to YOU and to teachers! Think of all the different ways they help you learn at home, such as thinking about other people in the house, learning

Handout 14-2
A General Description of Some School Employees

PEOPLE WHO HELP ME LEARN: A GENERAL DESCRIPTION OF SOME PEOPLE AT SCHOOL

how to help with chores, how to get your homework done, and other lessons that are more fun. Parents are really busy teachers – they help you learn about being part of a family and help you to do well in school. Parents talk to teachers so that everyone can help you learn! Teachers really want parents to know what is going on in school so that parents can continue teaching the same lessons at home. Remember, your parent is one of your very best teachers!

4. All schools have teachers who help students learn about things that are super hard for them. These teachers are called:

a. SPECIAL EDUCATION TEACHERS

b. SPEECH LANGUAGE PATHOLOGISTS

c. OCCUPATIONAL THERAPISTS

d. PHYSICAL THERAPISTS

e. ADAPTIVE P.E. SPECIALISTS

f. PSYCHOLOGISTS

g. PARAPROFESSIONALS

h. INSTRUCTIONAL ASSOCIATES

i. _____

j. _____

k. _____

Circle the different types of helpers you work with and then find the page that describes what they do with you.

Handout 15

Special Education Teacher

Many kids who have special education teachers can be very smart in many things and then have more trouble learning other things. Did you know that even Albert Einstein had trouble learning certain things? Your special education teacher is the one who helps with the areas you have trouble learning. Your special education teacher's name is:

_____.

Your teacher helps you learn about:

_____

_____

She can help you in your regular classroom or by having you come to her own classroom to teach you. Special education classes have fewer students than the regular classrooms so your special education teacher can spend more time with you and the other students.

If you are learning in the regular classroom, your special education teacher will work closely with your other classroom teacher(s) so that you can do as well as possible! All teachers talk to your parents as well, because people at home and school work together to teach you!

Your special education teacher will sometimes change a homework assignment that your regular classroom teacher gave you. This is OK because she is trying new ways to help you learn. Sometimes students don't like it when they have to do work that is different from the other students in the class, but it is important for you to let the teacher try different ways to make it easier for you to understand.

If you still feel it is hard for you to learn or you have a question in any of your classes, you can talk to both your parents and your teachers. Everyone is there to help YOU! What words can you use to tell someone that you don't understand what to do?

_____

Handout 16

Instructional Assistant or Paraprofessional

People who help teachers to teach students can be called "paraprofessionals" or "instructional assistants." These are people who really like to work with kids. They are like a "teacher's helper." Paraprofessionals can be very good at what they do! Their boss is the special education teacher but they also can get information from the regular classroom teacher. You may have more than one paraprofessional working with you. The name(s) of the paraprofessional(s) you work with is/are:

_____

Your paraprofessional works with you every day during:

_____

Like other adults at school they will talk to all of your teachers to learn how to better help you. Many times they make decisions about how best to help you with certain lessons both inside and outside your classroom. Sometimes your paraprofessional will help by changing your classroom lesson to make it easier for you to learn and be good at learning. Sometimes your paraprofessional will work with you on learning to pay attention and work as part of the group, even though those are not lessons that any of the other children are working on. Sometimes paraprofessionals will go with you when you play with other kids during recess if learning to play in a group is something you are working on. Paraprofessionals are really cool people. Your paraprofessional is working with you to help you learn:

_____

_____

Your paraprofessional expects you to also try to work on many things by yourself. She thinks you are ready to do some things all by yourself:

_____

Handout 17

Speech Language Pathologist (SLP)

The name of your speech language pathologist is:

_____

Speech language pathologists (SLP) usually don't work with kids every day because they work with students at different schools. Your SLP sees you _____ times a week on these days: _____. The SLP helps students improve their speaking or anything related to language.

The SLP works with some kids on learning to say sounds or words clearly; she works with other kids on how to put sentences together; sometimes she helps kids listen or write better; or how to use their language to make friends and work with other people.

Your SLP works with you on:

_____

_____

Even though you don't get to see your SLP every day you still have to work on the lessons she or he is teaching you every day! You can do this by:

_____

_____

You should work on this (circle the ones that are correct):

In your other classes	At home
During recess	At lunch

Your SLP also talks to all your teachers and even your parents. Since talking and understanding what people say is really important, she can teach you some really cool stuff!

Handout 18

Adaptive Physical Education Teacher (APE)

The name of your adaptive physical education teacher is:

_____

Since those are a lot of words we call them "APE" teachers for short. Your APE teacher helps kids whose bodies and brains have a harder time working together to do big body movements. This can include running, throwing, skipping, hopping and games with balls. Sometimes kids just have trouble getting their bodies to do a bunch of different movements at once (running and catching.)

Your APE teacher helps kids:

1. Learn how to make our muscles stronger.

2. Learn how to make our bodies move faster or for longer periods of time (this is called endurance). The heart is one of the biggest and most important muscles in the body, and it feels stronger when we can move for a long period of time!

3. Learn how to move our bodies in the exact way our brains tell them to. This is called "coordination," and this is when our bodies and brain work together. Throwing and catching balls takes a lot of coordination.

4. Sometimes our muscles or nerves (the things that carry the message from our bodies to our brains and back to our bodies) don't work very well. That's when our APE teacher teaches us other fun ways to play different types of games with our bodies.

You are working with your APE teacher on:

_____

_____

Your APE teacher works with kids at many different schools so you don't get to see him or her every day. You see your APE teacher on _____. Since keeping your body healthy is important there are things your APE teacher wants you to practice every day.

Things you can work on by yourself include:

_____

_____

Handout 19

Occupational Therapist (OT)

Your occupational therapist is _____.

To make it easier to say, an occupational therapist is called an "OT."

An OT helps people's bodies and minds work together by teaching the body to listen to the brain. They often help us learn how to do little movements of the body we have difficulty with like writing, getting dressed, and catching a ball. The OT does this by teaching you how to break down body movements into smaller parts so you can understand how all the movements work together. Your OT may also need to help you make some muscles stronger so it is easier for you to use your body. Did you know that writing with a pencil also means your tummy, back, and shoulder muscles have to be working to hold your wrist in place on the paper?

Sometimes our brain gets really, really busy trying to pay attention to all the stuff going on around us, and it gets tired of working so hard! Each of us is supposed to be able to use our brain to concentrate on what we are learning, but that is not always easy. OTs can teach us ways to help keep our bodies and brains calm so we can learn.
Your OT talks to your classroom teachers so they can also try the different ways to help your brain and body stay calm.

Your OT works with kids at a lot of different schools, so you don't get to see him or her every day. You see your OT on _____.

With your OT you are working on:

_____

_____

Even when you are not with her, you should still try to work every day on:

_____

_____

School Psychologist

School psychologists help figure out what type of learning strengths and weaknesses students have. School psychologists also can help work with kids on learning about themselves and how they can do their best in school. They may even work with students who are having other problems at home or at school.

Your school psychologist is _____.

If she tests you, she is doing it to see how best to help you, or to see how much better you have gotten over the years. Once she learns about you she meets with your teachers and your parents to help everyone develop a plan on how best to help you learn. Some people see their school psychologist each week to talk about how things are going in their lives. It is also possible that you don't see your school psychologist very often, but he or she keeps learning about how you are doing by talking to your teachers and parents.

It is really cool that so many people are here to help you!

The next time you are going to see your psychologist is

_____.

Section 4:
Writing Goals for the Child to Understand

The inner workings of the IEP are based on the written IEP goals and possibly the related benchmarks. Educational placement and services can only be discussed after the IEP goals have been included in the IEP document. This is the core section of the IEP, yet the student is often poorly informed about his IEP goals.

To follow is a series of real IEP goals and how they were simplified in the Me Binder to help the student understand what he should work on.

Example 1

IEP Goal: When instructed, Roger will work independently for 20-minute intervals with two or fewer verbal prompts, 80 percent of the time.

Me Binder Goal: You (Roger) will do your classwork without needing the instructional assistant to keep telling you to pay attention to what you are doing.

Example 2

IEP Goal: Roger will be able to describe problems pictured or read about, then answer "why" or "what should/could happen" questions with 80 percent accuracy.

Me Binder Goal: You (Roger) will think about problems in stories or pictures and then make guesses about what could happen next.

Example 3

IEP Goal: Roger will improve gross motor planning and skills for academic success.

Me Binder Goal: You (Roger) will practice playing on the swings, bouncing balls, and moving your body so that your body starts to know what to do without having to think so much about it!

Section 5: Behavior Care Plan Information

The information provided in this section helps students learn a plan was developed to teach them how to use more appropriate behavior in various settings at school. Having sat through many meetings to discuss a student's behavior and help develop a plan, I have come to the conclusion that behavior care plans must be written so that the student understands them as well. It makes no sense that we adults spend many hours devising behavior modification plans, when all the student usually sees from these meetings is a reward sheet. I firmly believe that learning to change behavior is an educational process the child needs much more information about!

We also know that consistency is crucial to the success of any behavior care plan. If a student's plan is written so he or she understands it, then we know that not only the child can interpret it, but so can the instructional aides, mainstream teachers, parents, and others. Consistency only happens when there is mutual agreement on what to do.

It is important to clearly define the child's behaviors that need to be modified. "Behavior problems" are any behaviors that prevent the student — or nearby students — from learning. These "behaviors" include blurting out in class, self-distraction, or refusing to complete assignments in class. Clearly, we need to discuss and deal with behaviors a child exhibits prior to the behaviors escalating toward aggression, severe depression, and so on.

⧗

Caleb was in middle school and had the same excellent paraprofessional work with him for many years. However, the paraprofessional told me that Caleb no longer had a behavior problem since he was no longer aggressive nor verbally abusive. When I observed Caleb in class, he did sit quietly in the group but he drew pictures all around the edges of his paper and refused to be re-directed by this paraprofessional. Clearly, Caleb still had a behavior problem, but it was only affecting his own education and not the education or safety of others.

The previous chapter on Social Behavior Mapping describes a plan for helping children learn about their own behaviors and how they affect other people, the consequences they receive, and ultimately how their behavior affects how they feel about themselves.

Figure 16 is an example of a more traditional behavior plan written so that the student understands it. . The child had difficulty following classroom lessons, accepting direction from the instructional aide or even agreeing to stay in the classroom during instructional times.

Figure 16-1

A Behavior Plan Written for the Child to Comprehend

WHAT FRED NEEDS TO LEARN IN SCHOOL, PAGE 1

Kids come to school every day to learn information about subjects like history, science, math, writing, and reading. The teacher is in charge of helping students learn. There are a lot of children in one class. In order for the teacher to teach all the children, the children have to be ready to learn. Being ready to learn means that a child has to:

1. Stay in class where the work is being explained and practiced.

2. Work on the task the teacher is talking about.

3. Listen to the teacher.

4. Let the teacher decide what work is to be done.

Some students have a special helper like you do. Brian is your instructional aide. He is there to help you be part of the class. You have a lot of good ideas and can be very smart, but some things are harder for you to do, like handwriting. Brian is there to help you when the work is being taught to you in class. Mrs. Heart is your teacher. She talks to Brian and helps him know what you should be working on. The only person who decides what work you are to do and how much of it you have to do is Mrs. Heart.

Right now Brian and Mrs. Heart are worried that you are not coming in to class ready to learn. For you to be ready to learn, you must:

1. Stay in class.

2. Do the work Mrs. Heart decides you need to do that day. (Brian is there to make sure you understand how to do the work.)

3. Do what Brian asks you to do. Brian can help you find easier ways to do the work. Brian can play games with you, but it is totally up to Brian how much work you are to do before you earn playing a game with him. You can choose the game, but you cannot choose how much work you will do in order to play the game.

Figure 16-2

A Behavior Plan Written for the Child to Comprehend

WHAT FRED NEEDS TO LEARN IN SCHOOL, PAGE 2

It is important that you understand what your job at school is.

Tell me three things you need to do at school to help yourself learn:

1.

2.

3.

We have made a schedule that will help you get ready to learn. Brian has that for you to review with you each day.

If you need help with getting ready to learn about your assignments, Brian and Mrs. Heart are there to answer your questions. You can ask for help by looking at Mrs. Heart and raising your hand to get her attention, or by looking directly at Brian and then saying, "I don't understand this; can you help me?"

Your reward is that when you do your schoolwork in class:

1. You feel good about what you have accomplished!

2. Brian and Mrs. Heart are proud that you are learning.

3. You earn time to go for a walk or play a game with Brian.

You can do it!

Section 6: Incorporating Specially Developed Materials into the Me Binder

Social stories and visual organizers are often used to help students with social cognitive deficits better understand the inner workings of the world that surrounds them. The development and use of these strategies is FANTASTIC; however, once developed they are often difficult to access. It takes effort to share them with the rest of the student's educational team. Individually created strategies can be placed in this section of the Me Binder; this helps make the information more readily available to others. This section will need to be updated on a regular basis.

Social Stories were created by Carol Gray to help children learn social cognitive information about specific environments. Social stories consist of three paragraphs:

1. Description of the setting: what is happening in the environment

2. Description of the perspectives of those around the child in this setting

3. Directive: A description of what the child should do in this setting to succeed.

Social stories are also written in the language of the child so that he can understand the expectations placed upon him. Carol Gray has written many books related to the topic of social stories; one is written for preschoolers and has corresponding pictures. It is entitled: *My Social Story Book* (2002), and is available at www.thegraycenter.org..

Goals for Addressing Concepts in this Chapter

1. Nick will describe the difference between three of his different educators at the school, with 80% accuracy.

2. Nick will describe the goals he is working on in his special education program and why he is working on the goals, with 80% accuracy.

3. Nick will explain when and where he is to practice the information being taught to him across the home and school day.

Summary

The concept of a Me Binder is reviewed to provide students with clear information about why they are receiving extra assistance from special educators. The Me Binder's purpose is twofold: 1) to explain to the student the focus of his program, and 2) to provide simplified, relevant information about the student and his or her educational program to other educators and parents who want to learn how to help the student.

The Me Binder includes a review of the student's schedule of services, the student's strengths and weaknesses, the different roles of the various educators and service providers who work with the student, a student-friendly version of his behavior plan and a section containing specially developed therapeutic materials such as *Social Stories*.

Chapter 10
About the Social Thinking Dynamic Assessment Protocol®

Good dynamic assessments are essential in designing individual, appropriate, effective intervention programs for students with any type of challenge. Good assessments encompass much more than testing for and identifying deficits. They also spotlight students' strengths and often reveal students' preferred learning modality. Good assessments bring all this information together within a context that allows us to see the child as a whole entity, not merely dysfunctional pieces, and appreciate the exquisite interrelationship of these parts.

Assessing social cognitive strengths and weaknesses in students can be a daunting task for education and service-related professionals. At present, no formal assessment protocols have been written and accepted for use in this area for children or adults. Without such standardized tests, educators are often ill equipped at incorporating formal social thinking goals and objectives into a child's therapeutic plan or individualized education program (IEP). Yet, those of us in the daily trenches of working with or parenting this population know these social challenges are very real and deserve more formal recognition and attention.

Furthermore, because of the nature of social cognitive challenges, existing assessment tests often fall short in accurately evaluating the level of social-thinking difficulty students possess. More often than not, our standardized language and communication tests return scores that indicate a far higher level of functioning in our students than they actually possess in real-life environments. We must broaden our perspectives towards communication and include evaluation of the dynamic social use of language as a separate and equal partner in assessing total communication functioning.

Many of these ideas are discussed in more detail in this chapter, especially attention to the limitations of current standardized tests in assessing social cognitive difficulties. The Social Thinking Dynamic Assessment Protocol® is presented, along with suggestions on functionally assessing a student's social cognition and related social pragmatic skills. The protocol is the result of more than 20 years clinical experience with these students, in both public and private practice. We regularly use this protocol in our clinic and have "field tested" it with other professionals involved in social pragmatic work with students, with positive results. Time and again we have found that the protocol gives us real-world, functional information on a student — the exact type of information that can then become the foundation of the student's social thinking treatment program.

Adopting a Healthy "Perspective" Towards Social Assessment

Students with social cognitive deficits require applied therapeutic intervention that focuses on **practical** knowledge and the **functional** application of skills across various environments. For this reason and others, our assessment of these socially-driven concepts needs to take place in a more natural, dynamic setting — one that allows the give and take, reciprocal nature of social interaction to unfold as it would in daily life. This is uncomfortable ground for many "testing people" who prefer standardized tests to be just that — standardized. It also presents inherent challenges in interpreting results.

While a one-test-fits-all approach may be appropriate for assessing skills such as math or vocabulary, by its very nature it is the antithesis of an appropriate environment for testing social cognitive skills. A new perspective towards assessment is needed if our goal is to help these students achieve success.

Expanding the Definition of Communication

Many parents and professionals define communication as the systematic development of expressive and receptive language skills. We think of communication and "talking" to be the same. Yet, talking is just one small part of communication. Consider the last conversation you had with another person and the nonverbal ways you supported your message: how you oriented your body, your tone of voice, gestures, facial expression, how close you stood or sat to the person, eye contact, etc. Communication is ever-present; everything we do (or don't do) sends a message to others around us. Merely sharing space with another person can send a strong message of liking that person (we stand close or orient towards him) or being aloof and nonsocial (we stand apart or turn away).

Once we add language to the communication, a tacit social expectation exists that we each will then monitor our own communication (verbal and nonverbal) in relation to others in the conversation. We become responsible for interpreting people's intentions, emotions, and desires in light of the context. For example, a student saying "shhh" to a peer in his classroom may be an attempt to stay out of trouble with the teacher; that same "shhh" on the playground may be playful in nature, to quiet a bystander while the child sneaks up to surprise another child.

Communication and conversation is a dynamic process. It unfolds over time and involves much more than assembling words into sentences and vocalizing a message or response. It requires an ongoing assessment of the speaker's intent, as carried through his spoken words, nonverbal cues, the context and your existing knowledge of the person's personality or personal expectations of the interaction. This process is communication.

To make matters even more complex, social knowledge continually evolves across our lifetime, involving increasing levels of nuance and sophistication starting as early as the third grade. The appropriate communication or social pragmatic skills for kindergartners are radically different than those for teens, which are quite different than those for persons in their 30s. Socially-appropriate communication reflects the age of the speaker, perceived belief systems, the context of the situation while also employing increasingly abstract syntax and semantics.

Given the complexity of communication, it is obvious that its assessment needs to be equally dynamic, analyzing much more than simple syntax or vocabulary. However, our current standardized tests fail to capture the many related aspects that contribute to functional communication.

Understanding the Limitations of Standardized Tests

Professionals - be they psychologists, speech language pathologists, counselors, educators, etc. - are taught the importance of using standardized tests to evaluate students' levels of functioning. By comparing them to a larger sample of similarly aged students, the exploration of social pragmatic/social language skills based purely on the results of standardized tests are insufficient for understanding the depth and complexity of social processing and social skill production (e.g. communication skills). (Simmons-Mackie & Damico, 2003; Tetnowski & Franklin, 2003; Bishop, 1998).

Very often the results of standardized tests of language competencies for students with normal intelligence, yet social pragmatic deficits, fail to represent that the student has a significant problem. The student tests "within normal limits." This can be very frustrating for the student, his or her parents and classroom teacher, who all observe serous problems in how the student is relating to others, participating in the classroom, handling abstract homework assignments, etc. Relying on standardized tests to measure a student's total communicative proficiency is a misjudgment that can follow a child through all years of his or her development, from preschool through adult years.

Our existing standardized language and pragmatics tests have yet to capture the depth and complexity of communication to the extent that they accurately assess our students with social thinking challenges. Some of the ways these tests fail this population are reviewed below.

1. Standardized tests are developed to measure specific skills, and in order to do so, remove competing variables. However, social pragmatic/ social language competencies are a function of social responses provided in natural, not artificially simplified environments. Stripping away competing variables radically minimizes the complexity of real-life communication and produces social pragmatic assessment results that are skewed at best.

Consider this scenario: A student having great difficulty attending to the classroom teacher's lectures is referred to the speech language pathologist (SLP) for possible challenges with auditory processing. The SLP, in order to "validly" assess the student's hearing, removes him from the natural classroom environment to a small quite room, with no competing variables, to conduct the mandated auditory test in the prescribed manner. No other person can be in the room at the time of the test, nor can the room have more than 25 decibels of background noise. It is no wonder that in this "sanitized" listening environment the student passes the test at the 30th percentile. However, to qualify for services in the public schools, the student would have needed to score no higher than the 7th percentile! The SLP reports to the parent and teacher that the student's

hearing is within normal limits. These results are accepted as "valid" since the testing protocol was followed as directed. However, the test failed to validly measure the teacher's concern: the student's ability to hear, attend to and process oral information and instructions while in the classroom. The result? The child fails to qualify for services. This idea is explored in more detail in the excellent article by Minshew and Goldstein (1998), "Autism As a Disorder of Complex Information Processing."

2. Standardized language subtests most often assess the student's technical knowledge and processing of language at the word and sentence level, and rarely address pragmatics – the use of language.

In university training programs, speech language pathologists learn that language consists of content (semantics), form (syntax), and use (social pragmatics). However, in clinical work, speech language pathologists traditionally focus only on the content and form of language, assuming that mastery in these areas will intuitively result in the student being able to use these skills to communicate effectively. And therein lies the cause of many a misstep in evaluating the communication abilities of those very students who need our help. *For students with social cognitive learning challenges, social pragmatics is not intuitively learned!* Many of our smarter students do well on tests, especially those that measure only semantics and syntax, and falter in the social use of language. Yet this part of communication is generally excluded from formal testing.

The assumption that a student who does well on the more technical aspects of language is equally competent on the social use of the language is an error of enormous proportions. The ability to socially use language requires an even more complex set of skills and social knowledge than the ability to develop basic expressive and receptive language skills. Many students with Asperger Syndrome and similar social-cognitive disabilities will pass the majority of language tests, yet have significantly impaired social language skills. Without remediation these pragmatic challenges will negatively impact not only their social relations, but their ability to self-advocate, participate in work groups in the classroom, and develop the self-awareness and people-awareness skills necessary to guide them through post-high school education, employment, and other adult situations.

3. Social communication can be viewed as a social executive function task; the nature of standardized tests minimizes the application of executive function skills. (Dawson and Guare 2004). Minshew and Goldstein (1998) also speak to this issue, explaining that autism is a complex information processing disability. It is not a disability easily captured by a set of specific subtests.

To this writer's knowledge, the Autism Diagnostic Observation Scale (ADOS; Lord, et.al., 1999) is the only standardized dynamic assessment instrument currently available that takes into consideration the complex nature of communication and the child's "Theory of Mind" abilities. However, the ADOS is a tool used only for diagnosis – it does not establish treatment recommendations based on the results. Furthermore, extensive training and practice is needed in order to properly administer and score the test and relatively few professionals are qualified to do so.

4. Communicative success is dependent on timing and interpretation. Observe a conversation among fifth graders or a classroom discussion and it is immediately apparent that

communication falls apart if a partner delays his or her response by more than two to three seconds. Social communication thrives or dies with the timeliness of responses, yet there are few subtests of language skills that require a timed response.

Communicative success is also dependent on the ability to listen and respond to another's words, in context, while simultaneously interpreting the meaning and intention of the message through both verbal and nonverbal communicative cues. These are exactly the skills expected of students in a classroom, and it is also expected that they be carried out with proficiency among a group of 20 or 30 other students. However, there are currently no standardized tests on the market that explore this dynamic process.

5. Various social adjustment and emotional processing psychometric assessments exist; however, these fail to measure social pragmatic/ social thinking deficits. Virtually all these tests are designed to determine whether, or to what extent, the student has deeper mental health challenges. Many bypass social learning altogether. While many new research studies demonstrate that persons with social learning challenges end up with mental health problems such as anxiety and depression, these are often the byproduct of inattention to their social learning challenges and not a coincidental co-existing diagnoses (Stewart, Barnard, Pearson, Hasan and O'Brien, 2006; Abell and Hare, 2005; Hedley and Young, 2006).

In summary, standardized tests often contribute relatively little meaningful information to help parents and professionals better understand their students' social pragmatic challenges. While the benefits and accuracy of standardized tests are loudly touted to many professionals, including administrators, the reality is that we continue to fail our students in accurately assessing social communication challenges. Until such standardized tests exist, it becomes necessary to design other functional, meaningful ways to evaluate students' pragmatic functioning and drive the programs and services needed to alleviate these challenges.

Conducting Functional Social Assessments

To begin with, assessment of students who are suspected of having social thinking challenges *must be multidisciplinary in nature,* with information contributed by most, if not all, of the following team members:

- Parents

- Mainstream classroom teacher

- Special education teacher

- Speech language pathologist

- School psychologist

- Occupational therapist

- Physical education/adapted PE teacher

- Other: physical therapist, vision therapist, etc., if working with the student

Social language and perspective taking are at play in all environments, from school to home to community. A child may function adequately in one environment – for instance, a school classroom – through rote repetition of learned skills, yet be floundering in all other arenas of his or her life where social thinking and social actions happen "on the fly." An accurate picture of the child's social thinking abilities can only arise from input gathered from multiple sources and across different domains.

Second, *use a variety of assessment tools.* To qualify for speech and language services in public schools, students must score below a specified performance level that indicates the student has a "severe" deficit.

It is generally accepted, if not strongly mandated that this "severe deficit" is to be determined through the administration of standardized testing or through language samples that demonstrate insufficient language skills combined with low test results. At the same time, the educator/speech language pathologist is a professional who should be considering the whole child and how his functional skill level serves him currently in his educational environment, as well as how his communication skills will serve him as he moves towards the complexity of adulthood. Federal law states it is also possible to qualify a student for school services based on the discretion of the professionals who have fully assessed the student, along with consent from the student's IEP team.

The following chapter reviews a variety of standardized tests used with students who exhibit social cognitive challenges. The strengths and weaknesses of each test are discussed in relation to it being part of an overall social thinking assessment. In many cases an IEP team will require standardized tests. It behooves professionals to understand the limitations of those available when using these instruments for assessment.

It is critical that in any assessment, whether or not standardized testing is included, we explore the *use* of language as an entirely separate and valid domain of functioning. The social thinking protocol explained in this chapter and provided in the appendix emphasizes social pragmatics. Readers will come to appreciate that it is possible to test pragmatics and base our assessment equally on this area of functioning. In doing so, we will capture more accurate information about a student's communication abilities – not just his mastery of speech.

Third, since language samples are a common means of assessing a student's functioning, it is a reasonable professional judgment that testing can consist of a *social pragmatic language sample.* Simply put, a social pragmatic language sample is a descriptive observation of a student's functional language, which encompasses not only spoken words, but all the nonverbal means he uses (or doesn't use) to support the intent of his message: eye contact, body orientation, body language, etc.

Multiple observations in various environments are a requirement. The sample should consist of observations of a student throughout his school day, with particular attention paid to how he relates to his peers during free time outside the classroom, and how he relates to others during more structured interactive experiences in the classroom (group work or circle time).

Pay particular attention to the student's interactions with his or her peers. Typical peers do not generally facilitate success for students with social cognitive deficits — adults do. Adults help create communicative success and often compensate for a student's weaknesses to prevent an awkward moment, even during assessments, without realizing they are doing so. Therefore, it is crucial to observe a student's interactions with his peers in various settings and under various conditions of calm/stress, order/chaos. After all, the desired goal of all treatment programs is that the student can adapt and communicate effectively within his or her peer group and the world at large.

Documenting multiple observations may sound like a time-consuming process. It is, but consider this: so is standardized testing. The good news is I discourage the blanket administration of standardized tests of receptive and expressive language. Many of our students are so good with these technical aspects of language that these basic tests are literally a waste of time. They will not accurately assess the student's social thinking deficits. A more productive approach is to complete a social pragmatic observation as well as the social thinking protocol described in this

chapter.

It is also extremely beneficial to talk to the student's classroom teacher(s) as part of this social pragmatic observation. However, take note that teachers are often unskilled at spontaneously describing social pragmatic skills or deficits. It is wise, therefore, to ask the teacher specific questions about the student. We have found that questions based on the I LAUGH framework return relevant information. Some suggestions include:

- How does the child indicate he needs help when he is stuck on something?

- Is he overly literal compared to his classrooms peers?

- Is there a difference between his reading decoding and reading comprehension skills?

- Does he struggle with holding a pencil and writing clearly?

- Does he struggle with composing paragraphs?

- Is he thoughtful of others when playing games or having to work with others in class?

- Does he anticipate when it should or should not be his turn to talk, or does he blurt out information?

A short, simple one page Teacher Questionnaire (included in the Appendix) can be used to learn more about a student's social functioning within the classroom. The most interesting and revealing question on this form is "How would his or her peers describe this student?" By asking teachers to share the impressions of peers, we often receive true-to-life information, rather than the politically correct answers teachers may feel compelled to give. Students will ultimately be judged their entire lives by their peer group. It is important to consider the reactions of this group to the student as part of the overall assessment.

The Social Thinking Dynamic Assessment Protocol®

The Social Thinking Dynamic Assessment Protocol® is a means of identifying and quantifying, in real-life terms, a student's social cognitive/social language skills. The results of the assessment provide not only a better understanding of the student's pragmatic language skills and his social interactive functioning, but also his ability to effectively apply social knowledge to the academic curriculum. A well-done assessment can guide the team in designing specific and tangible social and academic goals. It also gives teachers and educational staff a more thorough understanding of the "unseen" challenges the student grapples with on a daily basis that affect learning and his ability to confer benefit from the rest of his educational program.

Use of the Protocol as part of a social thinking assessment provides information critical to the development of the treatment program by:

1. Observing the student's social behavior in comparison to his or her same-aged peers, across a variety of different environments.

2. Pinpointing areas of relative weakness and relative strength.

3. Illuminating the importance of these social thinking and pragmatic language skills to achieve success in academic, social, community, and recreational arenas, and how vital they are to the future success of the student beyond high school.

4. Exploring the similarities between social thinking within conversation and social thinking within academic assignments. For example, a student with a limited ability to interpret the intentions of his conversational partners will have the same problem when asked to read a book and interpret the intentions of the characters. (Winner, 2005).

5. Prioritizing the student's weaker conceptual areas so that treatment can be targeted to first work on skills that most affect the student's current functioning level.

6. Describing a treatment plan that provides direct teaching of social cognitive concepts and related skills that can generalize across social and academic settings.

Informal social assessments can be paired with formal assessments; however, it should be noted that the results can be in strong contrast to each other. As mentioned previously, a student may score extremely well on all subtests of IQ and language, yet perform quite poorly on dynamic measures of communication. In our years of experience we find that the Social Thinking protocol, because of its dynamic nature and natural setting, yields results more reflective of the student's social-cognitive functioning. Armed with this information, we can systematically address a student's weak dynamic communication skills and design treatments to teach him to be more socially aware. Without this formal training, these students will most likely struggle significantly as they approach adulthood, and be socially impaired the rest of their lives.

Setting the Stage for the Social Thinking Assessment

Professionals who conduct student assessments generally establish rapport with a child before engaging him or her in standardized tests. While we want children to be at ease and free from stress, we rarely consider that this very process of "helping" the student may have an impact on the test results. Nowhere is this more a consideration to be taken into account than in the area of testing for social thinking impairments.

211

To conduct an objective social assessment, keep in mind that adults do more to structure and create coherent conversation with individuals with learning disabilities than peers will do for each other. When working with students, pay close attention to how much "work" you do to maintain a conversation or interaction:

- Monitor the number of follow-up questions you need to ask to keep the child engaged in the conversation. I write a bent arrow on my page every time I ask a follow-up question. If the child volunteers information on his own, my notes will be free of bent arrows, demonstrating the child's ability to flow with the back-and-forth nature of conversation.

- Monitor the content of the conversation. Is the student only willing to talk about a limited number of topics? What does he do when you try to change the topic? What type of questions does the student ask you? Does he demonstrate an interest in you/the new topic, or is the question intended to steer you back to talking about the student's desired topic(s)?

- Monitor the student's nonverbal body language and facial expressions. Is he turned toward you, with his body, face, and mannerisms showing engagement, or does his eye contact and body position indicate disinterest? Note if he can readjust when you give him direct verbal cues such as "When you turn your body away from me, I think you are not interested in what I have to say."

Where does the social assessment take place? Pretty much anywhere people naturally gather together. It can be completed in an office at school, in a private clinic, at home, etc. Just remember that the elements of the location become part of the assessment itself. Choose a place that doesn't have outside distractions, like a park, unless the parent is requesting intervention because of challenges in a specific setting. We usually conduct our assessments in a room at our clinic. There are also no rules as to who can accompany the student into the assessment room. I usually encourage the student's parents to join us at the table. We want to observe the student in as natural a setting as possible, and parents can become part of the assessment itself, as noted in the descriptions that follow.

The assessment is structured and guided by the professional, but the informal nature of it allows for a great amount of flexibility. At any point the professional can help the student work through a challenging moment, use humor, introduce story telling, or prompt a student as he works through a specific issue. Keep in mind at all times that our purpose in conducting the assessment is to learn more about the student's social pragmatic functioning. *Virtually anything we do with the student provides feedback in that regard.* Many students describe the assessment as an extended conversation and play, rather than being "tested."

At times we have tried out social pragmatic therapy concepts during an assessment to get a sense of how the student responds to them. For example, I recently assessed a 14-year-old boy, and as part of the assessment had him practice entering in and out of a communicative exchange I was having with his mother. Just as his mom reported, he had very little awareness of physically adjusting his body to enter into a group. We then talked about the Four Steps of Communication and practiced each step. I monitored how he processed this information and whether or not he incorporated it in later parts of the assessment. This teaching-learning strategy became part of the assessment itself. It indicated the teenager was willing and eager to learn this more meta-cognitive process for improving his communication.

Overview of the Social Thinking Dynamic Assessment Protocol®

The Social Thinking Assessment Protocol® is included in the Appendix. You will want to refer to it as you read the remainder of this chapter, which describes the informal assessment process in greater detail. The Protocol is not a written-in-stone tool – it can be modified or expanded, and I encourage professionals working in this area to do so. However, when used as is, it will provide a detailed picture of the student's social thinking capabilities and deeper insights into these "smart but socially weak" students.

The Protocol describes the task being probed and includes checklists to record observations that assess how the student responds to the test prompts. Interpretation and implications of results are also included in various sections.

Before using the Protocol for the first time, it is a good idea to go through some of the test prompts with a few age-matched neurotypical peers. This will give the examiner insight into ways neurotypical students respond to these questions, making it easier to spot social thinking challenges in students with suspected deficits. Professionals are often "blown away" by how revealing and truly challenging these social thinking probes are for our students with social cognitive deficits.

The assessment is comprised of the following sections:

Section 1. Getting to Know the Student

a. Questionnaires for parents and teachers

b. Review reports from school educators and private professionals

c. Meeting with parents

Section 2. Welcoming the Rubber Chicken

Section 3. Writing Sample

Asking for help

Section 4. The Double Interview

Part 1: Interviewing the student: explores the social dynamics of communication when it is focused on the student's life, including the student's use of narrative language

Part 2: Preparing to switch roles: Interpreting pictures about the evaluator's life

Part 3: Shifting perspective by having the student interview the evaluator

Section 5. Thinking with our Eyes

Exploring the student's ability to read eye-gaze and transfer this information to social thought

Section 6. Picture Sequencing

Sequencing and defining a picture story with an age-appropriate theme

Section 7. Social Scenario Pictures

Reading social scenario pictures to assess perspective taking

Section 8. Assessing Organizational Skills

Using narrative descriptions to explore the student's problem-solving skills and ability to adjust his behavior in the classroom

Note: the Social Thinking Assessment Protocol® is most useful, as is, for students functioning as "High-Level Emerging Perspective Takers" or "Impaired Interactive Perspective Takers" who are over eight years old. These designations were described in earlier sections of this book.

Protocol tasks can and should be modified significantly when the student is younger and/or appears to function at the level of an "emerging perspective taker." With preschool and early elementary school students the assessment is done more within play than through conversation. We might explore narrative picture story books, gauge the child's ability to accomplish basic Theory of Mind tests, watch how the child uses his body and eyes with others while engaged in play, or explore the student's ability to engage in parallel and then group shared imaginative play. Further comments and suggested modifications are described in sections of the protocol.

A dynamic social cognitive assessment — as well as the related treatments — are part science and part art. While the scientific research points us toward exploring aspects of social pragmatics (Winner, 2000); relating to the student and adapting the assessment to keep him engaged in a social relationship with the examiner is an "art." The value of the professional's "art" will never be adequately quantified by scientific evidence, but its importance cannot be undervalued (Ratner, 2006). You cannot reliably assess a student if he does not want to participate, nor can you provide treatment if the student refuses to come to the next session.

Section 1.
Getting to Know the Student

The assessment process begins with gathering information about the student from people who work with/know him.

Parents and teachers are asked to complete the "Teacher Questionnaire", which solicits information about the child's social behavior.

Review reports/assessments previously written about the student. Note whether test scores are stable across time, the child's general IQ range, the level of expressive and receptive language functioning and any test results related to the student's adaptive social-emotional functioning. Note the various diagnostic labels the child has been given and his overall behavioral adaptations across the years.

Interestingly, many professionals discuss in their reports a child's very weak social abilities but because the child performed well on standardized tests they refused to qualify the student for services within the school. This can be very frustrating for parents, and cause apprehension at having yet another assessment done. It is a wise professional who keeps this in mind when first meeting with parents.

Meet with the child's parents to learn more about their concerns and observations. When the assessment is held at my private clinic, I always spend time with parents prior to the evaluation to explore their concerns and solicit feedback on the child's challenges and abilities. Parents can offer invaluable information about the child's social emotional functioning across many different settings. Common questions I may ask the parents include:

- How is your child doing today? Does he know why he's here? How does he feel about having to go through the assessment?

- Describe your child in a social situation, such as a family party or at school in his classroom. How does he act? What does he say? Is he engaged or aloof?

- What concerns do you have about your child's social development?

- How is your child doing academically in school? Which subjects are the easiest/hardest? How does he feel about school?

- How does your child handle homework? If the child is in fifth grade or older, I usually ask additional questions about the child's ability to manage short and long term homework assignments.

- What questions do you have?

Take a bit of time to explain the evaluation process and why the informal nature of it is appropriate to assessing social thinking skills. Many parents are relieved to learn of the more true-to-life nature of the assessment and welcome the narrative, descriptive format.

Section 2.
Welcoming the Rubber Chicken

In my first book, *Inside Out: What Makes a Person with Social Cognitive Deficits Tick?* (2000), we tout the benefits of introducing a rubber chicken into the therapeutic setting when working on social thinking skills with students. Briefly, the rubber chicken is used when a student or an adult in the room makes a social error, which we are all prone to do from time to time. When we do something that "earns us the rubber chicken," we lightly tap ourselves on the head to demonstrate we've made a social blunder. The chicken brings humor into the situation and helps our students understand that we all make mistakes in our social interactions. (Rubber chickens are available at our website, www.socialthinking.com)

I also use the rubber chicken during my assessments. At first I just have it on the table, in large part to suggest that humor will be appropriate during the evaluation and to help the students relax. Students are permitted to fidget with the chicken as long as it does not become a distraction. While this may sound a bit bizarre, our students have difficulty making transitions to new environments and grow leery over time of all the professionals who test them. The rubber chicken introduces a novel element into the assessment and can later be used in many ways to assess the student's various social-emotional skills.

For example, I was working with a 14-year-old high school student with persistent depression because his peers don't interact with him. He explained to me he will talk to someone only if that person first talks to him. He went on to describe that this generally happens when, by good luck, his teacher puts him in a group with other students who like heavy metal or punk music. He waits until the other students start to talk about music, but even then will not join in because he thinks they may not want to talk to him. He often looks away since he feels awkward, and if they talk to him, he then jumps into the conversation. Not surprisingly, he is often unsuccessful in his mental bids for conversation.

Before I discussed how important his body and eyes are for communication, I handed him the chicken and explained he had just "earned the rubber chicken." I showed him how we can lightly tap ourselves on the head when we make a social error. He laughed and tapped himself on the head. I explained the error, helping him understand that he has to make people think he is interested in them if he wants them to communicate with him! He used the rubber chicken from that point on to acknowledge his social errors and laugh at himself. I, of course, made errors that allowed me to tap myself in the head with the chicken as well.

Section 3.
Writing Sample: Asking for Help

The first task asked of students, school aged or older, is to fill out a form. It requests basic information such as their name, the date, their birth date, home address, parents' names, etc. (For a kindergarten student I may only ask the child to write his name.)

At first glance this task may seem too simple to provide relevant information on the student's social functioning. However, it is deceptively simple. By having the student complete the form, the interviewer learns about:

Penmanship: The majority of our students have fine-motor planning problems that affect their handwriting. When I poll my conference audiences about various written language problems, including poor handwriting, about 80% of the audience indicates their students have these problems. Most students seem to have large, bulky handwriting, although a few have exceptionally small handwriting. Because writing is so laborious for them it can lead to behavior problems in the classroom. Problems with written language extend beyond just handwriting. Students also have trouble with planning and organizing their thoughts so their writing has coherence. We often overlook the many tasks involved in transferring our thoughts onto paper. It appears our students get easily overwhelmed with the multitasking nature of even a simple request. No wonder behavior problems arise!

Ability to ask for help: In general, students on the autism spectrum or those with other diagnoses that include a social thinking impairment have difficulty asking for help and/or clarification. Asking for help is a pivotal social skill; it clarifies the world and forms the basis for self-advocacy as a teen and young adult.

When I ask the student to complete the form, I mention we are here to help him, but only if he asks for assistance. I then intentionally withhold help, even if the student struggles, to better assess what, if any, strategies are used.

Observe the student: if he is not quickly and efficiently filling out the form, record what behaviors emerge when he is unsure of what to do. Monitor how long the student sits without writing or asking for help. If the student is visibly stuck at least 20 seconds, ask the student to think about how he can ask you to help him. Offer help once he forms a question, or help him develop a strategy to request help. Observe if the student uses the strategy once it is discussed, both here and during other parts of the assessment.

Once the task has been completed, ask the student, "What do you do at school when you get stuck? Do you usually ask for help or are you usually really quiet?" Make sure to confirm the student's response with the parent and teachers to determine if the student perceives his actions accurately.

Sunny was a second grade boy who was having significant behavior problems in the classroom. I asked him to fill out information about his family, along with the date. I also told him if he needed any help he was to ask for it; the adults in the room would not volunteer to help him unless he specifically requested it. When Sunny got to the line to write in the date he kept his head down, started to poke his pencil into the paper and said aloud to himself, "I don't know the date." He continued to repeat this and more aggressively poked the paper; however, he never looked up or directly asked for help. Three minutes passed before I interjected, "Sunny if you did want help, who would you ask?" He replied, "My mom," at which point it took him another 45 seconds to formulate the question, "Mom, what is the date?" This interaction indi-

cated that he likely had difficulty requesting help when he was writing, which quite possibly leads to increased behavior problems during this type of task in the classroom.

General knowledge and abilities: It is interesting to observe how much basic, personal information our students possess, particularly when they move into fourth grade and higher. A number of our "bright" students can speak about a range of academic topics, but are unable to spell their parents' names, or write their full address. This little task helps us keep the information we teach students in perspective. If a fifth-grade student is considered "very smart" but doesn't know his home phone number, we may be sacrificing functionality in the name of teaching academics.

Section 4.
The Double Interview

One of the most informative exercises in the Social Thinking Assessment Protocol is The Double Interview. It consists of me interviewing the student about his life at home and at school, then turning the tables and asking the student to interview me. More detailed discussion on each part follows.

The Double Interview - Part 1: Interviewing the student to explore the social dynamics of communication, including narrative description, when conversation is focused on the student.

Most people are more comfortable and capable talking about things familiar to them, or on which they feel knowledgeable. After the writing sample is taken, I tell the student I want to get to know him better, and to do so, am going to ask him a series of questions — I'm going to interview him. As I ask the questions listed below I take notes on the student's social pragmatic skills related to:

- Body language: maintaining eye contact; keeping his body, shoulders, and head turned towards me, etc.

- Ability to modulate his volume and tone of voice: Does he talk too loud or too soft? Is his prosody (vocal inflections) within normal limits, or does the student speak in a monotone?

- Does the child use sufficient narrative language skills to answer questions? For example, in response to the question, "Do you have a pet?" a student who simply says "yes" does not understand the nature of the question or that offering information in response to a question facilitates the back and forth nature of conversation.

- Are the student's responses related to the question asked or tangential to the topic?

- Does the student have one particular topic he is eager to talk about or that he constantly shifts the topic back to? Does the student seem bored or disinterested, or have lifeless expressive language skills during the interview unless he is talking about his area of interest?

Interview questions I use follow; feel free to supplement this list with your own.

1. What are your hobbies?

2. Do you have pets?

3. Do you have siblings?

4. What chores do you have to do?

5. What is your favorite thing to do at school?

6. What is the hardest or least favorite thing for you to do at school?

7. What do you do during recess or lunch time? Ask the student for specifics. For example,

many students mention they spend time with friends. Probe deeper by asking him to describe what they did together yesterday during lunch. If the student is not sure how to answer the question, ask him if he likes to be with other people or prefers to spend his free time alone. Explore the student's response further to gauge whether or not he has friends.

8. What do you like to do after school? Do you call people on the telephone? If not, why not?

9. If your mom got a day off from being a parent and could do anything she wants to do for the day, what would your mom choose to do? (The purpose of this question is to determine if the student can think about his mother as having interests other than those defined by her role as mother.)

10. If your dad could do anything he wants for a day, what would he choose to do?

   Interestingly, in my clinical experience, students generally know what their fathers like to do for "free time" but less frequently know about their mother's interests. It is unclear if this is true just for students with social cognitive deficits or if this pattern is consistent across all children!

During this part of The Double Interview keep in mind your focus is asking questions; avoid adding your own thoughts or comments when the student is talking. Model how to conduct an interview that is focused on the other person. When you get to Part 3, this will be important to the student.

Remember to take notes on the student's social pragmatic behavior while he is talking, along with summarizing his responses. Use bent arrows to indicate times you had to encourage further responses with a follow-up question.

The Double Interview - Part 2: Preparing to switch roles by using pictures as an information source for questioning the evaluator.

Turning the tables and asking the student to interview us gives us an opportunity to assess how the student communicates when forced to actively take the perspective of another person, rather than being solely focused on his own thoughts and preferences when in the company of others. Many students will not be comfortable with this part of the assessment. To prepare the student for interviewing me, I introduce three photographs of my family and myself.

I start out by verbalizing something like the following:

"I interviewed you by asking you questions and I learned a lot about you today. I learned you have a brother. You have two pets, you love to play with your Gameboy when you are home, and you have a friend who lives next door and you sometimes play together. I also learned you really like math but hate to write. You have two friends at school you hang out with during recess, but you are not sure they always treat you nicely. Your teacher's name is Ms. Draa and you like her a lot. I learned a lot about you!

But you know very little about me. You were told to come to my office and talk to me but you do not know much about me. To be fair, I am going to let you find out about me. I just interviewed you by asking you questions about yourself; now you get to interview me. Everything in this office belongs to me, including the pictures. You may ask me questions about anything you see in the office or any other questions about myself you might be wondering. Let's look at these pictures to help you get started."

The three photographs on my office table portray:

1. My father and me

2. My two teenaged daughters and me

3. My two daughters dancing in their marching band performance.

I begin by asking the student to tell me about the people in each picture. Most students are able to quickly identify that the pictures show various members of my family. However, on occasion a student will not be able to figure out the relationships in the pictures or recognize the same face in different pictures.

While the purpose of this task is simply to help students think more about me, this task can, at times, identify students who cannot recognize faces. It also helps screen students who over-focus on details, missing the bigger picture or gestalt. For example, when a student looks at the picture of my daughters standing with me in a typical family portrait and describes the picture as being of me and "two girls," the student is missing the concept of family. When I ask how the two girls know each other, a person with social thinking deficits might respond, "they are friends" rather than sisters. While this alone is not sufficient to diagnose a social-cognitive disorder, it is interesting and should be considered in the broader context of the information gathered about the student.

Having completed hundreds of assessments over the years, student errors in interpreting the pictures seem to fall into four general categories:

1. Limited ability to shift perspective

2. Difficulty reading others' faces

3. Limited accounting for contextual cues

4. Limited ability to make inferences

Limited ability to shift perspective

The most consistent error made by students is using their own personal framework in assigning relationships among the people in my photos, illustrating a difficulty in shifting perspectives. For instance, I used to show students a photo of my husband and myself. Most students thought my husband was my father. They saw a man roughly the same age as their own fathers and labeled him as a "father" based on their perspective, rather than as a "husband" based on my perspective. This error is understandable for very young elementary school children, but many 10- to 12-year-old students made that mistake, and then persisted in their description, even after corrected. This is a fascinating clue to how narrow their ability to take the perspective of another person can be and how hard it may be to interpret the world around them in any way other than their own.

Troy was a 10-year-old boy with an above-average verbal IQ. His educational testing did not show any significant discrepancies beyond a 10-point difference between his verbal and performance scale IQs, with his verbal IQ being higher. He had recently been asked to leave his private school due to mildly unusual social behavior. When he was presented with my pictures he described the man and woman (my husband and I) as "your grandparents." After asking him to make a different guess to see whether he could correct himself, I finally had to tell him the pictures were of my husband and me. Nevertheless, in all seriousness he persisted in labeling them "your grandma and grandpa" despite numerous reminders.

Difficulty reading others' faces

Some students, but not the majority, have a marked deficit in recognizing other people's faces; this is called facial agnosia.

⧗

Joe, a 42-year-old man with Asperger Syndrome, told us he could rarely identify people by their faces until he gets to know them very well. When I first met him we spent two hours together in deep discussion at my house. He then attended an all-day workshop where he watched me speak for six hours. Finally, he came to work with me at my office. When he arrived at my office he commented, "I am glad your name is on your door. I never would have recognized you!" Joe explained that he usually recognizes people by their tone of voice.

Any degree of difficult reading others' faces will severely impact a student's social abilities. Imagine the fear and insecurity a student might feel not being able to recognize his teacher, or the principal, or new classmates, or later in life, his boss or a new romantic acquaintance. If a student I am assessing does not recognize me in my photos, I probe more deeply into the degree of this difficulty, including his ability to read the facial expressions of others.

Limited accounting for contextual cues

The ten-year-old boy who thought my husband and I were my grandparents clearly had difficulty not only taking perspective, but also using contextual cues. The pictures show us in modern dress. My husband and I were in our late 30s and early 40s when the pictures were taken. We did not have gray hair.

In another assessment, I used a picture of my husband playing his trombone in a jazz band. I asked a seven-year-old student to explain why I had the picture of the jazz band on my table. His response was, "Those are all your children." Students with social cognitive deficits generally lack an appreciation for contextual cues that provide meaning and define relationships. Be sure to note these deficits on your assessment, as this affects the student's social success in all areas of life.

Limited ability to infer

It is not uncommon for students to have difficulty making inferences when looking at the photographs – i.e., guessing at the relationship among the people in the photos. Many miss the family ties altogether. Students fail to infer that the two girls sitting with my husband and me are my daughters. When asked who the girls are, students respond with answers such as neighbors or friends. Or they respond by saying, "I have no idea who those people are!" A bright, science-minded middle school student, who was teased often in school, could not assign a family value to any of the people in the photographs. He recognized me but then quickly gave up, saying he had no idea who the other people were.

By the end of the photograph description task, I make sure every student has a clear understanding of all three pictures and the relationships among the people in each.

Advice on selecting photos

Any type of socially themed photograph can be used for this part of the assessment. In our clinic we've tried all sorts of different pictures, some with more success than others. In general, we have found it most beneficial to use photos that show the evaluator's life in the pictures. This sets the stage nicely for the next part of the interview.

When gathering family pictures to show students, make sure the pictures:

- Clearly show the faces in the photographs

- Have minimal visual clutter so the student can focus on the people and not be distracted by other interesting objects in the picture.

- Do not contain pets/animals. Students are usually enamored by pets and will focus on them rather than the people.

The person doing the assessment should be in at least two of the three photos. If the third photo excludes this person it should be clearly connected to the evaluator's life. For example, my daughters are with me in one of my pictures, and then I have a photo of them dancing in their marching band as the third picture. This provides the visual connection and also suggests my daughters like to dance.

Double Interview - Part 3:
Shifting perspective by having the student interview the evaluator

Once the photograph task is finished, I review the next part of the assessment, where it becomes the student's turn to interview the evaluator. It is important to again explain the process: the student is responsible for finding out about me by conducting an interview with me, that an interview is a time when one person (the interviewer) asks specific questions of the other person (the interviewee) to find out information about that person, and that the job of the interviewer is to only ask questions that reveal information about the other person's life. We then review what constitutes a question if there is any concern the student is not aware of the difference between a question and a comment.

Many of our students are weak in question generation, whether they are children, teens, or adults. Therefore, I discuss with students the Wh-type words we use to initiate questions (e.g., who, what, when, where, why, how, do you…?), and if needed, write them down. It continues to surprise me how many older students need this written list before they can proceed with the interview.

The student is reminded that I interviewed him and he can use a similar format. I also again remind the student to use any visual information in the room, including the pictures we discussed, to think of questions to ask me about my life.

Strategies for helping the student with the interview

Once the student is asked to start the interview it is critical that the evaluator initially do nothing to foster the student's success in creating a good interview. Neurotypical children can usually ask a question within one to three seconds when given this level of structure. If the student indicates this task is stressful or overwhelming, or does nothing at all for more than 10 seconds, then the evaluator can help by:

1. Drawing four boxes on a piece of paper, explaining it as a visual framework of the number of questions the student is to ask before the task ends. Each time the student asks a question, place a check mark in a box. The interview is completed once each box has a check mark.

2. As mentioned above, the examiner can write out the list of words used to start questions, such as "who, what, when, where, why, how, do you…?" Place the list in front of the student to help him initiate questions.

3. Pointing to the pictures on the table or objects around the room and reminding the student he can ask questions about anything he sees. In many cases, I simply slide one of the pictures forward, asking the student to formulate a question about that picture. Remarkably, most students can immediately formulate a question once you provide the extra visual or auditory scaffolding to this task. This makes me strongly suspicious that our students' rapid responses to pictures in our speech and language therapy sessions do not generalize to an ability to think about people and formulate responses or questions as a natural part of conversation.

4. Directing the student to a specific topic he can ask about. For example, "In this picture I am with my daughters. What question can you ask me

about my daughters?" This generally solicits a question, but the student will often fail to follow up this question with another one still tied to the same topic. The student may need another prompt, such as, "Hmmm, do you wonder what school they go to?"

These cues are generally provided in the above order, from less to more facilitating. It is important to keep careful notes of the prompts you had to use so you have a clear picture when you later review the data collected and write the narrative report.

On my data collection form, I write down the questions the students ask about my life, along with a brief notation of my response. That way when reviewing my notes later I can see if my response helped the student formulate the next question or whether the student generated a new question. Remember to use some symbol (like a bent arrow) on the page to indicate each instance you had to give the student a cue or ask a follow-up question in order for him to produce a response.

Common student responses

It never fails to surprise me how challenging this task is for students with social cognitive challenges, no matter what their age. Responses to this task have been varied, and include: When asked to start interviewing me, a 21-year-old adult with Asperger Syndrome slumped over on the table and sighed, "I can't do that!"

- *Marty, a young adult, began the interview by saying, "Why did you get into this career?" and "Where did you go to school?" He then proceeded to say, very thoughtfully, "I may be able to think of two more questions and then I will be completely spent."*

- *George, an 8-year-old, asked to use my yellow pad and pen, the same tools I used to record his responses. He then positioned himself as a reporter and asked me virtually the same questions I asked him. (Some of our kids are very good at imitation!)*

- *David, another 8-year-old, also asked to use my pen and paper. He then drew a picture of me, and next to it he wrote comments based on his own thoughts like, "She's a nice teacher." He was unable to formulate a single question – he only drew pictures.*

- *Tom, a 13-year-old, began his interview by saying, "I see you have brown hair, I see you have a husband, I see you have daughters. That is all I need to know about you!"*

- *A number of teenaged boys have said, "No offense, but I am not interested in you." I respond by saying, "No offense taken; do it anyway."*

- *Ten-year-old Peter asked me, "What type of computer do you have?" Once I answered, he started to tell me all about his computer and the games he likes to play on it. All of the questions he asked me related to his own area of interest. Despite my directly stating, "We are only supposed to be talking about me right now," he was still unable to talk about anything other than his special interest.*

- *Joe, 9-year-old boy with a history of expressive, receptive language problems, looked at the list of question words, avoided eye contact and said "What do you…?," "What do you…?," "What do you 'blank'?" Clearly this child had learned a question formulation strategy but he did not know how to fill in the blank with actual content based on thinking about another person!*

Evaluating Part 3 of The Double Interview

In the many years I have been conducting this Double Interview, it has been fairly unusual for a student with social cognitive deficits to interview me with what I would consider a "healthy" set of questions. The vast majority of students' attempts result in vague questions about me, at best. Table 16 outlines the response patterns we have observed and the social thinking deficits these behaviors reflect.

Table 16
Student Responses When Asked to Interview the Evaluator

Response Patterns	Possible Social Thinking Deficits
Commenting on what the student knows about the evaluator rather than formulating questions to find out more about the evaluator.	The student is attempting to make sense of what he knows, but lacks the ability to seek more information about another person, probably because he doesn't understand how to fuse perspective taking with question formulation. This may be an executive function breakdown. **Basic Deficits:** 1. Inability to shift perspective to think about the evaluator. 2. Difficulty formulating questions.
Only asking questions related to the student's area(s) of interest.	If the student does ask questions, the questions are often about what the student wants to talk about, e.g., "Do you know much about carnivorous plants?" **Basic Deficits:** 1. Inability to shift perspective to think about the evaluator. 2. Difficulty formulating novel language unrelated to his area of interest.
Inability to formulate any questions at all.	Awkward silence or sighs of exasperation with the assignment. **Basic Deficits:** 1. Inability to shift perspective to consider the evaluator. 2. Inability to organize thoughts on what to ask the evaluator. 3. Inability to formulate language to talk about the evaluator.
If questions are formulated, they remain shallow. Student generally fails to provide a follow-up question about the same topic. (Follow-up questions gain deeper information about the topic and are key to moving from small talk towards a fuller conversation.)	A few questions are asked, and none solicit deeper information about the same topic; inability to produce follow-up questions. For example, the student may ask, "What are your children's names?" and once I respond to the question, he says, "That's it; I do not have anything else to ask." **Basic Deficits:** 1. Lack of perspective taking. 2. Inability to establish a shared imagination about the topic. 3. Inability to organize information well enough to formulate questions on a single topic.
The student asks a question of the evaluator, allows the evaluator time to respond, but then quickly diverts the topic back to his own area of interest, making comments only about himself.	For example, the student asks, "Where did you go to school?" The evaluator replies and then the student comments: "I go to Herbert Hoover. I play trumpet in the band. Have you ever played trumpet before?" **Basic Deficits:** Difficulty shifting perspective to think about the evaluator's experience.
The student asks the evaluator the same questions asked of him when the evaluator interviewed the student.	The student repeats the same questions previously asked of him: "What elementary school did you go to? What did you like to do during school? Who were your friends? What were your hobbies?" **Basic Deficits:** Creating novel questions to fit the present context.

Interpreting the results of the student's interview

A student's social thinking deficits are readily apparent in this part of The Double Interview. Many students who are incredibly verbal when talking about themselves and their own thoughts and interests become nonverbal or minimally verbal when directed to focus on and talk only about someone else. Their inability to think about the perspective of another person and formulate relevant questions is quite noticeable.

Furthermore, it has been my clinical observation that this deficit carries over into all areas of the students' lives. The vast majority of students who struggle with this task in the assessment setting demonstrate this same weakness in trying to form friendships with peers. These social deficits also impact students in the classroom and affect their ability to succeed at academic work that requires the student to compare/contrast or think about character motivation or reasoning.

Interestingly, the great majority of my students with social thinking challenges have strong social desires to establish and maintain healthy social relations. The fact that they cannot do this and other tasks well should NOT be interpreted to mean they lack the desire to do so. Instead, I strongly believe these assessment results illustrate that the social language tools they have to work with are insufficient in spite of having a social desire.

The narrative that follows describes how a "mildly challenged" child fared with The Double Interview. Some clinicians may find it interesting to try this task with typical students in addition to their students with perceived social cognitive deficits.

⧖

Fred, a 10-year-old boy diagnosed with a very high-level form of Pervasive Developmental Disorder-Not Otherwise Specified (PDD-NOS) had been moved to three different private schools in an attempt to find a setting that was comfortable for him given his mild but pervasive social awkwardness and attention difficulties. His family was about to move him into the public school system, in search of a team of individuals who would be willing to work with their son and his unique personality.

Standardized assessments did not clearly reveal any specific weakness. During the first half of The Double Interview Fred freely talked about himself as I asked him questions. During this time I noted his conversation quickly became tangential, and the more tangential it became the less he made direct eye contact. However, he was easily redirected back to the topic at hand.

During the second part of the task when he was to interview me, he continued to ask me bridging questions that explored only his areas of interest, such as "What computer games do you like to play?" He immediately replied to my responses with verbose and tangential comments about himself, once again with eye contact shifting away from me.

I used very direct cues to help him regain focus on the task of interviewing me, such as "I think we are talking about what you like to do, but your job is to find out what I like to do." All to no avail; he persisted with his verbose, tangential, and self-centered pursuit.

The double interview clearly summarized many of the issues peers and teachers experienced with him at school. His father, who was also watching, explained that the verbal behavior he demonstrated during The Double Interview was typical of the problematic behavior he exhibited in all other settings. Nevertheless, the standardized tests administered to him after completing The Double Interview failed to demonstrate any significant deficits.

As an assessment tool, The Double Interview explores students' breakdowns in social thinking and social executive functioning skills, highlighting their weaknesses in:

1. Shifting perspective from thinking about themselves to thinking about others.

2. Organizing their thoughts and then verbalizing them in a way that moves in a purposeful direction in conversation with another person.

3. Formulating questions and using follow-up questions to explore another person's thoughts and/or interests.

These results can be instrumental in designing appropriate services for the student, no matter what his level of social thinking turns out to be. From my clinical experience, The Double Interview is very challenging for students with impaired interactive perspective-taking (IIPT) skills and almost impossible for students who function more at the level of emerging perspective takers (EPT).

Information gained in The Double Interview can also be helpful in writing social thinking goals into the child's IEP. Goals can address helping the student learn to think about others, how to form questions to indicate interest in another person or to expand conversation, or goals that help the student use contextual cues to initiate or maintain conversation. (See similar goal recommendations found in other sections of this book.)

⧗

Joe, 15, was a sullen teen not pleased to have been brought for today's evaluation. During the first part of The Double Interview, I noted that when asked to talk about himself, Joe's responses were brief and bland. His mother had earlier mentioned that this had always been Joe's style of communication.

When asked to do the second half of the interview, Joe responded by saying, "No offense, I am just not interested in talking to you." I responded by saying, "No offense taken, but do it anyway." I then set up the four boxes on the paper explaining that once he had asked me four questions the interview would be done. I also reiterated that the pictures were on the table to give him clues about things in my life that are interesting to me. Joe then went on and asked four questions with moderate facilitating cues from me, such as showing him one of the pictures and saying, "Ask me a question about this picture."

At the end of the task I asked Joe if he had trouble asking questions of other people. He quietly admitted it was difficult, in fact he elaborated that he "never knows what to say to people." I then told him we could specifically study conversation skills like this and practice asking questions.

I taught Joe some basic skills for thinking about what people might want to talk about next. Joe became far more motivated to participate with me knowing I was not there just to survey his weaknesses but that he would also gain valuable information from the assessment itself. Most older students are eager to learn practical strategies and will be more cooperative during the assessment if you demonstrate, in some tangible way, you can help them in their own struggles to feel like they belong. Humor and the rubber chicken usually help as well.

Some preliminary research was done on *The Double Interview* (Miller 2002, Zweber 2002), which is posted on my website for public sharing.

Section 5.
Thinking With Our Eyes

Eye gaze is an integral part of social communication. It is also an important nonverbal cue to figuring out the thoughts and intentions of another person. The task that follows screens how well a student understands the role our eyes play in a communication exchange, specifically in establishing joint attention and figuring out what other people may be thinking.

This task requires no equipment and can be conducted in the assessment room while sitting at the table with the student.

1. Tell the student you are going to play a game with your eyes. Remove your glasses if you wear them.

2. Ask the student to look at your eyes and tell you what you are looking at.

3. Stare at a specific object or person in the room, such as the door handle, the clock, the child's parent if present, a poster, etc. At least once stare at the child.

4. Using your peripheral vision, note if the child looks in the direction you are looking and then "checks back" to confirm where you are looking. Checking back is a normal developing skill in children after their first year of life (Jones and Carr, 2004).

5. Conduct four to five trials and record on your data sheet whether the student was correct or in error.

6. If the child scored 50% or more correctly, proceed to the second half of the task: Explain to the student you are still going to play a game with your eyes, but this time, "I want you to tell me what I am thinking about."

7. Repeat looking at each object, waiting to see if the child can tell you what you are now thinking about. For example, if you look at the clock, the student should say, "You are thinking about the time." If you look at the student, the student should respond, "You are thinking about me!"

Interpreting the results

The eyes are the doorway to social interaction. Students should be able to quickly and efficiently consider others' thoughts based on rapidly reading their eye-gaze direction. One important caveat to this task: it is mainly about assessing joint attention, rather than a student's interpretation of emotions or intentions. That is a higher-level social thinking skill than what is being assessed through this simple task.

Most students who function at the level of IIPT or higher are able to quickly and efficiently perform both parts of this task. However, they may not be as finely tuned in their ability to read the precise location of your eye-gaze as are typical individuals and may therefore need an extra guess to first get in the general area.

These students are also generally able to tell you what you are thinking about if they are willing to make guesses. Children with social thinking challenges are often hesitant to offer information for fear of making a mistake. It is not uncommon for students with IIPT to resist making any related guesses. These students may respond by saying, "I couldn't presume to guess what you are thinking about." I then explain it is their job in this task to presume my thoughts and encourage them to make a guess. Once they make a guess, they are generally correct, but I note on my data sheet they are not fluent in "reading other people's minds" without hesitation and prompting.

Most students who function in the level of EPT may struggle significantly with the second part of this task, often responding with obviously increased anxiety or distracting behaviors when asked to tell me what I am thinking about. Note their struggle on the data form, as it is likely very significant to their overall ability to take the perspective of others quickly and efficiently.

Students who can fairly easily identify eye-gaze direction but struggle with figuring out related thoughts will benefit from direct instruction on the concept that each person's eyes help tell us about their thoughts. Review these concepts discussed in the earlier chapters of this book, and incorporate appropriate goals into the child's IEP. More ideas are also provided in my book, *Think Social!* (2005).

We have worked with some students who are unable to follow the direction of another person's eyes to any degree. These students have very impaired eye contact and will not be able to accurately complete the first part of the task. Instead, they will just make guesses about anything in the room. These students are not cognizant of the social function of eye-gaze and need to be taught how eyes are used to communicate. Strategies for doing so are found in Chapter 6 of this book.

Section 6.
Picture Sequencing

Section 6 uses pictures to assess the student's gestalt processing – his ability to see the big picture and relate pieces to an overarching thought or concept. It also sheds light on a student's basic-level ability to arrange items into a logical flow, which is important in many aspects of academic functioning. These skills are tested by presenting the student with a group of pictures and asking him to organize them in a sequence that tells a story or lays out the steps in performing some daily living skill, such as tooth brushing. As this task unfolds, the student is also asked to narrate the story or describe the task pictured.

Students, even those in early elementary school, should be able to sequence socially themed pictures and then narrate the story, using emotion in addition to providing a factual account. Students should also be able to create an appropriate and relevant title for the story.

Materials and Instruction

Sequence card sets are widely available online and through various publishers. They come in different numbers of steps, and vary widely in how clearly they illustrate the action. This is an important quality to keep in mind, especially for students who are challenged by social situations.

I regularly use two sets of social-themed picture cards that have very clear, real-life photographic sequences:

- **Sequences: 6- and 8-Step for Children (2005)**

- **Sequences: 6- and 8-Step for Adults (2005)**

These two red-boxed sets were originally published by Winslow Press, UK, and can be ordered through the publisher (www.winslow-press.co.uk). They, along with other good picture sets called "Color Cards," are also available through Speechmark (www.speechmark.net).

For older students (third grade and above) who function within the average or above range of intelligence, I present an eight-picture social sequence such as a birthday party or a car breaking down while a family is on vacation. For younger students or those with recognizable cognitive limitations, I may still use the birthday party sequence but start with only the first four critical pictures of the story. If the student sequences them successfully, I give him the other two cards to integrate into the sequence, one at a time so as not to overwhelm the child.

Some students with limited Theory of Mind/perspective-taking skills may only be able to organize daily living sequences, such as the steps involved in tooth brushing. Their more severe social thinking challenges preclude their ability to conceptualize how a social scenario would unfold (Baron-Cohen, Leslie and Frith 1985). Educators should choose life skills card sequences for them accordingly.

Administering the task

1. Show the student the set of disorganized pictures and explain: "This set of pictures tells a story. I want you to look at all the pictures and then try to put them in the correct order to show the story."

2. Mention that this task needs to be done quietly, without asking questions or making comments about what they are thinking. I developed this instruction because many students would verbalize their thoughts then start to question whether they were doing the task correctly, understandably afraid they might be making a mistake. By allowing language, we found the adult would often, unintentionally, help them figure out the task.

3. Explain that the student may lay the pictures out across the table if it helps to have that larger workspace.

4. Once the student begins the task, observe his problem-solving strategies and how easily he is able to complete the task. How does he go about organizing the pictures? Does he have the mental flexibility to rethink his own errors and correct them without any cues? If a student appears completely overwhelmed when working with eight pictures, I remove four and encourage him

to start again. I then hand him back each of the remaining four pictures to integrate into the mini-sequence he has started, making note on my data record of the extra cue needed.

5. Once the student indicates he is done, do not correct any errors. Proceed by asking the student to narrate the story supporting his picture sequence. Observe whether he recognizes the mistake(s) he made, and if not, how he accounts for his mistakes in his narrative description. Include the student's narrative story as a language sample in the assessment.

6. If the student sequences the pictures correctly, give him a "high five" and let him know he did the task correctly. If the student made an error, still congratulate him for his good work and mention he made one or two errors, without revealing them. Wait to see if the student can figure out the error without help. If he cannot, point to the pictures out of order and observe if he can re-think the sequence. Most students can recognize their error and self-correct with the initial cue. However, some students become completely disorganized once they try to fix their error and the sequence falls apart even further. This clearly indicates an acute executive functioning deficit; they cannot maintain a gestalt. Instead they try to re-think the sequence piece by piece. Help these students as much as needed so they can finish the task correctly, but note they needed "maximum cues" to correct their mistakes.

7. Once the sequence is 100% accurate, ask the student to label or create a title for the sequence. It should be relevant to the story.

8. The final step in this task is to have the student explain what people in each picture might be discussing, given the context. For example, in the first picture of the vacation sequence, the girl and her father are talking about sports they will play on vacation, since one is holding a tennis racquet

and the other is putting golf clubs into the car. In the second picture the husband has the hood of the car lifted and is staring at the engine; his wife is asking him why the car broke down. This part of the task allows you to assess how well the student can form language in context. Our higher functioning IIPT students generally do quite well on this task, but those with EPT often have trouble with this part of the assessment.

⧖

Recently a seven-year-old boy with PDD-NOS completed a four-picture daily living sequence with 75% accuracy. However, when asked to create a name for the picture story he could only repeat the actions in each picture. This demonstrated he had little cognitive ability to link details into a concept. In my report on this boy I noted he will have significant challenges in reading comprehension and written expression, given his over-reliance on details coupled with his inability to conceptualize the big picture of the task or story. Recommendations were made to help him practice summarizing activities in play, talking, writing, and reading. It is interesting to note that this boy had developed fairly strong language skills but he only spoke about topics of interest to him. He was also not able to judge when his talking time was appropriate and when it was not. As a result, in the classroom he was often off task.

Interpreting the results of the sequencing task

1. No significant errors: effortless positioning of the pictures and accurate telling of the story. The student is able to comprehend simple socially themed stories and does a sufficient job understanding the contextual cues and inferences in each picture. They perform well at a basic level of static organization.

2. Difficulty organizing the pictures in sequence: the student appears overwhelmed by the information, which implies a need to probe the following potential deficits more deeply:

   - Understanding the relationship of parts to the whole

   - Organizational problems, understanding sequences presented in classrooms, and possible reading comprehension issues

   - Recognizing contextual cues

   - Understanding inferences

   - Interpreting the meaning of people's body language; implies difficulty understanding contextual cues as well as abstracting social intentions displayed through nonverbal body language. For example, the final picture in the birthday party sequence is of a boy leaving a party with a bunch of balloons, walking toward a car with his mother, while turning back to the people who hosted the party and waving. This photo is commonly misinterpreted as a picture of a boy coming to the party.

3. Difficulty establishing the relationship between people in the pictures: the student is not able to determine who the people are (mother, grandmother, birthday boy, friends) or their purpose in the interaction. I have experienced teenagers and young adults who insisted I had tricked them by giving them two different card sequences mixed together because the characters in the pictures wear different clothing halfway through the sequence. My clients thought that because of the different clothing, the people were completely different; therefore, it was impossible for the sequence to continue, regardless of the fact that the activities in the picture were taking place with the same contextual cues in the background (party table, balloons, etc.). It was remarkable to note that these clients functioned at the level of IIPT and were not being recognized as having any real functioning deficits other than behavior regulation problems at school, since they scored so highly on standardized tests.

Errors in this part of the task indicate potential deficits:

- Lack of perspective taking: unable to understand the social order and associated implications of these social relationships

- Difficulty reading faces and body language

- Inability to consider context as a meaningful information source in social interactions

Adapting the picture sequence task for younger or lower-functioning students

When assessing much younger students or those with limited intelligence, it is better to use a shorter sequence (three to six steps) to explore their organizational and gestalt abilities. A basic prerequisite skill is that a student understand the concepts of "first, then last"; otherwise the student will not comprehend the task.

From my clinical observation, students who function at the level of emerging perspective takers (EPT) have a very difficult time organizing socially themed pictures since they represent other people's experiences. These students do far better sequencing daily living activity pictures (pictures that show the stages of tying a shoe or pouring orange juice). This makes sense because these students have trouble comprehending how people relate together socially. They miss the hidden social themes and underlying motives presented in stories about other people.

When a student cannot logically organize socially themed information, yet is able to sequence daily living pictures, it alerts me to the probability that the student will have significant difficulty reading grade-level literature. Literature is socially themed beginning as early as preschool books. In fact, a California state educational standard is that kindergartners will be able to sequence pictures to tell a story and make predictions about the pictures.

Students who struggle with this task will need to be further assessed for reading comprehension challenges. It is also highly likely they will struggle with journal writing to narrate their own social experiences in early elementary school. Narrative language can be further explored through the use of some qualitative and standardized assessments, such as SNAP or Dynamic Assessment and Intervention: improving children's narrative abilities.

Students who struggle with narrative language may do better when treatment begins with a focus on function rather than interpretation. Start with the student and how activities occur in his or her life. Teach the student to understand and organize his own life and his own experiences before moving into the realm of socially themed pictures. This may well mean NOT using the standardized school reading curriculum for his age group (which is socially themed) and instead using a digital camera to take pictures of the child within his own socially themed environments. The teacher then develops written language to tell the story of the child's own experience, followed by teaching the student to write about his own experiences. This may need to occur prior to expecting the child to actively participate in more generalized school tasks. As the teacher, you need to establish the relationship of the part (the child) to the whole (the classroom) in order for the child to be able to associate what he learns about himself in various environments to his place with others in those same environments.

Without this level of assistance, we merely reinforce a student's decoding and writing skills, absent written expression that sequences their own experiences into narrative language. In providing this alternative curriculum we are developing language for both social interaction and academic instruction.

This type of specific social instruction may seem foreign to a teacher. And, in a way it is. We do not need to teach neurotypical children this way because they enter school with active "social software" embedded in their thinking. This inherent social thinking allows them to consider, sequence, and discuss other people's experiences without having to have experienced it themselves! Not so for our social-thinking challenged students! We must think differently if we are to teach them in a way that is meaningful to them.

More strategies for helping students with reading comprehension can be found from:

- Story Grammar Marker® (www.mindwingconcepts.com)

- Articles and chapters written by Dr. Carol Westby

For further information on written expression, explore:

- The EmPower™ Writing Program developed by Dr. Bonnie Singer and Dr. Anthony Bashir (www.architectsforlearning.com/id12.html)

- Step Up to Writing (www.sopriswest.com; click on "shop" to find product)

Section 7.
Reading Social Scenario Pictures to Assess Perspective Taking

Visual cards depicting social scenarios are also used in this part of the social thinking assessment to:

- Determine the students' ability to take the perspective of others, and

- Gauge how proficient they are at recognizing a range of emotions in themselves and others.

Materials and Instruction

My favorite source of social pictures is a boxed set of full-color photo cards available through Pro-Ed, Inc. (www.proedinc.com; product ID 11043), called "Emotions and Expressions." The 5" x 7" cards depict 48 different emotions in a range of settings and can be used with school-aged children through adults.

The pictures I particularly like from this box include:

- The boy pulling salt in the sugar bowl.

- The boy about to hit his brother's Lego® structure with a book.

- The man who has no money to pay a bill at the restaurant.

- The girl who is stealing shampoo from a store.

- The man who split his pants while bending down.

- The man sitting alone on a park bench, near folks having a picnic.

Social scenario pictures like these can also be found in newspapers and magazines or can easily be taken with digital cameras. If taking your own pictures, make sure the background is free of visual clutter and/or distracting elements.

Each picture is presented to the student with the request that the student explain what is going on in the picture. Some of the pictures are fairly obvious (a man and woman arguing), but a number of the pictures require far more "reading" of subtle contextual and interpersonal cues to determine the meaning. For example, one picture shows a man purchasing his take-out food, realizing he has no money with him. Another picture takes place at the breakfast table where a girl is pouring milk on her cereal. Her brother stands behind her, with a mischievous look on his face while he pours salt in the sugar bowl. A person with weak perspective taking will find it difficult to interpret many of these pictures. Persons who lack the ability to think about others' thoughts or what they know have a very difficult time interpreting the picture of the brother putting the salt in the sugar bowl.

In addition to assessing perspective taking, these pictures also help the examiner perceive how well a student uses contextual cues in the environment as an information source in interpreting social interactions.

⧖

Tom, a 13-year-old boy with no clear diagnosis, had recently become school phobic and was referred for an assessment. In this part of the social protocol Tom had difficulty interpreting the picture of the man in the café who realized he had no money. The waitress is a woman about the same age as the man. She stands behind a counter and is handing the man his bill while she looks at him with a concerned expression.

When I asked Tom to describe this picture to me he adopted the voice of the woman and said, "Honey, I told you we were going to run out of money some day!" Clearly Tom had not accounted for the contextual cues in the restaurant that indicated the woman was a waitress and not the man's wife.

Reading social cards also measures students' capacity to discuss and describe emotional responses. Many of our students have limited emotional vocabularies. They may recognize very basic emotions such as being happy or sad, but are unable to notice more subtle emotions in themselves or others. The pictures demonstrate concepts such as worry, concern, embarrassment, anger, concentration, being mischievous, etc. I am always interested in whether a student is actively aware of the concept of embarrassment, which should emerge by the time a child is eight or nine at the latest. If a student is not able to identify that the man in the restaurant who forgot his money is embarrassed, then I help him use the word to describe the man. I then ask the student

if he ever feels embarrassed. If a teenaged boy or girl tells you they never feel embarrassed, it is a strong indication they are unaware of the range and varying intensities of emotions and visual cues that indicate these emotions in self or others. Typically developing teens actively modify their behavior in an attempt to avoid embarrassment.

⧖

Sid, an 11-year-old boy, mentioned he never feels embarrassed and then quickly asked me, "Is that bad?" I gently explained that that is kinda bad, because when you feel embarrassed you recognize people may be having weird thoughts about you. I told Sid that it is OK to feel embarrassed since you then know what behaviors you should avoid doing in the future if you want people to have "normal or good" thoughts about you. He seemed very interested in this frank discussion.

As you present the various cards to the student, note how well your student performs in the following areas:

- The ability to use contextual environmental cues to decipher social meaning

- The ability to consider nonverbal social cues to interpret emotion and intent

- The ability to label and describe a variety of emotions, with increasing sophistication as children age

- The ability to pull all these details into a logical gestalt to formulate a conclusion about the picture

Students exist in the midst of social scenarios every moment of their day. Most social scenarios demand immediate simultaneous interpretation and response utilizing all these variables and others. The scenarios presented in this assessment are still quite artificial in that they allow the student to study and focus on the picture for as long as necessary.

It can be reasonably inferred that a student who is weak at quickly and efficiently reading these social scenario pictures will be even weaker at interpreting the social environments at school, home, and in the community. Gathering more information about his functioning across these different domains will help validate your findings in this part of the assessment.

Section 8.
Assessing Organization Skills

A student's ability to organize himself, his personal environment, his thoughts, even his reactions are a segment of "executive functioning skills" discussed in previous sections of this book. Organizational skills are pivotal skills; deficits in this area can affect various aspects of the student's social and academic functioning. Most persons with social cognitive deficits will have accompanying problems with organization.

The Social Thinking Assessment Protocol® includes an extensive list of questions you can use to facilitate a discussion about the student's organizational skills. These questions are appropriate for students in fourth grade or higher. They elicit information in a number of different areas:

1. Motivation to work for good grades

2. Time-management skills

3. Willingness and emotional response to homework

4. Daily homework study habits

5. Long-term homework study habits, including procrastination

6. Ability to organize and prioritize homework assignments

7. Ability to ask for help

8. Ability to take meaningful and relevant notes in class

9. Ability to gather relevant study materials: planning skills

Many of the questions relate to homework and the student's study habits, because these are areas in which our socially challenged students are often unsuccessful. Unfortunately we have few organized programs in our schools and even in our private practices to teach students good homework strategies. Yet, homework is required of all students and good study habits result in better learning.

Less-than-desirable homework skills often go unattended during elementary school, where teachers are more willing to make accommodations for students with cognitive and/or social-thinking challenges. However, this picture changes quickly and dramatically once students enter middle school. Teachers are less flexible and more homework is assigned. Homework becomes a prerequisite in order to meet education standards to graduate. Impaired organization skills will become a more noticeable problem during these years. Even with our "smart" students who plan to go on to higher education, homework assignments that are continually amended or severely modified in volume or intensity will render the student unable to succeed once out of high school. Homework goes far beyond academic performance; it teaches time-management for less than enjoyable activities we have to do as adults, such as paying bills, filling out forms, etc.

We witness many recurring problems in students with social thinking deficits once we start questioning them on their organization skills. Students are easily overwhelmed by long-term assignments. They are unable to break large assignments into smaller, manageable parts, organize these parts in a logical sequence, prioritize each part and then allocate time needed to complete each part and the assignment in total. Their growing frustration with these tasks makes motivation difficult to sustain. Instead, they usually resort to procrastination strategies, including avoidance and argument, to delay doing what they actually do not understand how to do.

While this questionnaire is designed for direct use with students in fourth grade and up, parents of younger students should be questioned about their child's emotional tolerance and ability to complete homework assignments. It is important that we actively recognize and help students with time-management and organization difficulties so these foundation skills are in place well before they move into middle school. More information on this topic is available in my DVD and Workbook, *Strategies for Organization: Preparing for Homework and the Real World* (2005).

One standardized assessment described later in this chapter, called BRIEF: Behavior Rating Inventory of Executive Function, is a useful tool to explore a range of executive functioning skills applicable within a school environment. The test receives high marks from practitioners for its accompanying practical strategies associated with the test results.

Additional Social Thinking Assessment Protocol Strategies

As the student becomes more comfortable with you and the conversational nature of the assessment, you will find many students relaxing and exhibiting a more natural (to them) way of functioning. Of course, anything that occurs during the assessment is indicative of their strengths and weaknesses in social interaction, and notes can be made on anything that happens. However, over the course of doing these assessments for many years now, we notice commonalities in students' actions. Some of these follow, along with useful strategies for the practitioner.

Dropping a Pen to Check Social Thinking

Some of your students will be very anxious and excited to talk with you about a very specific topic that interests them. By this point in the assessment, you may have noticed they try and slip this topic into the discussion at every opportunity.

When I have a student anxious to tell me about what appears to be their perseverative topic, I let him know we will have time to talk about it later. When this time finally comes, (usually after the social pictures tasks), I set a visual Time-Timer to two minutes and let the student know he has two minutes to tell me about the topic.

Once the student starts to talk, I act out the following steps to further assess his social thinking abilities:

1. I start by showing active listening skills while the student is talking.

2. I then knock a paperclip or pen off the table with my elbow, while the students continues to talk.

3. I distractedly start looking around for the object I dropped. If the student does not adjust his speaking to notice my attention is no longer completely on him or her, I then:

4. Leave my chair and go under my desk to retrieve my dropped object. I then remain under my desk, timing how long it takes for the student to stop talking or at least shifts his attention to notice I am no longer sitting in the chair.

5. If 30 seconds have passed and he does not notice (yes, this happens), I then get back in my chair and try to stop the student from continuing his lecture. Often this requires me to wave my hands in front of the student to disconnect his speaking.

6. I mention he did not notice I was not present while he was talking. We then explore the idea that when one person talks to another the speaker is supposed to think about his conversational partner and adjust his talking based on his partner's attention.

7. Retry these steps and see if the student notices when you leave the chair. If so, reward him socially by praising his ability to appropriately shift his attention.

This assessment task allows you to ascertain whether or not the student is aware that communication is an active exchange that requires constant monitoring of other people's thoughts. A conversation is considered "successful" when each partner is aware of the shifting thoughts and perspectives of the other(s). Students who talk on and on about their favorite interest or don't notice I am no longer in my chair are not having "conversations" with me. They are "downloading" information stored in their brains. If you are sitting under a table while the student continues to talk for any longer than a couple of seconds – and certainly when it stretches to 15 to 30 seconds – this child has a dysfunctional communication style and should qualify for an IEP!

This is a fascinating task and one that helps parents and professionals gain a clearer picture of the student's perspective taking challenges. It's difficult to overlook such an obvious example of how our students miss the social connections required in any reciprocal social situation. Recently I received an email from a psychologist who had attended one of my conferences during which I mentioned this assessment strategy. He was assessing a high school student with good language and academic test scores who nevertheless was known to have significant social communication challenges. However, they could find no assessment tools to capture these challenges and justify his need for services. After

hearing me describe this task, he tried it with the student, who continued his long-winded soliloquy well after the psychologist crawled under the table. This task is deceptively simple, yet opens many doors to better understanding our students' social thinking challenges.

Observations of the Student in Different Settings

Once the protocol has been completed, evaluators may find it beneficial to observe the student in various social settings at school or in the community and document these observations as part of the overall social thinking assessment. In many cases these additional observations will further support the need for formal therapeutic intervention to teach social thinking and social pragmatic skills.

Strange Stories

In her book, *Autism: An Introduction to Psychological Theory* (1998), author Francesa Happé suggests the use of short targeted paragraphs called "strange stories" to help students interpret the intent of a message through context and figurative language.

The "Strange Stories" included in Happe's book are presented in Table 17-1. The original stories were accompanied by small cartoon drawings that are not reproduced here.

In our clinical experience, many students with Asperger Syndrome who display IIPT (impaired interactive perspective taking) to normal social thinking skills can read and interpret these stories correctly, despite obvious and significant social issues. "Strange Stories" are often used as one of a battery of tests to determine if a person has an autism spectrum disorder. I urge caution when including these stories as part of a diagnosis, because the results are often misleading and indicate a higher functioning level than actually exists with these individuals.

From a social thinking perspective, the real value of "Strange Stories" is in assessing the extent to which students have EPT (emerging perspective taking) skills. "Strange Stories" are consistently challenging for this group, as these individuals are usually extremely literal and have serious reading, narrative, and social comprehensive challenges as well. Therefore we limit use of "Strange Stories" in our assessments unless we think the student functions at the EPT level.

Table 17
Strange Stories (Happé, 1994)

Irony

Ann's mother has spent a long time cooking Ann's favorite meal: fish and chips. But when she brings it in to Ann, she is watching TV and she doesn't even look up, or say thank you. Ann's mother is cross and says, "Well that's very nice, isn't it! That's what I call politeness!"

Is it true, what Ann's mother says?

Why does Ann's mother say this?

White Lie

Helen waited all year for Christmas because she knew at Christmas she could ask her parents for a rabbit. Helen wanted a rabbit more than anything in the world. At last Christmas day arrived, and Helen ran to un-wrap the big box her parents had given her. She felt sure it would contain a little rabbit in a cage. But when she opened it, with all the family standing round, she found her present was just a boring old set of ency-clopedias, which Helen did not want at all! Still, when Helen's parents asked her how she liked her present, she said, "It's lovely, thank you. It's just what I wanted."

Is it true what Helen said?

Why did she say that to her parents?

Lie

One day while she is playing in the house, Anna accidentally knocks over and breaks her mother's favorite vase. Oh dear, when her mother finds out she will be very cross! So when Anna's mother comes home and sees the broken vase and asks Anna what happened, Anna says, "The dog knocked it over; it wasn't my fault!"

Was it true, what Anna told her mother?

Why did she say this?

Table 17 (*continued*)
Strange Stories (Happé, 1994)

Double Bluff

During the war, the Red army captures a member of the Blue army. They want him to tell them where his army's tanks are: they know they are either by the sea or in the mountains. They know the prisoner will not want to tell them, he will want to save his army, and so he will certainly lie to them. The prisoner is very brave and very clever; he will not let them find his tanks. The tanks are really in the mountains. Now when the other side asks him where his tanks are, he says, "They are in the mountains."

Is it true what the prisoner said?

Where will the other army look for his tanks?

Why did the prisoner say what he said?

Persuasion

Jane wanted to buy a kitten, so she went to see Mrs. Smith, who had lots of kittens she didn't want. Now Mrs. Smith love the kittens, and she wouldn't do anything to harm them, though she couldn't keep them all herself. When Jane visited she wasn't sure she wanted one of Mrs. Smith's kittens, since they were all males and she wanted a female. But Mrs. Smith said, "if no one buys the kittens I'll just have to drown them!"

Was it true, what Mrs. Smith said?

Why did Mrs. Smith say this to Jane?

Figure of Speech

Emma has a cough. All through lunch she coughs and coughs and coughs. Father says, "Poor Emma, you must have a frog in your throat!"

Is it true, what Father says to Emma?

Why does he say that?

Other Tasks Useful for Assessing Students with EPT

Special challenges exist in assessing very young students, or those who function at or below the EPT level. As mentioned, these students are very literal in their interpretation of language, are often inflexible thinkers, and may possess limited verbal abilities. Further strategies to assess this type of student follow.

Cause and Effect

Students with very limited social cognitive skills who have emerging language should also be assessed in their understanding of cause and effect. This can be done during play activities and through pictures showing cause and effect reactions. More severely impaired social thinkers cannot determine that a specific situation, as demonstrated in pictures, can result in specific outcomes. This understanding is an integral part of social learning and has a dramatic effect on academic success.

Attention Regulation

We often use the following block building task to assess a young student's attention regulation abilities (reprinted from my 2005 book, *Think Social: A Social Thinking Curriculum for School Aged Students*).

We work as a group to build one block tower, with each "builder" using nonverbal communication to instruct another person how he should add a block to the tower. Children can use eye contact, pointing, and gesturing, but not words.

Instructions: The block "tower" being constructed should have multiple blocks at the base to encourage a range of "building" choices.

1. Explain to the students they are going to play a "no talking game." Pass around a cup and have them pretend to put their voices in the cup, to reinforce no talking during the activity. You, as the leader, are allowed to talk to give instructions as needed during the activity.

2. Explain they can only show each other whose turn it is by using their eyes to "talk" to someone else.

3. Ask one of the students to pass out five blocks to each person at the table including you, the educator.

4. At first, allow each child to build his or her own tower with the blocks.

5. Explain they can all use their blocks to build one bigger, more interesting tower together.

6. Tell students the rule is that once a child puts his block on the tower, no one is allowed to move that block for the rest of the game.

7. You (educator) start by taking your block and putting it in the center of the table.

8. Similar to the game "Who wants the ball?" start by telling students they should look at you to show you they want to put one of their blocks on the tower. Whomever you look at next gets to take a turn.

9. Look at one child. The child then puts his block on the tower.

10. That child looks to see who is looking at him, looks back at one child and gives the next child a turn.

11. Continue having students take turns. Compliment students who are doing a good job showing they want a turn by looking with their eyes at the student who just put his block on the tower. Also compliment students who took a turn and then successfully looked at another child in the group.

12. Coach students who are not paying attention. Remind them that in order to get a turn putting a block on the tower they have to focus their attention on the child placing the block, and "think with your eyes."

13. When everyone's blocks are gone, talk about how great/ awesome/ cool the tower looks since everyone worked together to build it.

14. Count to three and let everyone knock it down together.

Narrative Language Skills

We often ask younger children, or those with more severe social challenges, to narrate a wordless picture story as part of the assessment. Any of the stories in the Mercer Mayer series of picture books works well. Searching online for "wordless picture books" provides many more resources.

If you do not have an extra person in the room when doing your assessment, place a doll in a chair. Tell the student he needs to tell the picture story to the doll so she can understand it. Tape record the student's narrative while also listening for the student's ability to tell a story that has coherence, appropriate use of pronouns, describes the critical elements of the story, and includes not only the actions but the intentions and emotions of the creatures or persons in the story.

Students assessed with significant narrative language problems will need to work more explicitly on these story-telling skills, building language complexity as they progress to describe more sophisticated mental imagery for the listener. For more information on this topic refer to:

- Story Grammar Marker® (www.mindwingconcepts.com), developed by Maryellen Rooney Moreau. Provides a tangible tool for instructing learners in narrative development.

- Team Up with TIMO® Stories: a computer program designed by Dr. Lauren Franke and Pamela Connors for 3-8 year olds to help build reading comprehension and social relations. (www.animatedspeech.com).

- Information in the field developed by Dr. Carol Westby.

- Narrative language assessments and treatment programs described in the next chapter.

Play and Related Skills

Younger children communicate through play, and play is the environment within which many of the child's social-emotional skills develop. By using simple play activities with a student, you will be able to monitor and assess the child's ability to:

- Establish and maintain joint attention

- Share space and materials

- Engage in shared pretend play using a shared imagination and not a predetermined script the child brings into the session focused on his or her area of interest

- Use different functions of language coherently to comment, question, explain, share.

At times we will blindfold a puppet to gauge early Theory of Mind skills: can the student predict what the evaluator sees and knows in the environment, versus what the evaluator's puppet sees and knows?

Assessing Your Older Student with IIPT

(Any student in fifth grade or higher)

The majority of social encounters experienced by students do not occur while individuals are seated at a desk. Be sure to get up and move around with your student while conducting the assessment. Discuss some tasks while standing or walking down the hall to get a drink of water from the water fountain.

Take note of how well the student understands and uses body language, stance, physical proximity, etc., to maintain the communication between you. Can he physically adjust when communication requires the student to stand and interact? Is he equally able to use social thinking skills during a moving conversation, as he is when seated at a desk?

When assessing IIPT students, especially teenagers and young adults, be prepared to encounter deep and often negative emotions associated with their social cognitive challenges. Most of these students are aware they are "different" from their peers and deeply feel the rejection and sense of futility that often accompanies a social thinking disorder. While most of us conducting the social assessments are not trained counselors or psychologists, we cannot probe into social emotional/social pragmatic functioning without touching on the emotions involved in social relationships. Create an opportunity to discuss students' feelings in regard to friendships, work loads, class work, working as part of a group in the classroom, etc. Be supportive and understanding while assessing how they think and process concepts related to their social interactions.

If a student appears to have significant depression, anxiety, increased obsessive-compulsive tendencies, anger, or sexual issues, note these and make appropriate referrals in your report. As valuable as it is to help students develop a more sophisticated foundation of social thinking and related social skill development, we cannot and should not ignore these social-emotional issues that are often a by-product of their inherent social thinking challenges.

Throughout my many years of working with these individuals, I have come to the following realization: there is NOTHING more important than helping a teen or young adult with social thinking challenges get through the precarious stages of adolescence with healthy, stable mental health. School admin-

istrators do not readily accept that mental health issues are intricately intertwined with social thinking deficits. It is, therefore, critical that a trained mental health professional who also understands social processing problems be part of the student's team. Cognitive behavior strategies — those that emphasize the role of thinking in how we feel and what we do — can help students learn to "think differently" (and as a result act differently) in response to their stressors.

I also counsel a student's parents, asking them to consider their child's mental health as part of the overall educational plan for the child. Placing a "smart" but socially stressed junior with poor homework management skills in four advanced placement classes may not be best for the student's mental health. Encourage parents to watch for signs of increased anxiety and make adjustments when needed to re-establish balance in the student's life, even when the student denies feeling upset.

Be wise, be careful and be respectful of our students' emotions. A social communication/social pragmatic deficit even in its mildest form can be devastating to a pre-teen, teen, or adult.

One final word of advice based on my own clinical experience and observation: A student moving towards, or in the middle of, a mental health crisis does not make good decisions. He will argue to keep his life just the way it is, even if it is ultimately quite harmful to them. Parents have full decision-making power to guide their children through these rough spots until the child is 18 years old. Parents who are actively learning to help their children with social thinking challenges should continue to be actively involved in decisions affecting their lives until they legally are no longer allowed to do so.

Unfortunately, I have seen too many good parents step back from making decisions when their child became a teen. While it is good to let children "test the waters" and learn the value of choices and consequences, parents must be aware that social thinking deficits will usually prevent their teen from seeing all the variables involved in a choice, and as a result, in many cases the child will make a bad decision. At times, the child's own self-defeating choices can turn into a full-blown crisis that takes years to work through.

Summary

The Social Thinking Dynamic Assessment Protocol® outlined in this chapter and presented in the Appendix is a practical, functional tool to obtain accurate, meaningful information about a student's social thinking abilities. The results provide a more realistic picture of the social thinking strengths and weaknesses exhibited in a child or adult than do formal, standardized tests alone.

Professionals conducting social assessments are encouraged to use a variety of assessment tools in evaluating a child. By doing so, we are able to capture a realistic picture of the student's social thinking skills and gather information from which an appropriate treatment program can be generated.

Chapter 11
Standardized Assessments: Comments & Critiques

An Overview of Assessment Procedures

This book concludes with a brief overview of various formal assessment procedures that can assist in evaluating the social-cognitive functioning of a student or adult. These instruments were originally designed not to evaluate social thinking, but language/communication or executive functioning skills. Still, there will be times when a formal, standardized test is needed. It behooves professionals to appreciate the limitations of these tests and why they may fail to reliably predict the social pragmatic deficits of the student being assessed.

Ideally, a comprehensive social assessment will include standardized tests coupled with the Social Thinking Assessment Protocol described in the previous chapter. I have found this combination of assessment techniques to provide the most holistic picture of the child and his social thinking abilities, and it is useful in designing services that can realistically and effectively meet his or her needs.

Communication by its very nature is complex. In our attempt to understand it well enough to test for its presence or absence, we oversimplify the process. We create subtests that look at select aspects of communication under individual microscopes. However, these pieces by themselves are not communication. Communication only succeeds when all parts not only work together, but do so with speed and synchronicity that matches the communicative exchange. Ultimately, communication is best understood as a qualitative process rather than a quantitative process (Simmons-Mackie and Damico 2003).

In this book we have discussed that communication is an interactive process consisting of:

- Perspective taking

- Eye contact

- Body language and facial expressions

- Language interpreted and used in context to decipher and code meaning

Furthermore, communication is dynamic and evolves over time; the rules and related nuance and sophistication of the message change as children become adolescents and then adults. Ideally, how we assess social knowledge and related social skills should also be sensitive to these changing dynamics, rather than being inflexible and standardized across settings and age groups.

While not required by public law, the use of standardized tests to measure a student's abilities is common practice. Standardized or quantitative measures of communication are abundant, and their inclusion in the assessment process is mandated in almost all public school evaluations.

Structure facilitates success

Standardized tests are tools of choice during assessment proceedings because they have recognized validity, established by their research-based norms, and are relatively easy to use. These assessment instruments compare test subjects' performance to that of their typical peers – a frame of reference that is meaningful and comfortable to most of us.

As we pointed out in the previous chapter, problems with standardized tests arise when the test itself does not fully capture the nature of the student's deficit. It can be argued that for individuals with strong language skills and social cognitive deficits, standardized tests return a very limited picture of the student's social cognitive functioning. The very nature of standardized testing tips the scales in favor of these students. Well-defined tasks presented in highly structured settings is an artificial environment, one that strips away the competing variables often experienced in the complex milieu of the classroom. This is true for intelligence testing as well as every other form of standardized assessment (Frith 1989).

Questioning Test Validity

Before administering any standardized text, practitioners need to make sure the test they are using is relevant to the perceived deficits in a student. Many tests do not adequately assess the range of skills in specific domains they purport to assess. For instance, the TOPL, the Test of Pragmatic Language (Phelps-Terasaki and Phelps-Gunn 1992) is a standardized test for assessing pragmatic language skills in students up to 13 years old. This test assesses what I call superficial social understanding in that it mainly explores social greetings and other forms of politeness.

While this can be a very useful test for students with more limited perspective-taking abilities or lower intelligence, it fails to capture the complexity of social pragmatic language deficits of students who have mild but pervasive perspective-taking challenges and those with impaired interactive perspective taking abilities. Our higher-functioning students understand this elementary level of social relatedness, at least from a cognitive level. Most have learned social manners, acceptable polite remarks, etc. Thus, these students — who have few friends, are picked on in school, and have academic difficulties in the classroom — usually score in the average range on this test. Evaluators less familiar with pragmatic language assessments sometimes summarize in their reports that a student diagnosed with Asperger Syndrome "does not have social pragmatic deficits based on his average performance on this test." Did the test really measure what it purports to measure?

Yes, but at the most superficial level of functioning in a child, and certainly not in a way that returns meaningful and valid information about the student's overall pragmatic language proficiency. This experience can be extremely frustrating for parents (and teachers) who have witnessed the child behaving in socially awkward and odd ways for years, yet having to deal with standardized test scores that deny the child the very services he needs.

It is an astounding fact within the field of language and communication: there is not a single standardized assessment instrument available to clinical speech language pathologists that measures the use of language through direct communication with another person.

The Strengths and Weaknesses of Published Assessment Instruments

There continues to be a steady stream of new assessment tools and checklists that can be potentially useful with our students. Many of these assessment tools are increasingly sensitive in measuring the nature of our students' social thinking problems. The majority of the tests that follow can provide greater insight into the nature and extent of a student's learning challenges. However, please keep in mind that for our students a "good test score" does not imply functional competence!

It is certainly reasonable to include some of these standardized measures in the assessment process. However, when assessing students with social cognitive deficits, it is never reasonable for an entire evaluation to be based on standardized measures.

It is critical that an evaluation of a student with social pragmatic deficits always include three components: Observation, Interview, and Testing.

Note: the following sections describe some of the tests used (or recommended not be used) to assess students with more abstract social cognitive performance. The brief comments about each assessment instrument are based on clinical experience. These descriptions are not intended to identify the "best" and "worst" options available, but to heighten awareness of the possible strengths and weaknesses presented by the assessment tool. This is not a comprehensive list of standardized tests available. Exclusion from this list in no way indicates that a test should not be used if the professional perceives it has potential value for understanding the more abstract nature of students' social communicative deficits. We urge professionals to carefully review any test before using it with students with social thinking and pragmatic language challenges.

Diagnosis of Autism Spectrum Disorders

Autism Diagnostic Observation Schedule (ADOS)

Lord, Rutter, DiLavore, and Risi
Ages: Toddlers through adults of differing developmental levels
Western Psychological Services, 1999

This assessment was originally designed as a research tool, but in recent years has been transformed for use by diagnostic clinicians in private and school-based practices. It is a standardized observation tool designed to assess behaviors, comparing those of the student to behavior profiles of differing levels of the autism spectrum. Diagnosticians must be trained on assessment tasks and scoring before administering the test.

Clinical Observations: The ADOS, while expensive, is considered the gold standard for tests that assess symptoms related to social communication challenges. ADOS-trained diagnosticians report it

is highly useful for assessing lower- and moderate-functioning individuals on the autism spectrum, but is less reliable when used with higher-functioning but socially challenged students.

It is a good idea for at least one member of any autism diagnostic team to be trained in this assessment instrument.

Autism Diagnostic Interview, Revised (ADI-R)

Rutter, LeCouteur, and Lord
Ages: 5 - 18 years
Western Psychological Services, 2003

This former research tool has evolved into a clinical assessment interview tool useful for diagnosis, treatment and educational planning. It assesses three functional domains: Language/communication; Reciprocal social interactions; and Restricted, repetitive stereotyped behaviors and interests. Administering the protocol requires extensive training and practice; the interview itself requires 1.5 - 2.5 hours to complete with a family.

Clinical Observations: Persons trained in administering ADI-R say that while learning to give the ADI-R is time intensive, the quality of the information gained through using the tool is excellent. They mention how much they learn about the student, helping them to immediately understand the appropriate channels for treatment. In addition, the interview questions facilitate deeper thinking on the part of the parents, helping them better understand their own child's strengths and weaknesses. ADI-R is another gold-standard instrument that promotes a deeper overall understanding of the student with social cognitive challenges.

Asperger Syndrome Diagnostic Scale (ASDS)

Myles, Bock, and Simpson
Ages: 5 - 18 years
Pro-Ed Inc., 2001

The ASDS is designed to specifically determine the "likelihood" that a student has Asperger Syndrome. The tool can be completed by any adult who knows the child; it consists of 50 yes/no questions that focus on the student's behaviors across five functional domains (Language, Social, Maladaptive, Cognition and Sensorimotor).

Clinical Observations: The ASDS contains interesting questions, but some may be confusing to the person completing the test. More accurate results are possible when it is administered in the presence of a professional who understands the disability and can clarify the meaning of questions as needed, rather than being administered by a parent or practitioner to complete on their own. I recommend only using this instrument when interviewing caregivers face to face to seek more specific answers about a student's behavior.

Gilliam Asperger Diagnostic Scale (GADS)

Gilliam
Ages: 3 - 22 years
Pearson Assessments, 2001

The GADS also focuses specifically on the diagnosis of Asperger Syndrome. It is comprised of a 32-item questionnaire for parents and professionals and breaks information into categories that explore Restricted Pattern of Behavior, Cognitive patterns, Pragmatic skills and Early development. Standard scores and percentiles are provided.

Clinical Observations: The same comments for the ASDS apply to the GADS.

Social Responsiveness Scale (SRS)

Constantino
Ages: 4 - 18 years
Western Psychological Services, 2005

This scale is useful in identifying Autism, PDD-NOS, Asperger Syndrome and Schizoid Personality Disorder of Childhood. Sixty-five questions prompt the caregiver to rate the answers on a scale from 1-4. This graduated scale not only identifies the presence, but also the extent of impairment across domains such as awareness, cognition, communication, motivation, and mannerisms.

Clinical Observations: This test asks some very interesting questions, mostly about the child in natural settings. Scoring can be done by hand or via computer. I have not had personal experience with this test; however, other professionals have found it useful.

Executive Functions: Organization, Written Expression, Problem Solving and Pragmatic Language Skills

Behavior Rating Inventory of Executive Function™ (BRIEF)

Gioia, Isquith, Guy, and Kenworthy
Ages: Child and adolescent
PAR: Psychological Assessment Resources, 2000

This is a standardized assessment instrument completed by caregivers and educators. It consists of 86 questions that fall into two validity categories: behavior regulation and meta cognition. Different scales further evaluate a student's behavior within the eight domains of executive functioning: Inhibit, Shift, Emotional Control, Initiate, Working Memory, Plan/Organize, Organization of Materials, and Monitor. The data can be interpreted on the computer, which then provides a detailed list of educational treatment suggestions and modifications based on the student's assessed challenges.

Clinical Observations: Educational psychologists strongly support the use of this test because it provides such functional information through its computer analysis and report generation. The majority of students with social cognitive challenges also have marked challenges across a range of executive functions. This is another test that can become part of a professional's core battery of tests administered during an assessment.

Test of Problem Solving 2-Adolescent (TOPS-2)

Bowers, Huisingh, and LoGiudice
Ages: 12 - 17 years, 11 months
LinguiSystems, 2007

This assessment instrument consists of problem-solving passages and open-ended questions that require critical thinking, much of it socially oriented, on the part of the child or adolescent.

Clinical Observations: This assessment tests students' ability to recognize the gestalt of a scenario, interpret the meaning, and then formulate their own responses to specific questions. This is a preferred test to administer to older students. It is fascinating to watch the student work through formulating his response. When scoring, make sure the student has not "talked around" the answer but has actually produced the target response requested in the manual. Even if our students score within normal limits, they often offer some very unique responses that illuminate their social thinking challenges. For example, after reviewing a scenario that described a family's pet dying, a high school student was asked why children like to bury their dead pets. He responded by saying, "So you don't trip over them in your home."

Test of Problem Solving 3- Elementary (TOPS 3)

Huisingh, Bowers and LoGiudice
Ages: 6 - 11 years, 11 months
LinguiSystems, 2005

This tool also consists of open-ended questions, but the situations are presented through full-color photographs rather than text. It addresses critical thinking abilities based on students' language strategies, using logic and experience. Questions focus on a broad range of thinking skills, including clarifying, analyzing, generating solutions, evaluating, and affective thinking.

Clinical Observations: This is the newest edition to the TOPS assessment tools for elementary school students, and I find it a big improvement over the last edition. It contains some challenging critical thinking questions embedded in the tasks, requiring students to draw upon various aspects of social knowledge. Furthermore, in addition to an overall test score, TOPS 3 now returns standardized scores in a range of thinking areas: Making Inferences, Sequencing, Negative Questions, Problem

Solving, Predicting and Determining Causes. This is an excellent test to include in the core battery of assessment tools we use for younger students with possible social learning challenges.

Test of Pragmatic Language (TOPL)

Phelps-Terasaki and Phelps-Gunn
Ages: 5 -13 years, 11 months
Pro-Ed, 1992

The TOPL includes 44 items, each of which establishes a social context. Students are asked to explain how they would handle the social situation. The test explores six subcomponents of pragmatic language: physical setting, audience, topic, purpose (speech acts), visual-gestural cues, and abstraction.

Clinical Observations: This assessment instrument has marked limitations. It assesses social thinking at only the most superficial levels and is best used only with students with impaired intelligence or more significant deficits in Theory of Mind. Higher-functioning students will regularly test in the normal range, despite prevalent and pervasive social thinking deficits. In no way does this test fully assess a person's social pragmatic language skills, and therefore should never be used as a sole assessment of whether a child manifests social pragmatic deficits. Unfortunately, I have observed far too many speech language pathologists in public schools rely on this assessment's findings and write reports saying, "This student has been given a diagnosis of Asperger Syndrome; however, the results of the TOPL demonstrate he has normal pragmatic language function. Therefore he does not qualify for services."

Comprehensive Assessment of Spoken Language (CASL)

See description in
Expressive and Receptive Language.

Test of Written Language, Third Edition (TOWL-3)

Hammill and Larson
Ages: 7 years, 6 months - 17 years, 11 months
Pro-Ed, 1996

This standardized and well-known test measures skills such as spelling, vocabulary, syntax and grammar, plot, character development, and general composition. A subtest of this assessment tool probes a student's ability to produce written language from a picture prompt during a timed writing exercise. Responses are analyzed based on contextual conventions, contextual language, and story construction.

Clinical Observations: Many educators have reported this assessment to be useful in identifying deficits in spontaneous written language. The subtest is the most useful portion of this tool as it replicates more realistic classroom conditions: requiring a student to write about a topic, not of his choosing, with only a picture prompt, within a specified time limit. Other subtests in this assessment explore the student's knowledge of writing conventions without timed testing. Many of our students will score quite well under this condition; they are "book smart" about elements of written language, and their test scores will suggest they are competent writers, when in reality they cannot engage in the more complex, executive functioning task of actually doing written work. When these test scores demonstrate competence, yet the student is still functionally incompetent, we need to probe deeper and use additional test instruments to better understand the nature of the student's challenges.

Test of Early Written Language, Second Edition (TEWL-2)

Hresko, Herron and Peak

Ages: 3 - 10 years, 11 months

Pro-Ed, 1996

This instrument, suitable for younger children, also measures a child's ability to construct a story when given a picture prompt.

Clinical Observations: I have not administered this assessment but teachers recommend the writing sample subtest, which measures such areas as story format, cohesion, thematic maturity, ideation, and story structure. See the above description of TOWL for additional considerations.

Expressive and Receptive Language Skills

Comprehensive Assessment of Spoken Language (CASL)

Carrow-Woolfolk

Ages: 3 - 21 years, 11 months

American Guidance Services, 1999

This instrument includes a variety of subtests that explore receptive, expressive, and pragmatic language for various age groups and skill levels. Many subtests explore abstract language using non-multiple choice formats — a positive feature as it requires students to provide self-generated responses. This returns more relevant information about a student's level of functioning than does a multiple-choice option.

Clinical Observations: While this test is expensive, it is a reliable instrument to include in your battery of tests. It offers a fairly typical assessment of expressive and receptive language skills for younger students. A more interesting set of high-level language subtests for older students delves into such areas as nonliteral language, deriving meaning from context, inference, and ambiguous sentences.

One weakness of the test should be noted: the paragraph comprehension subtest uses a multiple choice picture stimulus format. Students read a passage and then choose the picture that best describes their response. It can be argued that this may result in students with social thinking challenges either being able to "guess right" or otherwise score higher than if they had to generate their own responses to verify their understanding of the material. Many of my "bright" students will still score within normal limits on the abstract language sections of this test even though they functionally demonstrate significant social communication errors in their daily lives.

In my opinion, the best part of this test is the Pragmatic Judgment subtest. As the title implies, it assesses "judgment" — a more relevant aspect of functioning in the topsy-turvy social environment of daily life. This subtest generally returns a more accurate assessment of students' relative weakness in this area than does the TOPL. That said, keep in mind that this should be only one part of a comprehensive assessment that includes both formal and informal procedures to measure a student's social thinking/pragmatic language abilities.

Clinical Evaluation of Language Fundamentals® Fourth Edition (CELF®-4)

Semel, Wiig and Secord

Ages: 5 - 21 years

Harcourt Assessment Inc., 2003

This test is widely recognized in the field as one of the best basic assessment tools for exploring receptive and expressive language. However, it is not one I recommend be included in your standard battery of tests for students with Asperger Syndrome or similar disabilities. Many students with social pragmatic language impairments, but strong vocabularies and language structures, will do fine on the vast majority of these subtests. On a whole, it will not reveal their inherent challenges.

Clinical Observations: The CELF-4 has added an interesting subtest that explores language production within a timed context, more closely mirroring a normal communicative exchange. However, this subtest requires the student to recall presented sequential information rather than generate truly spontaneous communication based on thinking about and monitoring the exchange with the communication partner. Nevertheless, it is a start towards adding time constraints to our language tests. In addition, this updated CELF also provides a pragmatic checklist that many school-based professionals find very helpful. The checklist is not extensive, but it does encourage more thought and attention to this abstract form of language as a component of overall language proficiency.

In my opinion, the entire CELF-4 should be used only when a student's **technical** expressive and receptive language skills are of concern.

Test of Language Competence - Expanded Edition (TLC-Expanded)

Wiig and Secord
Age level 1: 5 - 9 years
Age level 2: 10 - 18 years
Harcourt Assessment, 1989

This test consists of subtests that explore the more abstract elements of receptive and expressive language. The subtests include:

- Ambiguous Sentences

- Listening Comprehension: Making Inferences

- Oral Expression: Recreating Speech Acts

- Figurative Language

- Supplemental Memory

Clinical Observations: This test is highly regarded in our field. The Oral Expression subtest is particularly interesting. While this test can be useful, practitioners should realize that a student with a high verbal IQ may score within normal limits on this test, despite significant social pragmatic deficits. Professionals untrained in the nature of social pragmatic challenges mistakenly assume that a student who scores well on Making Inferences (or any of the other subtests) will be able to fluidly execute this ability in real world situations. That is generally not the case. Also, consider that school-eligibility criteria are often so low (for instance, in the state of California it is 7th percentile or lower!) many students who desperately need social thinking intervention miss out because of scores on tests like this.

Diagnostic Evaluation of Language Variation ™ (DELV ™) — Norm-Referenced

Seymour, Roeper, and de Villiers
Ages: 4 - 9 years, 11 months
Harcourt Assessment, 2005

This newcomer on the market is designed to assist clinicians in distinguishing normal developmental language changes and patterns of variation from true markers of language disorder or delay. Valuable subtests in this tool explore a student's developing syntax, semantics and pragmatics.

Clinical Observations: This new test appears to be very promising. The authors respect the complex nature of communication and explore the links between language and social thought. Also, it is a far more challenging test than those typically given to younger children. Co-author Jill de Villiers' in-depth knowledge of the complexity of psycholinguistics in early language formation is apparent in the test design. While I have not yet widely used this test in my clinic, I think it should become an integral component in assessing a younger student's language-based communicative development.

Narrative Skills

Assessment of story-telling skills provides further insights into our students' ability to comprehend and express socially themed ideas. I have found this type of assessment quite useful in better understanding our students' functional expressive and receptive interpretive skills. The tests described in this section help quantify abilities, but should be combined with informal assessment methods (such as narrating wordless picture books as described in the previous chapter) to gather a truer picture of students' deeper processing problems.

The Strong Narrative Assessment Procedure (SNAP)

Carol Strong
Ages: Elementary and middle school students
Thinking Publications, 1998
(now sold by www.superduperinc.com)

SNAP evaluates narrative language and story comprehension by having a student retell a story from one of four Mercer Mayer wordless picture books included in the package. SNAP provides an in-depth analysis of a student's ability to formulate written and oral responses in a narrative form and addresses language fluency, length, syntactic complexity, cohesive adequacy, and story grammar usage. The evaluator can then analyze the language sample using assessment protocols, the results from which can guide the development of goals and related treatment strategies.

Clinical Observations: The picture format of the Mercer Mayer books encourages students to narrate not only story progression, but also the characters' related emotions, intentions, and thoughts. This type of informal assessment provides a more functional analysis, useful in helping teachers and parents further understand the extent to which social knowledge influences reading comprehension. This is a practical, user-friendly assessment tool.

Dynamic Assessment and Intervention: Improving Children's Narrative Abilities

Miller, Gillam, and Peña
Ages: elementary school students
Pro-Ed, 2001

This "dynamic" assessment tool differs from others in that it allows the examiner to assist the student during the assessment process. Like SNAP, this protocol is also based on the narration of wordless picture stories. However, the dynamic nature of it allows for a deeper analysis of the narrative information, which can then create more realistic goals and a more tailored treatment program. Post-treatment assessment is also encouraged.

Clinical Observations: This assessment/treatment tool provides a clear, structured approach to gain insight into children's narrative abilities. The stories are unique and involve social understanding of relationships. Wordless talking bubbles encourage students to create narrative dialogue. The instruction manual offers an easy-to-follow format for completing the initial assessment and developing instructional strategies. The one drawback is how the story books were designed. They are cute, but each page contains a lot of distracting visual information, making it difficult for some students to discern the critical information.

Social Competency Checklists

Scales or checklists that explore social pragmatic/social communication skills are being published with greater frequency now than ever before. Some of these are described below and may be of value to anyone conducting assessments. However, readers are cautioned against using any of these scales exclusively when determining a medical diagnosis or when establishing school eligibility. It has been my experience that when the scales are sent to caregivers to be scored, parents and teachers often do not understand the intent behind some of the questions, thus they give misleading responses. These checklists will be of most benefit when the clinician is present with the parent or teacher to discuss their answers as they rate a student's behavior.

Children's Communication Checklist (CCC-2) Second Edition

Bishop

Ages: 4 - 16 years, 11 months, who speak in sentences and are English users.

Harcourt Assessment, 2003

This 70-item rating scale explores a child's functional communication skills. The questions address a range of domains: speech, syntax, semantics, coherence, initiation, scripted language, context, nonverbal communication, social relations, and interests. Each domain yields its own score in addition to the general communication composite score.

Clinical Observations: Dr. Bishop's work in the field is impressive and insightful, and this scale gets excellent reviews from researchers as well as practicing clinicians. The 10 domain scores help identify areas for further exploration and treatment.

The SCERTS™ Model
A Comprehensive Educational Approach for Children with Autism Spectrum Disorders

Prizant, Wetherby, Rubin, Laurent, and Rydell

Ages: All ages

Brookes Publishing, 2006

This is a dynamic assessment tool that measures skills across time in the areas of social communication, emotional regulation, and transactional supports (e.g., "SCERTS"). Detailed checklists identify areas of strength and weakness in each child, and the assessment structure aligns directly with the multidisciplinary SCERTS program, resulting in easier identification of relevant treatment strategies for the student.

Clinical Observations: The SCERTS model and the social thinking concepts reviewed in this book work hand-in-hand in helping students with skill development while also increasing caregivers' understanding of these students' unique needs. The recent release of two excellent books by Prizant et. al., describing their assessment and treatment process is helping tremendously to further define the complex needs of our students.

Social Skills Rating System (SSRS)

Gresham and Elliott

Ages: 3 - 18

Pearson Assessments, 1990

Three different questionnaires evaluate various aspects of social functioning: social skills, academic competence, and problem behavior. Rating forms are included for parents, teachers, and students themselves. Gender-based norms are available, making this even more interesting. A separate computer scoring add-on program provides recommended treatment ideas aligned to the results.

Clinical Observations: The Social Skills Scale measures positive social behaviors such as cooperation, empathy, responsibility, self-control and assertion. A Problem Behaviors Scale measures behaviors that can interfere with the development of positive social skills. It assesses behavior in three subscales: externalizing problems such as poor temper control; internalizing problems, such as anxiety and sadness; and hyperactivity, such as fidgeting and impulsive acts. Given this tool's flexibility and detailed norms, many clinicians gravitate towards using it. It is an expensive assessment tool, but may be worth it given the options it offers.

Vineland Adaptive Behavior Scales Second Edition (Vineland-II)

Sparrow, Cicchetti and Balla
Ages: Birth - Adulthood
Pearson Assessments, 2005

This assessment has long been recognized as an excellent tool, and the second edition has only made it better. The test is relevant for a wide age group and offers multiple information gathering tools: teaching rating form, parent rating form, and an interview format that probes various life skill domains.

Clinical Observations: Vineland test results continue to be considered a reliable assessment of a student's self-help skills across a range of domains: communication, daily living skills, socialization, motor skills, and maladaptive behaviors. Because of its probing nature, it is not uncommon for a student with good scores on more traditional tests to receive surprisingly low test scores on the Vineland.

School Participation Checklist: A Tool for Measuring Basic Student Classroom Behavior

Lighthall
Ages: Preschool - 8th grade
www.autismandbehavior.com, 2005

This product is unique in that it asks educators to compare a targeted student's behavior to another "typical/average" student already being educated in the targeted setting (matched for gender and age). By doing so the IEP team is better able to compare the student's specialized needs to those of the other students in the classroom. Educators complete the school participation checklist for the student and also for an "average" neurotypical student in the class. Based on the results, checklists can then be filled out to identify areas of treatment and modifications needed for this student at school and/or within the classroom.

Clinical Observations: I have not yet used this tool, but the idea upon which it is based is very clever. By establishing a real-life, real-time "norm," educators can be more realistic in meeting the academic and social learning needs of students who "stand out" among their peers. Author Candace Lighthouse is collecting grade-by-grade norms for classroom expectations. Future results should be interesting and relevant to our understanding of social expectations in today's school environments.

The Walker-McConnell Scale of School Competence and Social Adjustment; Adolescent and Elementary Versions

Walker and McConnell

Ages: Elementary version: K - 6th grade
Adolescent version: 7th - 12th grade

Thomson Learning, 1995, ISBN: 1565934954

These scales explore a range of behaviors across the school day. The elementary version explores behaviors in three subscales: Teacher-Preferred Social Behavior, Peer-Preferred Social Behavior, and School Adjustment Behavior. The adolescent version explores behavior across four subscales: Self-Control, Peer Relations, School Adjustment, and Empathy. Both provide standardized scores, as well as useful descriptive information about the behaviors a student presents.

Clinical Observations: This tool is easy to use and includes interesting questions to explore student behavior across a range of contexts. The standardized scores make it attractive to schools and a useful component within a larger social behavioral assessment.

New Thought About Qualifying Students for Services

Most educators in the public school system are taught that a student meets IEP eligibility requirements for services only when he scores more than one-and a-half standard deviations below the norms on standardized tests. In California, speech language pathologists must return test scores of less than 7%, across two different tests or subtests, to qualify a student. Regardless of whether the student's full scale IQ is 150 or 70, all students must qualify under the same low 7%. Clearly this makes it much more difficult for a student with above normal intelligence to qualify for an IEP. Does this mean these "smart" students are not in need of services? Not from my experience, and certainly not within the realm of social thinking challenges. So what is an educator to do?

Think outside the box! Incorporate new ways of "seeing" this student's functioning, identifying his social/relationship impairments and reporting them within your assessment. In addition to test scores, consider the following:

1. Peers are the quickest to diagnose quirky or non-assimilation behaviors with regards to social communication, since students with weak social skills tend to stand out in the minds of students. Is this student "well known" within the school or his classroom, but not because he is gifted or a star athlete? **If the students have diagnosed a peer, the professionals should consider doing so as well!**

2. Observe the student in various settings, like the classroom, on the playground, in the hallway between classes, etc., where other typical kids are around. Does his behavior help him blend in with the rest of the kids, or make him stand out as odd, different? Remember, to score below the

7th percentile means this student functions in the bottom 6.9% of every 100 students. If your student stands out as less functional with regard to social communication skills in his classroom of 35 students, you can easily argue he is in the bottom 7th percentile!

3. Every IEP team, by federal law, is permitted the option of making a child eligible for an IEP based on team agreement and not just test scores. Clearly, this agreement needs to be documented in the report, but don't overlook this avenue for obtaining services for your bright but socially challenged student. Narrative reporting works well here. Just make sure it clearly defines the social cognitive weakness and how it affects the student's ability to learn and be part of the school environment.

The Social Communicative Assessment Report

You've tested your student, observed him in various social settings, conducted your own social thinking assessment as outlined in the previous chapter. You've gathered all the data – now how do you put it all together into a professional, coherent whole so it best represents the students and his needs? Good question!

Speech and language pathologists working within the U.S. public school system traditionally base their report on the result of standardized tests, coupled with some qualitative notes describing the impact of the student's communication skills on learning and functioning across the school day. This report goes back to the IEP team, who make a determination as to whether or not services are to be provided.

Our goal – and our challenge – is to create a report that meaningfully describes the student's social and language-processing issues. Yet we know that if we rely solely on standardized tests, we will fail miserably in describing the very real social thinking and

social learning impairments affecting many of our brighter students. Therefore, a combination of test scores and narrative reporting of the various social assessments works best. Our job is further exacerbated, however, in needing a relevant format for the narrative portion of the assessment so we are not, in essence, recreating the wheel for every student we assess.

One framework that has worked well in our clinic is using the I LAUGH model introduced in my earlier book, *What Makes Students with Social Cognitive Disorders Tick?* (Winner 2000). The I LAUGH framework helps a professional analyze and report on the observations made within the informal social tasks. It also helps parents and professionals understand and appreciate the impact of social thinking/social skill deficits on academic learning and classroom participation.

Do realize that these reports will take longer to create; however, by using the I LAUGH model you can keep the extra time to a minimum. Oftentimes these narratives are comprehensive and practical in nature, but this is exactly what they should be! Individuals with social cognitive deficits have complex problems that are not easily understood by educators or even the assessment teams. In many cases your role is not only to explain the student's challenges but to educate the IEP team as well!!

Simply using diagnostic terms to describe a student (e.g., Asperger Syndrome, PDD-NOS, High Functioning Autism, Nonverbal Learning Disability), especially one we realize clearly has social thinking challenges, is not enough. Our assessment reports need to explain how the applied label or IEP eligibility category placement manifests within the student – this student specifically – rather than use global language that may describe the disability but not how it affects this one child. An often-quoted saying within the autism community goes, "if you know one person with Asperger Syndrome, then you know one person with Asperger Syndrome," meaning there is a HUGE disparity in how this syndrome plays out in real life from person to person. While students with social cognitive deficits may have similar core challenges, they demonstrate these in very individual ways.

As we define the abstract nature of our student's challenges in more concrete terms, we set the stage for developing a more functional, relevant and meaningful treatment approach for the student. When we can discuss in IEP meetings the specific deficits the student presents, we will be far closer to understanding his need for services and writing IEP goals that address the student's specific NEEDS.

To follow is the assessment reporting template I developed based on the I LAUGH model for understanding social thinking impairments. We use this template in our clinic when we conduct student assessments and find it works well on two fronts: 1) it gives us the flexibility we need to describe a student's unique challenges; and 2) it reports our findings in a way that can be easily understood by all members of the IEP team, regardless of their expertise in social thinking impairments. Feel free to use and adapt this template to meet your own needs.

Note to the evaluator: Your assessment report should include your narrative and all your formalized test results. It is a good idea to discuss the formal test scores in relation to your other informal social assessment findings, especially when they are in stark contrast to one another. Use some of the explanations mentioned earlier in this chapter as to why this testing disparity occurs. If the test results align with the informal assessment findings, men-

tion them under the appropriate part of the I LAUGH model. For example, if the student did poorly on abstract language testing, you can mention that under the abstract and inferential section; if he exhibited executive function problems, mention that under the gestalt processing section, etc. By combining test scores and narrative, you create a cohesive picture of the student and relate behavior to social thinking, thereby presenting a more global understanding of how this child's strengths and weaknesses are interrelated.

Handout 21-1

Sample Social Assessment Report Template

Student's Name _____

Age _____ Grade _____ Referred by _____

This student was referred for evaluation/assessment for the following reasons:

_____

_____

_____

These concerns indicate the student may have deficits in social cognition and social communication. Challenges in these areas are often not revealed through traditional standardized tests, and at present, there are few reliable tests that specifically assess social thinking. Therefore, this student's functioning was assessed across a range of contexts, using a combination of assessment procedures:

- Informal interaction with the student

- Having the student participate in informal assessment tasks

- Observation of the student with his peers during free time as well as in the classroom

- Discussion of student's skills with his teacher(s) or having them complete a social behavior checklist

- Interview with the parents or having them complete a social behavioral checklist

- Administration of standardized assessments:

_____

_____

_____

The results of these assessment tasks will be reviewed and discussed using the I LAUGH model of social understanding as a framework. I LAUGH is an acronym describing social communication components that affect the student's social thinking and his ability to engage in academic curriculum that requires social thinking, such as reading comprehension, written expression, group work, perspective taking, etc. Each of the components will be described along with the student's strengths and weaknesses noted across the assessment. Using the I LAUGH framework encourages a more specific description of the possible areas of deficit.

Sample Social Assessment Report Template

I = Initiation of Language: The ability to use one's language skills to seek assistance or information. A student's ability to talk about his own topics of interest can be in sharp contrast to how that student communicates when he needs assistance. Students with social cognitive deficits often have difficulty asking for help, seeking clarification, and initiating appropriate social entrance and exit with other people.

(Add aspects of the assessment that describe the student's functioning in this area.)

_____

_____

_____

L= Listening With Eyes and Brain: Most persons with social cognitive deficits have difficulty with auditory comprehension. Listening, however, requires more than just taking in auditory information. It also requires that the person integrate information he or she sees in context, along with noticing nonverbal cues of the other people in the group to fully interpret the spoken or unspoken messages. Classrooms depend heavily on having all students attend to both verbal expectations and the nonverbal "hidden" expectations in the classroom. Being a "good listener" is attending to both verbal and nonverbal cues.

(Add aspects of the assessment that describe the student's functioning in this area.)

_____

_____

_____

A = Abstract and Inferential Language/Communication: Communicative comprehension depends on one's ability to recognize that most language/communication is not intended for literal interpretation. To interpret adequately one must be able to flexibly make smart guesses about the intended meaning of the message. At times one must pursue the analysis of language/communication to seek the intended meaning. Abstract and inferential meaning is often carried subtly through verbal and nonverbal communication. This skill begins to develop around kindergarten and continues across our school years as the messages we are to interpret, both socially and academically, become more abstract. Interpretation depends in part on one's ability to "make a guess." It also depends on one's ability to take the perspective of another. Abstract and inferential language is heavily part of our language arts, social studies, and science curriculums. It is also a skill heavily used in play and conversation.

_____

_____

_____

Handout 21-3

Sample Social Assessment Report Template

U = Understanding Perspective: This is the ability to understand the emotions, thoughts, beliefs, experiences, motives and intentions and personality of yourself as well as others. Students begin to acquire this skill in early development, intuitively. Neurotypical students have acquired a solid perspective-taking ability between the ages of 4-6 years old, and continue to refine their knowledge across their lives. The ability to take perspective is key to participation in any type of group (social or academic) as well as interpreting information within an academic context that requires understanding other people's minds such as reading comprehension, history, social studies, etc. It is also key for formulating clear written expression. Weakness in perspective taking is a significant part of the diagnosis of social cognitive deficits.

(Add aspects of the assessment that describe the student's functioning in this area.)

G=Gestalt Processing/Getting The Big Picture: Information is conveyed through concepts, not just facts. When participating in conversation, participants intuitively determine the underlying concept being discussed. When reading, one has to follow the overall meaning (concept) rather than just collect a series of facts. Conceptual processing is another key component to understanding social and academic information. Furthermore, difficulty with organizational strategies is born from problems with conceptual processing. This skill, like all others above, is an executive function task. Weaknesses in the development of this skill can greatly affect one's ability to formulate written expression, summarize reading passages, and manage one's homework load.

(Add aspects of the assessment that describe the student's functioning in this area.)

H= Humor and Human Relatedness: Most of the clients I work with actually have a very good sense of humor, but feel anxious because they miss many of the subtle cues that help them understand how to participate successfully with others. It is important for educators/parents to work compassionately and with humor to help minimize the anxiety these children are experiencing. At the same time, many of our clients use humor inappropriately, not understanding timing and subject matter and the subjective quality of humor. Direct lessons about the appropriate use of humor are often required to assist with social functioning.

Sample Social Assessment Report Template

All of the skills noted in the I LAUGH framework are critical components involved in the student's ability to personally problem solve and communicate with peers and teachers, particularly during times of stress.

Students with social cognitive deficits such as those described above typically benefit from therapy that identifies/explains the social skill in clear, concrete terms and breaks down concepts into smaller, more manageable pieces. Social interactions are complex, involving multi-channel information processing (i.e. auditory, visual, sensory, perspective taking) and can be overwhelming for the student! By breaking these complex structures into smaller parts we help students understand their significance in social interaction and class work.

Deficits in social communication and social thinking affect every aspect of the student's functioning, limiting the student's ability to participate effectively in groups, do his school work, and use critical thinking to problem solve personal or academic challenges. These weaknesses will seriously impact his transition to adulthood and need to be actively worked on now to help him succeed in school and as he evolves into an adult. I recommend the student receive the following services: (List plan of service delivery.)

Students with social communication/social thinking deficits tend to demonstrate them across all environments: home, school, and in the community. Once the IEP goals are agreed upon, the student will be more successful in acquiring new skills when parents take advantage of "teachable moments" outside the school setting. Parents are welcome to contact us any time during the school year to discuss the student's progress or brainstorm ideas for continuing the therapy in home and/or community settings.

The therapy program and services outlined above are intended to help the student gain self-awareness and improve his/her ability to use social thinking and related social communication skills. The program is not intended to "cure" the student of his disability; however, with progress, the student will be better able to interact and function within the world around him. Please realize that this progress may take time. Our social world is complex and often confusing. Help the student celebrate achievements, no matter how small, along the way.

Evaluation prepared by:

_____

_____

(evaluator's name and date)

Handout 22-1

Sample Social Assessment Report

The following sample report was written about a second grader experiencing problems in her classroom. The assessment was conducted by a clinician in private practice who reported her findings in an expanded version of the I LAUGH model described above. Note: this professional may have had more time to devote to the narrative than would a typical educator within the school system.

History

Cathy is enrolled at Blackwood Elementary School in the Joy School District. She has received speech and language therapy through the school district since she was 5 years old. Cathy was placed in a special day class in kindergarten and then transitioned into 1st grade without significant issues. Her first grade teacher noted Cathy had difficulty with peer interaction, maintaining her attention to what is going on around her as well as personal issues (getting a Kleenex as needed). However, she was well liked by her peers and was working at the general expected levels with her curriculum. When Cathy was nearly 5 years old, Dr. Betty Leat diagnosed her with high-functioning autism. At that time testing revealed a discrepancy between her visual motor skills (good) and language interaction and fine motor skills (weak).

She has remained eligible for IEP services because of her speech and language difficulties. Cathy lives at home with her parents; she has no siblings. Her parents report she had significant behavior problems when she was younger. She has not had these problems at school.

Current Status

Cathy participates in a 2nd grade class, mainstreamed with the exception of pull-out resource services up to four times a week to work on handwriting and math skills. She is also pulled out for speech and language services two times a week for up to 60 minutes. Her goals currently relate to:

- Producing grammatically correct sentences

- Answering wh-questions

- Initiating and maintaining conversation with teachers and peers

- Auditory processing

- Handwriting using the "Handwriting Without Tears" program

- Basic math facts

Cathy's father, Mr. Madrigal, volunteers in her classroom on a weekly basis. He is concerned about her social and academic development at school and in the home. He notes that at the beginning of the school year she was easy to distinguish from the other children given her tendency to "space out" when stressed, mainly because she had not adjusted to the new school routine. He feels she has improved. Her strengths are with fact-based work. Schoolwork that involves creativity, interpretation, or interaction

Sample Social Assessment Report

with her peers is more challenging for Cathy and causes her to lose her attention span. Her father says that when he is observing in class, if she spaces out, he taps her on her shoulder as a cue to pay attention, which she responds to. She generally does not raise her hand in class to ask for help, but she will go stand next to the teacher to gain assistance at times. Her father also indicated that she has difficulty with written expression as she cannot generate a topic to write about. He reported that the students are encouraged to write a journal entry in class each day, and Cathy tends to write the same thing over and over again unless someone gives her a different topic to write about. Her teacher apparently told the parents, "I have some concern, but I am not alarmed (about her writing)."

Cathy's parents are concerned that she is not keeping up with her peers socially and academically now that they are a year older. Her parents keep her very active by participation in ballet, singing, and drawing during after-school activities. She enjoys pretend play with her Barbie dolls when playing by herself.

Assessment

There are few standardized tests available, particularly for younger children, to assess their social pragmatic knowledge. I attempted to administer the Test of Problem Solving-Elementary (TOPS-E) to Cathy. During this test she was to look at pictured scenarios and then answer open-ended questions about the pictures. Cathy was unable to complete this test; after she was shown the 7th picture and answered only 5 of 36 questions correctly, I decided to discontinue the test. Cathy had significant difficulty understanding how the test questions related to the pictures. She was able to understand the general concept of most of the pictures, but could not grasp the meaning of the questions posed to explain them. For example, after seeing a picture of a boy on the ground surrounded by paramedics with the verbal explanation that the boy was in a bike accident, she was asked, "The paramedics said 'stand back.' Why did they say that?" Cathy responded, "Fire".

In the interest of time, further standardized testing was not administered. If the school SLP wants to further assess her abstract language skills the Test of Language Competence may be a good choice.

Informal Assessment

I also conducted an informal assessment to further evaluate Cathy's social cognitive knowledge and related skills.

- Cathy had virtually no eye contact throughout much of our session. I asked her to look at what my eyes were looking at and guess what I was thinking about. She had difficulty with this task, requiring cues to look to my eyes to direct her to what I might be looking at or thinking about.

- When asked to fill out a form where she needed to write her name and date, she had large awkward writing, even for a 2nd grader, and she was unable to fill out the date efficiently. She did not know how to write down the date on the paper, and when I segmented the information into "month", "day" and "year," she continued to require moderate-maximum cues to write down the information as it was requested.

- I asked her to interview me after I completed my interview of her. I helped her understand this process by showing her pictures of my family and by writing down the wh- words she might use to ask questions about me. She required minimum-moderate cues to interpret the pictures of my family; she required a language lesson to label my "husband." She appears to continue to be weak in her use of pronouns. When I then encouraged her to use the pictures to ask me questions about my family or myself, her first question was, "What family are you in?" She then asked, "How many children do you got?" Neither of these questions sought novel information different from what was already pictured. With further cueing she was able to ask me my daughters' names.

- I asked her to sequence eight pictures telling the story of a birthday party. She did a good job ordering the pictures, with the exception of a picture that shows a boy and his mother leaving the birthday party at the end; she placed this picture in the middle of the sequence. She appeared to enjoy the visual nature of this task and was quite proficient at it.

- I presented her with a number of different social scenarios where she had to explain what was going on in the picture. She accurately was able to describe that a girl felt sad because her mom was leaving the house and in another picture that a man had split his pants down the back seam. However, one picture showed a boy who was trying to deceive his sister by pouring salt in a sugar bowl, knowing she was going to put sugar on her cereal. Cathy recognized that the boy had an "evil" look on his face, and she understood that the boy was putting salt in the sugar bowl. She even explained that the salt would taste bad. However, she was not able to understand that the girl did not know this was going to happen. Thus, while she understood the boy was up to no good and she could see what he was doing was wrong, she could not understand that the boy was going to trick his sister. Given her lack of interpretive information she could not understand that the boy and the girl in the picture had different sets of knowledge. This is a critical developmental milestone, one which typically developing children generally acquire by 6 years old. This demonstrates a lack of perspective taking or "Theory of Mind" which is a foundation skill upon which further understanding of our world develops.

- Throughout the assessment, Cathy attended to all of the tasks, but would easily give up or become more "spacey" if she perceived the work to be too hard. However, her mood across the morning was cooperative and compliant, even if some of the tasks were challenging.

Sample Social Assessment Report

The I LAUGH model is a framework that explains social cognition and how it affects students' social experiences as well as their academic day. Based on the above information, Cathy's profile is reviewed below:

I = Initiation of language: This is the ability to initiate socialization or requests for help across the day. This use of language is not related to one's expressive language proficiency.

Cathy is noted to have weak initiation skills both for initiating play and for seeking assistance, as reported by her father and observed across difficult assignments she was given during this assessment. This is an important skill for social and academic growth towards independence.

L=Listening with your eyes and brain: This speaks to the fact that in classrooms children need to not only process auditory information, but they also need to use the knowledge gained from what they see to help make sense of their surroundings.

Cathy is weak in both her auditory and visual comprehension of the three-dimensional world around her. While she enjoys looking at pictures and books visually, it appears she has difficulty processing social relationships and the subtle social cues within them. When Cathy becomes overwhelmed she shuts down and loses her ability to pay attention.

A=Abstract and Inferential Language: Students are constantly required to "take what they know and make a guess" in classrooms and in social relationships. Reading often involves inferencing, which becomes more predominant in 3rd and 4th grade when students move into chapter books. Peer relationships also become more complicated at this time as the peer group becomes more savvy and sophisticated in their interactions.

Mr. Madrigal indicates that Cathy has difficulty in the classroom when she has to figure things out for herself; this is when she often needs assistance. When I gave her the TOPS-E, she either gave me a one word factual response or she said, "I don't know." She did not try and create a response by piecing together information. When I presented her with my family pictures, she had difficulty formulating questions to learn novel information about me. Her deficits in this area, I am sure, also affect her ability to choose a topic to write about when the teacher assigns open-ended journal writing tasks.

U=Understanding Perspective Taking: This is the ability to understand the moods, emotions, thoughts, intents, and motives of other people through your interactions or observations of them.

Cathy demonstrated difficulty both in her ability to formulate questions about me to seek novel information and in her difficulty interpreting the picture of the boy with the salt. She also continues to struggle with pronoun identification. Cathy clearly struggles with considering the perspective of others, which affects her ability to intrinsically understand the dynamics of the classroom or playground. It has been my experience that students can improve in their knowledge/skill areas through some direct teaching of these concepts across all environments in which they participate. This deficit is one of the more unique features of persons on the au-

tism spectrum. Cathy's difficulty distinguishing between the concepts of what others "think, know, and guess" in the pictured scenarios I presented would be a good starting place to work with her.

G=Getting the Big Picture/Gestalt Processing: This is the ability to take the information you have and understand it in terms of a larger concept. For example, reading comprehension requires us not only to understand the facts that are presented, but to also apply those facts to how characters feel, their motives, how they solve problems, etc. In social relationships, underlying concepts are woven throughout conversational language, play, or even your desire or lack of desire to be with another person.

Cathy demonstrated difficulty with her conceptual thinking. She was unable to successfully complete the Test of Problem Solving-Elementary, since she did not seem to be able to conceptually understand how the questions related to the pictures. Her teacher has also described her as missing a lot of what is going on around her, due to the fact that she appears more likely to focus on details and miss the "big picture." On the other hand she was very successful at sequencing seven of eight pictures correctly to describe a birthday party, indicating she is able to create concepts at a more simple, non-language-based level.

Recommendations

1. Cathy's parents have been pleased with the school district-provided services since preschool. However, they have recently been concerned that she may be falling behind her peers in ways that are difficult to measure through traditional educational standards of achievement. Cathy's parents report that she has a diagnosis from medical professionals of high-functioning autism, but the school personnel see her now as better fitting the diagnosis of Pervasive Developmental Disorder-Not Otherwise Specified. I can understand their preference for this diagnosis since Cathy has the ability and desire to relate to others, as long as she does not have to initiate it herself. Nonetheless, both diagnoses are part of the autism spectrum, and the school district has the responsibility to determine the most appropriate eligibility category to qualify her for an IEP. Cathy has always qualified for an IEP through the eligibility of speech and language, and while she will likely continue to qualify under that eligibility category, I don't think it properly reflects the more unique struggles Cathy is experiencing due to her social cognitive deficits. For this reason I recommend her eligibility be changed to "autism," which in the state of California also describes students with "autism-like" conditions. This eligibility category will provide the opportunity for services Cathy needs that are outside the traditional model for students with only speech and language disorders.

2. A member of the IEP team should observe Cathy both in the classroom and on the playground to better understand her functional skill levels in these environments. Although she does not have a significant behavior problem, this assessment demonstrated there are a number of red flags that indicate she may be having difficulty participating in her classroom, learning as part of a large group, asking for help, and establishing social relationships commensurate with her peers. As the curriculum progresses from the concrete to the more abstract and more demands are placed upon her to keep up with the class independently, she may have an increasingly difficult time. Students like Cathy, who

have tolerant personalities, may keep up during 1st and 2nd grade but become really overwhelmed in 3rd grade, where the curriculum and peer expectations become much more demanding. Cathy's parents are wondering if she would benefit from the structure provided by a 1:1 aide in the classroom. The Madrigals would prefer Cathy be able to succeed without an aide, but realize this setting may be too overwhelming for Cathy. Is it possible for Cathy to share an aide with another student with similar needs in her class?

3. Discuss with the IEP team the best way to balance Cathy's IEP program. Unlike the typical student, Cathy needs to learn two curriculums: the traditional academic curriculum required of all students and the social curriculum, which involves teaching her cognitively what other students have learned intuitively.

   a. The speech language pathologist may consider modifying goals to include direct teaching about perspective taking. Playing some games in the clinic to help Cathy think about what other people think, know, and don't know is a good place to start.

   b. It will also be important to work with her on the fact that "eyes have meaning," and you can "listen with your eyes." Cathy needs to learn that eye contact provides information to the observer about what the other person may be thinking.

   c. The speech language pathologist should consult with the classroom and special education teachers on how to help Cathy achieve success with the above-mentioned skills and take more notice of what goes on around her throughout the school day.

4. The resource specialist may consider adding to the IEP that Cathy use graphic organizers as a tool to help her with the writing process. Because Cathy has demonstrated difficulty with conceptual and inferential thinking, graphic organizers can help her visually see how information connects to specific topics. It will also be important for the resource specialist to work with the mainstream classroom teacher to develop alternative strategies for Cathy during journal-writing time. Can she use a topic choice board, where she chooses between three or four fixed topics each day?

5. While Cathy is a good reading decoder and comprehends fairly well at this phase of development, I anticipate she will miss out on critical conceptual information as the text becomes more demanding and moves away from picture books. Work with Cathy to become more successful in "making guesses" when she reads or works out math problems. Students like Cathy feel very challenged by the idea of guessing and prefer information that is "black and white." Anxiety arises when problem solving involves thinking in the gray area, i.e., taking what you know and making a guess. Graphic organizers used for reading comprehension can also be very effective in visually establishing a bridge from facts to conceptual knowledge.

6. An occupational therapist should evaluate Cathy for services that will help her with written language or in other relevant educational areas.

Summary

In summary I have made the following recommendations:

1. The IEP team transfer her eligibility from "speech and language disordered" to "autism."

2. One or two members of the IEP team observe Cathy's ability to work/learn as part of a group in the classroom, during group time with peers, and on the playground. Consideration should be given as to whether she needs to at least share a 1:1 aide now or whether it will become more necessary as she enters 3rd grade.

3. The IEP team needs to realign Cathy's IEP, taking into account that she functions as a person on the autism spectrum, which involves social relatedness impairments alongside academic challenges. This may require re-prioritizing IEP goals in speech and language, emphasizing Cathy's ability to learn about the perspective of others, the value of understanding someone else's eye contact, and her role in developing continued social relatedness with peers.

4. The resource specialist needs to consult regularly with the classroom teacher with regard to written expression, comprehension, making guesses/inferencing, etc. Goals may be considered for these areas.

5. An occupational therapist should assess Cathy to determine if direct service or consultative services would be beneficial.

6. The entire IEP team needs to communicate with each other, including the parents. Cathy requires additional non-traditional opportunities to help her learn more about the "social curriculum" of school. Social thinking impairment affects all parts of Cathy's day. By making all team members familiar with the social goals and concepts Cathy is working on, they can reinforce these lessons in all settings, resulting in a more comprehensive treatment approach. The Madrigal's appear to be very interested in helping Cathy and seek to be proactive by addressing her social thinking challenges now, before the social expectations of teachers and peers become too overwhelming for Cathy to handle as she moves from grade to grade.

Please feel free to contact me if you have any questions or need further explanation of anything included in this report.

Michelle Garcia Winner, CCC-SLP

Final Thoughts

IEP meetings are stressful times, especially for parents of "smart" students with social cognitive deficits. These parents know their child has significant "social thinking" problems that are not being understood. Understandably they come to the IEP meeting worried the team will not "get it" and will overlook or trivialize the pervasive nature of the child's deficits and the impact they have on his or her ability to learn and succeed. These challenges affect far more than the student's social world of recess or peer relations; for many they also impact the student's academic abilities as well as their mental health and, often, the mental health of the entire family.

Making it doubly difficult is the fact that these students' strengths and weaknesses are usually not accurately represented by traditional test scores, and we live and work within an education system that relies heavily on this means of assessment. At present our schools and administrators are not well equipped to understand a child who falls outside this norm.

Furthermore, all parents of students deserve an **honest** assessment of their child's functioning. IEP members are often compassionate but the teams are not always "honest" about a child's social functioning abilities. Curiously, we can talk about a child's learning disabilities for math and reading decoding, but we don't have a vocabulary for talking about social challenges. Or we don't feel comfortable using our vocabulary in front of parents. Very often teachers are honest in the teacher's lunch room, but do not report the real difficulties of educating the child at the IEP meeting. This prevents the entire team from developing an IEP that is realistic and centered on the student's most pressing needs. I encourage therapists and educators working with these students to use "honest compassion" as much as possible, but never compromise a realistic assessment of the child in favor of not hurting parents' feelings.

Alongside this honestly, we need to become more mindful of the messages we convey to parents. At times we make well-intentioned but misleading statements that sound like the child will be cured once treatment begins or that huge amounts of progress will be made. I often hear statements like, "Your student is so smart, he should do better this year with a one-on-one aide" or "We have a really good teacher who will help your student model normal behavior in the full inclusion environment." These statements dismiss the depth and complexity of social thinking problems and set up unrealistic expectations in both parents and other members of the IEP team who work with the child.

We cannot "cure" these students of their social thinking impairments, but we can make them more functional and more socially savvy. We do our parents and peers more service by acknowledging the reality of situations and being positive and proactive. Better responses might be along these lines:

- "The fact that your child is going through this is a bummer; none of us wants this for him, and we cannot quickly fix these problems. But we can make some suggestions to help him continue to learn to function a bit better."

- "The social problems we need to address at school are part of a larger problem he has across every part of the day. We also need you, his parents, to actively work on these same concepts at home."

- "We are going to help your child learn to do these skills better at school as part of our goal to help him work towards being more independent. However, we don't expect him to become 100% independent in this particular skill."

Unrealistic expectations are often born out of misinformation or lack of education on the part of parents and professionals. Sometimes it's simply because we don't want to accept our children as they really are. Many IEP team members do not fully understand the depth and complexity of a child's social communication issues. They see a super-smart student doing well academically, often with impressive verbal expressive skills, being educated in a mainstream setting and don't for one moment question the appropriateness of that setting. Many parents and professionals believe that social thinking deficits are best addressed within an inclusive setting, and that "normal models" will help our students learn the most.

This idea is strongly reinforced within the autism community. I remember attending an IEP for a student with "classic autism" who was minimally verbal. The parent's advocate insisted that the child receive "full inclusion 50 percent of the day" even though the mother had just explained that her child can only learn in an intensive one-on-one setting. Curiously, the IEP team immediately tried to accommodate the advocate's suggestion without questioning why we would place a child who cannot attend to more than one person at a time in a group of 30 children and expect that child to actively learn!

We must, at all times, keep in mind that these students will not intuitively learn from their peers. This just isn't part of their brain processing. Even our higher-functioning students, those who receive the bulk of their education in the full-inclusion environment, will strongly benefit from learning about social thinking and social understanding in a small group or 1:1 setting, away from the complexity of the classroom. Never underestimate the stress these students work under trying to "fit into" the social world around them. It can be exhausting. These smaller simpler settings provide an oasis of relief in their day.

Through the years I have attended hundreds of IEP meetings for a cross section of students ranging from extremely socially impaired to those with more moderate social thinking challenges. I worry at times that the IEP – an individualized education plan – is being replaced by a PEP – a "political education plan" based on educational ideology assumed to benefit all kids, rather than the one with special needs. Not all kids learn the same way. When school administrators tout that all kids must be educated in "full inclusion" settings in their schools, I become concerned that we have lost sight of meeting a student's **individualized** needs.

And, in the End...

The clever person who stated, "We are strangers in a strange land" understood the social challenges we each face every day living in our own neighborhoods. Our students with social learning challenges feel this more, perhaps, than any of us will ever realize. Yet, they want to belong and feel part of the larger world around them. By recognizing that their challenges arise from a different way of thinking, rather than behaving, we set upon the road to a shared perspective that will, ultimately, benefit us all.

Appendix

The Social Thinking Dynamic Assessment Protocol®

Section 1. Getting to Know the Student

Evaluator's name _____ Today's date: _____

Student's Name _____

Student's birth date _____

Obtain the following information from the student's parent(s):

School Student Attends _____ Grade_____

Contact at School_____

Classroom Teacher _____ _____

Classroom Setting (circle one): Mainstream - Resource - Self Contained class – Other: _____

Name of OT   _____

Name of SLP   _____

Other professionals working with the student at school: _____

_____

Private Practitioners currently working with the student:

_____

_____

_____

Previous treatment programs the child has participated in: _____

_____

_____

_____

Parent's primary concerns they would like to have explored during this assessment?

_____

_____

_____

Is the child on any medications? _____

_____

_____

Does the child have a history of sensory integration issues? _____

_____

_____

Does the child have a history of behavioral problems? _____

_____

_____

Is the child being treated for any significant mental health problems, or had past hospitalizations?

_____

_____

_____

Other information pertinent to the assessment _____

_____

_____

Section 2. Questionnaire for Teachers & Related Services Professionals

Dear Professional,

We are exploring the social-communication and organizational skills of the student listed below in order to develop social teaching strategies aligned with his/her unique strengths and challenges.

Your knowledge of this student's functioning levels is very important. Please complete the following chart and return it to me by the date indicated below. Feel free to contact me with any questions. Thank You!

_____ Date _____

Telephone (____) _____ Email _____

Child's Name _____ Return form by _____

Your Name _____

Relationship to the student _____

Place a check mark in the box that best describes this child; add comments here or on the reverse side.

SKILL	Comments	Above grade level	At grade level	Below grade level	Not observed
Math					
Reading Decoding					
Reading Comprehension					
Written Expression					
Large Group Participation During Class Discussions or Lectures					

Section 2. Questionnaire for Teachers & Related Services Professionals

SKILL	Comments	Above grade level	At grade level	Below grade level	Not observed
Small Group Participation in Class					
Making and Keeping Friends During Free Time					
Ability to Ask For Help in Class					
Organizational Skills While in Class					
Org. Skills from Home To School and Back					

Does this child stand out as unique in his interpersonal skills, either in class or out of class?   Yes or No (circle one)

If Yes, please explain why: _____

_____

_____

_____

Do you anticipate this student will encounter more challenges in future school years and/or adulthood?   Yes or No (circle one)

If yes, please explain why: _____

_____

_____

_____

How would his/her peers describe this student? _____

_____

_____

_____

Section 3. Writing Sample: Asking for Help

(Ask the student to complete this section)

Student's Name _____

Today's Date _____

Student's Birth date _____

Parents' first and last names

_____

_____

Home Mailing Address

Please write the address as you would write it on an envelope to mail at the post office

_____

_____

Phone Number   (_____) _____

THANK YOU!

Section 3. Evaluation

Evaluator Tools for Recording and Analyzing Findings: Section 3

Checklist for Student Activity: Completing Form and Asking for Help

Did you observe any of the following while the student was filling out the form?

❏ Student did this task effortlessly, needing no help.

❏ Student's writing was awkward. He held his pen oddly; writing is difficult to read.

❏ Student complained that he hates to write or that writing tires him.

❏ He did not ask for help, but instead delayed filling out a section(s).

❏ Asked for help effortlessly.

❏ Was familiar with all information requested.

❏ Is an older child (4th grade or above) but did not know basic information such as his address, phone number or date of birth.

❏ Writing task went well but parent has significant concerns about the student's ability to express him or herself in writing or refuses to engage in writing tasks in the classroom or at home.

Other comments on the child's writing skills or ability to ask for help:

_____

_____

_____

(If you are concerned about the student's writing, ask parents if the child is working on keyboarding skills at home.)

Sections 3. Evaluation

Evaluator Tools for Recording and Analyzing Findings: Section 3 *(continued)*

Errors in this section may imply:

- Difficulty with the physical act of handwriting. Student may easily fatigue and become stressed by physical load of the task.

- Difficulty asking for help. Student may not indicate that he needs help and instead becomes more stressed by the task. Or, student may become agitated or act out because he does not know how to ask for help.

- Student is limited in basic functional, personal knowledge. (address, phone number, etc.)

Recommendations based on weaknesses in this task:

- Possibly seek a consult from an Occupational therapist with regards to written language concerns.

- Explore the use of technology to teach keyboarding, etc.

- Teach student specific strategies to ask for help. Also explore with student why each of us asks for help. Make sure strategy is implemented by all teachers!

- In spite of student's possibly strong intelligence, make sure attention is paid to teaching functional life skills such as address, home phone number, etc.

Impact on different academic and social elements in a day:

- Student may fatigue easily with writing assignments, but may be unable to explain this and display behavioral problems as a result

- Student may become school phobic because of his inefficient motor system; may not want to have to sit at his desk and spend so much time on written tasks.

- Student may become easily frustrated at school since he or she does not naturally ask for help.

Section 4. The Double Interview

The Double Interview – Part 1. Interviewing the Student

What are your hobbies?	Student response	While the student is describing his life in this interview, observe the following skills and check if they are problematic for this student:
Do you have siblings?	Student response	❐ Avoids eye contact ❐ Body or shoulders are turned away from you ❐ Prosody of voice fluctuates too much ❐ Voice is monotone
Do you have pets?	Student response	❐ Voice is too loud or soft ❐ Looks very nervous ❐ Looks depressed ❐ Is using echolalia
What chores do you have to do at home?	Student response	❐ Has odd mannerisms: _____ _____
What are good things about school?	Student response	❐ Provides very limited, unelaborated responses ❐ Pronoun confusion ❐ Tries to tell a story or sequenced information but you cannot follow the story, poorly narrated.
What are harder things you have to do at school?	Student response	❐ Talks a lot about a specific topic: _____ _____

Section 4. The Double Interview

The Double Interview - Part 1. Interviewing the Student		
Who are your friends? What do you do with them at lunch or recess? Describe:	Student response	While the student is describing his life in this interview, observe the following skills and check if they are problematic for this student: ❐ Constantly talking, but not regulating to the interviewer
If your mom had a day to herself, when she did not have to focus on being a mom, what would she choose to do on that day?	Student response	❐ Language is tangential. Appears very literal, needs explicit instruction to stay with the task ❐ Fails to read your body language or facial expression ❐ Fails to read your intentions
If your dad had a day to himself, when he did not have to focus on being a dad, what would he choose to do on that day?	Student response	❐ Is very self-oriented ❐ Laughs inappropriately

Other comments/observations

_____

_____

_____

_____

The Double Interview – Part 2. Picture Interpretation	
Picture One of You/Family	Student response
Picture Two of You/Family	Student response
Picture Three of You/Family	Student response

Check off which of the following observations were most accurate:

- ❑ Student described all pictures in a timely manner, appropriately.

- ❑ Student struggled to figure out the people and/or relationships in the pictures.

- ❑ Student could not infer the theme of the picture (family portrait, party, etc.)

Other comments/observations:

_____

_____

_____

_____

Section 4. The Double Interview

The Double Interview - Part 3. The Student Interviews the Evaluator

Begin by reviewing the steps involved in an interview. Remind the student he was just interviewed by you, and he can ask questions about the three pictures you just discussed with him, or anything in the room.

Record the question(s) the student asks you. Note if you had to prompt any part of the question(s).	Briefly note your response to the question

Section 4. Evaluation

Evaluator Tools for Recording and Analyzing Findings: Section 4

Checklist for Analyzing The Double Interview

Check off which of the following observations were most accurate:

❒ The student generated novel questions easily, within 1-3 seconds.

❒ The student was noticeably uncomfortable during this task when compared to the first part of the double interview.

❒ The student could not initially generate a question; you had to write out the wh- questions to help him think of ways to start questions.

❒ You needed to draw four squares on a piece of paper to remind the student that the task would end once he had asked four questions.

❒ The student was unable to generate a question so you gave him a visual cue (showed him a specific picture).

❒ The student was unable to generate a question so you have him a verbal cue or started to form the question for him.

❒ The student told you he had no interest in talking to you.

❒ The student commented on what he or she knew about you but did not ask questions.

❒ The student asked the same questions you asked him.

❒ The student asked a question but failed to ask any follow-up questions.

❒ The student mostly asked questions about his own areas of interest.

❒ The student went on to talk about what was interesting to him, ceasing to interview you.

❒ The student shut down with body language and eye contact; you had to help the student through the entire process.

❒ The student told you he couldn't do it and refused to participate in the task.

❒ Other: _____

_____

_____

Section 4. Evaluation

Evaluator Tools for Recording and Analyzing Findings: Section 4 *(continued)*

Errors in this section may imply:

- Very weak narrative language skills if the student had a lot of difficulty explaining his or her own life in part 1 of the interview. An underlying problem may be very inefficient perspective-taking skills; the student cannot figure out what the listener needs to know or wants to know.

- Very ineffective use of his own body language and facial expressions, minimizing his or her own communicative effectiveness.

- Problems with eye-contact, limiting his or her communication effectiveness and may impact processing of other people's messages.

- Difficulty with prosody, tempo and voice loudness. This can be a significant diagnostic indication of language and social deficits, and the team should prioritize this for treatment, accordingly.

- Difficulty reading people's faces quickly enough to distinguish them from others.

- Limited ability to generate language, specifically questions, to learn about other people's interests (limited perspective taking).

- Inability to ask follow-up questions, thus conversation about other people's interests remains fairly shallow; inability to turn small talk towards conversational language.

- Limited ability to self-monitor how his or her language is interpreted by others.

- Difficulty self-regulating his talking time.

- Inability to share an imagination; only talks about what he knows.

- Student may not realize that conversation involves both what you know about someone and what you think they may want to talk about.

Recommendations based on weaknesses in this task:

- Identify the problems noted above; prioritize for this student, based on developmental age and functional needs, then write specific IEP goals to address those topics. Play and sharing of an imagination should always be worked on before addressing conversational language. See ideas suggested in *Think Social! A Social Thinking Curriculum for School Age Children* (Winner 2005).

Impact on different academic and social elements in a day:

- Student may appear uninterested in others either because he appears shy and talks to very few or because he is gregariously engaged in topics that only pertain to his areas of interest or his own life events.

- Student can be a challenge in the classroom, either because of lack of participation or over-participation; the child tangentially relates all subjects back to his own experiences or preferred topics.

- Student likely will encounter challenges with written expression as the student displays limited expressive language skills to meet the needs of the communicative exchange.

- Student fails to work well in group work classroom projects.

Section 5. Thinking with Our Eyes

Mark a "+" in the box if the student easily can follow your eye gaze, or a − if the student struggles with the task or provides an incorrect response.

Student looks at your eyes and where you are looking to determine what you are looking at.	Evaluator looks at the student	Evaluator looks at the clock	Evaluator looks at another adult in the room or some other object.	Evaluator looks at the door handle
Student tells you what you are thinking about based on where you are looking.				

Evaluator Tools for Recording and Analyzing Findings: Section 5

Checklist for Analyzing Thinking with Our Eyes

Checklist for analyzing student's actions:

❐ The student was able to easily and quickly engage in all parts of the task.

❐ The student required explicit redirection to stay connected to the task.

❐ The student does not appear to understand reading the direction of eye-gaze, or does so with poor accuracy.

❐ The student could read the eye gaze direction but was far less sure of how to answer when having to guess the thoughts of the evaluator.

❐ Recommend further work in this area.

Section 5. Evaluation

Evaluator Tools for Recording and Analyzing Findings: Section 5 *(continued)*

Errors in this section may imply:

- Difficulty understanding that eyes are used to convey information about thought and emotion among people.

- Difficulty quickly and efficiently using eye-gaze to interpret what people are looking at and what their related thoughts might be.

Recommendations based on weaknesses in this task:

- Work with student to practice identifying eye-gaze direction.

- Work with student to practice making "smart guesses" about what people might be thinking based on what they are looking at.

- Work with student on interpreting what people mean when they say "I caught a glimpse of ...." What does that mean in terms of what they now may know?

Impact on different academic and social elements in a day:

- Student has difficulty regulating around others given that he is not efficient at reading other's thoughts.

- Student may have extreme difficulty learning in a large classroom setting where one is expected to actively track the eye-gaze direction of fellow teachers and students.

- Student is likely to be unknowingly tricked, given that he cannot read people's intentions as conveyed through their eyes.

- Student is likely to have significant to severe problems with socially relating to all others and particularly peers, who understand how eyes are used in social situations as early as elementary school.

Section 6. Sequencing Pictures

Children 2nd through 5th grade

Select a set of pictures (preferably 6-8 pictures) to present to the student to sequence. Create interest by saying something like this to the student: "You get to do some magic! You are going to magically create a story out of these pictures by putting them in the correct order." Remind the student this is a non-talking task while creating the sequence. Observe the student's organizational and problem solving skills during the task. Does the student verbally mediate the task? What strategy is used to figure out the sequence? Is the student able to move pictures around effectively or does he get lost in the process?

To follow is a picture sequence from the set, Color Cards Sequences: 6- and 8-Steps for Children (2005, www.speechmark.net). Professionals can select other picture sequences or develop their own, using a framework similar to the one below.

Social Theme: Sharing Wheels

A. Mom and boy leave house with bike	E. Boy and girl play
B. Mom and boy go to playground	F. Boy and girl trade wheels
C. Boy sees girl	G. Boy goes home with scooter
D. Boy and girl talk	H. Boy and mom get to house with scooter

Mark above which pictures were placed in error by putting a slash through the letter corresponding to the picture(s).

Next, ask the student to narrate the story; do not interrupt or make any corrections.

If an error(s) has been made, tell the student he did a good starting job, but that he has to fix a couple of spots. See if the student can figure out what to fix. If not, touch the pictures incorrectly sequenced. Observe how the student goes about fixing the sequence: can he hold the main idea, or does he get lost?

Ask the student to create a name for the story. You can also describe this as creating a title, like for a book. Does the student understand the gestalt of the story, or is he tangential in his title? With reference to the above story, an example of a gestalt title would indicate that the kids traded or shared their wheels, e.g., "Kids Trade Toys". A tangential title would be something like "Mom and Son Go To the Park." Make notes if you have to cue the student to create a title that is more on target. Write down all examples they generate.

Student's story title(s): _____

Once the picture story is properly sequenced, ask the student to give you an example of the type of conversation that may be happening in each picture of the sequence. Notice if the student understands that conversations are contextually bound.

Section 6. Sequencing Pictures

Pre-teens through Adults

Present the older student or adult with a set of pictures (preferably 6-8) to sequence. Tell the student, "You get to create a story from these pictures by putting them in the correct order." Remind the student this is a non-talking task. Observe the student's organizational and problem solving skills. Does the student verbally mediate the task? What strategy is used to figure out the sequence? Is the student able to move pictures around effectively or does he get lost in the process?

Below is an example from Color Cards Sequences: 6 and 8-Steps for Adults (2005, www.speechmark.net).

Social Theme: Coffee Stop

A. The woman walks to the outdoor café

B. She sits at a table

C. She orders a drink

D. Enjoys her coffee and pastry

E. Pays the bill

F. Leaves her wallet on the table; a boy sees it

G. Boy takes the wallet

H. Boy give it to the woman

Mark above which pictures were placed in error by putting a slash through the letter corresponding to the picture(s).

Ask the student or adult to narrate the story; do not interrupt or make any corrections.

If an error(s) has been made, tell the student he did a good starting job, but that he has to fix a couple of spots. See if the student can figure out what to fix. If not, touch the pictures sequenced incorrectly. Observe how the student goes about fixing the sequence: can he hold the main idea, or does he just get lost?

Ask the student to create a name for the story. You can also describe this as creating a title, like for a book. Does the student understand the gestalt of the story, or is he tangential in his title? With reference to the above story, an example of a gestalt title would be "People Acting Nicely". A tangential title would be something like "Going to the Coffee Shop." Make notes if you have to cue the student to create a title that is more on target. Write down all examples they generate.

Student's title(s): _____

Once the picture story is properly sequenced, ask the individual to give you an example of the type of conversation that may be happening in each picture of the sequence. Notice if the student understands that conversations are contextually bound.

Section 6. Evaluation

Evaluator Tools for Recording and Analyzing Findings: Section 6

Checklist for Analyzing Sequencing Pictures

Checklist for analyzing student's actions:

❐ Student sequenced pictures, narrated story, summarized title and identified conversation as expected for his age.

❐ Student could not sequence the pictures but successfully reorganized them with an initial cue.

❐ Student required significant cues to help sequence the pictures appropriately.

❐ Student was able to narrate the story appropriately.

❐ Student's narration was tangential, hard to follow.

❐ Student was able to efficiently label the story.

❐ Student's title was tangential.

❐ Student could appropriately identify the conversation being held in each picture.

❐ Student could not identify the conversation from the social context.

Errors in this section may imply:

• Difficulty understanding that eyes are used to convey information about thought and emotion among people.

• Difficulty quickly and efficiently using eye-gaze to interpret what people are looking at and what their related thoughts might be.

Section 6. Evaluation

Evaluator Tools for Recording and Analyzing Findings: Section 6 *(continued)*

Recommendations based on weaknesses in this task:

- Student may need to work on identifying the context and learning how that helps us interpret people's intentions.

- Student may need to explore how specific gestures and facial expressions carry meaning in context.

- Student may need to work on more elaborate cause and effect, understanding how social themes play out in a fairly predictable way based on our own knowledge from our life experiences.

- Student may need to learn to explore how language is generated from specific contexts.

- Student may need to work on recognizing the main idea.

- Student may have difficulties problem solving because he has difficulty holding information along a continuum.

- Student may have difficulties with overall executive function tasks including all tasks related to organizational skills. Explore this area more completely.

Impact on different academic and social elements in a day:

- Reading comprehension of age appropriate stories may be overwhelming; the student cannot hold together a theme.

- Written expression using narrative language may be very challenging; student cannot sequence ideas well.

- Student may have real challenges interpreting intentions and perspective taking; he will have difficulty interpreting language in context both socially and in reading comprehension.

- Student's expressive language may be tangential; he will need to work on holding to the main idea in both spoken and written language.

- Student's expressive language may be literal, resulting in weaknesses in interpreting and producing abstract language.

- Student may have difficulty making inferences in reading comprehension where that inference involves interpreting social information.

Section 7. Social Scenario Pictures

During this next part of the assessment, social scenario pictures are shown to the student, one at a time. The student is asked to "explain what is happening in the picture." The evaluator is listening to determine if:

1. The student accurately captures the overall social theme in the picture.

2. The student is able to appropriate label the environmental context.

3. The student is able to identify any emotions while describing the pictures.

I use social scenario pictures from ProED's "Emotions and Expressions Cards" (www.proedinc.com), but evaluators can use any social picture card that clearly illustrates and social theme.

Present the student with four pictures total, selected based on age and developmental levels. Write a brief summary of the pictures in the left column, and the student's response in the right column. An example follows.

Man with ripped pants	
No money when in a restaurant	
Salt in sugar bowl at breakfast	
Stealing from a store	
Mom leaves child in care of a baby sitter	

Section 7. Evaluation

Evaluator Tools for Recording and Analyzing Findings: Section 7

Checklist for Analyzing Social Scenario Pictures

Check off which of the following observations were most accurate:

- ❏ Student is able to quickly and efficiently interpret all pictures.

- ❏ Student struggled to identify the environmental context or roles of the people in some of the pictures.

- ❏ Student could not easily identify the intentions of one of the persons in the picture (e.g. could not see the boy was planning to trick the sister, could not see the big brother was about to smash the little brother's Legos), meaning the student was not easily picking up on the nonverbal cues of the character's body and face.

- ❏ Student did not use a range of emotion words to describe how the characters felt in the different scenarios, even when directly asked about their feelings.

Errors in this section may imply:

- Difficult reading contextual cues in the environment

- Difficulty reading nonverbal body and face cues

- Difficulty synthesizing nonverbal and contextual cues to understand a main idea.

- Limited range of emotion words to express feelings in self, others or in fictional characters.

Recommendations based on weaknesses in this task:

- Student may need to work on identifying the context and how that helps us interpret people's intentions.

- Student may need to explore how specific gestures and facial expressions carry meaning in context.

- Student may need to work to expand his or her emotional vocabulary.

Impact on different academic and social elements in a day:

- Student may have limited ability to read social contexts needed for navigating the school day.

- Student may have difficulty interpreting social information in order to process inference.

- Student may be tricked by peers because he cannot easily read people's intentions.

- Student may have difficulty with written expression that requires him to incorporate social knowledge (writing in dialogue, etc.) or writing about his own feelings.

Section 8. Assessing Organizational Skills

For Students in Fourth Grade or Higher

This final segment of the social assessment is used to gauge the student's organizational and other executive functioning skills. This is done through dialogue with the student, rather than a set of tasks. Remember that everything that transpires throughout the assessment can be commented on as part of the social assessment. As you go through the following list of questions with the student, make note of how easily the student converses with you, body language and tone of voice, motivation/interest, ability to stay focused and on topic, level of stress/calm, etc. These are all indicators of the student's social thinking strengths and weaknesses that can be included in your written report.

Name _____   Date _____

1. How important are grades to you?

2. What are your classes and what are your grades?

        a. _____

        b. _____

        c. _____

        d. _____

        e. _____

        f. _____

3. How do you take notes in class?

4. How do you study for tests?

5. Do you write down your assignments?

6. Do you refer to your assignments once you write them down?

7. Do you ask for help in the class?

8. Do you call any students to ask for help?

9. Do you study in the same place each day?

10. Do you type pretty well? Which do you prefer, handwriting or keyboarding?

Section 8. Assessing Organizational Skills

For Students in Fourth Grade or Higher

11. Do you have a study/homework schedule?

12. Is there a difference between studying and doing homework?

13. How much time do you spend doing homework/studying each night?

14. Do you have any tricks to motivate you to keep on studying or doing homework?

   a. Do you take any breaks when you study?

15. How do you prepare to study?

16. Do you guess how long each homework assignment will take to complete?

   a. Yes/No

   b. If you do make a guess, how accurate are you at guessing?

17. Are you better with assignments that are due the next day or ones that are due later in time (two weeks later, etc...)

   a. Why?

18. Do you wear a watch?

19. Do you monitor time while you study?

20. How do you feel when you finish your homework?

21. Do you study/do homework each night?

22. Do you monitor time when you do your own hobbies?

23. Do you ask for help at home?

24. Do you have an organized backpack?

25. Do you have many binders? How do you organize them?

26. Do you always turn in the work you completed at home?

27. How much of your homework do you actually complete? (percentage)

28. Do you complete your homework:

   a. Quickly

   b. Slowly with a lot of interruptions/breaks

   c. Thoughtfully

Section 8. Evaluation

Evaluator Tools for Recording and Analyzing Findings: Section 8

Checklist for Organizational Skills

Check off which of the following observations were most accurate:

❐ Student does not appear to have organizational skills challenges beyond those his peers are also experiencing.

❐ Student lacks motivation to participate in the classroom/homework process. Has little concern about grades or his performance.

❐ Student does not have a set study routine.

❐ Student does not predict time for his homework assignments.

❐ Student does not write down homework assignments predictably.

❐ Student does not bring materials for homework from school to home reliably.

❐ Student does not create a study plan each night.

❐ Student cannot break down larger tasks into smaller chunks.

❐ Student does not know how to prioritize workload across a week, a day or an hour.

❐ Student does not take frequent work breaks, but becomes ineffective continuously sitting to do homework.

❐ Student does not understand that once homework is completed he will have free time, but instead cries/complains at length about assignments that are relatively easy to complete.

❐ Student does not ask for help from teachers, parents and/or peers.

❐ Student does not use the phone to network with friends on harder assignments.

❐ Student does not turn homework in once complete.

❐ Student makes a lot of excuses for why homework is not done.

Section 8. Evaluation

Evaluator Tools for Recording and Analyzing Findings: Section 8 *(continued)*

Errors in this section may imply:

- Student is overwhelmed by homework tasks; may have behavioral or motivational problems.

- Student has executive function problems; cannot break down abstract tasks into more concrete sub-tasks.

- Student may not know how to study even if he tries to study. Studying requires the intuitive ability to develop, modify and re-prioritize plans on a regular basis.

- Student may not ask for help, which means he may not have the tools to develop self-advocacy as he ages.

- Student may be getting depressed as the workload increases and he lags farther behind, despite knowing he or she is "smart".

- Student needs IEP goals written to address specific aspects of the organizational process that are challenging. Student must work on these IEP goals as he transitions from school to home and back again with differing assignments.

- Parents need to learn about and then teach organizational skills at home during teachable moments, and to further generalize skills.

Recommendations based on weaknesses in this task:

- Break down the organizational tasks for homework and consider teaching explicit aspects related to:

  - Motivation

  - Knowing what needs to be done

  - Structuring the homework environment

  - Time prediction

  - Segmenting the task

  - Prioritizing the task

  - Exploration of attention span for task productivity

  - Visually mapping assignments due across months, weeks, and days

  - Taking perspective of others about the assignment

  - Communicating (asking for help/clarification) about the assignment

  - Personal reward system to push self through task and larger reward at the end of the task

- For more information about the above:

  - DVD and related handouts: "Strategies for Organization: Preparing for Homework and the Real World" (www.socialthinking.com)

  - Book: Sper, M. (1993) Crach Course for Study Skills. Linguisystems: Illinois (www.linguisystems.com)

Section 8. Evaluation

Evaluator Tools for Recording and Analyzing Findings: Section 8 *(continued)*

Impact on different academic and social elements in a day:

- Student does not do homework.

- Student may appear to have a bad attitude about school, when in reality he is overwhelmed by the task demands

- Student may not think he can talk about his challenges with school work and/or homework since he is supposed to be "smart".

- Increased frustration may result in student having behavior problems at home and/or school.

- Student may shut down and become depressed over his or her inability to participate in the daily curriculum.

Final Notes

Final notes or other assessment tasks done with this student:

Use this section to record other tasks incorporated into the assessment, or general notes about the evaluation that will be pertinent to include in the written report.

Bibliography

Research Publications and Informative Books

Abell, F. and Hare, D. (2005). "An experimental investigation of the phenomenology of delusional beliefs in people with Asperger Syndrome." *Autism: The International Journal of Research and Practice, 9 (5)*, 515-531.

Adderholt, M. and Goldberg, J. (1999). *Perfectionism: What's Bad About Being Too Good?* Minneapolis, MN: Free Spirit Press.

American Psychiatric Association. (2000). *Diagnostic and statistical manual of mental disorders (4th ed., text rev.).* Washington, DC: Author.

American Psychiatric Association, (1994). *Diagnostic and statistical manual of mental disorders, 4th edition (DSM-IV).* Washington DC: American Psychiatric Association.

American Speech-Language-Hearing Association. (2005). *Evidence Based Practice in Communication Disorders (position statement).* Available at http://www.asha.org/members/deskrefjournals/deskref/default

Attwood, T. (2006) *The Complete Guide To Asperger's Syndrome.* Jessica Kingsley Publishers: Philadelphia, Pennsylvania www.jkp.com

Attwood, T. (1998). *Asperger Syndrome: A Guide for Parents and Professionals.* Philadelphia, PA: Jessica Kingsley Publishers.

Baron-Cohen, S. (1995). *Mindblindness: An Essay On Autism And Theory Of Mind.* Cambridge, MA: The MIT Press.

Baron-Cohen, S., Jolliffe, T., Mortimore, C., and Robertson, M. (1997). "Another advanced test of Theory of Mind: Evidence from very high functioning adults with autism or Asperger Syndrome." *Journal of Child Psychology and Psychiatry, 38*, 813-22.

Baron-Cohen, S., Leslie, A.M., and Frith, U. (1985). "Does the autistic child have a 'Theory of Mind'? *Cognition, 21*, 37-46.

Baron-Cohen, S., Tager-Flusberg, H., and Cohen, D. (2000). *Understanding Other Minds: Perspectives from Developmental Cognitive Neuroscience.* New York, NY: Oxford University Press Inc.

Bishop, D. (1998). "Development of the Children's Communication Checklist (CCC): A method for assessing qualitative aspects of communicative impairment in children." *Journal of Child Psychology and Psychiatry, 39 (6).*

Bloom, L. and Lahey, M. (1978). *Language Development and Language Disorders.* New York, NY: John Wiley & Sons, Inc.

Civardi, A., Hindley, J., and Wilkes, A. (1979). *The Usborne Detective Handbook.* London, England: Usborne Publishing Ltd.

Crooke, P., Hendrix, R, and Rachman, J. (2007 - in press) "Measuring the effectiveness of a teaching social thinking to children with Autism spectrum disorder." *Journal of Autism and Developmental Disorders.*

Dawson, P. and Guare, R. (2004). *Executive Skills in Children and Adolescents. A Practical Guide to Assessment and Intervention.* New York, NY: The Guilford Press.

Dobson, K. and Dozois, D. (2001). "Historical and philosophical bases of the cognitive-behavioral therapies." In K. Dobson (ed.) *Handbook of Cognitive-Behavioral Therapies* (pp. 3-39). New York, NY: The Guilford Press.

Durand, V.M. and Merges, E. (2001). "Functional communication training: A contemporary behavior analytic intervention for problem behaviors." *Focus on Autism and Other Developmental Disabilities, 16(2),* 110-119.

Emery, N.J. (2000). "The Eyes Have It: The neurothology, function and evolution of social gaze." *Neuroscience and Biobehavioral Reviews, 24,* 581-604.

Everly, N. (2005) *Can You Listen with Your Eyes?* www.linguisystems.com

Frith, U. (1989). *Autism: Explaining the Enigma.* Cambridge, MA: Basil Blackwell Inc.

Gevers, C.; Clifford, P., Mager, M., and Boer, F. (2006) Brief Report: A Theory-of-Mind-based Social-Cognition Training Program for School-Aged Children with Pervasive Developmental Disorders: An Open Study of its Effectiveness." *Journal of Autism and Developmental Disorders, Vol. 36, No. 4.*

Goleman, D. (2006) *Social Intelligence: The new science of human relationships.* Pg 11, Bantam Books: New York, New York.

Happe, F. (1998). *Autism: An Introduction to Psychological Theory.* Harvard Cambridge, MA: Harvard University Press.

Hedley, D. and Young, R. (2006). "Social comparison processes and depressive symptoms in children and adolescents with asperger Syndrome." *Autism: The International Journal of Research and Practice, 10 (2),* 139-153.

Howlin, P., Baron-Cohen, S. & Hadwin, J. (1998) *Teaching Children with Autism to Mindread: A practical guide for teachers and parents.* West Sussex, England. John Wiley & Sons, Ltd.

Jacobson, P. (2003) *Asperger Syndrome and Psychotherapy: Understanding Asperger Perspectives.* Jessica Kingsley Publisher: England. www.jkp.com

Jones, E.A. and Carr, E.G. (2004). "Joint attention in children with autism: Theory and intervention." *Focus on Autism and Other Developmental Disabilities, 19 (1),* 13-26.

Levine, M (2002) *A Mind At a Time.* Simon and Schuster; New York, New York.

Lord, C., Rutter, M., DiLavore, P., and Risi, S. (1999). *The Autism Diagnostic Observation Schedule.* Los Angeles, CA: Western Psychological Services.

McEvoy, R., Rogers, S., and Pennington, B. (1993). "Executive function and social communication deficits in young autistic children." *Journal of Child Psychology and Psychiatry, 34(4),* 563-578.

Miller, A. (2002) "The Double Interview Task: Assessing The Social Communication of Children with Asperger Syndrome." Masters dissertation. University of Kansas.

Minshew, N. and Goldstein, G. (1998). "Autism as a disorder of complex information processing." *Mental Retardation and Developmental Disabilities Research Reviews, 4,* 129-136.

Myles, B., Bock, S., and Simpson, R. (2001). *Asperger Syndrome Diagnostic Scale.* Austin, TX: Pro-Ed.

No Child Left Behind Act of 2001, 20 U.S.C. § 6301 et seq.

Ozonoff, S., Pennington, B., and Rogers, S. (1991). "Executive function deficits in high-functioning autistic individuals: relationship to Theory of Mind." *Journal of Child Psychology and Psychiatry, 32 (7),* 1081-1105.

Paxton, K. and Estay, I. (2007). *Counseling People on the Autism Spectrum: A practical manual.* Jessica Kingsley Publishing. Philadelphia: Pennsylvania. www.jkp.com

Prizant, B., Wetherby, A., Rubin, E., Laurent, A. and Rydell, P. (2006a) "The Scerts Model: A comprehensive educational approach for children with autism spectrum disorders." *Vo1 1, Assessment.* Baltimore, MD: Paul H. Brookes Publishing.

Prizant, B., Wetherby, A., Rubin, E., Laurent, A. and Rydell, P. (2006b) "The Scerts Model: A comprehensive educational approach for children with autism spectrum disorders." *Vo1 II, Program Planning & Intervention.* Baltimore, MD: Paul H. Brookes Publishing.

Ratner, N. (2006) "Evidence-based practice: an examination of its ramifications for the practice of speech-language pathology." *Language, Speech and Hearing Services in Schools.* Vol. 37. 257-267.

Rogers, K., Dziobek, I., Hassenstab, J., Wolf, O. and Convit, A. (2007) *Who cares? Revisiting empathy in Asperger Syndrome. Journal of Autism and Developmental Disorders,* V37, N4, p709-715.

Simmons-Mackie, N. and Damico, J. (2003). "Contributions of qualitative research to the knowledge base of normal communication." *American Journal of Speech-Language Pathology, 12 (2),* 144-154.

Sofronoff, K., Attwood, T., and Hinton, S. (2005) "A randomized controlled trial of CBT intervention for anxiety in children with Asperger Syndrome." *Journal of Child Psychology and Psychiatry.* Vol 46(11), p1152-1160.

Stewart, M., Barnard, L., Pearson, J., Hasan, R., and O'Brien, G. (2006). "Presentation of depression in Autism and Asperger Syndrome." *Autism: The International Journal of Research and Practice, 10 (1),* 103-116.

Tager-Flusberg, H. (2000). "Language and understanding minds: connections in autism." In *Understanding Other Minds,* S. Baron-Cohen, H. Tager-Flusberg, and D. Cohen (ed.s). New York, NY: Oxford University Press Inc.

Tetnowski, J. and Franklin, T. (2003). "Qualitative research: Implications for description and assessment." *American Journal of Speech-Language Pathology, 12 (2),* 155-164.

Thorndike, E. (1920) "Intelligence and Its Use." *Harpers Magazine 140,* pp 227-35.

Wellman, H. and Lagattuta, K. (2000). "Developing understandings of mind." In *Understanding Other Minds,* S. Baron-Cohen, H. Tager-Flusberg, and D. Cohen (ed.s). New York, NY: Oxford University Press.

Weschler Intelligence Scale for Children-Third Edition. San Antonio, TX: Psychological Corporation.

Wing, L. and Gould, J. (1979). "Severe impairments of social interaction and associated abnormalities in children: epidemiology and classification." *Journal of Autism and Developmental Disorders, 9,* 11-20.

Winner, M. (2000). *Inside Out: What Makes The Person With Social Cognitive Deficits Tick?* San Jose, CA: Michelle G. Winner. www.socialthinking.com

Zweber, K. (2002) "The Double Interview: Assessing The Social Communication of Adolescents with Asperger Syndrome." Masters dissertation. University of Kansas.

Treatment Materials

(not all of which have been noted in this book)

Activities and Events (Six sequencing stories, each with eight picture sequence cards) (1991). United Kingdom: Winslow Press (www.winslow-press.co.uk).

Beyer, J. and Gammeltoft, L. (1998). *Autism & Play.* Philadelphia, PA: Jessica Kingsley Publishers.

Bosch, C. (1988). Bully On The Bus. Seattle, WA: Parenting Press, Inc.

Buron, K. and Curtis, M. (2004) *The Incredible 5-Point Scale: Assisting Students with Autism Spectrum Disorders in Understanding Social Interactions and Controlling their Emotional Responses.* Autism Asperger Publishing Company: Shawnee Misson, Kansas. www.asperger.net

Civardi, A., Hindley, J. and Wilkes, A. (1979). *The Usborne Detective Handbook.* London, England: Usborne Publishing Ltd.

Duke, M., Nowicki, S., and Martin, E. (1996). *Teaching Your Child the Language of Social Success.* Atlanta, GA: Peachtree Publishers.

Everly, N. (2000). *Can You Listen With Your Eyes?* East Moline, IL: LinguiSystems.

Emotions and Expressions (Photo cards). (1995). Austin, TX: Pro-Ed Inc.

Faherty, C. (2000). *Asperger's: What Does It Mean To Me? A workbook explaining self awareness and life lessons to the child or youth with High Functioning Autism or Aspergers.* Arlington TX: Future Horizons.

Franke, L. and Connors, P. (2000). *Team Up With Timo: Stories* (Software). San Francisco, CA: Animated Speech Corporation.

Gajewski, N., Hirn, N., and Mayo, P. (1998). *Social Star Series,* Books 1, 2 and 3. Eau Claire, WI: Thinking Publications.

Gajewski, N. and Mayo, P. (1987). *Transfer Activities: Thinking Skill Vocabulary Development.* Eau Claire, WI: Thinking Publications.

Gajewski, N. and Mayo, P. (1998). *Social Skill Strategies: A Curriculum for Adolescents,* Books A and B. Eau Claire, WI: Thinking Publications.

Gray, Carol. (1994) *Comic Strip Conversations.* Arlington, Tx: Future Horizons.

Gray, C. and White, A., eds. (2002). *My Social Stories Book.* Philadelphia, PA: Jessica Kingsley Publishers.

Gutstein, S. (2000). *Autism Aspergers: Solving the relationship puzzle.* Arlington, TX: Future Horizons.

Gutstein, S. and Sheely, R. (2002). *Relationship Development Intervention with Children, Adolescents and Adults: social and emotional development activities for Asperger Syndrome, Autism, PDD and NLD.* London and Philadelphia: Jessica Kingsley Publishers.

Gutstein, S. and Sheely, R. (2002). *Relationship Development Intervention with Young Children: social and emotional development activities for Asperger Syndrome, Autism, PDD and NLD.* London and Philadelphia: Jessica Kingsley Publishers.

Hindley, J., Travis, F., Thomson, R., Amery, H., Rawson, C., and Harper, A. (1999). *The Usborne Spy's Guidebook.* London, England: Usborne Publishing Ltd.

Leaf, M. (1939). *Fair Play.* New York, NY: Frederick A. Stokes Company

Mayer-Johnson LLC (2001). *Boardmaker®* and *Speaking Dynamically Pro®* communication software. Solana Beach, CA: www.mayerjohnson.com or (800) 588-4548.

McAfee, J. (2002). *Navigating The Social World: A Curriculum for Individuals with Asperger Syndrome, High Functioning Autism and Related Disorders.* Arlington, TX: Future Horizons.

Miles, L. (1996). *Secret Codes.* London, England: Usborne Publishing Ltd.

Moreau, M.E. (2005) *Story Grammar Marker Kit.* Springfield, MA: Mind Wing Concepts, Inc. www.mindwingconcepts.com

Myles, B., Trautman, M. and Schelven, R. (2004) *The Hidden Curriculum: Practical solutions for understanding unstated rules in social situations.* Shawnee Mission, KS: Autism Asperger Publishing Co. www.asperger.net

O'Brien, E. and Riddell, D. (1997) *The Usborne Book of Secret Codes.* London, England: Usborne Publishing Ltd.

Prizant, B., Wetherby, A., Rubin, E., Laurent, A., and Rydell, P. (2005). *The SCERTS™ Model - A Comprehensive Educational Approach for Children with Autism Spectrum Disorders.* Baltimore, MD: Brookes Publishing.

Sims, L. and King, C. (2002) *The Usborne Spy's Guidebook.* London, England: Usborne Publishing Ltd.

Spector, C. (1997). *Saying One Thing, Meaning Another: Activities for Clarifying Ambiguous Language.* Eau Claire, WI: Thinking Publications.

Speechmark (2005) *Sequences: 6 & 8-Step for Adults.* United Kingdom: Speechmark Publishing, Ltd. www.speechmark.net

Speechmark (2005) *Sequences: 6 & 8 Step for Children.* United Kingdom: Speechmark Publishing, Ltd. www.speechmark.net

Story Grammar Marker® Kit (2005). Springfield, MA: MindWing Concepts, Inc.

Time Timer (timer) www.timetimer.com

Toomey, M. (2002). *The Language of Perspective Taking.* Marblehead, MA: Circuit Publications.

Vermeulen, P. (2000). *I Am Special.* Philadelphia, PA: Jessica Kingsley Publishers.

Winner, M. (2007). *Social Behavior Mapping.* San Jose, CA: Michelle G. Winner. www.socialthinking.com

Winner, M. (2002) *Social Thinking Across The School and Home Day,* DVD. San Jose, CA: Think Social Publishing, Inc. www.socialthinking.com

Winner, M. (2007). *Sticker Strategies to Teach Social Thinking and Organization.* San Jose, CA: Michelle G. Winner. www.socialthinking.com

Winner, M. (2005). *Strategies for Organizaton: Preparing for Homework and the Real World.* San Jose, CA: Michelle G. Winner. www.socialthinking.com

Winner, M. (2000). *Think Social! A Social Thinking Curriculum for School-Age Students.* San Jose, CA: Michelle G. Winner. www.socialthinking.com

Winner, M. (2005). *Worksheets! For Teaching Social Thinking and Rekated Skills.* San Jose, CA: Michelle G. Winner. www.socialthinking.com

Assessment Tools

(not all of which have been noted in this book)

Bishop, D. (2003). *Children's Communication Checklist (CCC-2), Second Edition*. San Antonio, TX: Harcourt Assessment.

Bowers, L., Huisingh, R., and LoGiudice, C. (2006). *The Listening Comprehension Test 2*. East Moline, IL: LinguiSystems.

Bowers, L., Huisingh, R., and LoGiudice, C. (2007). *TOPS 2-Adolescent; Test Of Problem Solving 2-Adolescent*. East Moline, IL: LinguiSystems.

Bowers, L., Huisingh, R., and LoGiudice, C. (2005). *TOPS 3: Elementary; Test Of Problem Solving 3: Elementary*. East Moline, IL: LinguiSystems.

Carrow-Woolfolk, E. (1999). *Comprehensive Assessment of Spoken Language*. Circle Pines, MN: American Guidance Service.

Constantino, J. (2005). *Social Responsiveness Scale (SRS)*. Los Angeles, CA: Western Psychological Services.

Gilliam, J. (2001) *Gilliam Asperger's Disorder Scale (GADS)*. Bloomington, MN: Pearson Assessments

Gioia, G., Isquith, P., Guy, S., and Kenworthy, L. (2002). *Behavior Rating Inventory of Executive Function™ (BRIEF™)*. Lutz, FL: Psychological Assessment Resources, Inc. (PAR).

Gresham, F. and Elliott, S. (1990). *SSRS: Social Skills Rating System*. Bloomington, MN: Pearson Assessments

Hammill, D. and Larsen, S. (1996). *Test of Written Language, Third Edition (TOWL-3)*. Austin, TX: Pro-Ed.

Hresko, W., Herron, S., and Peak, P. (1996). *Test of Early Written Language, Second Edition (TEWL-2)*. Austin, TX: Pro-Ed.

Lighthall, K. (2005). *School Participation Checklist: A Tool for Measuring Basic Student Classroom Behavior*. www.autismandbehavior.com

Lord, C., Rutter, M., DiLavore, P., and Risi, S. (1999). *Autism Diagnostic Observation Schedule (ADOS)*. Los Angeles, CA: Western Psychological Services.

Miller, L., Gillam, R., and Peña, (2001). *Dynamic Assessment and Intervention: Improving Children's Narrative Abilities*. Austin, TX: Pro-Ed.

Myles, B., Bock, S., and Simpson, R. (2001) *Asperger Syndrome Diagnostic Scale (ASDS)*. Austin, TX: Pro-Ed.

Phelps-Terasaki D. and Phelps-Gunn, T. (1992). *Test of Pragmatic Language (TOPL)*, Austin, TX: Pro-Ed.

Prizant, B., Wetherby, A., Rubin, E., Laurent, A., and Rydell, P. (2005). *The SCERTS™ Model - A Comprehensive Educational Approach for Children with Autism Spectrum Disorders*. Baltimore, MD: Brookes Publishing.

Rutter, M., LeCouteur, A., and Lord, C. (2003) *Autism Diagnostic Interview, Revised (ADI-R)*. Los Angeles, CA: Western Psychological Services.

Semel, E., Wiig, E., and Secord, W. (2003) *Clinical Evaluation of Language Fundamentals®-Fourth Edition (CELF®-4)*. San Antonio, TX: Harcourt Assessment.

Seymour, H., Roeper, T., and de Villiers, J.; with contributions by de Villiers, P. (2005) *Diagnostic Evaluation of Language Variation™ (DELV™) – Norm-Referenced.* San Antonio, TX: Harcourt Assessment.

Sparrow, S., Cicchetti, D., and Balla, D. (2005). *Vineland Adaptive Behavior Scales, Second Edition (Vineland-II).* Bloomington, MN: Pearson Assessments

Strong, C. (1998). *The Strong Narrative Assessment Procedure (SNAP).* Greenville, SC: Super Duper® Publications.

Walker. H. and McConnell, S. (1995). *Walker-McConnell Scale of Social Competence and School Adjustment, Adolescent Version, 1st Edition.* Belmont: CA: Thomson Learning, Thomson Wadsworth.

Walker. H. and McConnell, S. (1995). *Walker-McConnell Scale of Social Competence and School Adjustment, Elementary Version, 1st Edition.* Belmont, CA: Thomson Learning, Thomson Wadsworth.

Wiig, E. and Secord, W. (1989). *Test of Language Competence–Expanded Edition (TLC–Expanded).* San Antonio, TX: Harcourt Assessment.

Games

(not all of which have been noted in this book)

Apples to Apples. (2000). Madison, WI: Out Of The Box Publishing.

Charades For Kids. (1999). New York: Pressman Toy Corporation.

Mayo, P. and Waldo, P. (1986). *Communicate: An Educational Activity to Reinforce Social Communication Skills During Adolescence.* Eau Claire, WI: Thinking Publications.

Guesstures. (1990). Milton Bradley Company.

Imaginiff. (1998). Buffalo, NY: Buffalo Games, Inc. (www.buffalogames.com)

Waldo, P. (1986). Problem Solver (PS). Eau Claire, WI: Thinking Publications (www.thinkingpublications.com)

DVDs/Videotapes

Hess, J. and Hess, J. (2004). *Napolean Dynamite.* Fox Searchlight Pictures

Pingu (2005) Canada: The Pygos Group www.pingu.net

Wallace & Grommit in Three Amazing Adventures. (2005) Universal City, CA: Dreamworks. www.dreamworks.com

Social Thinking Products by Michelle Garcia Winner

Available from: www.socialthinking.com

DVD/Video: "Social Thinking Across The Home and School Day"

A Michelle Garcia Winner DVD/VIDEO produced by Carol Gray's "The Gray Center." This four-hour presentation consists of:

- A two-hour workshop reviewing the critical aspects of social cognition that impact social and academic skills. Michelle describes the I LAUGH model of Social Cognition.

- A two-hour demonstration of educational lessons in both group and individual sessions with older and younger students showing how to put theory into action.

Use this indispensible video/dvd to educate teachers and parents about Michelle's ILAUGH model of social cognition. Observe Michelle in a clinical setting, engaged in related educational lessons with students!

DVD/Video + Workbook: "Strategies for Organization—Preparing for Homework and the Real World"

Organizational skills are traditionally broadly defined and broadly taught. For students with challenges in the areas of multi-tasking or executive functioning, homework management can be overwhelming to the point of meltdown!

Using her warm and engaging teaching style, Michelle presents 10 steps for organizing and producing homework, beginning in early elementary school. While the DVD focuses on how to complete daily homework; the skills learned apply throughout our lives and extend to managing chores, jobs, vacation planning, and more.

The DVD is accompanied by an easy-to-use workbook that includes a project planning guide, time estimation tables, action plans, and problem-solving strategies.

Book: "Sticker Strategies:
Practical Strategies to Encourage Social Thinking and Organization"

Sticker Strategies includes more than 80 fundamental teaching concepts/student strategies, all printed on color-coded 4x6-inch stickers for application onto a spiral-bound set of index cards. Students use the cards and stickers at their desks while at school or home. This tool allows teachers to help students determine which strategies or social thinking reminders work best for them; a small book of strategies is then developed based on the individual student's needs that the student can transport around campus.

This new product helps students, parents and teachers work towards having students "own their own strategies." The color-coded Strategy Stickers help students learn to be better social thinkers and organize themselves in home and school environments. Blank stickers allow for the creation of individual, customized stickers. Use this book as a launching pad to create your own strategies!

Book: "Social Behavior Mapping –
Connecting Behavior, Emotions and Consequences Across the Day"

One of the most successful tools used at Michelle G. Winner's Center for Social Thinking is the Social Behavior Map (SBM). Michelle developed the SBM as a cognitive behavior strategy to teach individuals about the specific relationship between behaviors, other's perspective, other's actions (consequences), and the student's own emotions about those around him or her. The SBM is a visual tool that displays these abstract concepts through a flow chart.

Now, Michelle and her team of talented therapists have created a collection of more than 50 Social Behavior Maps covering a range of topics for home, community and the classroom. *Social Behavior Mapping - Connecting Behavior, Emotions and Consequences Across the Day* is geared for use by parents and professionals to help those with social thinking challenges understand what behaviors are expected and unexpected in a way that makes sense to their way of thinking.

Available from: www.socialthinking.com

Book: "Think Social!
A Social Thinking Curriculum for School-Age Students"

This curriculum publication documents how lessons are introduced at Michelle Garcia Winner's Center for Social Thinking clinic. It demonstrates how to develop a social thinking vocabulary with which to teach children, parents and teachers across the years. It starts with lessons on 'Being Part of a Group' and continues into self-monitoring behavior, the development of language-specific skills, awareness of language meaning, and the development of imagination and wonder towards play/conversation. It introduces ways to explore complex issues of problem solving, hidden curriculum, and social rules as they change during our lifetimes. Eight sections incorporate more than 100 detailed lessons that can span years of treatment.

Book: "WORKSHEETS!
for Teaching Social Thinking and Related Skills"

The *Worksheets!* book breaks down abstract social thinking concepts into concrete lessons for students to work on in individual sessions or as part of a larger group. Lessons are organized into categories that include friendship, perspective taking, self-monitoring, being part of a group, effective communication, making plans to be with others, problem solving and more. Use these Worksheets! at school and at home. Many of these lessons are helpful for all students, not just those with clear social challenges.

Book: "Inside Out:
What Makes the Person with Social-Cognitive-Deficits Tick?"

This book reviews a comprehensive model that helps us understand the social cognitive deficits of persons with diagnosis such as Asperger Syndrome. Included are worksheets that can be used in classrooms and in small group settings to help students learn a variety of concepts, including perspective taking. This book covers content presented in her "Social Thinking Across the Home and School Day" workshop.

POSTERS!

to Stimulate Social Thinking Skills at Home and at School

Experience a life-size "Boring Moment." See what "Being Part of a Group" looks like in the big picture. Use wall-hung "Social Behavior Maps" to guide students through appropriate behavior and responses. Check out these popular posters on line at www.socialthinking. com or at one of Michelle Garcia Winner's conferences.

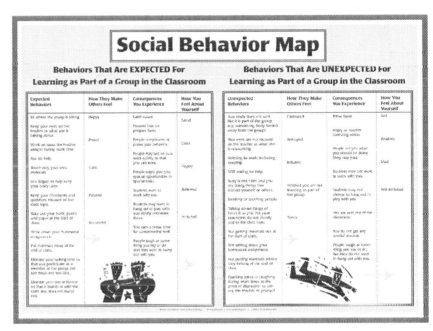

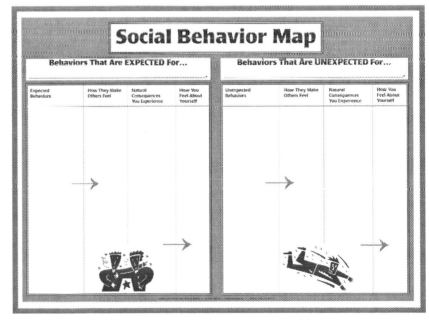